Religions in Africa

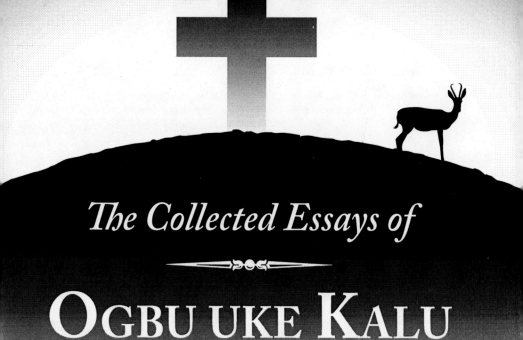

The Collected Essays of

OGBU UKE KALU

Volume 3

RELIGIONS IN AFRICA:
Conflicts, Politics and Social Ethics

Edited by
Wilhelmina J. Kalu, Nimi Wariboko, and Toyin Falola

Africa World Press, Inc.

P.O. Box 1892
Trenton, NJ 08607

P.O. Box 48
Asmara, ERITREA

Africa World Press, Inc.

P.O. Box 1892      P.O. Box 48
Trenton, NJ 08607   Asmara, ERITREA

Book and cover design: Saverance Publishing Services

Library of Congress Cataloging-in-Publication Data

Religions in Africa : conflicts, politics and social ethics / edited by Wilhelmina J. Kalu, Nimi Wariboko, and Toyin Falola.
    p. cm.
Includes bibliographical references and index.
 ISBN 1-59221-778-8 (hard cover : alk. paper) -- ISBN 1-59221-779-6 (pbk. : alk. paper) 1. Africa--Religion. I. Kalu, Wilhelmina. II. Wariboko, Nimi, 1962- III. Falola, Toyin.
 BL2400.R45 2010
 200.96--dc22
                      2010028816

Table of Contents

Table of Contents

Preface

The book you have in your hands is part of a three-volume set of Professor Ogbu Kalu's essays. It is proper at this juncture to show how this particular volume fits into the whole set. The three volumes cover the major areas of his scholarship: *Pentecostalism* (Volume I): The first volume gathers essays on African Pentecostalism. It is largely interpretative as he fights what he perceived as Western distortions on what has and is happening with regard to Africans' charismatic embrace of the third Person of the Trinity. There is a significant display of the craft of the historian in dealing with primary data but it does not constitute its main strength or focus. The first volume is attempting to provide the proper lens—polishing and enlarging its angle all the time—to view, interpret, and evaluate the Pentecostal experience in the continent. He berates scholars who reject the alternative trans-national discourse that is sensitive to local identities, appropriations and contestation of global processes and instead opt to interpret Pentecostalism as the religious vehicle for Western global cultural influences in Africa.

Mission (Volume II): In the second volume, we have collected together some of his contributions to mission history and interpretation of its historiography. In the mission-volume he supremely displays the craft of a historian in the collection, analysis, and interpretation of primary data.

Social Analysis (Volume III): The final volume collects together very insightful essays of on intersection between religion and social issues in African. It is a virtuoso display of political and ethical analyses of the flow of events as Christianity penetrated Africa and sustains itself in multiple forms. Here he displays the sensitivity of a great historian coupled with an eye for ethical issues.

In all, he is always fighting to correct distortions, agitating for the proper historiography and lens; and struggling to preserve the past for future generations in ways that will inspire them for greatness. His use of African proverbs and myths is a joy to read; his narrative style very impressive and easy to follow, and his mastery of the Christian history of the continent and the scholarship across the centuries and decades are formidable and intimidating. When he even disagrees with other scholars he is very respectful and mindful of their work and reputation. He criticizes them so as not to humiliate them, but to move his argument forward as friends are wont to do in a banter.

No one who is familiar with Kalu's impressive body of work will fail to notice how he retrieves, deploys, advances and frames ideas—both old and new. He is always thought-provoking, entertaining, probing, advising and amusing. He uses ideas as a graceful dancer uses movements, to flow and arrest, push and pull, rise and crouch in disappearing gestures. As the ideas danced they are transfigured, shining as polished blade of a sword held up to the African noonday sunlight. The thought—now elegant and sharp—becomes tactical African proverbs and proverbs illuminate his thought. Kalu's thought never fails to cut deep into the crust of knowledge to excavate gems of excellence.

The editors decided not to make changes to these essays, except in some cases of obvious typographical errors.

Biography
Wilhelmina J. Kalu

Ogbu Uke Kalu (June 2, 1942 – January 7, 2009)

Ogbu Uke Kalu was born in Ohafia, Abia State, Nigeria, in 1942, to the late Elder Kalu Uke Onwuchekwa and Mrs Margaret Uzumma Uchendu Kalu. He received his primary education at the Ohafia Central School, later studying at Hope Waddell Training Institute, Calabar (1955-1961). Ogbu started his higher degrees at the University of Toronto, Canada. He obtained B.A. Hons., History; M.A. *summa cum laude*, McMaster University, Hamilton, Ontario; and Ph.D. History, University of Toronto (1968-1970). He studied at the Institute of Historical Research at the University of London and graduated with a Master of Divinity (M.Div.) from Princeton Theological Seminary, New Jersey. He was awarded Doctor of Divinity (DD) *honoris causa* (1997) by the Presbyterian College, McGill University in Montreal, Quebec, Canada. After completing his study abroad, he returned to Nigeria in 1974 as a lecturer in the Department of Religious Studies, University of Nigeria, Nsukka, and became a professor of church history in 1978. Until 2001, he served in different capacities at Nsukka including dean of the Faculty of the Social Sciences and Director of the General Studies Division, University of Nigeria, Nsukka.

In 2001, Dr. Ogbu joined the services of McCormick Theological Seminary as the first Henry Winters Luce Professor of World Christianity and Mission. This Chair was created through a grant from The Henry

Luce Foundation, Inc., in honor of Dr. Henry Winters Luce, a Presbyterian missionary in China in the early 1900s.

Over the years, Ogbu served as visiting professor at several institutions. These include Harvard Divinity School and Center for the Study of World Religions; Bayreuth University, Germany; University of Toronto, McGill University, University of Edinburgh, University of Pretoria, and Presbyterian Theological Seminary in Seoul, McCormick's partner seminary in Korea.

Professor Ogbu Kalu was a prolific writer. His publications covered a wide range of subjects in the humanities and social sciences. He published more than 15 books and over 150 articles in journals and edited volumes. His books include *African Pentecostalism: An Introduction* (2008), *Clio in a Sacred Garb: Christian Presence and African Responses, 1900-2000* (2008), *African Christianity: An African Story* (2005), *Interpreting Contemporary Christianity: Global Processes and Local Identities* (2008, with Alaine Low), *African Christianity* (2007), *Power, Poverty and Prayer: The Challenges of Poverty and Pluralism in African Christianity, 1960-1996* (2000), *Shaping Beloved Community: Multicultural Theological Education* (2006, with David V. Esterline), *The Embattled Gods: Christianization of Igboland, 1841-1991* (1996), *History of Christianity in West Africa* (1981), *The History of Christianity in West Africa: The Nigerian Story* (1980), *African Church Historiography: An Ecumenical Perspective* (1988), *Divided People of God: Church Union Movement in Nigeria 1875-1966* (1978), and *Readings in African Humanities: African Cultural Development*. Some of Kalu's publications have been republished widely.

Professor Kalu's life was full of service to God and humanity. He chaired several ecumenical organizations focusing on the development of the Church in Africa. He served on the editorial board of several academic bodies including the Caribbean and African Journal of Theology, and he served on the advisory boards of several church-related institutions and organizations in the Nigerian Church and Society in Ibadan. Kalu served as an examiner with the West African Examination Council and as an external examiner to various universities in Nigeria and worldwide.

Ogbu was a man of deep Christian faith and conviction. He was an ordained elder in the Presbyterian Church in Nigeria where he held several offices. He played an active role in the world church. For many years, Professor Kalu provided leadership in theological education in Africa. His work in theological education was especially important to him and the community he so faithfully served. Ogbu acted as Secretary-General of WAATI, the West African Association of Theological Institutions (WAATI) and as the founding chair of the Conference of African Theological Institutions (CATI). Until his death, he was Director of the Christianity in Africa

Project. He held several leadership positions in the Church. He was on the membership committee of the General Assembly Board of Faith and Order. In Chicago, he was an active member of The People's Church, a Progressive Community Center where he passionately enjoyed teaching adult education classes.

Ogbu Uke Kalu is survived by his wife, Dr. Wilhelmina Josephine Kalu (nee-Dowuona-Hammond), and their four children: Engineer Edward Uke Kalu, Dr. Stella Uzumma Egwim (nee-Kalu) (Pediatrician), Dr. Jayne Eberechukwu Codjoe (Dentist), and Ms. Patience Orie Kalu (Psychologist/MBA). Professor Kalu is also survived by his siblings, Mr. Kalu Uke Kalu, Mrs. Nnezi Anyaegbu, Mr. Obiwe Uke Kalu, Mrs. Onyemma Kalu, Mrs. Ngozi Onwuka, Mr. Okoro Uke Kalu, and by two step brothers, Mr. Awa Kalu and Mr. Onyeani Kalu.

Tributes
and
Testimonies

Jehu J. Hanciles
School of Intercultural Studies
Fuller Theological Seminar

Ogbu: A Great Man

Few scholars have done more than Prof. Kalu to put African Christian scholarship on the world stage and nurture a whole new generation of African scholars. His prolific writing relentlessly explored new horizons of knowledge and showcased an African perspective. In classrooms, countless seminars, numerous conferences/consultations, and innumerable personal encounters around the globe, his profound grasp of African realities, uncanny insight into African Christian trends, unparalleled bibliographical knowledge, and pithy wit penetrated the dense fog of academic misperceptions and challenged received wisdom. His irrepressible humor disarmed interlocutors even while his sharp mind assailed arguments. He rarely left an audience without adding to their understanding of the issues under discussion. But it is for his warm personality,

down to earth insights, generosity of spirit, and gift of friendship that so many budding and growing African scholars will mourn his passing. When I met Prof Kalu for the first time (in 1992/3, as a young PhD student at the University of Edinburgh) he made an immediate impression— matter of factly instructing me to start publishing. In a matter of weeks a strong rapport developed that flourished over the years into in a deep friendship and close professional relationship. Prof. Kalu impacted my life in profound ways, through his thoughtful counsel, mentoring support, and warm affection (extended to my family). I mourn his passing deeply; and with the growing band of African scholars I ponder the indelible gap in African scholarship he leaves behind while also giving glory to God for his legacy. Through his life and work the road we tread has been made that much more accessible and promising.

Joel Carpenter
Director, Nagel Institute
Calvin College

━━━━◗◉◉◖━━━━

Ogbu: The Great Scholar

This year a group of us at Calvin College are reading books on African Christianity from the perspective of several fields: theology, history, political science, and anthropology. In October we read Prof. Kalu's African *Pentecostalism: An Introduction* (Oxford, 2008). We found it to be a very rich and mature scholarly offering, and I wrote Ogbu after our discussion, playfully chiding him for mis-titling the book as "An Introduction." It is, in fact, a definitive statement by the leading scholar of the field, addressing all of the main interpretive issues. We are not surprised to learn that African Pentecostalism won the annual award from the African Studies Association, but we were surprised and saddened to learn of our friend's illness and departure.

It is fitting that Ogbu ends African Pentecostalism with a chapter on "Reverse Flow," the movement of African Christians into the global North, bringing this gospel of grace and power with them. Ogbu embodied the reverse flow for many of us. He questioned our long-held assumptions within the contemporary human sciences favoring "methodological atheism," and he insisted that truly Christian scholarship demanded a deeper approach. Ogbu modeled spiritually attuned intellectual work in his own writing, and at least we have it to learn from, now that he has departed. There will be a day, we fondly hope, when we can take up this conversation with him again.

Kanayo K Odeluga, MD. MPH

Oke Osisi: A Tribute to a Great Igbo Son

In the summer month of June, 1942 a seed was sown into the soil of Alaigbo in Nigeria. This seed was named Ogbu Uke Kalu by his proud and grateful parents. This seed was nurtured in the cross cultural city of Calabar by his parents who were part of the emerging Igbo elites that

spread out to various parts of Nigeria during the colonial era. His father, as an Igbo community organizer was active in the Igbo Union and provided leadership for Ndi Igbo in the City of Calabar. As an unflinching supporter of western style education his father sent away to Enugu for his primary education while living with an uncle. He attended the great Hope Waddell College where he came under the tutelage of the great Igbo sage, Dr. Okanu Ibiam as principal, who later became the fi rst premier of Eastern Nigeria. As this seed was nurtured and watered, it grew into a colossal tree (Oke Osisi) with deep roots and widespread branches that born good fruit. He is rooted in a deep faith in God, acceptance of cultural identity as nwa-afo Igbo and spirit of excellence in the pursuit of his life work and mission. Many have found shelter and rest through their life journey under this tree. Many have also eaten of the fruit of his life and have been strengthened and refreshed.

On the eve of his departure from Nigeria to travel to Toronto Canada to pursue college education in 1966, he escaped assassination by Nigeria armed forces that were ordered to kill any Igbo person following the murder of General Aguiyi Ironsi. He saw his survival as a sign that God has great plans for his life. While in Canada, he joined the Biafran Student movement serving as secretary. He poured himself into the Biafran cause and organized various campaigns to raise money for humanitarian mission to relieve the hunger and suffering of those caught the civil war. At one point he quit school for a year and donated his scholarship money to the humanitarian cause.

He returned to Nigeria after his education at University of Toronto and Princeton University to teach in the University of Nigeria, Nsukka – a center of Igbo scholarship and learning. Suffice it to say that within a short period, he distinguished himself as a Christian, mentor, reformer, inspiration and change agent within the University community. He became the youngest person to attain professorship in the University when he "out-published the publishers in town". As a dedicated and hard working academic he was pro-lific in his writings which were published in several distinguished academic journals, textbooks and magazines. His humility showed in the way he dealt with his colleagues, students and staff of the various departments where he served at UNN. As a scholar, he believes that there is no wall between the ivory tower and the public square or market place. He was comfortable in the citadels of learning, the "ama" (the Igbo public square), the podiums, pews and pulpits of this world. What he learnt he taught and used to shape public policy, opinions, views of those he comes in contact with so as to seek a better life for humanity. His scholarly advocacy for Ndi Igbo not only runs through his work and writings but can also be seen in the way he immersed himself in the Igbo community activities and politics wherever he is. Many will not forget his invaluable services as a leader of the Igbo Desk at the last Nigerian constitutional conference under General Abacha under the auspices of Mkpoko Igbo sponsored by Izu Umunna and Aka Ikenga. He gave himself to his community in various projects and activities to promote welfare of all. Here in Chicago, he became the brain behind the annual Igbofest Symposium, gave the inaugural keynote speaker at the first Ndi Igbo Couples' Nite, participated in Igbo Cultural Connection Series organized by Umuigbo Alliance and was a mentor to many young Igbo intellectuals and professionals.

His scholarship is unique. He is a historian with a heart enlightened by love of God and the gospel of his Lord Jesus Christ. He viewed history as the story of God's dealings and interactions with His creation. In his work, he chose to explore the interaction between man, his environment and worldview, so as to help find solutions to his problems and answers to his questions. In his writings, he tells the story of his subjects from their perspective – a paradigm shift in African historiography. He is a master in the distinguished Igbo art of story telling.

Within the arena of Church history, Prof Ogbu led the way and dis-tinguished himself as a world renowned authority in African Christianity. In this generation, he has given voice to the Holy Spirit and His work among Africans and people of African descent. He has a special burden for the African Diaspora and strived to understand their circumstances so as to walk with them in support and solidarity. Following his 2008 visit to Columbia and meeting Afro-Colombians, he expressed to many around him and anyone who cared to listen, how deeply he was touched by their plight and sufferings. He started immediately to mobilize support and funds to help build a Day care Centre in Bogotá to care for children of widows displaced from rural communities by Colombian rebels and mul-tinational corporations interested in their land for cultivation of coca and maize respectively so that they can pursue work to support their families. He was supposed to visit them early this January with his wife Dr. Willy but God had a different plan.

Professor Ogbu Kalu:

Oke osisi ka obu.
O di uko na mba.
O di iche.

We will never forget him. We will forever eat of the fruit of his life and work here on earth. Today, Prof Ogbu Kalu lives in the bosom of His Father God, the lives of his wonderful children, in his work and life mission and our collective memories. His mantle shall not fall to the ground.

Andrew F. Walls
Honorary Professor University of Edinburgh;
Professor of the History of Mission,
Liverpool Hope University;
Head of the Department of Religion,
University of Nigeria, Nsukka, 1962–65

The Late Professor Ogbu Kalu

Blessed is the man who does not walk in the counsel of the wicked ...or sit in the seat of mockers. But his delight is in the law of the LORD.... He is like a tree planted by streams of water which yields its fruit in season and whose leaf does not wither...

Ogbu Kalu was like the Psalmist's fruitful tree: upright, solid, productive, full of sustenance for others. The source of these qualities also recalls the Psalmist's words; this was a man who deliberately turned his back on self-seeking and cynicism in order to follow the teaching of the One whom he knew as the Lord.

The fruit was abundant. For one thing, he was Africa's premier Church historian. In this area he was both a ground breaker and a master builder, combining great range with depth of insight. He had begun with years of research into British history; when he turned to Africa he produced both valued works of synthesis and indispensable works of exploration, detailed studies of Nigeria and magisterial continent-wide surveys. He was a skilled and sympathetic interpreter of the religious reality of Africa; his seminal works on the process of Christian conversion in Igboland and, most recently, on Pentecostalism in Africa open up whole fields for investigation and comparison. African Church history has long been a marginal subject in the Western academic world; the present place of Africa at the heart of the World Church has brought it into the academic mainstream, a topic of importance for all who care about the Christianity in the twenty-first century. If the topic of African Christian history is now better serviced, better resourced, better interpreted, better understood than previously, an immense amount of the credit for this belongs to Ogbu Kalu.

He was not content to carry out his work as a detached scholar. For decades he was an inspirer and facilitator for the work of others, and a leader and driving force in team activity. More than twenty years have passed since the Nairobi workshop on African Christian history supported by the World Council of Churches as part of a project towards an ecumenical Church history. Ogbu led the workshop and edited the collection of papers on African Christian historiography that emerged from it. Latterly, in collaboration with the South African scholar Professor J W Hofmeyr, he organized the writing by a group of scholars from all over Africa a major work with the significant title African Christianity: an African story.

No one has done more to ensure that the history of African Christianity would be written, studied and pondered by Africans. And, though an internationally recognised scholar, his position as a servant of Africa, and of Nigeria in particular, has never been in doubt. In the last few years he has been based in the United States, and one outcome has been the almost staggering flow of significant writing that he published. But for over a quarter of a century before that he taught at the University of Nigeria, Nsukka, also serving as Dean and in other administrative capacities, through some of his country's bleakest years. The difficulties of maintaining the scholarly life in such a situation are overwhelming, and they defeated many; but Ogbu demonstrated how high standards could be maintained, and taught and researched and wrote and published and kept the scholarly flame burning in the Department. The tree continued to bear fruit in season, even when the streams ran dry.

For behind the productive scholar and the stimulating teacher and the lively lecturer, underlying and informing all this activity, lay the straight-forward, warm-hearted Christian that we remember now with affection and gratitude. We thank God for all that Ogbu Kalu did, but still more for what he was. So we commend to the Father's loving care and comfort those who knew him best and loved him best, and whose loss is therefore greatest, his dear wife Dr Wilhelmina Kalu and their children. For the rest, let us pray the Lord of the harvest to send new labourers, inspired by the work and example of Professor Ogbu Kalu, into the field in which he laboured so mightily

J. Akuma-Kalu Njoku, Ph.D.
Associate Professor, Folklore and Ethnomusicology
Western Kentucky University

Our Teacher, Master, and Friend

Professor Ogbu Kalu was my teacher at the University of Nigeria, Nsukka in the 1970s. He became my senior colleague when the University hired me, and since then, my master and friend. Over the past thirty-two years, I came to know Professor Ogbu Kalu as a man of noble lineage in Ohafi a, a highly distinguished Igbo man, and a scholar of no mean order. We have shared stories of childhood experiences, swopped jokes and made each other laugh. He always seemed to have a different appellation (Ikom, Akparawa, Onye oke, etc.) for me; never called me by my first name. I remember him most as a teacher. The last teaching moment was in September 2009, when he sent me a manuscript entitled "OSONDU" Patterns for Igbo Quest for Jesus Power" to review for him. Me, review a manuscript for Ogbu Kalu who has written well over 20 books and published more than 100 articles? "Well," I said to myself: "Prof. is trying to tell me something now." I wrote the review; just one page. He responded wondering how I was able to pack into a paragraph the research he had done for ten years. He went ahead and wrote several instructive pages unpacking my response.

I knew that Professor Ogbu Kalu was at his best as a teacher when answering questions you asked him in the attitude of learning. In our last conversation, in November 2009, I asked what he thought about a manuscript in which I was using "neo-traditionalism" as a conceptual focus for modifying the Ohafi a heritage of headhunting in ways that will cause new generations of Ohafia achievers to bring new kinds of trophies to their village Ikoros in the 21 century. He suggested that I replace "neo-traditionalism" with the term "revaluation." He told me why. He even used his own name Ogbu (The Killer) to demonstrate the point. Then he pointed me to many different directions to explore. During that discussion he gave me the telephone number of a potential publisher—The Africa World Press—and promised to call the publisher himself. Before I knew it, he died. Sai! I have lost me a teacher, master, and friend.

Ukachukwu Chris Manus
Department of Religious Studies
Obafemi Awolowo University

Kalu: Our Great Friend

Sisters and brothers,

There is no doubt that no one individual is indispensible on this planet. Nevertheless, the appearance of persons like Professor Ogbu U. Kalu on our earth to contribute his own quota in its firmament of life supposes the truth that even if no one person is that indispensable, some one like Ogbu Kalu had lived to make an incomparable difference. Indeed as the old adage goes, 'a tree cannot make a forest' but surely contemporary ecologists and environmentalists agree that the disappearance of certain species of trees; especially the irokos and the mahoganies render a forest barren. Thoughts like these reflect some of the extraordinary hard facts of life.

It is exactly for this rationale that I, Professor Chris Ukachukwu Manus, your kinsman, friend and compatriot in particular, mourn your sudden exit from history. Despite the oddities your departure has created, I remember and salute you as an exceptional Guru, an icon in the world academy and a stalwart in the arena of the global knowledge industry. Your intimidating array of works, originality and creativity in research, grotesque affability and a high sense of duty have combined to attest that you belonged to the category of the erudites who had come to the world to make outstanding qualitative differences in knowledge creation and transmission in the tertiary educational system in Nigeria and beyond. It is exactly for these reasons that I remain very proud of your life.

For those of us, your colleagues who are still left in this bleak cosmos, your life which had impacted so much on us still remains an impeccable source of inspiration to march on. It will not be out of obsequies decorum to say 'thank you very much' for bequeating so much to us. You were indeed a role model, a titan, a trail blazer and a pathfinder in the fi eld in which we commonly ploughed. Your drive and initiatives will ever remain our guide.

In this year of your demise, we are theologically not bereft. We promise you that with God Almighty ever on our side, aluta continua. You were a gem, indeed an extraordinary scholar. May your gentle soul rest in the perfect peace of the Lord, Jesus, the Christ.

The Rev. Dr. Earle F. Roberts
Missionary in Nigeria, 1956 – 1970
Former Principal Clerk of the General Assembly of
The Presbyterian Church in Canada;
Moderator of the General Assembly of
The Presbyterian Church in Canada, 1993

➤◦◦◦◦◄

Dr. Ogbu Kalu, A Religious Man

At the time that I heard of Ogbu's death Psalm 23 came into my mind, especially the verses 'Yeah though I walk through the valley of the shadow of death, I will fear no evil, for Thou art with me, Thy rod and Thy staff they comfort me…'. Ogbu would have felt the power of those words at the moment of his passing.

When Ogbu first came to Canada, the two most influential people in seeing that Ogbu receive further education, outside of Nigeria, were the late Dr. Francis Akanu Ibiam and the late Rev. Dr. Edward H. Johnson, after whom Ogbu and Wilhemia's, (Willy's) son Edward Kalu is named.

I first met Ogbu in Nigeria in 1963, during the rainy season. He was in his final term at the Hope Waddell Secondary School in Calabar. I thought, 'here is one nice kid'. A lasting impression was he appeared to be an avid student.

Arriving in Canada in September of 1963, prior to the Fall opening of the University of Toronto, Ogbu showed a different approach to studying. He used to study the topic of what the professors were going to teach before it was taught! I had never before known a student to do that so it certainly made Ogbu stand out in my mind. He proved to be an excellent student, far surpassing all our expectations.

Upon graduation from the University of Toronto, Ogbu, because of his ability, had his choice of any university he wanted to attend and there were many outstanding universities who wooed him, however he felt God had placed a plan in his mind that he should follow and follow he did. Meeting and marrying his beloved Willy, turned out to be part and parcel of this Divine Plan.

Then came the day when Ogbu's Christian faith started to ignite. When it jumped ahead of him and empowered him, it was wonderful to behold. Willy's faith was a direct infl uence which impacted Ogbu's relationship with the Lord and God's plan for Ogbu's life.

God gifted Ogbu with the ability to write and he became a prolific author. Along with this came the recognition of him as a 'man with a message' and so from around the world he was sought out as a speaker. International organizations longed for him to be on their Boards and Committees. In all these demands on his life Ogbu never lost sight of an individual and their needs, never lost sight of his humble beginnings, never lost sight of saying 'thank you' to those he felt had helped shape his faith along the way.

Ogbu's life became a total dedication to God and the assignment he knew the Lord had given him.

We celebrate your Resurrection my brother. Earle

Dr. Waibinte Wariboko
Department of History and Archaeology
Faculty of Humanities and Education
Mona Campus – The University of the West Indies

Kalu, Mentor and Teacher

As a student at the University of Port Harcourt in Nigeria, I knew the late Professor Ogbu Kalu through his contributions to African Historiography generally, and to African Church Historiography in particular. Coming after the generation of scholars such as E.A. Ayandele and Jacob Ade Ajayi in African Church Historiography, Ogbu gave more breath and scope to issues dealing with the responses of the Igbo-speaking peoples to Christianity. As he advanced in his craft, however, he began to look at Nigeria within West Africa and the African continent, in order to provide more enriching analyses of the sociopolitical and cultural consequences of the missionary encounters with African societies. Most of us interested in this subject today certainly owe this man, including the generation immediately before him, an immeasurable debt of gratitude for the theoretical directions and narrative styles they have introduced in this subject.

I had the privilege, eventually, to meet this great scholar in the Campus of the University of Nigeria when I was collecting data for a study on West Indian Missionaries in Southern Nigeria. Without any prior notice, surprisingly, I was warmly received by the late Professor Ogbu Kalu in his sitting room to discuss my project. This unplanned meeting, which turned out to be very productive, was what gave me the best opportunity to appreciate the mind and social character of this man: he came across as very perceptive, unassuming, amiable and humble; and I went away from that encounter with a greater sense of admiration for his character and devotion to scholarship. Since then, unknown of course to him, I have held him as one of my heroes; and I do know that he is a hero to dozens of younger students of African Church Historiography within and outside of the ancestral continent. Without any exaggeration, his passing will be an irreparable loss to all students of African and Africana studies.

Cynthia M. Campbell
President, McCormick Theological Seminary

<hr/>

Professor Ogbu Kalu: A Thanksgiving

McCormick Theological Seminary joins colleagues, friends and family members throughout the world in giving thanks to God for the life and witness of Professor Ogbu Kalu. When Professor Kalu came to McCormick in the fall of 2001, he was already a distinguished international scholar. Widely known as one of the most important historians of the Christian movement in Africa, we were honored that he accepted our invitation to serve as the first Henry Winters Luce Professor of World Christianity and Mission. We hoped that Professor Kalu would bring to McCormick insights from the experience of Christians and the life of the church in Africa. What we gained was a colleague whose knowledge and personal experience was truly global in scope. All of us learned more about the church and its mission because of his presence with us. Professor Kalu had four primary commitments. He was a man of deep and abiding personal faith, a man of prayer, a man who loved God with his whole being. He was a man dedicated to his wife and wonderful family. He was a scholar of the very first rank whose commitment to research and writing was simply astonishing – by my count nine books (including edited collections) published since coming to McCormick. This is a legacy of scholarship that will endure and serve the current and future church for years to come. Finally, and by no means last, he was teacher deeply committed to students – to helping them learn and become the very best they could become as scholars and leaders.

The Bible tells us that those to whom much is given, of them much will be required. Ogbu Kalu was a man richly blessed by God –blessed with great intelligence, boundless energy, intellectual imagination and deep love for God and neighbor. All of those gifts he shared freely and generously with everyone with whom he lived and worked. We at McCormick are profoundly grateful to God to all that God has given us and the world through the life of Ogbu Kalu.

Robert A. Cathey, Ph.D.
Professor of Theology

━━━━━◗◖◖◗◖━━━━━

An Outstanding Colleague

I count it a great privilege to have served as a colleague and friend of Ogbu Kalu since 2001 at McCormick Theological Seminary. I will continue to be inspired by his example as a research scholar who combined boundless curiosity with endless energy. But I will also remember Ogbu as a person who took seriously the role of colleague among us as a faculty member. His warm-hearted friendship did not preclude honest expression of differences in opinion and the challenge to live and teach more faithfully.

I will never forget once when I was giving a guest lecture in one of his classes. I was making the case that all ecumenical christology began as someone's local christology (church teaching having to do with the Person and Work of Christ). Ogbu rose to his feet, walked to the black board and began to draw a kola nut. From the symbol of the kola nut he explained his belief that at the root of every authentic local christology was the Gospel of God. Deep within this critical historian was a bold believer who gave witness to the Gospel in how he prayed, how he made us laugh, and how he invited us into a much larger world of the Christian faith than we had previously imagined. We will miss the wonderful gift of his faithful presence among us. But now even ordinary things like kola nuts will become occasions to pause, remember, and give thanks for his life well lived in the service of the Gospel.

Dr. David D. Daniels III

Great mind. Great colleague. Great soul.

During the late 1990s, I participated in a conference on the Holy Spirit hosted by Emmanuel College, University of Toronto, where I first met Ogbu Kalu. Prior to our meeting, I had already heard good things about him; he was introduced to me as a superb scholar and phenomenal bibliophile. At this conference, I glimpsed his mind in action. He delivered an engaging, insightful, and encyclopedic lecture on an aspect of the Holy Spirit. Throughout my time knowing him, I have continued to be amazed by his intellect. What I admired highly about Kalu's mind was his ability to lodge Christianity within wider philosophical and social currents; the social and political significance of the Christian faith remained preeminent in his thought.

Kalu committed himself to expanding scholarship by writing on new topics in religious history and supporting the academic work of young scholars. His scholarly work regularly interrogated new primary sources, cited the publications of young scholars, enlarged the conversation of the topic, overturned the consensus on the subject, and crafted new interpretations.

As the dean of African Church history, he contributed to the theoretical rigor and sophistication of the discipline. His long list of publications has created a rich corpus of scholarship that will be mined by scholars for generations to come.

For almost a decade, Kalu and I co-taught a course on global Pentecostalism at McCormick Theological Seminary. In the course, we debated the various positions, rethought our analyses, and probed new approaches to study the topic. I learned much from him. In our classroom exchanges, we sometimes would have to be interrupted by the students so that our dialogue would expand into a class discussion. With love and grace, he took each student's question seriously and worked patiently with each student's paper. He freely loaned his books and ideas to students to strengthen their papers; he readily accompanied students to the library to show them where particular texts were shelved. Solid academic work genuinely excited him.

Kalu was a delightful human being with a deep Christian faith, wonderful spirit, compassionate heart, and endearing laugh. He loved God and people. A person of integrity, he touched so many people with his intellect and soul. The Christian faith shaped his life and relationships. His embodiment of the Christian faith witnessed to the grace-bearing life of the mind and of the Spirit.

David Esterline
Dean of the Faculty
McCormick Theological Seminary

Ogbu U. Kalu (1942-2009)

Professor Ogbu Kalu was a colleague and friend—generous and faithful to the point of redefining the terms. He was a mentor at times, a pastor at other times; he was always available, always ready to take on new challenges and additional responsibilities. It is difficult to think of continuing without him. Yet, along with the profound loss, there is also profound gratitude—for the years of learning alongside him, for the laughter, the prayers, the truly remarkable gift of his scholarship, and the lively grace of his life among us.

Professor Kalu came to McCormick in 2001 from the University of Nigeria at Nsukka where he had served as Professor of Church History since 1978. During the years at Nsukka he also served as visiting professor at universities and seminaries in nearly every part of the world, including Harvard, Pretoria, Edinburgh, the Presbyterian Theological Seminary in Seoul, McGill and Toronto Universities in Canada, and the University of Bayreuth in Germany. After coming to McCormick he continued to respond to invitations from around the world to lecture and to participate, usually in leadership roles, in research and publishing projects.

Dr. Kalu was a scholar like few I have ever known; his curriculum vitae runs to 35 pages of small print. It includes 18 books authored or edited on the history of the church in Africa, world Christianity, and Pentecostalism. One of the most recent, *African Pentecostalism: An Introduction* (Oxford University Press, 2008) was named the best book on Africa published 2007-2008 by the Association of Third World Studies. When I last spoke with Ogbu in the hospital, he told me about his next book, already more than half written, to be titled Eating the Crocodile: African Immigrant Pentecostalism. The title, he explained, comes from the expression that immigrants would use when they had survived crocodile infested waters and had safely arrived in Europe—that they had eaten the crocodile rather than the other way around. Beyond the books, his most recent c.v. includes 189 articles in academic journals and lists membership on 10 editorial boards. Prodigious hardly begins to describe Professor Kalu's scholarship.

Yet to know his published scholarship was hardly to know Ogbu. If you read his annual reports to the Board of Trustees at McCormick, among the academic accomplishments you would have also noted headings like "Taught pro bono" followed by a list of (often little known) colleges and churches in Nigeria and Chicago—an indication of the depth of his involvement and commitment to all aspects of the life of the church. Ogbu was a man of deep, profound Christian faith, faith that he lived out in local congregations as much as in university and seminary classrooms and in the academic guilds. His faith was the framework and foundation for his whole life as a scholar, member of church and community, and friend.

I miss Ogbu deeply. And I will always be grateful for his friendship and relentless encouragement, for the legacy of his scholarship, for the depth of his faith, and for all that he brought to us at McCormick. We will not be the same having had the gift of his life among us.

Ted Hiebert
McGaw Professor of Old Testament
McCormick Theological Seminary

———⟩◦◦◦⟨———

A Friend and a Gentleman

My favorite reason—out of a fairly long list of "favorite" reasons—for teaching at McCormick is the people here: the students, the staff, and my colleagues on the faculty. I find it hard to imagine—and I have had some experience with other faculties before coming to McCormick—a group of colleagues with a more wholesome combination of academic excellence, church commitment, worldly experience, and those simple traits that make them fun to hang out with (something academics are not necessarily known for but which makes working with them way better!).

That's one of the many, many reasons Ogbu's leaving us is so unspeakably heartbreaking. He leaves such a big, empty space among us that no one else can fill: a space now emptied not just of ideas but of friendship and heart and soul. McCormick's website pays tribute to Ogbu as "a towering figure in the fields of Global Mission, African Christianity, and Global Pentecostalism." He was, and I want to describe just one small experience of the many we have had that made him such a great man to be around.

When I went to teach English at Numan Teachers' College in the great savannahs of northern Nigeria after graduating from college, I discovered and taught Things Fall Apart, a ground breaking novel about the encounter between European missionaries and Nigerian villagers, by Chinua Achebe, Nigeria's great novelist. Living in Nigeria was my first contact with true difference—the difference between American and Nigerian, the difference between the city and the village, the difference between Christianity and traditional African religions—and I struggled mightily to figure out how to think about it. In an article about his work, Achebe taught me the most important thing I learned in those years—and I think that I have ever learned—about difference: the nonnegotiable place of human dignity. "The missionaries have contributed a lot to our culture, such as schools and hospitals," wrote Achebe (and I probably shouldn't even be using quotation marks here because I'm completely quoting this from memory), "but what they have taken from us is our dignity." This is when I recognized, as I have many times since, that the dignity of each person is where everything must begin.

Last year, on the fiftieth anniversary of Things Fall Apart, The New Yorker did a retrospective on the work of Chinua Achebe, which I called to Ogbu's attention for the simple reason that they are Nigerian compatriots. We had never talked about Chinua Achebe and African literature. "Yes, Chinua," Ogbu said, "he was a good and wise man." And for the next thirty minutes or so, Ogbu sat in my office describing his personal friendship with Chinua Achebe and bringing to life for me the character and mind of the man who had so influenced me years ago. How rare it is rub shoulders with those who can bring even deeper meaning to our deepest insights. How few people can bring us the world the way Ogbu was able to.

This spring I had hoped to introduce Ogbu to our daughter Mary Claire, who is studying English literature in Chicago this year and has studied African literature including Things Fall Apart, so that the three of us could sit around cups of coffee and talk about Achebe, colonialism, African literature, African Christianity, and what it means to be human. Now we will never have that conversation. And we will be much poorer because of that. But all of us who came to know Ogbu have already been immeasurably enriched because he was with us.

Luis R. Rivera, Th.D.
Associate Professor of Theology

⎯⎯⎯⎯◦◦◦⎯⎯⎯⎯

A Friend and a Mentor

It is difficult to write while mourning the unexpected death of a dear friend and without enough time to dig deep in the archives of heart and memory. The life of a human being is a profound mystery that no one can capture in few or many words; even the most complete biography could not convey completely what a life was or meant. These words are only an unfolding testimony of one who was touched and blessed by Dr. Ogbu Kalu.

Ogbu and I were assigned to lead a study travel seminar to Colombia on January 3-14, 2009. He was anticipating with excitement this second visit to Colombia and Latin America. But his journey took an unexpected turn. He was ready to travel south but his destination changed for a realm beyond. For this other trip and for this divine call, he was also prepared. I visited an emerald factory in Colombia. I saw the different shapes and cuts that make these stones shine in beauty to our eyes. I have no money or desire to have one of these precious stones, but I carry with me the treasure of having met, lived and worked with Ogbu, that precious African emerald! I have no precise words to describe the shape and cuts that made his life beautiful to family, colleagues and friends. I can only name some of those faces that stand out to me and that I am still contemplating from this side of the journey... a person of faith... a beloved husband and father... a premier scholar and teacher... a joyous person... a responsible and committed colleague in theological education... a generous philanthropist...an ecumenical Africanist... and a global citizen from Africa/Nigeria.

Ogbu's body will be buried in Ohafi a, Nigeria, but he lives in the hearts and minds of many people around the world. There are two places in Colombia that touched his heart and where he will also be remembered. The members of the Travel Seminar planted a young palm tree in memory of Dr. Ogbu Kalu on the main campus of the Reformed University in Barranquilla, Colombia. The group also donated a framed picture of Ogbu to the town of Palenque de San Basilio, the first free territory for African slaves in the Americas founded in 1603 by a runaway Zulu prince, Benkos Bioho. When Ogbu visited Palenque in August of 2008, there was a profound mutual discovery. He said to the people of Palenque, "I have found Africa in America." The people of Palenque said to Ogbu: "You are part of our family. Come to Palenque if you ever need a piece of land to live with your family."

When I invited Ogbu last year to co-lead the trip to Colombia, I was not aware that I was contributing to fulfill his dream of visiting Latin America for the first time. Our visit to Colombia in August, 2008 meant a lot to him. It was the beginning of a spiritual connection that will survive death as some of his projects for Colombia will be carried on by his family, colleagues and friends: the connection between McCormick Theological Seminary and the Reformed University in Barranquilla; a day care center for a displaced community; and the purchase of a pick-up truck for the economic development of Palenque.

The first thing I did after returning to McCormick from Colombia was to stand outside Ogbu's office. I contemplated through the glass window that space where we shared many time. I felt his absence and realized that I am coming back to a McCormick that is changing rapidly. I am committed to honor the memory of this friend and mentor and to fulfill some of his scholarly and philanthropic dreams. I pray for God's Spirit to bring peace and strength to Willy, her children and the rest of the family.

Kenneth Sawyer
Associate Professor of Church History
McCormick Theological Seminary

⚬⚬⚬⚬

Kalu: A Community Leader

Iknow Ogbu Kalu from his years with us at McCormick Seminary. Like so many others, I claim him as family, and, like so many others, I was blessed to have been claimed by him. We mourn his passing. We celebrate his gracious life and the gift he was to us. We witness the rivers of living water that fl owed so freely from his heart. From his first visit as candidate for the post of Luce Professor of World Christianity and Missions, we knew we would be fortunate to have so accomplished a scholar join us, but none of us could know what riches he would bring as colleague and collaborator. When Ogbu and Wilhelmina took up residence in Hyde Park in September of 2001, they fully joined this community, in study, service, and social life. In a special way, Ogbu took up residence in his office, with all things revolving round where he met with students, where his network of correspondence expanded, where he prayed and meditated and composed his essays. Though very busy, he considered his first years at McCormick a sort of sabbatical, before the scholarly world learned of his new post and availability for the ambitious new projects that he would complete in these years.

Ogbu was a great teacher, and he quickly reached out to students at Mc-Cormick, the Lutheran School of Theology, and the University of Chicago, all the while completing his work with a long train of students from across Africa, and with new students whose research touched on African themes. Students sought him out, recognizing his wisdom with applications, proposals, dissertation chapters, and publication projects. He cared about his students, and he took special care for his students. He recognized potential in graduate students, and he was a directive mentor responsible for the development of younger scholars. Likewise, Ogbu was a particularly caring colleague, with a fierce affection for his new coworkers. His appointment marked an important moment in the life of this community. His mandate was to profess the history of world Christianity and missions in this place, and he did so as a world Christian, not separating his Ohafi an, Igbo, Nigerian, African identity, but by connecting all that he was with all the conversations he had. He often described an unseen world to an unseeing people. He gave sight to the blind.

Ogbu and Wilhelmina Kalu joined us at Progressive Community Center, the Peoples' Church, by cheerfully folding themselves into our subcompact car with my wife and our three daughters, to drive for Sunday services, and for weekday meetings. Ogbu recognized the peculiar role of a seminary, in service to the whole Church, but needful of the accountability available only in a local assembly. From his place at Progressive, with his close relationship with his pastor B. Herbert Martin, Ogbu contributed to the life many congregations, including the Apostolic Church of God, Trinity United Church of Christ, and Edgewater Presbyterian Church, and he taught and preached and prayed in dozens of congregations – a true fulfillment of his office as a Teaching Elder in the Presbyterian Church of Nigeria.

Ogbu wrote that Church history is the "memory of the people of God, a pilgrim people,…constantly re-tell[ing] stories about the loving and reconciling acts of God in Christ and the Holy Spirit." Ogbu told the stories of the loving and reconciling acts of God in Christ and the Holy Spirit. But he also told how the promise and power of the gospel had been continually constrained and compromised by race, class, culture, and national story. Still he reminded us every day that the gospel means 'good news' and he showed how God had called all humanity to fullness of life. In his joy he taught us his discipline. In his singing he taught us his devotion. In his pride for his own children he taught praise and appreciation for God's grace. In his grief for his own parents, he taught gratitude for God's mercy. He told us a faithful narrative of the surprising work of God in our times.

He brought the burdens and ambiguities of tradition into conversation with the contemporary Church. He faced the challenges of our time, whether in assisting the defense of a Nigerian woman accused of adultery and threatened with stoning under Sharia law, or in his exposition of our current fears and fascinations. He reminded us that the Church is broader than our parochial preferences and prejudices. He helped us to distinguish some truth from much falsehood.

My family and I were the beneficiaries of countless acts of his kindness and care. My children knew his care and loving concern. He deeply cared for this community, and he fervently prayed God's blessing for each of his children, and for his colleagues, students, and McCormick staff, and for each of their children.

Finally, Ogbu honored us by sharing his graced life with us in these years. Ogbu is the son of Uke Kalu Onwuchekwa, and of Margaret Uzunma Uchendu Onwuchekwa. Their faithfulness was a gift to him which he shared with us. He honored those who had carried him, taught him, wept with him, danced with him, and prayed, taught, talked, argued, and laughed with him. He fulfi lled his calling with grace from the leading of the Spirit. Ogbu Kalu was with us long enough to learn some of his ways, long enough to walk with him for a time. Now he goes on before us. Thank God for our beloved brother and friend.

*Ogbu beginning senior lecturer appointment
at the University of Nigeria*

Ogbu at Village Send off to Canada, 1964

Ogbu as undergrad at Victoria College,
University of Toronto, September 1964

Ogbu with Stella and Edward

Ogbu and Willy with Edward and Stella

Ogbu at Jayne's Christening

Ogbu and daughter Jayne

Ogbu and daughter Patsy

Ogbu and Patsy in Village home Isiugwu Ohafia

Ogbu and daughters

Ogbu and daughter Stella

Ogbu and son Edward

Ogbu and Edward, Stella and Jayne

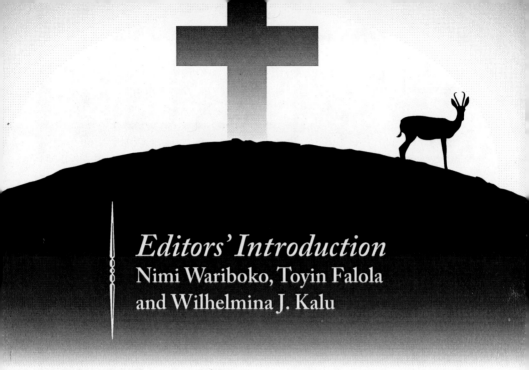

Editors' Introduction
Nimi Wariboko, Toyin Falola
and Wilhelmina J. Kalu

General Introduction

This volume is a serious reflection on the intersection of religion with the various other spheres of life. The essays, drawing from multiple disciplines, show how the metaphysical-moral visions of Africans equip them to respond to problems in the political, economic, and educational sectors and to construct social orders capable of promoting human flourishing. By diving deeply into social issues that confront Africans Professor Ogbu Uke Kalu lifts up the fundamental presuppositions which undergird politics, economics, culture, law, and family and thus lays bare the social-ethical outworking of African traditional religions, Christianity, and Islam.

In these essays Kalu repeatedly points scholars of African societies to the religious commitments that serve as the source of meaning beyond the political and economic spheres. The essays succinctly lay out the moral and spiritual sources that ground daily living and visions of the future. He goes beyond his primary training as an historian (displaying a formidable mastery of social theory) to advance the argument that the dynamics of the various spheres of life and social relationality in the African continent cannot be adequately understood without comprehending the religious dimension of social existence.

His analysis is very ethological. That is to say the essays reveal the ethos that informs actions and reflections in African societies; they are focused on the deep moorings of existential meaning, and they highlight the ways Africans morally and spiritually organize their lives. Like a good ethicist who understands the discipline of social ethics as the "science of ethos," his method is both longitudinal and cross-sectional. He combines historical analysis—tracing the development of issues over time—with cross-sectional interpretation of society. His cross-sectional analysis focuses on enduring patterns and dominant structures of interactions as they are observable today in the political economies he is investigating. These two methods of interpretation are executed in a tightly woven form and are always anchored to the inner logic of the values of the societies under study. The existential and ultimate questions that drive African socialities and agents are correlated with answers in religious message. Thus, the analyses are ultimately theological.

Indeed, in this volume he thinks and writes as a Christian social ethicist. The essays in their collective impact show how Christianity has interacted with the indigenous ethos of Africans. This is not all. They ask questions about what the mission of African churches should be in the twenty-first century as pertaining to forging of an ethos which can support sustainable economic development, social justice, peaceful coexistence, gender equality, and ecological conservation.

Summary and Relevance of Chapters

In stating the case for the relevance of these essays for contemporary scholarship we will try as much as possible to allow Kalu to speak in his own voice and endeavor not to impose much of our theoretical bias on the interpretation of his ideas. The sixteen essays in this volume are divided into four sections: (1) theology and politics; (2) religion, culture, and social engagement; (3) religion and violence, and (4) Theological education. The goal of this introduction is not to sum up the contents of the essays in this volume. Its limited purpose is to lift up the questions they ask and try to answer and connect such with the main themes in Kalu's scholarship and with the line of thought running through the three volumes.

Section I: Theology and Politics

Kalu was a prominent historian, theologian, and social analyst. His thought as exemplified by the essays in this collection was not one-part history, one-part theology, and one-part social science. His thinking on social issues was well integrated and hence each essay is also tightly woven together as one fabric. As a whole they are well blended because of the framework he applies to all of them.

This framework is like a five-sided star with each point bringing a distinct perspective to the whole and yet carefully guided to harmonize with the others. The sides of the star are context, periodization, culture, worldview, and ecology. Together, they constitute the hermeneutical lens through which he understands the patterns of human-divine relationships and the response to the gospel in Africa. In addition, they form the site in which theology, history, and human interactions happen and are sustained. This site-lens framework enables him to reflect concretely on what is happening to a people in their specific and particular gospel-people encounter. But since site and lens are always situated in a people's life and the people own them, by taking this approach to his investigation he is always compelled to ask and answer questions about the agency of the people.

In the two previous prefatory essays we mentioned that Kalu's scholarship is always concerned with highlighting the agency of Africans as they respond to the gospel. Now we can say that the essays in this volume reveal that this inclination was not simply a patriotic gesture or a reaction to distorted historiography, it was also methodological.

Chapter 1 succinctly lays out this framework, and in chapter 2 we see it at work. The question he asks about faith and politics flow from the African context in which the two are not necessarily understood as separate dimensions of human life. The roots of political ethics are nurtured in primal spirituality; and in a sense politics is political spirituality, and the political is a site of confrontation between the forces of good and evil. According to him,

> In Africa, the political realm is sacralized or enchanted and politics is a religious matter precisely because it is moral performance; it is about the undergirding values that determine how we govern ourselves or exercise power in the task of wielding the authority given to us.

He then shows how the linkages between culture, worldview, and ecology in the African context in the twenty and twenty-first centuries have worked to blur the boundaries between the sacred and the profane, and to interweave politics and faith in the public space.

Using the same argument that the roots of political ethics are nourished in primal spirituality, chapter 3 analyzes the acute legitimate crisis in Nigeria between 1993 and 1998. He posits that we cannot adequately understand the political crisis that engulfed the nation during this period if the role of religion is neglected. It was not only the military rulers and political elite that used it to patch up crumbling legitimacy, but also citizens used it as a coping mechanism in the face of the economic collapse that accompanied the political crisis. The oppressed citizens also deployed it to create the survival spaces to express themselves in the light of mounting intensity of material and psychological scourges that defined those crucial five years. The political elite tapped the resources of religion (especially from African traditional types) in their competition for economic resources and power in the modern space. The military leaders mobilized religious forces to give them the appearance of invincibility and to portray the state as enjoying divine approval.

The undertone of this kind of analysis which lifts up the availability of spiritual forces in the public spaces and shows how both rulers and ruled tap them for power and protection is a diatribe against Enlightenment rationalism. Put differently, his political purpose for writing the essay is perhaps to lessen the arrogance of Enlightenment rationalism. The academic interest is that the scholar who approaches politics, public morality, and public space with a "sanitized," disenchanted, rationalistic model will not penetrate the core of the intersection of religion and politics in Africa.

The interplay of politics and religion in Nigeria is warfare. The state is often an instrument of class struggle. The state is co-opted for the service of the dominant faction of the elite. There is an undue emphasis on capturing political power and an intense fear of losing to rival parties. For this reason, political competition assumes the character of warfare and has become a zero-sum game, "an anarchy of dedicated self-seeking."[1] The leaders are often engrossed in a struggle for survival. As in every war, human lives are at stake. Politicians organize their campaign as war-campaigns with religious forces fully summoned to assist in gaining victory and dominating the enemy. Often before the actual commencement of electioneering warfare, the electorates must be mobilized and sentiments whipped up. Religion is often used to align the relevant "foot soldiers" on the supposedly right side. This is the background he paints for understanding the case of a poor Muslim woman sentenced to die by stoning for committing adultery.

Exercising great sensitivity toward genuine Islamic piety, Kalu tells the ordeal of Safiyya Hussein with such compassion and elegant analysis that the reader can feel the pains of a hapless and helpless woman tossed around on a political chess game under the halo of a religious canopy. In chapter 4, using the Safiyya's saga as a jumping off point he shows how sharia laws in Nigeria have become a weapon of political warfare—just as Christian elites also use their religion for political gains. The political is also a sharp sword in the clutch of religious hands. Reality is always very complex and messy and to grasp it we must learn to use multiple lenses to examine it.

In this analysis of the interplay of politics and religion, as usual, Kalu keeps the focus on the religious dimension. He is generally impatient with scholars who reduce all crises in Africa as being engendered by socio-economic deprivations. He argues that the religious dimension is important for understanding crises in the continent and that it is a veritable key to grasping African politics. In reconstructing Safiyya Hussein's story and the ensuing controversy over the implementation of sharia laws in a supposedly secular country, he cautions against starting the analysis from a non-religious consideration. As he puts it:

> The paper argues that while political and socio-economic dimensions are important, the sharia question should be examined from a wider perspective that privileges the religious dimension. It is from this dynamic epicentre that the other enriching political, socio-economic, gender and global variables make sense and simplify a riddle. Sharia discourses that begin from the non-religious considerations run the risk of grabbing the stick from the wrong end to befuddle analysis.

The discourse in the next chapter (5) which treats how Pentecostal/charismatic rhetoric images Islam and sharia is another exemplar of the framework we have associated with his social analysis. In this chapter, as in the last one, we see that his analyses show how context (space), periodization (time), culture, worldview, and ecology are deployed to inform and explain space-time events. It is by paying close attention to the site-lens framework that he is able to show that the radicalization of Islamic politics in Northern Nigeria, contrary to what many commentators said at the time, was not induced by the recent insurgence of Pentecostal and charismatic forces. The roots of the radicalization go very deep into Nigeria's history and politics, and thus cannot be easily attributed to the "clash of fundamentalisms." At best, the explosion of Pentecostal/charismatic spirituality among Christians only partly contributes to it.

Pentecostal and charismatic group contributed to the tension between Christians and Muslims as they demonized Islam in their theology and practices. He advises that Nigerian Pentecostals need "to develop a concept of dialogue for the sake of a stable public space." He also contends that Muslims have "used the sharia as the lightening rod of their politics, a rallying cry." The players on both sides have "turned religious politics in Nigeria into a shark-infested waters" because they have rejected the "plurality in the worldview and cultural backgrounds of [their indigenous] communities."

The next two chapters, 6 and 7, explore the political-theological connections between Africans and African-Americans. The first discusses the famed African-American pastor, Jeremiah Wright and his political engagement with Africa. The chapter analyzes the social-activist theology of Jeremiah Wright, the former pastor of President Barack Obama. What Kalu brings into relief is Wright's effort to engage his church in the global public space and leading it to identify with the poverty, suffering, and crises that confront blacks all over the world. "Dr Jeremiah Wright's forte and legacy is this capacity to feel other people's pain of humiliation; this capacity to empathize, this capacity to respond to the individual and offer a hand that lifts up those pushed down into the miry pit by systemic social injustice."

Kalu also highlights Wright's theology of mission. The projects of Wright's church which are outside the United States are not merely programs for social justice, but are also concrete expressions of his theology of mission. His understanding of mission, is among other features, is

> characterized by the quality of being, saying and doing in community and for community of black folks. Second, it starts by building and nurturing a *koinonia* through worship and Bible study, teaching and preaching so that it embodies the presence of the reign of God in community. Third, from the black community at home it flows to all black people in Africa and in diaspora responding to the challenges of global issues of social justice and transforming social despair with hope. He perceives mission as a reciprocal activity between Africa and African diasporic communities.

Wright's story is used to shed light on the historic role African-Americans played in the evangelization of Africa in the nineteenth century. The participation of African-Americans in missionary activities in Africa fell into disrepute in the mid-twentieth century and now Kalu says with the Wright's engagement there is a "renaissance of a theme that suffered disaster along the pathway of black history."

Another important player in African-American re-engagement with African Christianity is James Cone. He has influenced theological thinking in South Africa with his black liberation theology. In chapter 7, Kalu tells the story of how the emergence of black theology in the 1970s inspired many South Africans and elicited a prophetic response from the church in South Africa. The awakening of the church to its prophetic mission to oppose oppressive structures and laws in South Africa is marked by the 1986 *Kairos Document*.

The scholarship of Cone is important for understanding how South African churches in the heat of apartheid sought to relate the black struggle for freedom and human dignity to God's justice. Kalu argues that Cone's prophetic scholarship inspired both blacks and whites in South Africa to appropriate their nation's resources for their own struggle and adapt them for their purpose.

> The contents [of the Kairos Document] resonated more with Cone's idea than with Marxist purists. It may not have the theological clarity or succinctness of Barmen but it theologized more elaborately and contained a deep social analysis of the state. It used a liberation theological model to engage in a trenchant description and critique of the contemporary regime. Its real title stressed a *"theological comment on the political crisis in South Africa"*.

Section II: Religion, Culture, and Social Engagement

What should be the relationship between church and culture (state)? This is an age-old debate in which many theologians have participated. Kalu in the five essays in this section not only takes a stance in the ongoing debate, but also shows how African churches engage with social issues in the modern public space. His stance is undergirded by his theologies of church and mission which he summarily states in chapter 8 as:

> From a theological perspective, we define the church less as an institution but as a people, a community of those who have been called out from their former lives into a new relationship with Christ. Institutional structures serve to organize but the story is about people who are inside the institutional canopy, who are mandated to share and proclaim the reign of God over the whole inhabited earth, to continue what God had started in the career of the man, Jesus. This reign is perceived in concrete terms as God's love that is a gift to be received and shared with the neighbor... The church's responsibility for the public space is rooted in its core identity and connection with the reign of God.

Based on this conception of church and mission, what should be the primary focus of African church's engagement with social issues in the continent? Taking as his point of departure the assertion that poverty is the primary concern of Jesus Christ and the most urgent existential problem facing Africans, he maintains that the church should focus on poverty alleviation. This argumentative position is both a prescription for the future and a flight of the Minerva owl or the backward glance of the African bird, *Sankofa*. Indeed, he holds that the economic and social woes in the continent have already compelled churches to articulate a Christian response to political stagnation and poverty. For instance, he writes that:

> The forms of engagement range from spiritual warfare and emergency relief to political activism. For instance, in Nigeria, Pentecostals have been the bulwark of the ecumenical body, Christian Association of Nigeria, and engaged in an enormous relief work in Liberia and Sierra Leone. In recent times, many Pentecostal groups have prayed their people into state houses as governors. They have also designed City Projects in which certain urban centres are targeted and the immoral qualities of the rulers of the city taken as "prayer point". Sanitizing the undisciplined cultures of large urban areas has been a viable political task.

Chapter 8, the first essay in this section traces the shifting emphasis from other-worldliness and conservative political ideology to social engagement. This is not all. The chapter also provides an analysis of the general pattern of African churches' responses to "the challenges of growth of state power and bowls of poverty." They are more engaged in issues of social justice since the 1990s than they were in the 1970s and 1980s. In the face of the recent colossal economic disasters African churches have been compelled to "bring faith inspired motivations and ethics in seeking for new answers to endemic problems such as poverty" and therefore redefining the role of faith in economic development.

Having declared poverty as the main subject of his theological ethics, in chapter 9 Kalu provides a historical survey of poverty in Nigeria. His analysis shows the roots of poverty as embedded in the structural faults of the colonial era. This historical survey provides insights about changing perception, causes, faces of poverty, and alleviation strategies that were tried in the past. One of the causes of poverty—which he believes even the post-colonial government inherited—is the lack of concern for the poor and the environment.

The survey is also helpful in its reconstruction of how indigenous communities understood the meaning of poverty and the efforts they took through local social and economic processes to combat it. Using language as the entry point into indigenous conception of poverty, he is able to profile it from strong cultural and historical perspectives and then goes on to show how it has changed under colonialism and post-colonialism.

Chapter 10, "Healing as the Children's Bread: Contested Coping-Healing Strategies in African Pentecostalism" examines an aspect of Pentecostals' engagement with poverty and other social issues. Ill health is a crucial dimension of what it means to be poor in Africa. This chapter focuses on the conception, theology, and practice of faith healing in Pentecostal churches. These churches bring a spiritual, supernatural perspective to sickness and disease. While their pastoral-care system provides an important coping mechanism amid ravaging health crisis and whereas it does not necessarily disdain the germ theory (as some scholars erroneously believe), the system is undergirded "with a worldview that places a causal connection between purity and danger, sin and sickness." Kalu, like many other scholars, finds this explanatory framework problematic. But unlike most of them, he affirms Pentecostal churches' recovery of the notion of the church as a healing community. In addition, he avers that the gulf between African Pentecostal concept of health and healing and that of modern science is narrowing.

Ecological disasters are premium causes of poverty in Africa. As we already learned in chapter 9, both colonial and postcolonial governments in Nigeria neglected the environment in their rush to implement ill-conceived economic development strategies. But the neglect of the environment by governments was not the only cause. There were ambivalences in African worldview that have "produced destructive eco-ethics." In the chapter (11) entitled "The Gods are to blame: Religion, Worldview and Light Ecological Footprints in Africa," Kalu examines how Africans perceive environmental disasters as a religious matter refracted through a primal cultural hermeneutic. Indigenous African spirituality as he puts it "celebrates an intimacy with the natural world" and it is always in "search for harmonious relationship with nature and awareness that nature carries hidden knowledge." Yet he argues that African worldviews do not often have the ethics of restraint. In this way, he brings into sharp relief the tension that exists between values of environmental conservatism and non-sustainability in African indigenous worldviews. This is a tension or dialectic that is often ignored by scholars who tend to romanticize African past or worldview.

In order to ease or resolve the tension there must be an inner transformation of African worldviews, he advises. The task for African religious ethicists is to craft an ethic of restraint and seek ways of incorporating it into the sacralized worldviews of various communities. This Kalu hopes will help move the communities to "more pro-active eco-care." He calls this task "cultural engineering" and proceeded to show how it can be done.

This section on church and society comes to a close with a discourse on feminist and womanist ethics in chapter 12, "Daughters of Ethiopia: Constructing a Feminist Discourse in Ebony Strokes." It is about African female theologians' response to the violence and discrimination meted out against women in Africa. He applauds them for developing theologies and social-ethical frameworks to highlight women concerns, but urges them to engage both with African-American theologians and African Muslim women thinkers.

Section III: Religion and Violence

In this section on religion and violence, Kalu works from the assumption that religion affects politics and politics is not immune from religious influence. The interplay between them is a key to understanding violence in the African continent. In fact, he argues that religion is the substratum of politics as well as its handmaiden in Africa. His stance is supported from several perspectives. For instance, he maintains that "in Africa, the sacralization of the cosmos legitimates the political space and the dynamics of the political culture." Religion-motivated violence also has a political purpose. Violence is an "attempt to grab, control, and redirect the dynamics of the forces [of the spheres of society] along vested interest."

In this section of three essays he pulled together divergent perspectives and multiple disciplinary methods to shed light on the connection between religion and violence in Africa. His overarching conclusion is that "theories of religious violence based on Western epistemology and enlightenment worldview may be unhelpful for many regions of the global south where religious violence is endemic." At the minimum their context, worldview, and culture are different and thus a one-size-fits-all theory is inappropriate.

Chapter 13 explores how religious and cultural roots of social orders inform and nurture violence in public spaces. The argument is that the most sustainable mobilization of interest groups and identities are often enacted and promoted through cults. They are thus powerful channels and sites for generating and distributing political violence. The analysis in this chapter on the one hand portrays religion as a weapon in the competitive, pluralistic public space and on the other it clearly shows religion as the substratum of politics. As Claude Ake once put it "reality is full of contradictions, and [that] we can not grasps it unless we learn to think dialectically." Politicians and elites resort to primal religious worldview and summon religious forces to confer on them "the illusion of invincibility, protection and numinous power to control others and destroy opponents."[1]

Given all this, it is not surprising that Kalu holds that the task of understanding the political landscape and theologizing about it and the violent confrontations it throws up must necessarily investigate the "importance of worldview and resilience of primal values in the modern public space."

Chapter 14 begins with the argument that theology or God-talk in Africa cannot be considered serious if it neglects reflecting on violence and the role of the church in securing justice and peace. The fact that violence has decimated resources, manpower, and ecosystems makes it imperative to examine God-human relationship from the perspective of violence. Thus, this chapter explores the power of emergent religious forms in generating loyalty and deep passions which often lead to violence and lost of lives.

From here the discourse moves to the "politics of Jesus" as well as models of conflict transformation rooted in indigenous knowledge. The result of his engagement with Jesus' politics and models of conflict transformations is a set of three prescriptions crafted to aid theological reflection on possible solutions to violent conflicts. As he puts it, the transformation of religious conflict would rest on a tripod:

i. re-imagining the public space (socio-economic transformation and good governance);

ii. healing the public space through projects such as truth commission and re-negotiating social contract through national conference;

iii. centering the religious space by promoting a culture of interfaith religious education through (a) creating dialogue contexts that mine the interior theological bases of various faith traditions, and (b) deliberately engineering salient ethics for peaceful existence in the entire continent.

He is careful to note that conflict transformation cannot be imposed from the top or by governments, but must flow from the grassroots and the churches which operate in the midst of the people.

> It will emerge from the quality of relationship generated by the common people and by paradigms of evangelization that enables the church to offer the water of life instead of being a river between communities. This may require new models of priestly/ministerial formation and the deliberate cultivation of a dialogical Christian presence.

Section IV: Theological Education

In chapter 15 Kalu revisits the Edinburgh Conference of 1910. He examines in details the conference participants' debates on the educational projects of Christian missions in Africa and set them within the context of actual practices of missionary education. His overall assessment is that Christian education and even the conference participants' reflections on it were in thralldom to the racist and imperial mentality of European empire builders in Africa. Missionary education was not geared to developing converts as Africans proud of their heritage, but to transform them into carriers of European worldview and cultural sensitivity. Such colonial-era education did not expand the beneficiaries' understanding of themselves through the identification with their social-cultural location. "Education became the strongest weapon in Western underdevelopment of Africa because of its power of eradication."

The Christian education enterprise was not a total disaster as it engendered some unintended good results. According to him, "education and translation would fuel both charismatic spirituality and nationalism and change the character of Christianity in the aftermath of the conference."

The final essay, chapter 16, examines the impact of education on contemporary African Christianity—especially on ministerial formation. The clergy educational process is under enormous strain. The rapid expansion of Christianity in the continent has yielded a large pool of candidates for ministerial education, but there are no adequate facilities to train them and the training most pastors receive is very shallow. "Many churches have resorted to de-schooling in theological education. Confident of a spiritual experience and a divine call, many people start their own ministries without formal training. It is dubbed as setting up an altar." In this scrambled pattern of ministerial formation, apprenticeship is all the rage. Such training on the job is been "imaged as gaining a mantle." Some churches go a step further by forming an in-house Bible college. The problem is that their pastors (almost always not formally trained themselves) teach all subjects and there is no effort made toward outside accreditation.

There is also some good news—at least there are some prospects looming in the horizon. There are now many Christian universities in Africa which are responding to the increased demand for an educated leadership who are locally trained. There are, however, concerns about them. They are not seminaries or divinity schools devoted to the study of comparative religions, are laboring under the heavy burdens of poor academic quality and accreditation issues, and are educating students with curricula that do not privilege African worldview and culture. So he raises serious questions about the ability of the new Christian universities to serve the cause of theological education in Africa in the twenty-first century. Nonetheless, he acknowledges that the experiment with tertiary education provides African churches with a new opportunity for the application of indigenous model of theological education.

Note

1. Claude Ake, *Democracy and Development in Africa* (Washington, D.C.: The Brookings Institution, 1996), 129.

Part I

THEOLOGY AND POLITICS

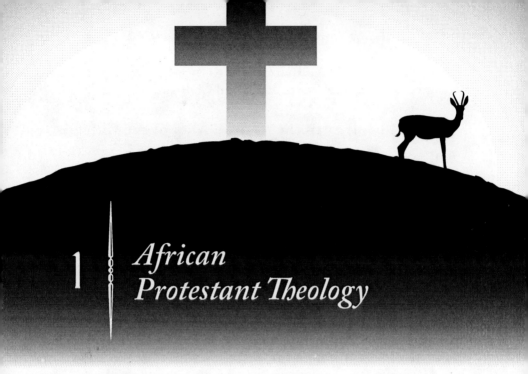

1 | *African Protestant Theology*

The Emergence of African Theology

In 1973, when John Mbiti heralded the authenticity of African Theology, many wondered whether there was an identifiable theology that could be branded as African. The riposte was that theology is a human enterprise, reflecting upon God's relationship to human beings and the world of nature. It is God-talk by human beings about their understanding of the nature of the triune God, the patterns of human-divine relationship, and the requisite ethics. People through the ages have provided conflicting answers to these deep things. In spite of Western efforts to systemize and define it as faith seeking reason, theology remains a process as each generation and context reflects differently on its particular experiences. Context (space) and periodization (time) constitute the framework for doing theology. Each theological enterprise has a background story shaped by the culture, primal worldview, ecology, and history. Culture encompasses the socio-economic and political structures, language, religion, and ways of life of a community. It constitutes the contested site in gospel-people encounters. Undergirding each culture is the worldview that enables the explanation, prediction, and control of space-time events. Culture is hewn from the rock of a community's responses to the challenges of the eco-system. This eco-system determines the economic structures which, according to Karl Marx, influence other aspects of the culture. Culture, worldview, and the ecology, therefore, act as the hermeneutical lens to understand God-talk.

African Theology in the African Map of the Universe

Africa constitutes a specific cultural context. In spite of myriads of sub cultures, there are common denominators and cultural signifiers that underscore shared identity, and denote the deep-level assumptions and allegiances that format the varied cultural ingredients and provide larger meaning. Africans appropriate the gospel through the lens of their worldviews. With a cyclical perception of time, life is a journey as the soul (Akan: *sunsum*) travels from birth to death, through the ancestral world before reincarnating back into the human world. The human world is a reflection of the spirit world; the sacred meshes into the profane. Ancestors, as the living dead, cross the boundaries freely, their presence being acknowledged through sacrifices, libations, and festivals when they visit the human world as masked guests. In the three-dimensional perception of space, spirits inhabit the sky, earth (land and water), and the ancestral world. It is a charismatic, alive universe, a precarious vision in which evil spirits essay to ruin human beings through witchcraft and sorcery. People fight back through rituals that ward off evil spirits with the resources of benevolent gods.

The story of African theology is about the intrusion of an external agent, Christianity into the cosmos. In the missionary enterprise, the civilization project built on Enlightenment's evolutionary worldview demonized indigenous religions and cultures. It challenged the viability of African culture to serve as an anchor amidst rapid change and a marker of identity. The clash of worldviews became the first concern of African theology. Slave trade and various brands of colonialism severely disfigured every aspect of African culture, religion, ecology, resources, and history. Admittedly, every culture contains life-threatening elements, and indigenes colluded in the destructive enterprise that created the loss of freedom and vulnerability. Often, it was "we on us." Efforts at liberation included primary resistance, nationalist struggles, armed rebellion, freedom wars, constitutional conferences, self-rule projects, coups, counter- coups, and ethnic wars. The concern here is the reflective, theological dimensions in the quest for identity, recovery of dignity, and the freedom to respond to the gospel using indigenous resources such as language, cultural production and indigenous knowledge.

[handwritten margin note: what of Egypt, Alexandria? → Patristic African theology]

4

The Goal of African Theology

The goal of African theology is to create the possibilities for the gospel to answer questions raised in the interior of African worldviews. It seeks to remove Western hegemonic structures and captivity in the modes of expressing the indigenous responses to the gospel; to declare that Western culture and theology are not normative. Epistemology is crucial in doing liberation theology. This task was ironically performed by Protestant missionaries when they translated the Bible into various vernaculars, and by African Americans, who returned to evangelize Africa in the 18th century before the first Western missionary organization was founded. They came with a fully-fledged anti-structural, charismatic theology articulated in the New Life movement. In the next century, the nascent African theology spilled into the Ethiopianism movement whose cardinal affirmations were articulated by McNeal Turner, Thomas Delaney, Alexander Crummell, and Edward Wilmot Byden. Declaring that *"God is a Negro"* and that they *"are no longer slaves,"* they explained that God's *providence* brought them to America so that they could return to redeem the motherland through Christianity. Indigenous revivalist movements such as Godianism and Afrikania would sprout to clothe African concepts of God in Western garb and rituals.

In the inter-war years, the pneumatic emphasis blossomed in the African Instituted Churches variously named as *Aladura* (western Africa), *Zion* (southern and central Africa), and *Roho* (eastern Africa). Before splintering into myriad groups, the classical forms used the resources of the translated Bible to appropriate the pneumatic resources of the gospel within the depths of indigenous worldviews. The Hebrew culture resonated prominently with African indigenous cultures and created inculturating pathways as they re-imagined God's saving presence in their wilderness and the healing power of Christ through the Holy Spirit. Emphases were on prayer, rituals and symbols drawn from indigenous African and Biblical roots, and a muscular ethical replication of Levitical practices. The theological achievements included the recovery of orality and narrative as a method of doing lived theology, articulated through ritual processes, dance, music, and lively liturgies that elicit participation. The psychology in the healing practices privileged the organic union of body, soul, and spirit. Spiritualized diagnosis betrayed the sensitivity to the numinous world where the presence of evil forces explained causality. Healing, deliverance (exorcism), visions, dreams, and the quest for material resources loomed large in the ritual repertoire that included the use of indigenous pharmacopeias. As the movement expanded, messianic, nativistic, and vitalistic genres emphasized elements that challenged Christian doctrinal purity.

African Theology:
From World Wars to Decolonization

The enlarged space for African culture set the stage for the challenges to the mainline churches in the post- Second World War era. A new crop of theologians trained in Western institutions joined the nationalist affray in a kerygmatic enterprise to convert African peoples and their cultures by turning these to the glare and judgment of the gospel. They argued that Africans should not be mere proselytes but truly converts; that Christ is in every culture and judges the life-denying aspects of all cultures; that the pilgrim and indigenous principles, the global and local processes must be held in tension. The enterprise went beyond cultural nationalism to interrogate how one responds to the gospel in a world in which the gods of the ancestors remained resilient. The character of African God-talk in the mainline churches in the colonial period elicited the quest for identity. John Parratt averred that African Theology could be divided into two streams: the emphasis on culture in western Africa and on the politics of social justice in central and southern Africa. Both dimensions remained relevant in all contexts. Each theme was privileged at different points in time driven by forces in the environments.

In the 1960s, Harry Sawyer led the quest for *indigenization* that contested missionary theology of *adaptation/transplantation*. He wondered whether ancestors could pass muster as communion of saints. E.B.Idowu (1962) studied the Yoruba concept of God (*Olodumare*) to decry the racism in missionary theology, arguing that Christianity should be an extension of African traditional religion. By the next decade, the limits of indigenization became obvious: God was in Africa before the missionaries but missionaries brought the gospel at known points in time; therefore, the task of theology should examine the patterns of traditioning or appropriation process better described by *contextualization* and *incarnation*. Concerns revolved around doctrine, culture, the foreign liturgies, and decision-making power monopolized by missionaries. How could one understand God, Christ, the Holy Spirit and other Christian doctrines with the backdrop of African deities, ancestors, and spirits? Mbiti's doctoral dissertation at Cambridge (1964) examined the concept of eschatology in the New Testament, as preached by missionaries, and as understood among the Akamba of Kenya from their indigenous conception of life after death. Christian Gaba (1974) examined the theology of salvation through the sacred scripture of Anlo people in Ghana; Gabriel Setiloane developed an African theology from Tswana indigenous concepts, and Kwesi Dickson hosted a group that compared African and Biblical concepts of revelation.

It became the staple diet of African scholarship to explore various Biblical themes either through ethnographic case studies or by painting with broad brushes. Debates on Africa theology moved from Botswana (1980) to Monrovia (1982) when Sergeant Doe's coup scattered the conferees! Some suggested the ancient method of "spoiling the Egyptians," conservatives like Byang Kato rejected the methodology that uses indigenous religion and culture as the basis for doing Christian theology. He compared it to confusing natural and revealed theologies. Catholic scholars from Kinshasha tended towards philosophical method while Protestants deployed anthropological approaches. Kwame Bediako's *Theology and Identity* (1992) likened the vibrancy of African theology to the first two centuries of Christianity in the Graeco-Roman world. The study of African traditional religion intensified driven by the theological task. As John Mbiti insisted, the kernel of the gospel remains the same everywhere; Christ redeemed African religions and cultures that served as *praeparatio evangelica*. Okot p'Bitek's *African Traditional Religion in Western Scholarship* accused him of "hellenizing" African traditional religion. Undeterred, Mbiti studied how Africans named God in many vernacular languages, and examined the use of the Bible in African churches to illustrate the large areas of resonance that served as pathways to reclaim identity, and demonstrate the nature and significance of African theology. He continuously repeated the Akamba proverb that cattle are born with ears, they grow horn later; that the sources for African theology are oral narratives, the Bible, inherited Christian traditions, and African experiences. In this enterprise Christ remained a sore finger in the African map of the universe; so younger scholars explored various imageries for Christ: *guest, ancestor, chief, king* and more. Each was limited by the ambience of cultural understanding and differences in usage.

By the 1980s, it became clear that decolonization was a form of passive revolution as the departing colonialists installed black representatives who soon established dictatorships. The challenge for liberation theology was to analyze the neo-colonial structures, expose the new forms of social injustice, and respond to the challenges of resilient covenants with the ancestors in the midst of modernity. Apartheid in southern and central Africa further challenged the churches. Vatican II and Uppsala 1968 changed the international Christian perspectives on Africa. But African American influence became crucial as James Cone visited Accra, Ghana, in 1977 with the message of a black liberation theology. Southern Africans grasped it as an exit. A debate ensued whether it was applicable in Africa. Four political positions emerged in South Africa based on nuanced understanding of black liberation theology: Luthuli and ANC, Sobukwe's anti-white

Pan African Congress, Steve Biko's Black Consciousness Movement, and Desmond Tutu's non-violent United Democratic Front. This theological trend led to the *Kairos Document* that became important in forcing the churches to theologically engage issues of social justice in the heat of the liberation of southern Africa. It sustained the guerilla movements by re-interpreting the gospel contextually and challenging "church theology" from the viewpoint of the oppressed. Its method was a prophetic social analysis with the mind of Christ's *sedaqah*.

Theology, Mother Tongue and Inculturation: From the 1980s to the End of the Second Millenium

The cultural identity theme did not fade but was tackled through increased recognition of the power of vernacularisation, experiments in ministerial formation, new models of theological education, and the concept of *inculturation* which enables Christian theology to be respectful, humble, dialogical, and postures the gospel as the good news that responds to the deepest aspirations of the people.

New concerns emerged as the economies of soft and militarized African states collapsed. World Bank's Structural Adjustment programs worsened the scourge of poverty at the micro-economic level. Faced with the implosion of the modern state, environment degradation, abuse of human rights, poverty, and pluralism, African theology was required to become a tool of hope, and a sign of God's saving grace and preference for the poor. In the late 1980s, a number of creative theologies emerged in Africa: Inus Daneel developed the Earth-keepers' Theology among traditional healers, AICs, and mainline churches in Zimbabwe. To counter environmental degradation and the lack of a viable eco-ethics of preservation, this theology utilized the indigenous concept that to cut down a tree without appropriate ritual is like killing a person. The *ngozi* spirit hovers and may become hostile until appeased. He designed the Eucharistic liturgy that enabled people to confess their abuse of nature, to present and bless tree saplings at the altar, and to plant the new trees. Mercy Amba Oduyoye mobilized a Circle of Concerned African Women Theologians to write theological treatises that contest patriarchy in African churches. The dominant method was the art of remembrance, an excavation of indigenous memory that searched the language (proverbs and folktales), and the cultures in matrilineal and patrilineal communities for images that degrade women. These narratives could be reconstructed in favor of women's roles in the past of communities. The enterprise benefited from the reconstructionist hermeneutics of suspicion in Western feminist theology but distanced itself in significant ways. For instance, its Christology painted Jesus as womanist-friendly because the maleness of Jesus does not matter in African language structures that do not differentiate according to gender. In every encounter with women, Jesus exposed some aspects of the meaning of the reign of God. Mariology became iconic in this ecumenical sharing as Evangelical and Catholic women found common grounds. Like African American "womanist" theology, the Circle members remained Trinitarian, believing in the church, challenging the flat reading of the Bible in African churches as the source of the patriarchal gender ideology, and therefore, called the church to deal justly with women.

Toward the end of the second millennium Africa experienced a rapid growth of Christianity. The cutting edge is the Charismatic/Pentecostal movement whose theological register includes word-faith, prosperity, deliverance, intercession, intense evangelism, and exercise of charismatic gifts. The charismatisation of the mainline churches all over Africa, and the decline of the numerical strength of AICs in West Africa indicate the acceptance of theologies rooted in indigenous spirituality, the reclamation of the pneumatic resources of the Bible, and privileging of experience. Experience serves as a cipher indicating the insertion of a contradictory opinion, a right to be heard, a contradiction of what authority says. It is an assertion of a self-authenticating autonomy deploying language symbols of resistance that appeal to inherited ideology. It demands that the gospel performs better than the traditional religions in responding to health and wealth challenges. It is sensitive to the untoward natural environment, and declares that Christianity is about power in the midst of a precarious worldview and threatening global processes. The new theology is based on the old cardinal principles of evangelicalism: intensely Biblicist, emphasizing conversion, eschatology, and social activism, rejecting cessationism, and recovering the pneumatic dimensions of the gospel muted in the racist effort to avoid confusion with the spirits of "pagans". It rejects some of the compromises in the earlier pneumatology of the *Aladura, Zionists, and Abaroho* especially appropriation of symbols and rituals from traditional religions. Charismatic theology enables African Christianity to regain the power in the gospel for coping and engaging the problems from both the indigenous worldviews and modernity. It is an experiential theology with a muscular Christology. It has reshaped the religious landscape of Africa. African theology is intensely charismatic because it reflects from a charismatic indigenous worldview.

Bibliography

Samuel Ngewa, Mark Shaw, Tite Tienou, eds. *Issues In African Christian Theology* (Nairobi: East African Educational Publishers, 1998).

John S. Mbiti, *New Testament Eschatology In An African Background: A Study of the Encounter Between New Testament Theology and African Traditional Concept* (Oxford: Oxford University Press, 1971).

K. Dickson and P. Ellingworth, eds *Biblical Revelation and African Beliefs* (Maryknoll, NY: Orbis Books, 1969); Kwesi Dickson, *Theology in Africa* (Maryknoll, NY: Orbis Books, 1984).

Kwame Bediako, *Theology and Identity: The Impact of Culture Upon Christian Thought In The Second Century and Modern Africa* (Oxford: Regnum Books, 1992).

G.H. Muzorewa, *The Origins and Development of African Theologies* (Maryknoll, NY: Orbis Books, 1985).

D.M. Gitari, *In Season and Out of Season: Sermons to A Nation* (Oxford: Regnum Books, 1996).

Allan A. Boesak, *Farewell To Innocence* (Maryknoll, NY: Orbis Books, 1977).

John Parratt, ed., *A Reader in African Christian Theology* (London: SPCK, 1987); *Reinventing Christianity: African Theology Today* (Grand Rapids, MI: Erdmans, 1993).

J. N. K.Mugambi and Laurenti Magesa eds. *Jesus in African Christianity: Experimentation and Diversity in African Christologies* (Nairobi: Acton Publishers, 1989).

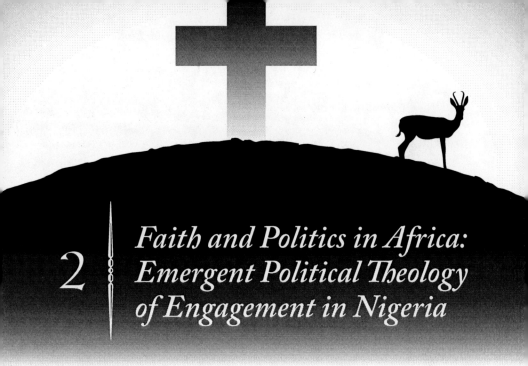

2 | *Faith and Politics in Africa: Emergent Political Theology of Engagement in Nigeria*

Theoretical Framework

It will not be pedantic to begin with theoretical musings because an old teacher taught me to ask simple questions about large issues. Why do we, for instance, speak of faith and politics as if both operate as separate dimensions and spheres of human life? This manner of posing the question that comes so naturally may possibly hide a worldview that may not be universally shared. It comes from a mental structure that puts the emphasis on the analytical mode of human reflection; it may jar with the feeling component in experiencing life. Western Enlightenment worldview drew the distinction that appears so natural to those brought up in its perception of reality. One dimension of globalization is that it is changing awareness of other worldviews. In Africa, the political realm is sacralized or enchanted and politics is a religious matter precisely because it is a moral performance; it is about the undergirding values that determine how we govern ourselves or exercise power in the task of wielding the authority given to us. Authority is legitimized or delegated power; every ruler is situated as a subsidiary entity. So, the questions of power are always: who holds power; for whom and to what end? While it is possible to answer these questions of power from humanistic perspectives, the moral dimension of power has not failed to assert itself. Indeed, there is always the problem of the source of authority and obligation. In pre-modern and Enlightenment Europe even kings appealed to God as the source of authority and themselves as mere viceroys.

Religion is intricately woven into the fabric of politics and provides the compelling touchstone of legitimacy or the love of the ruler by the ruled; the motive for exercising power; reason to be obeyed; the determinant of the moral standards and style of power and the engine that moves governance. In such contexts, the structure of governance had tremendous impact on the modes of religious expression and religion could not be conjured out of politics. The enlightenment project that sought to desacralize the political space and disenchant the worldview could only so dare with a myth that imagined three evolutionary stages of civilization shifting from the darkness of religion and philosophy into the blinding light of reason, science and empiricism. It conjured politics into a science and imbued it with secular morality and existentialist ideals. In spite of the vaunted claims, human nature remained resistant and theories of culture lag tried to explain the inexplicable. Why do people do horrible things to other people in spite of reason, technology and civilization? T.S Eliot could, therefore, re-imagine the post-world war period with the metaphor of the shadow in his *Wasteland* poems and Spengler moaned about the *Decline of the West* as the idea of progress suffered a defeat. The global village has brought people from high technological zones to revisit those from low technological regions where the world is still enchanted; religion colludes with magic to weave an organic perception of reality; and spiritual forces combine with humans to create a humane environment where human beings could be truly human. That is the goal of any viable political culture.

The emphasis here is that the linkage between culture, worldview and ecology has protected the centrality of religion in the public space in these non-Western contexts. Religion has not operated as an independent variable but has always been influenced by these other forces and in turn influenced them. In spite of the insertion of secularism, religion has remained resilient and the heart beat of non-Western cultures. The worldview in African communities is charismatic as gods operate in the sky, land, water and ancestral world. They destroy the boundaries between the profane and sacred; sacralize reality and gives religious value to everyday activities. Religion, culture and ethnicity become the organizing frameworks of human lives and the modern public space is constantly villigized through the use of cultic elements acquired from the primal sector of the culture.

Just as an illustration from an event that occurred in the first week of February 2003: a Nigerian newspaper reported an event in a state house of legislature located in the south-west region. A member was to be dismissed for indiscipline. On the fateful day, as the Speaker of the House announced the verdict, the member strode to the center of the house, brought out an egg from the folds of his *agbada* or long-flowing apparel and broke it on the floor with incantations; a pandemonium ensued as he brought out a pot full of concoctions and broke it on the floor. By this time, honorable members were scampering over the seats in the bid to escape from the foul-smell of the enchantment. Without resort to filibuster he was able to disperse his opponents. Even the security guards of the House of Legislature escaped for their dear lives.[1] Cultic power is employed freely in the public space and often buttresses political clout.[2] As the competition for dwindling resources intensify, religion, even if manipulated, becomes central in political discourse. It is this context that informs our reflections on faith and politics in Nigeria.

It may be added as a necessary digression that the current literature on secularism and religion in the West is like a war zone strewn with contesting claims of victory. Within 2002 four books could serve as illustrations of the battle lines: Steve Bruce argued in his *God is dead: secularization in the West* that the emphasis on scientific and technological ways of understanding reality has induced the precipitous decline of religion and emergence of societies characterized by diversity, pluralism, individual choice and relativism. Edward Norman joined by declaring *Secularism: the New Century Theology*. Others demurred: Philip Jenkins in *The Next Christendom* accepted the shift of the center of gravity of Christianity to the southern hemisphere and therefore the imperative of paying attention to the journey of the gospel through those cultures. He argues that Western secularist theorists have ignored the "browning" of World Christianity and its impact for the future. This "new Christian world of the south could find unity in common religious beliefs...(and develop)..a powerful Christian identity in culture and politics". But he made a special case for America, arguing that the pattern of decline witnessed in Europe does not apply here where a large percentage of the population still shows religious adherence; the strongest exception among industrialized nations. Reginald Bibby concurred in his *Restless God: The Renaissance of Religion in Canada*. Perhaps a large influx of immigrant population renews and revitalizes Christianity and saves its total collapse in Europe.[3] Commentators of many hues agree that there is a tremendous spiritual quest that may not be Christian but bound to affect the critique of socio-political culture. The resilience of religion in the politics of the Third World and especially of Africa that Jeff Haynes has argued so forcibly may reflect a wider trend requiring scholarly inquiry.[4]

Two other issues of larger significance deserve attention. The impact of western culture on Africa determines the relationship of politics and religion because Western culture has reconfigured the terrain. It created three publics: primal, external and emergent public that is neither fish nor fowl and imbued with ambiguous morality and value system. Nigerians refer to it as the white man's world. For instance, if one stole in the 'white man's world', the person is beyond the purview of traditional sanctions. The development of urban contexts created the ambiguous space for people who neither internalized Western values nor kept faith with the traditional. It has been argued that the indiscipline and corruption among the political elite could be explained by the gap. A politician who robbed the state could still dance to the big drum in the village as a warrior who had forayed out into the white man's world and returned with a piece of the national cake for his people. The battering of traditional models of social control and yet inability to install a viable Western alternative has many implications including the sensitivity in doing a different type of political theology.

But it provides the class factor in social analysis. Often attention is focused on what the elite say and write. Beneath elite politics is a vibrant infra-political zone where the ruled comment freely on their rulers. It has its own language, symbols and meaning system. It exhibits a large dosage of local vitality and hidden strategies of resistance; it creates a domain of self-assertion. Take for an example a case when a ruler dons a laborer's gear, picks up a spade and plants a seedling at the inauguration of an expensive program called, *Operation Feed the Nation*; the infra-political zone would quickly sense that the ruler is in fooling the people because his normal flamboyant lifestyle does not match the masking tradition of a laborer's garb. Indeed, he might be defrauding the treasury in a program that should be named, *Operation Fool the Nation* because after the inaugural ceremony, the project will be allowed to flop while the budget must be spent. Thus, *Better Life for Rural Women* was dubbed *Better Life for Rich Women* who benefited from the resources allocated to the project. NEPA does not mean *National Electric and Power Authority* but *Never Expect Power Anytime* for those urban dwellers who regularly fight with mosquitoes in the dark throughout the night. Political theology is about what the people are really saying on the moral quality of the exercise of power among them and not about the pronouncements of the elites. Political speeches by the ruling elites and media reports do not constitute the stuff of political theology. What the people are saying and doing at the level of infra-politics provide clearer guides and these implicate the church because the wide range of the associational life of the church makes it the leader of civil society in most parts of Africa.[5]

With these caveats we can now use the Christian case study to illustrate the relationship between faith and politics in an African context, Nigeria. The goal is beyond tracing the relationship between church and state to show that Christians in Africa have gradually reshaped their attitude and articulation of the gospel's relationship with the world. They have lost the fear of the world and would rather mix the fear of God with a luxuriant embrace of the world. The notion that life is not a destination but a journey invited differing options on how to live in the world. From the philosophical distinctions about matter and spirit to the doctrine of two kingdoms or two keys and the misconstrued adage about what belongs to Caesar or to God, Christian theology has labored under an inbuilt ambiguity. Applying a strong control with periodisation, the reflection will examine four time frames: *God as a stranger*: Pepper, Guns and God under Iberian Catholicism. This would cover the early encounters with Christianity between the 16th and 18th centuries. *God of the Empire*: the church in the civilization project will examine the period, 1841-1960. *The Ethnic God*: decolonization and indigenization will cover the period between 1960 and 1990 when the second liberation from homegrown dictators started. *God of this World*: theology of engagement will point to some new features in Nigerian political theology inspired by two impulses, the charismatic/Pentecostal insurgence and the challenge of Islam in the period between 1990-2003.

God as a Stranger: Pepper, Guns and God

European encounter with Nigerian communities started as a powerful political and commercial activity. Garbed in the crusading spirit, Iberians initiated the *reconquista* project to recover their native land from Arab domination and respond to the commercial and military challenges by the Arabs who occupied the Levant route to the sources of spices, seized the granary in the Maghrib and initiated a lucrative trans-Saharan trade in gold with the Futta Jallon and River Senegal basin of West Africa. Couched in religious rhetoric it was always obvious that the quest for national glory and gold predominated the service of God. Nigeria got enmeshed in the enterprise through the power of a myth about a sprawling empire of Benin in the interior that was rich under an enlightened ruler. The quest for the golden kingdom of Prester John fired imagination about such exotic places. The Portuguese found more than a rich empire, they found plenty of pepper. The Oba of Benin wanted guns and Christian priests were used as the mediators of a new relationship. The curious journey extended into Warri and the Olu was keen enough to send his son to Portugal to be educated who later ascended the throne as *Olu Sebastian*. But the repackaging collided with the ritual demands of a monarch; the effort to install a Christian God as the source of power could not be sustained and his reign was shortened. The court-alliance pattern of the encounter left the control under the indigenous ruler and Christianity sat lightly as a stranger, an instrument of diplomatic relationship and mediator of a new civilization. Neither the Franciscans nor the Capuchins scratched beyond the surface of the indigenous culture. By the end of the 17th century, only broken images signaled that Christianity once made a bid for political relevance in the culture theater.[6]

The explanations are simple: Portugal was more interested in pepper and the kings in guns. Portugal soon found more pepper in India and with greater accessibility, making Benin irrelevant and the journey to Warri tedious. When the Oba of Benin failed to get guns, he sent away the priests and closed the school that was in the palace. Portuguese presence clung safely to the coast except in the Kongo- Soyo kingdoms;[7] they preferred to trade from their *feitoras* and hugged the unpopulated and safe islands such as Sao Thome, Il Principe and Fernando Po. The cathedral built in Cape Verde for training missionaries for work in the mainland of Africa did not provide enough indigenous manpower to attempt daring relationships with Africans while the *padroado* agreements left the missionary enterprise under the sole control of the Portuguese monarch.

Geography and demography constitute important factors in the explanation. Portugal itself was too small to occupy the wide territories "discovered" especially in the face of competition from other Europeans such as the Danes, Dutch, French and English- the last two fought the Seven Years War while scavenging on Portuguese territories. Primal religion constituted the basis for governance; the monarch was a priest-king, an image that King James I of England strenuously sought to consolidate under the concept of divine rights of kingship. In this time frame, the force of the gospel was too weak to challenge a different conception of governance. Indeed, the gospel bearers soon started to enslave the prospective converts and slave trade not only overawed the character of Christian presence but gave it a bad press. In this period of the migration of the West to other lands, the ideal of Christendom soon lost commitment and remained mere rhetoric.

God of the Empire:
Godly Politics and the Civilization Project

This weak Christian presence changed significantly from the 19th century when abolitionists attacked slave trade and opened the space for evangelical revival to export a new spirituality into a wide range of cultures. Industrial Revolution provided more powerful technological tools that compelled a massive European migration into non-Western worlds. A certain feature was that evangelicalism was recruited as the civilizing component of the new endeavor. Thus, while it had the ambition of focusing on the sharing of the gospel in a more intentional manner than the Iberians dared in Africa, its political implication was just as compelling. Two contrary winds blew. Voluntarism in mission webbed a wide range of populations into the endeavor and enabled a different project that could counter the commercial self- interest in the imperial project. Colonialism had asset of identifiable goals; it set out to install a new economic order, legitimate trade and a new political order built on rational administrative structure that would be anchored with treaties with indigenous political leadership. But right from Fowell Buxton's proposal to Parliament, *African Slave Trade and Its Remedy* in 1841, Christianity was imaged as the civilizing yeast in the colonial enterprise. God and empire were ineluctably bound because the culture contact could not be articulated in secular terms; it must be a fulfillment of a covenantal manifest destiny, a redemptive endeavor. Rudyard Kipling distinguished himself in propagating the alliance and potentials for collusion of Bible, flag and plough.[8] But the reality showed that the two did not always agree: on cultural policy, the colonial enterprise was short of manpower and distracted by the unsettled geopolitics in the period 1906-1946.During this period, nations fought themselves, the economies crashed and the hubris about the idea of progress cracked. The colonial enterprise needed indigenous cultural vitality: its social networks; indigenous political system and social control models in a policy dubbed as the Indirect Rule. The gospel bearers sought to supplant the indigenous religion and transplant Christianity by first providing a new and sustainable cultural infrastructure. The instruments employed included a vast array of educational techniques; translation of the gospel into indigenous languages; engagement in cultural reconfiguration that touched every aspect of every day life-music, dance, art, agriculture, clothing, celebration of the rites of passage. In this cultural deconstruction, they were assisted by the fact that by the mid-century, specifically after the Berlin Conference of 1885 when the partition of Africa was conceived in the heat of national rivalries, European countries diminished the real powers of indigenous rulers and installed new structures of governance and personnel. Christian court alliances were now joined to a mass movement.

A second contested area was the content of education. Colonial governments wanted literate personnel for its offices and commercial agencies. Missions used schools as a means of evangelization and for creating an educated elite that would mediate the new civilization and gospel. Professor J.Ade Ajayi is quite perceptive in the subtitle of his book on Christian missions in Nigeria: *the making of an elite*.[9] Missions did not plan a high level of education and certain subjects for votaries. It was not that they dreaded the potentials of knowledge or presumed it to be a forbidden fruit that might open the natives' eyes. Education was a capital investment not a consumer good; they did not wish to encourage indulgence. The missions acquired much power through their control of social welfare apparatus. The empire removed its gloves and insisted upon peculiar versions of God. Christianities from different nations suffused Africa: some used a *volkschirche* ideology to experiment on indigenization; others simply assimilated. In the heat of the December sun in Nigeria, all sang the same song as in Europe about snow falling on snow in the bleak mid winter amidst howling frosty winds.

As imaged by His servants, the God of the Empire brought suffering and salvation. An iconoclastic trait demonized indigenous cultural produc-tion and implanted an Enlightenment worldview that separated faith and politics. The teaching was that a good Christian should avoid the political kingdom and seek first the kingdom of God. This did not mean that mis-sionaries were not involved in politics; much to the contrary they engaged in the politics of collusion. There are always exceptions as some missionar-ies took the interests of their people to heart. For most, the core of their political theology was to keep the natives from engaging in matters above their heads. An ideology of trusteeship supplanted the idea of indigenous capacity. Ironically, both the making of an elite and the translation project bore subversive, unintended consequences. The new indigenous elite soon initiated programs for self-esteem and self-fulfillment. The backdrop is the complexity in colonial cultural presence: at one level it relied on the adap-tation of indigenous African political institutions; at another, it diffused European institutions and at a third level, it disregarded subordinate African authorities, acknowledged no legal restraints on the exercise of power over Africans.[10] The despotic element resonated with the demonizing cultural policy of missionaries. The nationalists responded by employing the church as the free political space for voicing indigenous protests against white monopoly of decision-making processes; soon, some proposed an exit and formed African churches, a Christianity that dialogued more intimately with African cultural initiative. The genius of the movement was that it was not opposed to the God of the Empire or the cultural resources of the propagators; rather, it essayed to appropriate these for indigenous progress. Dubbed as "Ethiopianism", this form of racial and cultural nationalism had two impacts: it nurtured the resilience of primal vision that the policy of indirect rule had protected and missionaries attacked; it reared the new protagonists for political nationalism.

In the post World War II period, the missionaries' educated elite who were the scions and protégés of the Ethiopians became the protagonists in the struggle for political independence. Religion, therefore, was a key element in the politics of de-colonization. It was the God of the Empire who bred the political leaders for the new Africa. Some missionaries who thought that their indigenous agents were ungrateful by participating in the politics of independence soon changed tacks by assuming that their accession to power would benefit the mission. Rivalry ensued as each mission supported their people. The Catholics, for instance, saw the hand-writings on the wall clearly in the early 1950's and intensified a program of indigenous ministerial formation. In some places, political parties emerged along denominational lines. In Nigeria, denominational differentiation served as a key aspect of electioneering in the early politics of independence.[11] A new version of politics of collusion was choreographed as Christian churches waltzed with nationalists. The leaders were invited to the ceremonies ushering a new political dispensation and presumed themselves to be a part of the enchanted circle. Meanwhile, translation nurtured religious initiative as the African Indigenous Churches challenged the pneumatic traditions of the mainline churches.[12] From the middle 1920's, indigenous Christian initiative became a major feature of the Nigerian scariscape. However, neither its traditionalization of the gospel, liturgy and polity nor its eschatology yielded a theology of engagement but rather created safe havens where the victims of the colonial enterprise rebuilt their bruised bodies and spirits.[13]

The Ethnic God: Indigenizing God and Politics

Two major trends characterized the prevalent political theology of the post Independence period. Nationalism was so much in the air that T.A. Beetham wrote a book on *The New Africa* in which he wondered whether Christianity would survive or whether the renaissance of primal religion would overawe the young plant.[14] The God of Africa was a part of the nationalist rhetoric and propaganda. "Godianism" as a religious form emerged arguing that Africans had a concept of God before the white man tried to subvert it. It was as if there was a trend to return to the posture of God as a stranger but unlike the earlier period, this period co-opted the Christian God and essayed to image him as the ethnic God. E.A.Ayandele's study of the impact of the missionary enterprise in modern Nigeria captures much of the nationalist mood and glorification of the ethnic God. He gave a high profile to those who saw the pernicious character of the God of the Empire and opposed its unrestrained insertion.[15] Cultural theologizing predominated in the churches. It was called *indigenization* project but the concept continued to spin around *contextualization*, *incarnation* and recently *inculturation*. Each of the concepts signaled an awareness of the inadequacy of expressing what Africans wanted

19

to say and what Europeans wanted to hear. Indigenization was attacked as suggesting that the gospel was native to the soil of Africa when everybody knew who brought it, from where, when at what costs. Contextualization bore the imprint of liberation theologians who started from the context to the gospel and, according to some evangelicals as David Hasselgrave, ran the risk of undercutting the authority of the Scriptures, "consigning to them a secondary role in the contextualization process." [16]

Parratt has argued in his *Reinventing Christianity (1995)* that the cultural theologizing in much of Africa could be distinguished from the political theology that emerged in Southern Africa in response to racist ideologies and practices. There was more to it than that because what is termed as cultural theologizing had political overtones. It depends on whose lenses were employed. Many of the nationalists who participated thought that they were serving a higher cause by confronting the God of the Empire with the ethnic God. They quickly moved from there to design a new political space that sought to confine Christianity, by profiling it as a handmaiden of imperialism. One- party states and dictatorships soon emerged amidst African cultural and political nationalism. The implosion of 'theological' states that sought to monopolize every sphere of life engulfed the continent. They experimented with new transformative ideologies such as African Socialism and Humanism and drank pints of Marxist ideology and rhetoric without full commitment to the tenets. [17] Coups followed coups. Westminster structure was experimented in Nigeria between1960 –1966; then the calabash of blood broke, washing it away in a bloody fratricide till 1970; thereafter long years of military rule followed till 1999 with a brief interlude, 1980-84. The Moslem challenge to Christianity changed the political landscape because all the military dictators were Moslem and they ruled with fiat and decrees. The disengagement between Christianity and the new politics of independence is a significant factor in the political theology of the period. Christianity was no longer associated with the center of power; it was contested in an increasingly pluralistic context. The danger was whether it was conscious of the change of status and marginality and how it responded.

A number of trends ensued in the internal politics: the ecumenism among Protestants that was foremost in the period 1960-1965 vanished by the end of the civil war in 1970;as it was driven out of the center stage it indulged more and more in an intentional refurbishing of denominational profiles. [18] Meanwhile, the elite took part in conferences on African theology designed to plant Christianity into the soil of communities and thereby transforming their lives and understanding of the presence of the kingdom in their midst. In the 1980's the Moslem challenge compelled a different form of ecumenical enterprise and by the 1990's the scourge of poverty and abuse of human rights compelled the Roman Catholics to develop strategies for raising political consciousness among the laity. An aspect to this was the proliferation of NGOs. The end of the cold war changed the international political scene. Western countries moved against African dictators; by-passed corrupt military governments by channeling funds through NGO's to support civil societies; empower rural sectors and battered civil society and mobilize democratic forces. In this new dispensation the NGO-ization of churches became prominent because of the vast array of social network that could serve as a civil society's active force. Prominent was the church's lack of political consciousness. Years of collusion bred a laity that lacked the will and theology to engage the political space and utilize its numerical strength and its vast potentials.

There was another significant dimension best explained with the concept of social suffering. Just like individuals facing terminal illness, society responds to intense suffering by resorting to coping mechanisms that worked in past experience. Nigerians resorted to primal religious powers as enabling vitality for competing for scarce resources in the modern public space. The proliferation of chieftaincy titles marked the quest for legitimization by the elite; traditional medicine men would imbue them with supernatural powers; reinvention of traditional societies and cult groups followed apace; resurgence of membership in Western secret societies such as Freemasonry and Rosicrucianism; soon the public space was imbued by competing cults. To counter the membership of Christians in a number of these groups, mainline churches intensified the encapsulating strategy that compensated the elite with knighthoods clothed in rich symbolism rooted in an imagined history.[19] The password for knights, *diligence, devotion, and defense* served as a means of retaining members of the elite and mobilizing them as agents to covertly foster the church's influence in the public realm. A devoted knight pledged his fealty to respond to a brother in distress and to defend the church against its enemies.

God of this World: A New Theology of Engagement

This backdrop gives prominence to the new theology that emerged from the fringes of mainline churches and among the charismatic youth groups. Paul Gifford has argued that in Africa, the mainline churches had engaged in charitable institutions and were prominent in the Second Liberation of Africa that started as the western nations supported democratization and taming of predators.[20] In one country after another, conferences were held to negotiate new liberalized constitutions. Church leaders were selected to preside over such parleys. The perception here is that the dictators had decimated other arms of civil society; the churches survived because of their international connections; the new roles for the churches challenged them rather than confirmed their previous track records. In Nigeria, no such conferences were held as the dictator gave up inexplicably; some suggest that he was murdered; that his viagra was laced with poison as he breathed his last in the arms of Indian female consorts. More interesting is that Gifford imaged the charismatic and Pentecostal churches as led by vanguards of American right wing groups and supportive of dictators; that they were fronting for the American CIA.[21] The conspiracy theory has been rejected by most scholars and African creativity reaffirmed. The chronology of African charismatic and Pentecostal insurgence does not support an American origin.[22] But Gifford ignores the political theology that emerged. The perspective here is that the political theology at the center characterized by Christian Association of Nigeria that some described as "dangerous awakening" [23] was less radical than the theology that emerged from the fringes; and that the charismatic groups from the fringes soon radicalized the politics of the mainline churches.

Some explanations could be canvassed for rapid growth of charismatic and Pentecostal forces in the 1980-1990's: the fit into the primal worldview that accepted the spiritualized worldview and offered a new power in Christ to deliver people from witchcraft and other demonic forces; the instrumentalist perception that argues that the collapse of the economy and abuse of human rights made the upper and middle class just as vulnerable; all surged into charismatic churches that preached prosperity gospel and appropriated modernity; a religious perception traces the outpouring of the spirit in Nigeria from the 1970's and the increasing intensity that changed the shape of the religious landscape.[24] Two aspects deserve attention: the phenomenon caused the explosion of the numerical strength of Christianity in Nigeria. The character of the movement changed every decade: the emphasis on holiness and evangelism shifted to prosperity, upward mobility and faith/claim theology in the 1980's. By mid-1990's there was a sharp return to holiness ethics led by The Full Gospel Business Men's Fellowship and the Intercessors for Africa. For our purposes, the Intercessors serve as the exponents of a political theology that soon flowed into the mainstream of the movement.

The Intercessors developed as a ministry among University of Ife students with the mentorship of Pa G.Elton, a Briton who had come to Nigeria in 1937 under the auspices of the British Apostolic Church. It has African and international networks with the emphasis to change the lives of nations through prayer.[25] First, it perceives prayer as political praxis and that the social, political and economic fortunes of nations can be reshaped through the power of prayer. Second, hindrances to individuals and nations occur through internal sources such as the sins, pollution and acts of disobedience that offend God and attract punishment or withholding of benefits. Spiritual forces also externally attack the fortunes of a nation. Pauline images of the powers suggest the hierarchy of forces that war against human beings and determine life fortunes. There are a number of dimensions to this assertion: the first is that individual and communal responsibilities explain poverty and suffering. Human beings bring misfortunes to themselves. Repentance becomes the key weapon. The events in human life are connected to events in the spiritual or supernatural realm. The things that are seen are made of things that are not seen. Some may want to blame social structures for the suffering of the vulnerable. Pentecostals image social structures as being capable of being hijacked by demonic forces. People serve as tools of such forces. Thus, certain leaders could be profiled as being possessed. Deliverance strategies for discerning the powers and liberating individuals from them; and re-sanctifying communities have evoked emotional discussions among theologians.[26] Third, they insist that Christians are not to pursue only personal salvation but have obligations to engage in the restoration of their nations. This theology of engagement denies the doctrine of the two kingdoms; and reinterprets salvation to include liberation from material want, psychological needs; access to education or just about anything that dehumanizes or diminishes the full potentials of people. When Jesus asked the audience to look at the coin, he was drawing attention to the idolatry in the inscription that divinized the human Caesar and called for a return to a true unalloyed worship of God. It was not a diatribe against engagement with worldly affairs.

The embrace of the world includes a sensitivity about nature. There is a strand of ecological ethics in Pentecostal political theology of engagement. It is built on an understanding of a certain order in creation and human role as stewards; failure brings suffering. Within this perspective is a strong attention to land as gift and covenant. Sin and pollution break the covenant and compels the need for the deliverance of land.[27] Fourth, to explain how this works: Emeka Nwankpa, who is a lawyer, mines the primal worldview to show how our forefathers covenanted the land and all its people to various deities; how fratricide and collusion in slave trade polluted the land and how certain indigenous ethics such as the killing of twins brought evil upon the land. He moves from there to profile the forces within the land that could be the hindrances. It is a prophetic ministry that utilizes the full range of charismata as the tools for diagnosing the problems and proffering solutions. Another strong strand is the nationalist concern of the theology. Thus, Steve Okitika in his *The Battle for the Nations: Ministry of Interceding for Our Nation* catalogues the prophecies that the Lord gave them about Nigeria in a period of two decades. [28] As a priestly ministry of being watchmen for the nation, they listen and act out the spiritual guidance. For instance, in 1995, the Holy Spirit asked them to send intercessors to Liberia and they commissioned people who not only took gifts to the brethren in Liberia but also taught intercessory ministry and prayed for the recovery of the nation. [29] When the state intervened with military force under the ECOMOG program by West African nations, the saints sent a vanguard to deliver the land from the negative consequences from bloodshed and to invoke God to bring true peace.

Pentecostal theology is done in a Biblicist temper without the decorum familiar with critical scholarship and it uses the ingredients from indigenous religion to achieve contextualization. It mines the interior of primal worldview and images the entire structure of indigenous religion as the weave of covenants with the gods of the fathers. Ritual agents and rulers dedicate their lands and peoples to various deities. Festivals, rites of passage and the celebration of the agricultural cycle are rituals that re-energize the covenants periodically. Libations are tools for implicating the entire community, born and unborn to ancestral spirits. The conclusion follows that the poverty that has stunned the people and other misfortunes trailing families could be explained: they have offered to deities what belongs to God and the remedy is to confess, reverse the covenants and rededicate their lands to God so as to regain prosperity and recover the years that the locusts have eaten. In Village revival meetings, chiefs are invited to stand in the center of the congregations and confess the sins of idolatry in the past and commit the land to Christ.

Pentecostal cosmology links individual, social and political misadventures to the larger cosmic battle between God and His enemies. They declare that God has a purpose and counsel for individuals, families, communities and nations. By opening *doors* of the body and *gates* of communities and nations, demonic forces enter to possess, control and derail from God's munificent design. Contrary to some criticisms that Pentecostals see the devil in everything and refuse to acknowledge systemic evil, Pentecostals place responsibility on both individuals and social structures; on the rulers and the ruled. They also affirm that some of the problems are aspects of a larger cosmic consequence beyond human ken. Intercession becomes a strategy for self-reintegration, re-alignment of the path of destiny of society and nations; it serves as political praxis. Embedded is a veiled iconoclasm and demonization of indigenous culture; it asserts that the primal vision has failed and a new dispensation is needed. But because it works from the interior of the worldview, the rural populations appreciate its critique and often accept the proffered solution.

Intercession serves as a form of political critique at the national level. They accuse the military of shedding blood and militarizing the society. People begin to imitate its culture of force in social relationship. Using a certain exegesis, they explain that from Cain's example, when blood is shed, the earth withholds its increase or economic collapse occurs. They designed a program to teach civil servants and public officials how to govern with good conscience; their sins and corruption serve as lightning rod that brings hunger in the midst of plenty. They emphasized that born again Christians must become detribalized but re-organized to work as a new community. This attacks the dysfunctional force of ethnicity. From here it has been a short step to the insistence that Christians should pray the righteous into the corridors of power.

There is more: a certain nationalistic tinge rings through the rhetoric; expressed metaphorically that Africa is like a gun that God will use to deal with His enemies and Nigeria is located in the position of the trigger. Nigeria has a special place in God's redemptive will for Africa. Its huge human and mineral resources must be redeemed and made available for this noble use. Therefore, the poverty in the midst of plenty; disorganization in the midst of vast resources must be rejected. This is the generation to pray Nigeria into its proper place! Such rhetoric has captured imagination. But along with this is an internal debate about prophecy in political matters; whether personal predilections do not influence prophecies. Another angle is about false mercenary prophets who dupe the politicians. As the numbers of Charismatic and Pentecostal groups bulge, their political importance has not been lost on the political elite who urge prayers and political support. For instance, *This Day News* reported on 15th January 2003 about the crusade by Reinhard Bonnke:

> The leader of the Christ for All nations (CFAN) who has been organizing crusades in parts of Africa, on arrival headed straight for the office of the Governor Adeniyi Adebayo of Ekiti State where he was received by the Deputy Governor, Chief Paul Alabi. Bonnke prayed for the governor, his deputy, members of the state executive council and civil servants who stormed the state conference center to catch a glimpse of the evangelist. Chairman of the Local Organising Committee for the Great Gospel Crusade in Ekiti State, Rev. Kunle Salami, expressed appreciation to the state government for offering to host Bonnke during the crusade.

This report has many intriguing dimensions including the popularity of prayer crusade in the state; its value for elections; the specific role of the government in funding it and the salience of religious actors in the public space. Specifically, the protagonists in the center are of the charismatic Pentecostal type.

Nigeria entered the year 2003 with the drum beats of elections that will be held in April 2004. Unlike any election in the nation's experience, religion is at the center. One index is to follow the number of religious items that appear in all the newspapers: in the editorial column, letters to the editor, syndicated pages and other commentaries and specific articles about religious matters and religious leaders commenting on religious matters.[30] All newspapers carry an unusually large numbers of religious items daily because the Presidential and other elections are being fought on religious lines. The incumbent President, Olusegun Obasanjo, claims that he became born again during his years in prison under the former dictator Sanni Abacha. He has written two books including a collection of sermons. He constantly attends revival meetings and patronizes charismatic pastors and causes. For instance, in 2001, when the Gideon Bible had problems in clearing containers of Bibles from the wharf because of high duties, they appealed to a born again President. Instead of ordering the Port Managers to allow the goods without duties, he paid the three million *naira* (ca. $30, 000) duties from his personal purse. He is pitted to a Moslem retired General and former Head of State, Buhari. Once again, religion has been given a front seat in the Nigerian public space. The contest is heated because the Charismatic and Pentecostal forces have in the last few years become actively engaged in politics. The Pentecostal Fellowship of Nigeria as well as other mainline churches mobilized. The Lagos branch of the PFN announced that four million of their people registered during the Voters' Registration exercise of 2002.As one argued, they do not wish to pray down God's blessings on the nation only to allow unbelievers to benefit! Their political ideology images a God of this world and this is a long distance from the missionary political theology that they inherited. The Moslems are also politically conscious and assured that sharia will only be protected by a Moslem leader.

In conclusion: there has been a tremendous numerical growth of Christianity in Nigeria in the post-independence period. A significant part of the growth occurred after the civil war propelled by the charismatic and Pentecostal forces. All Christian forms have benefited. The charismatization of the mainline churches has a number of implications including the acceleration of growth and a higher level of faith commitment. Instrumentalist explanations do not negate the impact. Economic collapse in the last decade of the last millennium has decimated the middle class and the professionals. Religious commitment provided solace and a survival strategy; it bred moral integration and provided a caring network. The demographic shift in the class patronage of charismatic and Pentecostal groups has immense social and political implications. Christian population constitutes a critical mass in the election process. Their mobilized and committed ideological posture gives them an edge over centrifugal competing forces. As the movement has shifted into the rural areas, its mobilized power has increased and its ability to encompass the infra-political zone has enabled it to articulate a deeper level of political theology. It has also essayed to contest the power node of the primal religious leaders. Chiefs are imaged as the stumbling blocks if not the source of the misfortunes of the youth and upward mobile sectors of the population. Born again people urge their village chiefs to make open confessions and re-dedicate the land to God so that they themselves may succeed in the competition for wealth in the nation. They argue that if they prosper, the village will prosper; if they fail, their villages will be desolate.

There are a number of significant changes in the political space: in the quest to get Christians into positions of power, the discussion is hardly around denominational affiliations. The category has changed to the born again mark. It is as if the denominational politics of the 1960-70's failed and only the trans-ethnic, non-denominational categories will suffice. The political class has identified with charismatic and other Christian affiliations more than before. One explanation is that the political class is made up of professionals whose businesses collapsed with the economy and politics is the only avenue to recovery in a context in which the Federal Government controls the resources of the nation. Most of the elite live on one form of Government patronage or the other. Those without support from military Government failed. Indeed, most of the financiers of the political system in Nigeria are connected with the military whose members were able to accumulate vast wealth and therefore could control the political system. Thus, the demographic change in the patronage of charismatic religiosity means that people with influence could give it a higher political profile. The danger is that they could hijack the movement from its Godly cause unless the charismatic spirituality embeds a vigilant spirituality that could detect the danger. This was the point in the interview given by the Chairman of the Pentecostal Fellowship of Nigeria, Lagos State, Bishop Lanre Obembe on Friday, 10th January 2003. He warned against dupes and charlatans within the fold and politicians who may wish to exploit the organization:

from available records, over four million Pentecostal members registered during the last voters' registration exercise;…in the past, Pentecostal Christians suffered undue hardship as they were marginalized in the running of the state. But now, with the dynamic and responsive leadership that God has given PFN, it was ready for constructive negotiation to enable its people hold elective and political offices. We are open and ready to negotiate directly with political parties and contestants about sharing equitable distribution of offices and resources. PFN will no longer be marginalized.[31]

The intentional mobilization in the political arena and battle rhetoric provide materials for examining an emergent form of political theology in contemporary Nigeria.

Notes

1.   *The Guardian Newspaper* (Lagos, Nigeria), 2nd February, 2003:9.

2.   See, O.U.Kalu, " Harsh Flutes: The Religious Dimension of Legitimacy Crisis in Nigeria, 1993-1998" In T.Falola (ed) *Nigeria in the 20th Century* (Durham, NC: Carolina Academic Press, 2002): chapt.45; O.U. Kalu, *The Scourge of the Vandals: Nature and Control of Cults in Nigerian Tertiary Institutions* (Nsukka, University of Nigeria Press, 2001). Both works discuss the proliferation and impact of cultism in modern Nigerian public space including schools from the 1980's.

3.   Steve Bruce, *God is Dead: Secularization in the West* (Oxford, Blackwell, 2002); Edward Norman, *Secularization: New Century Religion* (New York, Continuum, 2002); Paul Jenkins, *The Next Christendom: The Coming of Global Christianity* (New York, Oxford University Press, 2002), see, p.11; Reginald Bibby, *Restless God: the Renaissance of Religion in Canada.*

4.   Jeff Haynes, *Religion in the Third World Politics* (Boulder, CO., Lynne Rienner Publications, 1994); and *Religion and Politics in Africa* (London, Zed Press, 1996).

5.   O.U.Kalu, *Power, Poverty and Prayer: The Challenges of poverty and Pluralism in African Christianity, 1960-1996* (Frankfurt, Peter Lang, 2000), chapt. 2.

6.   F.C.Ryder, *Benin and the Europeans, 1485-1897* (London, Longmans, 1969); Lamin Sanneh, *West African Christianity: its religious impulse* (Maryknoll, NY, Orbis, 1983); O.U.Kalu, *The History of Christianity in West Africa* (London, Longmans, 1980); C.R.Boxer, *The Portuguese Seaborne Empire* (London, Hutchinson & Co., 1969);J.H.Parry, *Europe and a Wider World* (London, Hutchinson & Co., 1966 ed).

7.   Richard Gray, *Black Christians White Missionaries* (New Haven, Yale University Press, 1990).

8. Andrew F. Walls, *The Missionary Movement in Christian History: Studies in the Transmission of Faith* (Orbis, 1996); *The Cross-cultural process in Christian History: Studies in Transmission and Appropriation of Faith* (Orbis, 2000).

9. J. F. Ade Ajayi, *Christian Missions in Nigeria: The making of a new elite* (London, Longmans, 1965).

10. Toyin Falola ed. *African Politics in Postimperial Times: the essays of Richard L. Sklar* (Lawrenceville, Africa World Press, 2002):507-508.

11. Elochukwu Amucheazi, *Church and Politics in Eastern Nigeria, 1945-1966* (Lagos, Macmillan Publishers, 1986).

12. See, Allan Anderson, *African Reformation* (Lawrenceville, Africa World Press, 2000).

13. O.U.Kalu, "The politics of religious sectarianism in Africa", *West African Religion* (University of Nigeria), 16, 1 (1975):13-25.

14. T.A. Beetham, *Christianity in the New Africa* (London, Pall Mall, 1967):ix.

15. E. A. Ayandele, *The Missionary Impact on Modern Nigeria, 1842-1914: a political and social analysis*(London, Longman, 1965) see a discussion on the historiography in O.U.Kalu, *African Church Historiography: an ecumenical perspective*(Berne, Switzerland, 1988), chapter 1.

16. Robert E. Coleman, ed., *Evangelism on the cutting edge* (New Jersey, Fleming H.Revell Co., 1986):75-88. see, p. 78.

17. J.C.McKenna, *Finding a social voice: Church and Marxism in Africa* (New York, Fordham University Press, 1997).

18. O.U.Kalu, *Divided People of God: church union movement in Nigeria, 1878-1965* (New York, NOK Publishers, 1978).

19. As an example of one of the knighthood orders, see, Christopher J. Kauffman, *Patriotism and Fraternalism in the Knights of Columbus: A history of the fourth degree*(New York, Herder and Herder, 2001).

20. Paul Gifford, ed., *The Christian Churches and Democratization in Africa* (Leiden, EJBrill, 1995); Kwame Bediako, *Christianity in Africa* (Maryknoll, Orbis, 1995).

21. Paul Gifford, *The New Crusaders* (London, Pluto Press, 1991) and *African Christianity: Its Public Role* (Bloomington, IN, University of Indiana Press, 1998); J. Marishane, "Prayer, Profit and Power: US Religious Right and Foreign Policy," *Review of African Political Economy*, 52, (1991):73-77; Sarah Diamond, *Spiritual Warfare: The Politics of the Christian Right* (Boston, South End Press, 1989).

22. O. U. Kalu, "Third Response: Pentecostalism and the Reconstruction of Christian Experience in Africa"*Studiae Historiae Ecclesiasticae*, University of Pretoria, 24, 2 (Dec.1998):1-34.

23. I.M. Enwerem, *A Dangerous Awakening: The Politicization of Religion in Nigeria* (Ibadan, IFRA, 1995); M.H.Kukah, *Religion, Politics and Power in Northern Nigeria* (Ibadan, Spectrum Press, 1994); S.O.Ilesanmi, *Religious Pluralism and Nigerian State*(Athens, Ohio, Ohio University Press, 1997).

24. O.U. Kalu, "The Pentecostal/Charismatic Reshaping of the African Religious Landscape, 1970-2000" *forthcoming in Mission Studies: Journal of IAMS*, 20, 1, 39, 2003.

25. O.U. Kalu, "The Practice of Victorious life: Pentecostal Political Theology in Nigeria, 1970-1996" *Mission: Jnl of Mission Studies (University of Ottawa, Canada)*, 5, 2 (1998):229-255.

26. See, *Pneuma, vol.* 13 is devoted to the controversy. Edward Rommen, ed., *Spiritual Power and Missions. Evangelical Missiological Soc. Series no.3*(Pasadena, William Carey Library, 1995).

27. Emeka Nwankpa, *Redeeming the Land* (Achimota, African Christian Press, 1994);Walter Wink, *Naming the Powers: the language of power in the New Testament*(Philadelphia, Fortress, 1984).

28. Steve Okitika, *The Battle for Nations: the Ministry of Interceding for our Nation* (Lagos, Moinab Ltd., 1996).

29. ibid., 160.

30. see, www.gamji.com that carries all the Nigerian newspapers. See, the Bonnke story in www.thisdayonline.com/news/20030115news20.html. There is an interesting long commentary on "The church and southeast politics"in www.mtrustonline.com/dailytrust/opinion1522003.htm.

31. www, guardiannewsngr.com/news/article23.

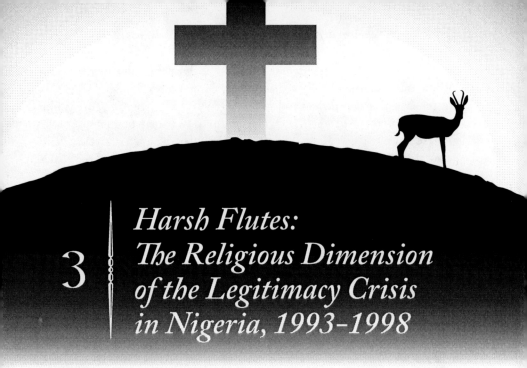

3 | Harsh Flutes: The Religious Dimension of the Legitimacy Crisis in Nigeria, 1993-1998

Anatomy of the Legitimacy Crisis

In 1993, the presidential elections, which would have ushered Nigeria into civilian rule as an end to a long praetorian regime, were annulled. Within a year, a new military regime under General Sanni Abacha took office and lasted until he died in 1998. It was a period characterized by a painful legitimacy crisis and much personal and social suffering which forced many in the international community to isolate Nigeria because of an appalling human rights record. The goal here is less an ambitious analysis of the entire Abacha rule than a focus on the religious dimension only.

Initially people made an acrostic of the general's name and joked, that *Abacha* meant, *After Babaginda Another Criminal Has Arrived!* This proved too prophetic, as a brutal reign was unleashed which brought immense suffering and decimated legitimacy, the engine that moves salient governance. This paper regards legitimacy as governance according to recognized principles; in accordance with established legal forms (rule of law) and practices. Apropos here are the structuralist indices such as clear procedures; rational, predictable management standards; citizen participation; degree of openness; transparency; accountability and the practice of democratic virtues. The World Bank Development Report of 1997, *The State in a Changing World,* echoed these indices in an attempt to revamp the state as the instrument for anchoring a modernization model. Legitimacy goes beyond governance to the degree of acceptance of the ruler by the ruled. Why should the ruler be obeyed and enjoy cooperation? Undergirding this are the questions of power and authority: Who holds power, for whom, and to what end? Authority is legitimized power. It may be rooted in religion, social norms, or force. Whatever the source, it must be packaged to be acceptable to the ruled and to achieve social order. Thus, when the ethics of power vitiate the responsibility of power, dissent may occur. This is a legitimacy crisis characterized by the breakdown of the rule of law, eliciting a lack of love and confidence by the ruled in the rulers. A permutation of political attitudes would follow: cynicism, disenchantment with the political issues of the day, fear or lack of trust, and sometimes self-doubt or pessimism about the capacity of one's people or race to govern itself. Afro-pessimism has become a familiar model in analysis of the modern African state. Dissent may follow either through liberation military insurgence or varied forms of passive dissent.

A legitimacy crisis destroys economic growth and breeds disquiet and suffering. In a praetorian culture, military fiats or decrees substitute for the rule of law and disenabling environment vitiates the capacity of the state to adequately fulfill the roles demanded by modernization model. The dominant political culture is characterized by patrimonialism, politics of the belly, clientalism and corruption. As the Cameroonians would say, "*The goat eats where it is tethered*" .(Bayart, 1993) In pidgin English, it is called, *I chop, you chop*. Nigerians have coined a new word, "*settlement*", as the rulers "*settle*" or give money and contracts to relations, cronies and supporters while the opposition is brutally attacked, killed or detained with Decree Number Two which, for security reasons, cannot be queried in the courts. Ouster clauses are used to hamper the judiciary. Instead of a legal rational authority, the patrimonial system borrows its idiom from primal society: The personal self and the official is not distinguished; loyalty is a core value and is encapsulated with the distribution of patronage. A hegemonic alliance or reciprocal assimilation of elites welds the dominant class. The military in Nigeria has turned into a prebendary one-party rule. Serving and retired officers use their enormous wealth to control. Inside Abacha's Nigeria, corruption turned into looting the public treasury. It is estimated that the general left an estate worth over ten billion dollars with a vast business empire controlled by his son and Lebanese brothers-in-law under the company logo, *C-&-C (Chougry &Chougry)*. A report entitled, "*Plundering and Looting Unlimited*", (Awodede, 1998:12-23) has catalogued the result of a current investigation on Abacha. To give one example: after the Russians assisted Nigeria in building the Ajaokuta Steel Mills, they were owed 2.5 billion dollars. Abacha's son negotiated to buy the loan and paid a half-billion dollars to the Russians. But he gave his father's government a bill for the full sum and pocketed two billion dollars in one contract. He forced ministers to pay him money for oiling access to his father. The mother controlled importation of petroleum products in the country and, therefore, the government refused to pay for the turn-around maintenance (TAM) of the four refineries in the country. Cars still queue for miles to buy petrol in an oil-producing nation. The Obasanjo government, in 1999, announced that they have recovered one billion dollars in cash from two of Abacha's bank accounts, in Brazil and Pakistan and Swiss banks have frozen over three billion dollars awaiting the court cases on the matter. Praetorian culture treats society itself as a military barrack and decimates civil society while the moral values of core segments such as the civil service, academy, judiciary, and traditional political nodes are compromised. (Bratton, 1989) Quite often, as the economy collapses so do basic infrastructure such as roads, water, electricity and health care delivery. The spiral effect moves from the urban to the rural sector as the populace becomes more vulnerable to power adventurers and anti-social bandits. The militarization of society evokes the increase of violence in the society as all means of legitimate survival are blocked. Meanwhile, the global market economy responds to the disabled economic environment by withdrawing investment and insisting on debt recovery. The World Bank imposed the draconian Structural Adjustment Program while other Western governments topped the icing on the bitter cake with sanctions. The Commonwealth suspended Nigeria for abuse of human rights.

At issue here are three other models of analysis: firstly, modernization theory explains both the inherited structures from colonialism as well as the frustration of the West with states such as Nigeria. Decolonization was built on the hope of creating vibrant markets. States are the core instrument in the enterprise. The pursuit of the ideal soon bred one-party states and authoritarian regimes designed to mobilize communities in the single-minded creation of consumer societies. Colonial regimes were authoritarian, exploitative, and created unviable nation -states. Having bequeathed a burdensome legacy, they paid scant attention to the power monopoly of their proteges. After all, little rats learn thievery from big rats. Secondly, in reaction to this model, dependency theory emphasizes the exploitative nature of the modernization model. Instead of economic growth, it breeds deepening dependence on the metropolis. Loans breed loan sharks. Dependence psychologically stultifies. Externality, or what Bayart considers as the extravenous factor, describes the despair in the dependency model that produces the feeling that *Uhuru* is worse than the yaws of colonialism. Thus, invitations go out to external forces to intervene in the failed economies and states. Analysts note an increase in the popular demand for Western foreign intervention. Much of this has come through the increased roles of Non-Governmental Organizations (NGO's). Efforts to bypass the corrupt state increase the presence of NGO's engaged in various forms of poverty alleviation programs and empowerment of civil society. NGO's may not always be angels but they find enthusiastic cooperation within civil society.

Ernest Gellner defined civil society as "the set of diverse non-governmental institutions which is strong enough to counterbalance the state and, while not preventing the state from fulfilling its role as keeper of the peace and arbitrator between major interests, can nevertheless prevent it from dominating and atomizing the rest of the society" (1994:5) Great optimism flowered on the value of civil society and associational life as rescue to bondaged people in authoritarian regimes but much doubt has appeared whether civil society is necessarily imbued with democratic values or serves the interest of society. (Fatton, 1995:67-99; Horn, 1996:43-69; Longman, 1998: 68; Gifford, 1998:19-20) Fatton prescribes a typology because much of the support for predatory regimes come from certain sectors of civil society. Longman argues that the role of the churches in the lake regions of Africa challenges the optimistic view. Others doubt that, given the history of the concept in Western socioeconomic life, it could be adequately applied in Africa where the legitimacy crisis has cultural roots.

A legitimacy crisis activates infra-politics, a realm where the people create apolitical world of their own and where they ridicule the wisdom of the rulers.(Fatton, 1992) For instance, Operation Feed the Nation (OFN), is known in that circle as *Operation Fool the Nation,* because the people are certain that the elite would predictably loot the funds for agriculture. The National Electricity Power Authority (NEPA) is referred to as *Never Expect Power Anytime* as communities are darkened in power outages. In the summer of 1998, when the outage occurred during the World Cup soccer tournament, the masses burned some power stations in retaliation. In Nigeria, voters charge the political candidates money to register or go to polling booths because if one does not collect from the big man at such crucial times, he will not be seen near the poor man again. Yet, when General Abacha tried to manipulate the elections of 1998, only 20 percent of the registered voters bothered to collect the money to vote. The depth of political cynicism created by legitimacy crisis acquired macabre dimensions. As the thirty-four members of the Multi-Ethnic Coalition of Eminent Nigerians observed, "*the deepening cynicism and apathy with which the general public now view the transition program has led to a state of unprecedented gloom and despondency in the land.*" (Babarinsa, 1998:7) The masses could afford to laugh at the rulers in their intra-mural fights. As Abiola was jailed, the masses read the moral that *even the rich* can *cry!* When the managing directors of failed banks were detained, the populace guffawed that, *it takes a thief to catch a thief. When Abacha leaves office, the decree will catch him!*. So, Abacha refused to leave office and, instead, tried to remove his army uniform and metamorphose into a civilian democratic ruler!

The capacity to laugh in the midst of suffering requires study. In pidgin English it is dubbed as *"shuffering and shmilling"*. Curative and therapeutic, it is a form of revenge on the *Vagabonds In Power* who would otherwise consider themselves as Very Important People. Fela Kuti, the Afro-jazz artist, assisted the masses in developing much of the language of dissent; it was he who dubbed the American giant communication company, ITT, as *International Thief Thief,* for colluding with Abiola to ruin Nigerian tele-communication services at a cost of one billion dollars. Ironically, the violence of the regime sedated the populace and turned Abiola into a hero as the streets filled with violent protesters at the news of his death in prison. Some may wonder whether infra-politics tends to trivialize suffering and enervates adequate engagement against forces that dehumanize. It may also generate a pressure that blows up at some point in time.

The temper of the legitimacy crisis that Nigerians call, *"political impasse",* as if to mystify a dark force with a foreign word, is beyond the political realm. It is as if the rulers declared war on those they ruled. They blew harsh flutes instead of the mellifluous music of "good company". They predated and cowed the people into subservience and sought to banish laughter. Emigration ensued as people suffered from a lack of material well-being and loss of dignity. The concept of "good company" is derived from Monica Wilson who said that among the Nyakyusa of Tanzania, there are a number of desirable political values known as "good company" which *"implies community, that is, the establishment and maintenance of harmonious relationships among people."* (Wilson, 1957 :66-90; Magesa, 1997: 259) Good company defines the meaning of legitimacy, political order and the values undergirding political leadership. These include dignity, decency and wisdom. As the Igbo say, *we own the king and the king owns us.*

Legitimacy crisis is, therefore, a moral condition which causes social suffering and blows harsh cultural notes. In traditional society, harsh flutes signify untoward times because, like the bugle in Western society, the flutist beckons to war, encourages the fighters, sings the praise of the strong as well as for the fallen. The air in the last five years of military rule was redolent with strident note of the harsh flute. Our people say that when the blood "enters the eyes" of a person, he can no longer distinguish between friend and foe in causing pain. Abacha always covered his reddened eyes with dark sunglasses. As a part of the government's "charm offensive," media consultants would produce photographs of the dictator in civilian clothes and without his dark glasses. This raises a crucial matter: how the media was used to repackage Abacha's image both internally and extra-locally in such a manner that through certain cultural representation of despotism and attendant social suffering, "experience is remade, thinned out and distorted" (Arthur and Joan Kleinman, 1996:2). Similarly, Misty Bastian has further illustrated the resort to sinister "corporate/state self-promotion in a period of systemic collapse" by examining the production and distribution of "Abacha Televisions" under the harsh regime.(1999) The disingenuous effort to embed despotism went beyond large billboards declaring that *Abacha Is The Answer!*, it sought to invade the private space of the sufferer and to convince that the oppressor is the answer to an unasked question. To implicate the elite, there were Abacha-brand name refrigerators and cellular phones.

Harsh flutes incite dark forces such as ethnic conflicts, armed robbery, and a virulent competition for scarce resources. The moral dimension draws attention to religion. Two concerns here: First, the boundaries of the religious factor in a political analysis of the modern state in Africa has often pinned the gaze on Islam and Christianity, especially their discordant notes. The government accentuates this impression by banishing the discussion of religion from the Constitution-making process. Arguing that disagreement over the inclusion of the Shariah laws in the Constitution would be disruptive, they leave the wrong impression that these religions are the key actors on the political landscape. Second, from this limited focus two patterns of discourse emerge: a) the fad of leftist social analysis that images religion as dysfunctional and, b) argues that religion has been manipulated by the undisciplined elite in their virulent competition for the diminishing resources. As the state provides a source of power and wealth entirely out of proportion to that available from any other organized force in a society, political power is fought with enormous ferocity; religion becomes both a contested field and an instrument of competition. (Usman, 1987; Ibrahim, 1991) The virulence of the competition is accentuated by the fact that Islam has a more profound sense of political power than the ambivalent Christian concept of Two Kingdoms. (Sanneh, 1996, 1997). Third, some aver that the problem with Nigeria is moral and that analysis should, therefore, mine the value systems of the competing religions and transform the salient values into empowerment ethics in the public square. (Kalu, 1986).

The position here is that the religious dimension is more pervasive and complex than a focus on Christianity and Islam would suggest. First, the *roots of political ethics in traditional worldview* open avenues for the resilient intrusion of primal spirituality in contemporary political dynamics. Second, the *villagization of the modern public sphere* by those who legitimate their power by appeal to ritual sources in traditional religion and culture is a common feature in Africa. Third, these two factors enable traditional secret societies such as *Ogboni, Nyamkpe, Owegbe,* and *Ekine* to serve as instruments for mobilizing economic and political power in the modern sector. The rise of indigenous cults in the dynamics of modern politics has been a function of the intensity of the material and psychological scourges caused by the legitimacy crisis. As rational institutions that enjoyed only a brief existence collapse, people resort to primal modes with greater zeal. The political elite go to the village for "medicine" and charms to enhance competitive force in the modern space. Fourth, proliferation of cults of power such as the *Mami Wata* cult not only have political significance but are creative cultural inventions to meet pulsating needs. Fifth, some political actors legitimate their quest to govern by appealing to political and ritual positions held in the primal space; hence the rash of chieftaincy titles and innovation of bizarre costumes. Sixth, there are varieties of other religious forms whose symbols, myths, and rituals may not be strictly political but soon assume political potentials as the votaries utilize the resources in the public square. The growth of Spiritual Science Movements that are foreign, theosophic religions such as the Ancient Mystic Order of the Rosae Crucis (Rosicrucians/AMORC), Freemasonry, Grail Message, Eckankar and Aetherius Society and Christian Science, to name a few, has often been ignored in the literature but they are burgeoning in numbers and some of them have much political importance. The cities of the nation are invaded by a multiplicity of secret societies and churches that celebrate the human search for well-being, a new mixture of idols. There is so much dependence on charms for everyday life that the Road Safety Corps took an advertisement to warn drivers to rely less on these and more on good driving practices. But how could they be expected to do so when the Oba of Benin still pilgrimages annually to Akpoba river on the Benin-Asaba road to offer sacrifices so that there will be fewer accidents on the bridge. We must plumb all these nooks while still holding to the dialogical enterprise as an antidote to the use of religion as an instrument in political conflict. The potentials and dilemma of pluralism in modern Nigeria are crucial models of analysis. (Kalu, 1996a; Ilesanmi, 1997)

A key concern is to explain the apparent explosion of these cults. Some may query whether there is an explosion or merely the resilience of primal religiosity that modernization theorists expected to die naturally. Instead, religion and ethnicity have rebounded with new vigor into the modern political space. (Haynes, 1996). The consideration of space is one mode of explanation recalling the Old Testament account in Exodus 31 where Leah takes her father's household god from the microcosm, where it underpinned reality to the macrocosm across the Euphrates noted for its rich religious cults and gods. Ordinarily, it would be suspected that the household god would be out of its depths! Similarly, as modernization created an emergent culture, the forces that sustained the primal space should lose potency. Indeed, this was Robin Horton's intellectualist explanation or "the rationality of conversion". (1970:85-108;1975:209-235;373-399) But the ironic predominates. Arthur Kleinman employs a different discourse based on the body-self- society model or, an understanding of social suffering through its socio-somatic effect. When the society is traumatized and sick, it affects the body and mind of suffering individuals. The evidence of the "the relationship between the outer force to the inner state" or the body-effect of socio-political events in the lives of the academics in a disabled university environment is illustrated by the death of more than a dozen academics in the University of Nigeria, Nsukka in the short period, 1997-1998. High blood pressure and heart attacks accounted for these deaths and were nicknamed *Abacha Fever*. People joked that one should be careful in hugging others because they may be suffering from an advanced level of the "Abacha Fever" or "Brief Illness." In such moments of social suffering, argues Kleinman in the William James Lecture, "it is in the local worlds that relational elements of social existence in which people have the greatest stake are played out. These include survival, status, power, resistance or loss. The fact that some things matter, matter desperately, is what provides local worlds with their immense power to absorb attention, orient interest and obj ective poles of experience" (Kleinman, 1997:327).

The village is both space and a reference group; in the past its cults served as a coping mechanism in pursuing the things that matter. Thus, how people cope under the present pressure is best understood by how they coped before. Kleinman points to another key aspect that will continue to inform our discourse: the tension between despair/ depression and hope/ struggle for survival is played out in the public space in the religious politics of synthesis or making meaning in collapsing contexts. Some will be overwhelmed and be chided as pessimists as if they bemoaned the pathology of the Nigerian condition without offering solutions. Others will emigrate and join the brain drain that has depleted the intellectual output from a country endowed with vast potential. The polluted land will spew out her people. Under Babaginda, the government was alarmed and countered with a television advertisement with a character called *Andrew* who was seen at the International Airport "checking out". The caption cajoled *Andrew* that Nigeria belongs to us all. We have no other land. Abacha would not even bother about Andrew. When the university staff protested in 1996 that a professor was paid about $100 per month, Abacha ordered that their salaries should be withheld unless each signed a paper declaring against a strike. Yet in the midst of enormous suffering, others will resist the lurking demoralization and despair with programs " *of regeneration and re-moralization.*" (Kleinman, 1997:331-4)The nation shall not die!

These cultic depths do not limit the fact that the Muslim-Christian rivalry is important in the political dynamics of Nigeria. Much to the contrary, the varieties of intra-religious competitions have immense political consequences. For instance, within Islam, the rise of fundamentalism especially pandered by the Shiites who want the nation to be governed with the Shariah laws caused divisions among the predominant Sunni and with other moderate Moslems such as the Ahmadiyya. The conflict between orthodoxy (e.g. *izalatu)* and the *tariqahs,* (Sufi orders), can be illustrated by the employment of foreign *marabouts* for the protection of Muslim political leaders with mystical powers and rituals. The indulgence of *mallams* in preparing charms and talismans for clients is worth exploring.(Oseni, 1988:236-253) There also is the conflict raging between the Yoruba (Southern) Moslems and the Northern Hausa/Fulani, between supporters of Saudi Arabia and the supporters of Iran. These played out in the denial of the presidency from Chief M. K. O. Abiola, a Southern Muslim, by Northern political Muslim elite represented by the Sultan of Sokoto, Alhaji Ibrahim Dasuki.

Similarly, the virulent rivalry between Roman Catholics and Protestants and among Protestant denominations determined the tensile strength of the Christian political force in the country, especially within the Christian Association of Nigeria (CAN).(Enwerem, 1995) Given the pneumatic emphasis and class content of the Aladura, it has often been speculated whether they understood the nature of political power and engagement. Yet scholars have noticed that the messianic type among the Aladura, who have openly incorporated occult teachings, (Hackett, 1989 :164) enjoys the fastest growth and that ritual agents in the neotraditional sector of the Aladura, just like the native doctors, provide "medicine" and cultic prayers for people operating in the political space. As Paul Gundani demonstrated with data from Zimbabwe, when Western medical facilities collapse and socioeconomic stress increase, the business of the indigenous prophets of the nativistic and vitalistic Aladura increases as cheap and efficacious coping mechanism.(1998:1-16) In the discourse of social suffering, health is generally perceived as a social indicator.

Finally, the salience of Pentecostalism in the modern scene raises questions about their political theology which has garnered force around five themes: Christian Zionism, the Beast in the European Union, Window 10/40 and AD 2000 and Beyond and prophetic imagination woven around the promise and restoration of the black race. To "redeem the land", intercessors for Africa, re-vision national histories, endeavor to break ethnic boundaries and conduct city walks that re-dedicate the cities of Africa to God. These have enormous political consequences. They can be perceived as a form of religious nationalism that affirms that the nation and the continent shall not die. Theirs is a politics of engagement designed to restore hope in the midst of social suffering. Is this gratuitous optimism or a process of remoralization? This reflection will elaborate this wider perception of the pervasive and complex role of religion in the legitimacy crisis that has engulfed Nigeria in the twilight of the second millennium. The cosmologies in Nigerian traditions are deeply religious, so the political culture has strong religious dynamics that provide salient leadership values, empower the predators and lift the poor from despair. The complexity is the focus: "how people make, negotiate and unmake meaning in human conditions especially in conditions of breakdown and disruption" (Kleinman, 1997, 317).

To recapitulate: The Nigerian state has been analyzed, employing certain political models as modernization, dependency, patrimonialism, the praetorian/prebendary model, civil society, extraversion, Afropessimism, and sociosomatic resonance. These weld together the contours of African political analysis in the last decade. The emphasis here is that the legitimacy crisis of the five years (1993-1998), which caused much social suffering, arose more from internal factors. Admittedly, the burdensome colonial legacy and the activities of the entrepreneurs of global economy weave the backdrop tapestry. As a poet put the matter, beyond the external factors, it is "*we on us*". The legitimacy crisis in Nigeria is, therefore, rooted in the moral and religious dimensions of our cultures. This explains the waves of moral renaissance programs under various presidents: Murtala Mohammed started an *Ethical Revolution* in 1975; Shehu Shagari followed *en suite* in 1979 with a half-hearted attempt which the Nobel-laureate Wole Sonyika lampooned in a satirical song which queried, "*etika revo wetin?*". General Buhari changed the caption in 1984 into *War Against Indiscipline* and General Babaginda modified it to *War Against Indiscipline and Corruption* (Oji, 1985). Even Abacha mouthed the obvious recognition of the religious roots but used it as a camouflage slogan in his looting of the nation.

What follows will first examine the sacralization of political order and ethics in primal society. Second, it is demonstrated that as the political elite tap the resources of primal religion in their competitions in the modern space, they provide an enormous opportunity for primal religiosity to influence the dynamics of modern politics. Legitimacy crisis merely intensified the process in a religious space bedeviled with an occult explosion. Third, it is argued that new spiritual science movements with political significance are forms of cultural invention, some deriving and all "consonant with the world-affirming and pragmatic orientation of traditional religious beliefs and practices." (Hackett, 1989: 164) Fourth, the role of the *Aladura/ African Indigenous Churches* in the impoverished conditions of legitimacy crisis is explored. Finally, the many facets of the Abrahamic religions in the political dynamics of Nigeria are revisited. What roles did the broad range of religious forces play beneath the political events of the last five years of Nigerian history?

Primal Religion in Modern Political Space

Masquerades are very important in Nigerian communities. Their presence is the heart-beat of every festival. As the flutist leads the masquerade into the village square, the recitation of the moral foundations of the community follows in majestic lyrics. The gods are guests to the human world; the organic worldview in which spirits dwell among humans is celebrated. Masquerades are a metaphor for the ubiquity of spiritual forces and the intervention of the supernatural and enchantment of human affairs. This explains the circle in the cyclical perception of time that surrounds the three-dimensional space. The gods in the sky, the Earth deity, the spirits on land and in water, and the ancestral spirits under the earth all impact humans (for better or worse) and imbue the whole of nature. Admittedly, there are many ethnic and sub-ethnic groups in Nigeria with more than two hundred and fifty different language groups but there are core cultural features that are shared. Ours is an enchanted universe in four components: in the sky, the Supreme Being operates through deities that become oracular, manifesting as sun, moon, lightning, thunder, and rain. The earth deity controls the morality of the land in the second component where other spirits governing the world of nature, animals and humans serve as patrons of professions and order the beauteous marine kingdom. The ancestors, conceived as living-dead, are guardians of communal well-being, ethics, and historical bonding. A fourth crucial component consists of ubiquitous spiritual forces that can be tapped and used to enhance life-force. Their activities are based on the belief that the world is a moral order in which good and bad spiritual forces compete. In a rather precarious vision, humans essay to win the protection of the munificent gods against the machination of the evil ones. Ritual activities and prohibitions or boundaries of purity and danger, are utilized to achieve the goals of an abundant life in material well-being and a long life with dignity.

Anthropological literature is replete with discussions of the vital force in African religiosity. From birth, rituals are employed to enhance the vital power of the person through life circumstances. The efforts may involve resort to "medicines", divination, spells, charms, prayer, and empowerment rituals. Causality, fate and destiny are linked to spiritual powers. Nothing happens by chance, so space-time events can be explained, predicted, and controlled by appealing to the activities of spiritual forces in the human world. Religious ardor is about power or obtaining the good offices of supernatural forces; it often involves the manipulation of the spiritual forces to promote one's good, protects one's path, and attacks or destroys the machination of one's enemies.

These four components interweave to sustain the political ethics of the community. Sacralization of the cosmos legitimates the political space within a moral order in which the oracular deities, seeing from above, uphold and punish infraction. The Earth deity along with the other spiritual forces and the ancestors are the predicates of authority. Rulers and the ruled act from a sense of their ultimacy and presence. This fact is seen in the four models of social control: the socialization process inculcates the acceptable norms of the community. Covenanting rituals, with what Victor Turner calls "forest of symbols" bond the child with the spirits at the gates of the community. Van Gennep has examined the physical, psychological, and sociological dimensions of socialization. Shorter adds that the process continues into adulthood, imparting the wisdom of the ancestors, religious wisdom, and wisdom for living well and fully for one's sake and for the sake of the community. The proverbs, riddles, songs, and dances exude with moral guidance.(Van Gennep, 1960: 165ff; Turner, 1967; Shorter, 1987).The ritual may involve withdrawal from the community and periods of exclusion and communion with the spirits of the land. The community restricts those who would flout salient values with prohibitions, gossip, joking relationship, satire and cultic action. Punishment crashes on the heads of the obstinate; the offended deities are then appeased with sacrifice and rites of purification. Those who uphold salient values are rewarded with honor, a chieftaincy title, praise names and an eagle's feather to the accompaniment of the flute and big drum. Political ethics in a traditional society are rooted in the social control models. The foundation is moral and sanctioned by the gods for the well-being of all. Truthfulness, decency, moderation, and wisdom are acceptable leadership values. There was no secular theory of obligation. To accede to authority roles, the individual must be "animated", imbued with a close relationship to the gods of the community. As a chief, the animation rites endow the "tongue of the tiger" . This is sharp and will judge rightly without favor nor swerved by patronage of the rich. Many studies have used the ritual of enthronement of rulers to buttress the religious roots of legitimacy in primal society (Olupona, 1991).

Our interest is not to mine the political structure of Nigeria cultures but to emphasize a certain ambience, namely, that modern political culture has sought to debauch primal ethics and yet, the spiritual dynamics of the primal order has invaded modern politics. Traditional cults are used in modern public space without the due moderation and boundaries because the modern space is supposed to be an unlimited and unbounded space. Rulers and the political elite source legitimacy from primal space without absorbing the salient values. For instance, in traditional society, the leader is a ritual agent even in the situations where there are priestly guardians of communal shrines. Priestly functions are invested in the paterfamilias, first sons, kinship heads, village, clan leaders, and female priestesses. Gerontocracy, the rule of elders, predominates because elders and ancestors are in close proximity. In any community, there would be ritual power nodes: diviner, seer, herbalist/healer, and witchcraft expert who provide protective enhancement and destructive medicine, charms, and amulets. General practitioners may combine some of these roles! An elastic structure enables the recruitment of spiritual forces from foreign communities for witchcraft detection and protective and achievement-enhancing medicine. Guilds and secret societies also co-exist sharing wisdom, craft, cult, and medicine. They mobilize around certain interests; for instance, healing, wealth, influence, esoteric knowledge, mutual aid, and entertainment. In some communities, leaders can only emerge from among the members of the secret society.

Underneath modern Nigerian public space is a political culture that, like a virus, feeds on the red blood corpuscles of the primal world; by so doing, they transfer to the modern political space dynamics imbued with a primal religious force. To explain: there are three "publics" in the Nigerian political and moral universe: the primal, the emergent, and the Western. In spite of decolonization, vestiges of the Western public survives in our present. Foreign education and global forces keep the character of the Western public in our present. But it is weak. The strongest is seemingly the emergent public that is neither primal nor Western, a veritable melange of both. One of Fela's songs dubbed it, *shakara* culture spawned in the urban centers. It has its own value system bred in the anonymity of the town. As a society is thrust into a larger or re-organized macrocosm, new lifestyles and ethical options appear.(Hefner, 1993) Colonial officers worried about "black Englishmen" who were neither English nor authentic Africans. Changing value systems ensured that people did things in the emergent public that they would not dare in the primal or Western publics. In the latter they would be imprisoned; in the former gods were the policemen. But the emergent public was regarded as the *white man's world*; there, people did the *white man's work*. To foray there successfully was an achievement to be celebrated with the flute and drum. People learned to loot in the emergent public without due repercussions in the primal context as long as they were not caught. The interplay of the two publics explains the moral collapse in the nation. The kinship, ethnic and clientele character of patrimonial culture from the emergent public overwhelmed primal values under indigenous rule. The victory of the emergent value system is illustrated by the expectation of villagers that their kith and kin should go to the emergent public and bring their own share of the national cake by hook and preferably by crook. If a fraudulent public official were prosecuted, his village elders would go on a delegation to protest. Dishonest individuals can now take chieftaincy titles without fulfilling the moral prerequisites. The immoral ethics of the emergent public have debauched the salient values of the primal culture and provided the fodder for power adventurers and predatory military rulers. Praetorian regimes both engender and exploit the collapse of the religious and moral force that propped up the society.

A closer look betrays the ironic villagization of the modern political space. Political actors pose as warriors from their villages to compete for national resources on behalf of their communities. They, therefore, seek legitimation in the primal political base. They undergo rituals of empowerment: chieftaincy titles, membership in cults and secret societies; they patronize ritual agents who provide protective charms and amulets. Thus "fortified", they are able to detect poison, ward off witchcraft spells, and operate with immense vital force. The emergent public is imaged as a precarious context in which success can be achieved only with magico-religious power derived from any efficacious sources.. The preparation for the foray into the emergent zone starts from the village. This has the benefit of building a grassroots support by showing the villagers that their political representative is one of them and shares the village's value system and cults. One can appear as a champion of African culture, dance with the masquerade, and pose as a nationalist of no mean order! In a context in which economic power is derived from political power, the elite utilize primal cult and spiritual force in self-aggrandizement. They assume titles which position them as the "the leopard which guards the village, the voice of the people, the light, the sun, the moon, the lightning that shows the way, the war leader" of the people. There is a teasing cluster of imagery of money, power, and light on the darkened path of communities. Armed with village legitimacy, they offer themselves as a good investment for the military leader who is in the market for clientele and ready to pay cash for some form of legitimacy. An intimacy of power is crafted. The parasitic relationship vitiates traditional institutions, robbing them of their salient values and disabling the rural masses of the will to protest. In the last five years, the inability of the political elite to withstand the tyrant and to protect the masses from the humiliations of poverty can be explained by the interconnection between the primal and emergent publics. The political elite proved to be the clay feet of civil society. The dynamics of our legitimacy crisis are rooted in religious culture.

Two further examples will suffice. These are powerful cults which emerged from the primal religiosity to dominate modern political space, the *Ogboni* from Yorubaland and the *Nyamkpe* from the Cross River basin in South-Eastern Nigeria. Both are powerful secret societies whose votaries developed through rungs or degrees of initiation. The *Ogboni* cult controlled Yoruba society and could discipline a king. It became dominant because Nigerian contact with whites, traders, commissars, or missionaries first took place in the Yoruba environment. The indigenous people used their secret society as a means of mobilizing adequate responses to the new dispensations. Gradually, other Nigerians sojourning in Lagos found that the society conferred protection, access to wealth, power, and upward mobility in professions and politics. It became a trans-ethnic religious force dominating modern sectors such as business, professions and politics. The judiciary, civil service, military, government, and even top ecclesiastical posts were lorded over by *Ogboni* members. In 1914, an Anglican archdeacon, Venerable T.A .J. Ogunbiyi, founded the Reformed Ogboni Fraternity in an attempt to remove the "pagan" rituals and enable Christians to participate without qualms. He emphasized the benefits of the bonding in the brotherhood. Each initiate swears to be *"in duty bound to help one another in distress, to succor, in adversity to warn against danger and be charitable under all circumstances"*. Thus, two *Ogboni* cults co-exist as a powerful secret society from the primal religion and serve as a power node in modern political space. The secrecy, class, wealth, and bonding enable them to wield enormous influence. *Nyamkpe* played a similar role among the communities of the Cross River basin but to a lesser extent. A cult of the Leopard spirit, it served as the political force, adjudicator, and enforcer of customs among many ethnic groups in the region. It was of Ejagham origin but gained much prominence because of the role of the Efiks of Calabar. Calabar was the port of early commercial contact with the hinterland. It soon housed the provincial commissioner, new courts and educational institutions. The secret society was first used to choose local rulers; then, served as a trade mechanism to galvanize indigenous traders and settle disputes, and finally a society for the wealthy and powerful class.

The entry fee increased as the society became more important both in the colonial and post-colonial dispensations. Like the *Owegbe cult* among the Edo of Midwestern Nigeria, secret societies became core instruments of political mobilization in Nigeria. As ethnic competition intensified, communities resorted to these mobilization systems. They served as pressure groups, secret enclaves where the fears and strategies of the community were discussed. They mobilized the elite, offering covenants of mutual support, wealth, cult security and protection in dangerous terrains, and political clout. Recently, those engaged in developmental and environmental struggles among the Ijaw have formed secret societies imitating the *Sekiapu and Ekine* society among other Niger Delta communities. Thus, at the federal level, there was a mushrooming of ethnic identities suffused in cults of the primal publics, and each struggling to serve narrow interests. Abacha found the scenario easy to maneuver, "settling" some, webbing others, and destroying any opposition that refused to be compromised. This explains the orgy of sycophancy around the dictator.

This is a worldview far removed from Enlightenment rationalism. People still believe in the availability of spiritual forces which can be tapped for vital force and protection in the public space. Thus, night guards, politicians, police officers, civil servants, soldiers, businessmen, academics ands students all could go to native doctors and acquire requisite medicine for protection, power, passing examinations, gaining promotions, making money, retaining good health, traveling safely, and winning in sports. Robbers seek bullet-proof medicine and smugglers seek medicine that will make them invisible and undetected by anti-drug or customs agencies. The amazing aspect is that there could be so much failure in spite of the charms that people carry with them. As rational social structures collapsed, there appeared to be an increase in the penumbra religious zone. Politicians would hire traditional rainmakers to scatter opponents' political rallies with heavy rains. Primal religiosity was employed in electoral pranks instead of using hostile advertisements. In the early 1990s witches took an advertisement in a newspaper to announce that they would be hosting an international convention in the ancient city of Benin. The leader of Nigerian witches started an annual prophetic declaration of major events of each new year-usually that a very important person would die! But the political focus of the prophecies reflected the disquiet in people's mind caused by the legitimacy crisis.

The proliferation of secret cults in the Nigerian public space started much earlier and has merely risen in intensity. The government outlawed them in the civil service and military with the Gazette of 1977. Perhaps the proliferation grew from the revival of indigenous religion during the civil war (1967-70) and the intense competition triggered by the oil boom thereafter. In universities, it turned into a scourge of educated culture when students formed innumerable secret cults, each outdoing the other in violent crimes. These were not fraternities or peer- support groups as in North American universities where the worst fate would be to drink oneself to death. Rather, the students visited native doctors, poured their blood in shrines, and established violent cults that intimidated fellow students, especially females, and faculty. The political dimension was soon obvious as the student cults rivaled one another to control the hall governments, students' unions and the National Association of Nigerian Students. Lacking in learning and morals, one could anticipate another blow on the vaunted civil society that will oppose predatory governments. They not only aided the disabling of the academic environment but during the mayhem of the last five years, many of the cult students became drug dealers, thugs for politicians and mobilizers of student support for the military oligarchy questing for legitimacy. Student recruits were richly rewarded in the poor academic environment as they became *"Youth Earnestly Asking Abacha" (YEA-A!)* to continue ruling the nation. Through them primal cults ascended into the ivory tower with devastating consequences.(Kalu, 1997) It should also be added that as legitimacy crisis intensified the savagery in competition for resources and political power, thuggery as a mechanism in politics increased. Thugs fortify themselves with charms, cultic, "powerful" prayers, concoctions, and incantations. Groups of thugs have their ritual chaplains.

Religion, Invention of Culture and Politics

Two religious groups come to the fore: the first, the *Mami Wata* cult is rooted in primal religion but is a good illustration of "invention of culture." It added foreign elements in the emergent culture. As R.W. Hefner observed, "the incorporation into a larger social order acts as a catalyst for reformulation of indigenous religion" *(1993:21)*. The other is completely foreign but is utilized like the secret societies of primal culture and proliferated as a means of surviving in the emergent public. The rise of the Spiritual Science Movement has not featured much in the academic analyses of religion and politics in Nigeria. Rosalind Hackett (1989:153) who coined the terminology was still confused about an adequate typology. She noticed a proliferation of them in Calabar in the 1980s. The focus here will be only in two such groups that are sizeable enough and have political impact on the environment: namely, the AMORC and Grail Message.
In current literature, much interest is lavished on the *Mami Wata* cults of Africa because of the interest of art historians fascinated with the rich

iconography and the influence of goddesses in gender studies. It is a female cult. In primal worldview, rivers were important. A world exists in waters where goddesses preside. They gave beauty, wealth, and fertility power. Women speak of dreaming that they went into the river during pregnancy and were given beautiful babies. Such marine deities as *Oshun* patronized divination, witchcraft, and sustained political power (Badejo, 1996). For power and wealth, people killed cows for *Idemili of Nnobi* and took the title of *Ogbuefi Idemili*, conferring a high social and political status. Communities built shrines and installed priestesses. Marine cults became rife. Ifi Amadiume (1985) has shown that if the river and its cult is crucial for the political life of the community, patriarchal ideology would intervene to place either a male priest or a male husband over the female priest. The idea grew that there was a queen in the water whose beauty was surpassing, who did not give fertility, health, long life or progeny or acted as mother; rather, she gave wealth, power in life pursuits and sexual prowess. She was more a lover than a mother whom votaries sought for gifts which bestowed allure, beauty, and grandeur. She was outside any social system and gave gifts with significance in the emergent culture. People gradually associated her with European goods. The traditional version entangled with the lore of sailors. The notion that she came in a canoe was added. Cults burgeoned in which the priestesses would divine and perform rituals to connect an individual with a mermaid spirit who would grant riches, monetary and material, and desires such as political victory and high position. The person would promise to observe certain prohibitions and give something precious in sacrifice to the spirit. Many of the political elite in Nigeria resorted to these shrines on the bank of rivers for the munificence of the mermaid. As professions such as engineering, architecture, banking collapsed, politics became the only means of making money or collecting the crumbs from the tables of military rulers. There could be a connection between economic collapse and the proliferation of *Mami Wata* cults. Shrines were consecrated in the homes of ardent votaries. As the pantheon of water spirits expanded and the number of devotees grew, their ritual paraphernalia and icons became more elaborate, incorporating foreign cultic features.

Drewal (1996:308-333) has argued that the cult was transformed from the traditional mode to serve the interest of the emergent public with the Euro-African commercial contacts in the 15th Century. This may explain dreams of a journey to a domain with white people, posh buildings and fineries. But African contact with Indians is also crucial. Her representation as a snake charmer grew from African interest in Indian prints of Hindu gods and goddesses and spirits. The lithographs of Buddha and other chromoliths are of Indian origin. In the colonial period, magazines and catalogues of Indian charms, spells, rings, candles, talismans, and perfumes proliferated in Nigeria. They promised easy paths to wealth and success and protection more powerful and expensive than the traditional "medicine." The dangerous proviso was that if one misused the directives, the person could become mad! Africans associated the success of Indian merchants with the potency of their religious cults. The impact of Oriental and exotic cults in modern Nigerian life deserves research. It is a key factor in explaining the resilience of nativistic and vitalistic religious enterprises. Popular religion thrives on it. In an emergent culture, they have always proved a resort for the desperate person who finds survival in the urban setting rather traumatic. *Mami Wata* cults promise materials for use in modern living, and money which could be used to purchase votes and power to enhance success in the modern political space. It is believed that after the person dies, a squabble would break out among his progenies, and all the wealth would be dissipated or "return" to the marine world. *Mami Wata* must engage in much recycling!

The evidence of the extent of this cult has emerged from the burgeoning literature on deliverance. For instance, in many monthly breakfast meetings of the Full Gospel Business Men's Fellowship International, a number of the elite give testimonies of their spiritual journey and their struggles to make money and gain power in the world. L. R. Rambo (1993) has discussed the impact of these biographical reconstructions in encapsulating the believer; many of these are published in gory accounts of sojourns with marine cults. The deputy governor of Rivers State in the Third Republic told the group how he was receiving occult materials from India. He would place an order for candles and other liturgical materials by writing the list on a paper and burning the paper in his shrine using appropriate incantations. The ordered candles and items would just appear in his personal shrine. It was his route to the governor's mansion. Through the prayers of his wife, he became "born-again" . He is now a preacher on the vanity of the endeavor. The expense in setting up a viable shrine indicates that this is a game that the rich play.

Similarly, the AMORC and Freemasonry are secret societies for the professional elite. They are much like *Ogboni* except that they originate from the West. The AMORC is an esoteric fraternal order founded by H. Spencer Lewis in New York in 1915. It claims continuity with an ancient Egyptian occult order and promises to help people discover the secret powers of inner vision and cosmic consciousness. The concern here is not with their "mystical philosophy" but with their political relevance. On the surface, they provide international linkage, a world-wide cultural fraternity, access to financial opportunities for professional elite, and spiritual solace.

They are bastions of political power in the state. At the cultic level, they constitute a similar invention of culture, the appropriation of new spiritual modes to serve functions already articulated in the primal religion. The symbols are, therefore, differently attuned to the Western magical tradition. Studies on Sierra Leone, Liberia, and Cameroon exposed how the Lodge (Rosicrucians and Mason) constitutes the nerve center of power in these countries. A thorough analysis of the intricate web of power and influence of the Lodge is provided by Abner Cohen's *The Political Culture of the Elite (1981),* a case study of the Creoles of Sierra Leone. Lodges are popular throughout the West African coast. Nigeria is rather too large and endowed with a centrifugal power structure but the Rosicrucians and Freemasons are very influential in the South. Many Christian groups are concerned that their important members are also members of these two religious secret societies. The Catholics, Anglicans and recently the Methodists have countered by giving elite members titles and bizarre uniforms and long parade swords within Knighthood Orders. On the surface it may appear that they do not appreciate the political and economic dimension to cult membership but some say that the liturgy of the Knight Orders resemble those of the Rosicrucians and the political function is the same.

There are over a dozen groups within the Spiritual Science Movement; most sprung up in the 1980s. One line of enquiry could explore the human conditions as a backdrop and why Nigerians appear to be so receptive. Some groups are from the West and many are Oriental. The Masonic Lodges are prominent because they were founded in colonial times and served as a contact between the rising African elite and the Europeans. Among the new ones, only the Grail Message has acquired some modicum of social importance because the leader in Lagos, Lawanson, was a rich professional and pitched a television campaign on the educated, professional elite. Emphasizing cleanliness in personal appearance and quiet demeanor, they built temples which stood out because of the flowers, exquisite architecture, and landscaping. Their canon, *In the Light of Truth,* is a-three volume teaching on spiritual knowledge concerning human existence in creation. Supposedly it is written by Abdrushin, but there is no such person because the founder was from Vienna. Some surmise the presence of ancient gnostic traditions. But there is secrecy which only the "sealed" know. It has mobilized a highly literate and professional elite in the South with access to wealth that could be exchanged for political power.

Magical Substratum of Scariscape and Politics

This effort so far has avoided a serious discussion on popular religion and has focused on instead the magical substratum that undergirds the religious landscape (scariscape) and how this either influences political ethics and practice or is influenced by the political trends and practice of the rulers. This method dethrones any religious tradition from posing as the convention precisely because people explore and exploit various religious forms at the same time. Each religion has both a formal node and an informal substratum or "supplementary religiosity" riddled with cult. Cult becomes the contested space in the pursuit of power and protection, themes that the legitimacy crisis intensifies.

This assertion can be illustrated by Christian and Islam ideology. The African indigenous churches have been heralded as an African response to the missionary message, a reaction to colonial Christianity, a creative translation of the message with African idiom, and Africa's creativity at the culture-gospel interface. The encomia abound to the point of romanticization. Much of this is right. Oosthuizen(1997:308-324) emphasized the socio-economic and political roles in the African environment. However, the movement is declining in West Africa. Gifford has some data from Ghana (1998:62-63). It was never strong in the Cameroon and the civil wars in Sierra-Leone and Liberia have taken tremendous tolls. The decline in Nigeria is obvious, too. Equally crucial is that in the development of the movement, some genres shifted away from the biblical roots and brought elements that are doubtful. (Kalu, 1996b: chapt.11)

Attention on four types indicates that the *Revivalist* type of indigenous churches such as Godianism, merely clothes primal religion with Christian paraphernalia. It is unimportant in contemporary scariscape. The *Messianic* type in which the leader claims to be one or the other of the Trinity is the largest and fastest-growing. An example is the Brotherhood of Cross and Star with headquarters in Calabar (Hackett, 1989). The leader promises to provide the special resources to meet the human condition: healing, wealth, power, protection. Rosalind Hackett argues that

> the exorcism of evil spirits and 'medicine' from homes and places
> of work, formerly undertaken by traditional specialists, is becom-
> ing more and more the responsibility of the spiritual churches,
> notably the Brotherhood of the Cross and Star." (1989:271)

He combines techniques from the metaphysical religions, witchcraft, and the Oriental occult. Of course, he quotes Scriptures. Hackett shows that the leader is close to the AMORC and works with the Subud Brotherhood of Indonesian origin. The members invest the letters of the leader's name with sacred, protective power. He is said to appear to those who knock their foreheads on the floor three times and recite certain incantations. The magical powers and miracles have political importance. The movement assiduously seeks to influence people in authority and to sponsor candidates for political posts at local and federal government levels. Many beneficiaries testify that their success came from "Papa" as they fondly refer to him. When Melford Okilo, a former civilian governor, was dragged to the Assets Recovery Panel in 1986, he donated much of his loot to the Brotherhood and miraculously was released. He is now a political agent of the movement. Examples abound but limited space deters.

As hinted earlier, the market for the prophets of the vitalistic and nativistic genres of *Aladura* has expanded in inverse proportion to the collapse of social infrastructure and economy. These prophets shop for the ingredients of their practice from the advertised "Merchants, Mystic Adepts and Master Occultists" who sell herbal products, Indian amulets, talismans, lucky jewelry, love-potions, secret biblical texts encased in leather pouches, oils, alums of various colors and Kabbalistic literature such as Sixth and Seventh Books of Moses. Some are itinerant mystical consultants and professors; others set up healing homes where "powerful prayers" can be given for different conditions. Their importance for thugs is pertinent. It is, therefore, palpable that these three genres are doing better in the untoward times than the Pentecostal Aladura (Christ Apostolic Church) and the Zionist (Cherubim and Seraphim).

The Enlightenment worldview and cultural policy of mainline Christianity tended to saccharine the magical substratum except in the bowdlerized rituals that use some symbols from Roman Catholicism in syncretistic formularies. Indeed, the attraction of Christianity at its inception was its technological power because of the association with colonial insurgence and the expansion of European hegemony. Thus, Paul Gifford argued that "the relative success of Islam was due to two things which missionary Christianity could not yet emulate: its magico-spiritual techniques through prayers and charms and its social affability" (1998:323). There was more: Islam had the prestige of its international networks and its political-military clout. The magical substratum in Islam has received inadequate attention in the discourse of Islam in national politics. Most scholars are concerned with Islamic influence over control of the military, political leadership of the nation, control of resources, and the struggle to write the Shariah into the Constitution. Moreover, there has been the tendency to treat the implosion of the cultic dimension in Islam as aberrant. For instance, when the Maitatsine movement, led by Mohammed Marwa Maitatsine, raged in Nigeria from 1978-1985, the commission of inquiry noted the appalling magical and violent aspects. They gained power through ingesting certain parts of the human body and killed many people for that purpose. The real threat was that they recruited from among the unemployed and indoctrinated them against wealthy Muslims who were insensitive to the poor and to orthodoxy. Maitatsine was highly political, operated in the infra-realm and with magic. It was a bloodsucking cult against both Muslims and especially Christians; they engineered riots in which thousands died for no just cause.

The concern here is power and cult in Sufism. Alwii Shihab would insist that this was a travesty of Islam. This is why Alhaji Shehu Gumi, the grand qadi, founded the *Jamaa Izalat al Bida wa Iqamat al Sunnah, a movement against innovation,* which between 1978-1980 terrorized the Sufi orders. In Nigeria, the dominant Sokoto Caliphate, founded as a result of the Usman Dan Fodio jihad of 1804, adheres to the *Quadriyya* Sufi order. The jihad extended into Yorubaland in the South in three stages: initial insurgence, 1840-1860; a consolidation lasting until 1894, and a third wave that reached a crescendo around 1908. In 1921, a new Sufi order, *Ahmadiyya,* came into Yorubaland through the Indian Ahmadi missionaries. The *Tijaniyya* gathered force with the arrival of the holy man, Ibrahim Niass of Kaolack, Senegal. Two political facets mattered: the Sokoto Caliphate was a key power node in Nigerian politics controlled by the feudalistic, autocratic descendants of the jihad leader. Their support of the Quadriyya created a second facet namely, the progressive scions of the oppressed turned the Tiyyaniya into a rival political party. They mobilized the *talakawas,* nobodies, around the intense spirituality of Niass, and this ideological division resulted in the formation of two political parties in the North. The Northern Peoples' Congress was Quadriyya, based in Sokoto while the Northern Elements' Progressive Union was Tijanniyya, based in the populous commercial city of Kano. The division between the radicals and the hegemonic conservatives in Hausa/Fulani politics has always played out in the rivalry of Sufi orders. Both rejected the Ahmadiyya as true Moslems. But this order established a number of schools with Western educational orientation and produced highly educated Moslems who operated in the modern sector with a proficiency that those with an Arabic education lacked. During the last decade, attention turned on the extent of cultic practices within Sufism. During the regime of General Babaginda, it was reported that seven rams were buried alive daily by *marabouts and seriki,* who controlled ritual protection for the general. In the recent investigations on the brutal Abacha regime, the former director of military intelligence alleged that the national security advisor, spent about two million naira quarterly to hire marabouts from Senegal, Chad, Morocco, and the Niger Republic to offer daily sacrifices and protect Abacha's star from being shot down by his many enemies. He buried live cows in Aso Rock in order to give Abacha the impression that he was loyal to the self-succession bid of the ruler. Like the mythologized vampire, for years he seemed to obtain a new lease on life and potency. The attention of commentators turned to the vast cost to the nation and missed the religious significance. This has been the concern of an intramural dispute in Islam. Sheik Gumi was concerned about relating doctrine and practice. As an intellectual renaissance occurred among the younger breed, there was immense concern about the moral decadence among the Northern political elite and the depth of cultic practices.

Reform took two routes: to attack Sufi brotherhoods and reestablish the preeminence of Islam in national affairs. The Muslim Students Society spearheaded the revival of orthodoxy. They scrawled "Islam Only" on walls of tertiary institutions and public places. But they, too, divided into Antidarika, pro-Saudi, Dawahwa and violent pro-Iranian Shiites. Both reflected the socioeconomic milieu of unemployment and the visible gap between the rich and the poor. The legitimacy crisis heightened matters by creating a confused political terrain and economic collapse. Soon, the Shiites declared that they would not accept any government that was not organized around Muslim principles. As Yakubu Yahaya said in an open court:

> We as Muslims, don't recognise the authority of the Federal Government, State Government, Local Government and any form of authority. We do not recognise them as our leaders. We are against them. What is between us and them is enmity, eternal enmity, fight, war, forever until the day they will come to the book of Allah...We are on parallel lines...they have their so-called decrees. After getting drunk they come to sit down, make their so-called decrees...We as Muslims have our law which is the Koran and Sunna, the traditions of prophet Muhammed and we execute them under the leadership of Mallam Ibrahim El-Zak-Zak-Zaky). (Kalu, 1996a)

El-Zaky who graduated in economics from Ahmadu Bello University had been one of the leaders of a campus pro- Iranian group. He was funded to mobilize a full Shiite program in Nigeria. On 30th September, 1996, they unleashed mayhem in Kaduna. General Abacha incarcerated them until he died. They were recently released under the new democratic dispensation. Extraversion explains this violent response to a violent regime as the revolutionary clarion of international Islam beckoned the young Muslims with harsh flutes of jihadist war. Jealous for his own flute, Abacha silenced competing ones. The prop for this scene was put in place when Babangida had surreptitiously, with the collusion of the Sokoto Caliphate, registered Nigeria as a member of the Organization of Islamic Countries in 1986. The furor absorbed the attention of the populace throughout 1987, causing enormously bitter religious politics. Bala Usman (1987) suggested the interesting hypothesis that it was a deliberate manipulation of religion to hide political and economic failures of the general. Another explanation can be proffered, namely, that the flagrant partisan activities and pronouncements of the Northern elite in the political arena were designed to recover lost legitimacy within Islamic ranks. There, votaries were concerned with: (a) the neglect of *ribah* prohibitions in the economic lives of the elite;(b) the destruction of the legal manifestation of Islam and abuse in the exercise of the Shariah; (c) despite the proliferation of mosques, there was little observance; religious piety was often vitiated by formalism; (d) the educated felt impotent to control deviance except by virulent attack on fellow Muslims; (e) and though the Pakistani businessman, Yusuf Fardi, richly endowed the Supreme Council for Islamic Affairs, the body remained ineffective because of the ability of the Military to manipulate the leadership. (Kalu, 1996a:106)

Just as in the South, the Northern political elite resorted to both traditional cults and Islamic cults for power and protection as they forayed into the national political scene. As in the case of vitalistic Aladura, the Muslim mallam is noted for cultic prayers, amulets, and charms for power, protection and control of space-time events. This is related to the affable cultural policy of Islam that tends to absorb exogenous primal religion and culture with less trouble; for instance, Yoruba *Ifa* divinatory techniques. (Abdul, 1970;Doi, 1971) Oseni has argued that the bad eggs among them practice sorcery and misuse such prayers as *Ya Sin* and *Suratu l-lahab.* (Oseni.1988:248) Mallams equipped people with bullet-proof charms and poisoned arrows for the attacks on Christian churches, one of the many dimensions of the political use of cult in Islam.

The Muslim-Christian Factor in National Politics

Lamin Sanneh has, in two works, *Power and Piety* (1996) and *The Crown and the Turban* (1997) set out the broad framework of the religious factor in political dynamics in African states. At one spectrum is the development of the concept of the nation state; at the other, its gradual bloom into a unitary, absolute, and comprehensive leviathan:

> The state authority aspired to the status of a metaphysical abso-
> lute, in which the will of the nation state became omnipotent
> and definitive of truth about human beings...Such a claim turns
> the state into an explicit rival religion bolstered by an impreg-
> nable system of rewards and inducements, as well as sanctions
> and penalties (1997:180-181).

The state would like to declare the public sphere a religion-free zone so as to tap its deep allegiances in legitimation. How did Muslims and Christians respond? At the conceptual level, both share a theocratic and patriarchal perception of power. But in its development, Islam clung tenaciously to the notion that there is no distinction between the public and religious spheres and that political power was essential for promotion of religion. It was quite prepared to fight any authority that muzzled this enterprise. This explains why each of the nine jihads in West Africa, culminating in the Usman Dan Fodio's, involved state formation. Meanwhile, the Christian West disengaged the coaches of state from religion. Citizenship no longer carried religious import. A history of ambiguous attitude to power was bequeathed to African Christians while the Muslims marched with confidence. History came to their further aid in the colonial policy of Indirect Rule. The defeat of the Sokoto Caliphate appeared inconclusive as it was followed by a *hijra*, and Mahdist revolts continued to loom threateningly. The British lacked the manpower and resources for an imperial rule, given the rumors and real wars in Europe. A certain romantic temperament, fascinated by Arabic culture, spawned Hamitic theories of the origins of the Fulani and produced the policy of protecting Islam, utilizing the emirs as administrative agents and restricting missionary insurgence into those quarantined territories. At decolonization, the British virtually inscribed that the North should rule. The mineral resources and sea-outlet were located among the educated Southerners. Religion acquired geopolitical and constitutional dimensions. Ethnic factors caused even more complexity because some ethnic groups in the North were not Islamized and some became Christian.

From this backdrop, the religious factor in national politics was characterized by conflicts over: (a) the Constitution: the Muslims sought to add the Shariah into the Constitution in 1978, 1989 and 1991; (b) international relations: as Muslim bodies organized, using the petro-dollar as a weapon, Nigeria was a crucial member of the OPEC and this loomed large in their calculation. This explains the membership of the OIC in 1986; (c) economy: the revenue-sharing formula, allocation of industries, and utilization of foreign loans became contested issues. Many alleged that an army dominated by the Northern Muslims was partial in these matters;(d) ethnicity: the riot in Zagon-Kataf in 1992 represented ethnic conflict with religious undertone. The Katafs in Southern Kaduna were not Islamized during the jihad and became Christians. But the feudal Caliphate placed Muslim rulers over them. The Katafs rebelled against these; the government conducted a kangaroo court and jailed the key citizens of the group. The Middle Belt ethnic groups, especially the Tiv, rebelled against the centralizing politics of the Caliphate, became strong Evangelical Christians, and formed their own United Middle Belt Congress; (e) political order: zealous speeches about the unwillingness of the North to share power with the Christian South became dysfunctional. Years ago, a Southern politician, Obafemi Awolowo, thought that the matter could be solved by giving a written undertaking to the Northern political elite that he would patronize Arabic schools, pilgrimages, and Northern control of key government posts. They ignored him.

In 1993, a Southern Muslim won the election but vested interests connived against him. The political life of the nation went into a spin from which it has not recovered. Moshood Abiola was opposed by some key players in the army because he had colluded with them to a point of hubris and they rebelled. The Northern elite also demurred. It is known that the Sultan of Sokoto mobilized the opposition within the Northern Council of Elders. Some adduce that their clash was based on conflicting business interests, given the propensity of both to make money from commissions in securing contracts for foreign companies. Some adduce that the Northerners despise the liberal Islamic tendencies among the Yoruba. Al-Ilori, a Yoruba Islamic scholar, averred that while the Southerners took spirituality seriously, Northerners nosed into the political power aspects. David Laitin put it aptly, arguing that religion is a principal cultural marker for politics in the North; he compares this with the Yoruba scene:

> religion and not tribe has become the leitmotif for northern politics as ancestral city (and not religion) has become in Yorubaland. Yorubas organize in terms of ancestral city for internal battle and tribe for Nigeria-wide politics; northerners organize in terms of religious brotherhood for internal battle and world religious membership for Nigeria-wide politics (1986:163).

A key factor in the fall of Abiola was the cooperation between Dasuki and Abacha. Later, it became clear that Abacha had his own personal ambition to rule, and he dexterously galvanized the military and religious opposition to Abiola. When he was firmly seated in the presidency, Abacha, like Stalin, ruined all his former allies and cleared the way for his self-succession as a civilian ruler. He desecrated the Sultan's stool by removing Dasuki

57

from office. Dasuki tasted what he had served to another person when he climbed over the rightful successor through the aid of General Babangida and Alhaji Abubakar Abubakar (a.k.a. Triple A*)*, a corrupt eye of the Caliphate in the government treasury. Dasuki's competitors wrapped themselves around Abacha like a cloth, offering a more secure allegiance. He gave them back the throne of their uncle, Siddiq Abubakar. This was the height of military manipulation of a powerful religious institution to secure legitimacy as the new sultan served his patron as a washcloth in the politics of self-succession.

How did Christianity respond to the pretensions of the state? Janus-faced: a weak theory of power, collusion in the civilization enterprise, uncreative cultural policy that packaged the message as hardware, and virulent internal rivalries combined to breed a weak political theology that legitimized the powerful. Yet there have been moments when the church aided the weak and essayed to be faithful to its mission to humanity. The Christian Association of Nigeria was formed to cure rivalry with social ecumenism and sharpen the response of the church to partisan political acts. As a counter to Jamatu Nasril Islam (Victory to Islam) and the Supreme Council of Islam, this body heightened religious competition in the public square. Many elections were fought on religious allegiance. It raised awareness to the tendency of Islamic fundamentalists to burn churches in Northern Nigeria. A rash of this occurred between 1981 and 1991. It has phased down. The Christians claim that the Scriptures provide that one should turn the other cheek. After that the Bible becomes silent, meaning that one could retaliate. The churches have engaged in a vast array of poverty alleviation programs, a virtual NGO-ization of the church. The external factor was equally crucial as many foreign bodies responded to the plight of Nigerians by sponsoring various projects. The Catholic Church has led in this measure that includes public enlightenment on democracy. An internal report prepared by the Inter-Church Coalition in Canada indicates, however, that the churches in Nigeria have been a weak voice in protesting the brutality of Abacha. Many in the pews were more concerned with "churchy" matters and the politics of survival. Daring individuals such as Matthew Hassan Kukah, a Catholic priest, raised their voices. When Bishop Emmanuel Gbonigi, the Anglican Bishop of Akure, declared in a public interview that Abacha is thoroughly wicked, that there will be a revolution, everyone expected that prison guards would soon be casting lots for his purple coat. But Abacha died a fortnight after, on the morning he planned to declare that he had accepted the people's "earnest desire" that he should rule. Seven weeks later, Abiola died. The exit in 1998 of the chief protagonists of the legitimacy crisis of 1993 alarmed the entire country. Many saw the finger of God in the affairs of the nation; others saw the gloved hands of American CIA. The close aides of the ruler are still busy "ratting" on one another about the two mysterious deaths.

Political Nationalism in Religious Stroke

Throughout the prolonged crisis, Nigeria was sustained by a certain form of nationalism with a strong religious undercurrent. Commentators note the heightened religious temper in the nation and explain it by its appeal to the straitened socioeconomic predicament. Rough times have always forced people to reexamine their spiritual roots. Religions are supposed to serve as balm in difficult times and answer ontic questions about existence. The argument here is that the heightened religious temper has political import as it expresses nationalism: the refusal to let the nation die. Ordinarily, nationalism tends to assume religious symbolism and dimensions. Political liberation is often moored to a strong religious ideology. Literature abounds on civil religion that sacralizes the public space for civil purposes. Space will not allow an excursus on civil religion in Nigeria though this falls squarely into the ambit of religious presence in modern politics. The quest for legitimacy by military rulers involved not only deliberate patronage of religious groups (hajj, pilgrimage, religious holidays) and activities, but the cultivation of civil religion.(Olupona, 1989:41-48) The declaration that Nigeria is a secular state has not implied a strict separation of religion and state as in Western countries. An official Nigerian government delegation goes to Mecca yearly on the hajj.

Of interest is how religious groups have operated during the crisis from a keen sense of nationalism: to assist the individual towards self-reintegration, rejection of pessimism, cynicism and the poverty which stares at noontide and to reformulate the destiny of the nation in contradistinction from the rulers. Within Islam, it was clear that such reformulation did not exist within the elite Muslim band. When Dasuki insisted that the presidential elections should be annulled because "we do not have any candidate," he represented a clique who wanted to continue to live as parasites off the state. The Shiites had a clearer vision, however narrow; so did the younger generation of the Northern intellectuals. This is important because the legitimacy crisis of 1993 inserted an interrogation of the very essence of nationhood into the daily consciousness of the ruled.

Within the Pentecostal band of Christianity, there arose a cogent revisioning from a broader perspective. It argued that God had a plan for the nation and had spoken promises for the good of the nation. Such promises cannot be annulled and have wider connections to the destiny of the black race. The size and resources of Nigeria were designed to assist her to fulfill the larger roles. Pentecostals blamed both the rulers and the ruled for polluting the land with greed, fraud, and violent bloodshed. God will forgive the nation for patronizing idols by hosting the Festival of Arts (FESTAC). God will restore and will install a leader. All acknowledge that the problem of Nigeria is leadership. Since God could use Cyrus, the leader does not need to be a Christian. From here, they moved to tackle the increase of violence in the cities and to denounce the encroaching poverty on cities that used to bustle with economic activities. Pentecostals took prophetic action in specific policy matters, conducted city projects, and asserted that in spite of all problems, God has not given up on Nigeria. Soon they developed the vision that the "brethren" should run for offices at all levels of governance. Outreaches now included mobilization for political participation. A political theology of engagement soon suffused the Christian environment. Their analysis blamed both rulers and ruled, the internal actors as well as the external forces: demonization of the World Bank, the European Union as the Beast, and Zionism in response to the influence of International Islam on the country. Through the impact of the Pentecostal movement, the ambivalence towards power in the Western churches has given way to a new consciousness about the need to bring strong Christian ethics into governance in Nigeria.(Kalu, 1998)This seeped into the mainline churches through the charismatic movements. Some have perceived this as "a dangerous awakening"(Enwerem, 1995). Some may even wonder whether the radical religiosity sufficiently challenged the structures of the praetorian regime. A vigorous response to the aftereffects of the legitimacy crisis cannot be denied. It not only provided the spiritual missing link in Christian presence but threw a challenge to all religious groups to mine the political values within their systems for the salient ones which could reformulate the destiny of the nation in positive ways. But this movement lacked an ideology of dialogue that could mobilize other religious forces in the face of predatory rulers. Instead, the progressives appeared as hostile fundamentalists.

Dialogue is not debate but living together in affirmation of the best in all religious traditions. Primal religion espoused salient political values before the Abrahamic religions suffused the emergent public. Islam and Christianity espouse ethics of love, humility, decency, transparent honest leadership, and the values that nurture "good company." Dialogue is to be rooted in one's traditions and open to others. The world religions whose dysfunctional presence has concerned social analysts should recognize a new pluralistic environment anticipated in the ethics of their canons. If dialogue prevailed as an antidote, military rulers would not have brought so much suffering to our people and with such impunity.

Bibliography

Abdul, M.O.A.(1970) "Yoruba Divination and Islam", *Orita,* University of Ibadan, 4, 1(June).

Amadiume, Ifi (1985) *Male daughters female husbands,* London: Zed Press.

Awodede, Obed (1998) "Plundering and Looting Unlimited", *Tell Magazine,* August, 24:12-33.

Babarinsa, D. (1998) "The Gun and the Pulpit", *Tell Magazine,* 21 May 25[th.]

Badejo, Deidre (1996) *OSHUN: The Elegant Deity of Wealth, Power and Femininity.* Trenton, NJ: Africa World Press Inc.

Bayart, J-F (1993) *The State in Africa: The Politics of the Belly,* London: Longmans.

Bratton, M.(1989) "Beyond the State: Civil Society and Associational Life in Africa" *World Politics,* 41:407-430.

Cohen, Abner (1981) *The Political Culture of the Elite,* University of California Press.

Doi, A.R.I. (1971) "An Aspect of Islamic Syncretism in Yorubaland" *Orita,* 5, 1 (June).

Drewal, H.J. (1996) "Mami Wata Shrines: Exotica and the Constitution of Self" in *African Material Culture,* ed. M.J. Arnoldi, C.M Geary, K.L. Hardin. Bloomington, Indiana University Press: 308-333.

Enwerem, I.M.(1995) *A Dangerous Awakening: The Politicization of Religion in Nigeria.* Ibadan: IFRA.

Fatton, R. (1992) *Predatory Rule: The state and civil society in Africa.* Boulder, Colorado: Lynne Reiner.

_____ (1995) "Africa in the Age of Democratization: The Civic Limitations of Civil Society", *African Studies Review,* 38, 2:67-99.

Gennep, A. van (1960) *The Rites of Passage.* Chicago, University of Chicago Press.

Gellner, E. (1994) *Conditions of Liberty: Civil Society and Its Rivals.* London: Hamish Hamilton.

Gifford, P. (1998) *African Christianity: Its Public Role.* Bloomington: Indiana University Press.

Gundani, P.H. (1998) "Independent Prophets and the Quest for Wholeness/ Healing: An Investigation of the Ministry of Selected Prophets in Harare, Zimbabwe," *Studia Historiae Ecclesiasticae,* 24, 1:1-16.

Hackett, R.I.J. (1989)*Religion in Calabar.* New York: Mouton de Gruyter.

Haynes, J (1996)*Religion and Politics in Africa.* Nairobi, East African Education Publishers.

Hefner, R.W. (1993) *Conversion to Christianity: Historical and Anthropological Perspectives   on a Great Transformation.* Berkeley, University of California Press.

Horns, J. D. et als.eds.(1996). "The Development of Civil Society in a Democratic State: The Botswana Model," *African Studies Review,* 39, 2:43-69.

Horton, R (1970) "African Conversion" *Africa, 41:85-108;* "On Rationality of Conversion" *Africa,* 45:219-235;373-399.

Ibrahim, J (1991) "Political Turbulence in Nigeria", *Journal of Modern African Stud.,* 29, 1:115-136.

Ilesanmi, S. O. (1997) *Religious Pluralism and the Nigerian State.* Ohio Univ. Center for International Studies.

Longman, T.P. (1998) "Empowering the Weak and Protecting the Powerful: The Contradictory Nature of Churches in Central Africa," *African Stud.Rev.,* 41, 1 April: 49-72.

Kalu, O. U. (1986) "Religion and Political Values in Nigeria: A Pluralistic Perspective", *Religious Pluralism in Africa,* Nairobi, August, 1986.

_____ (1996a) "Vines and Brambles: Christianity, State and Development in Nigeria, 1900-1994", *Studia Historiae Ecclesiasticae,* 22, 2, December: 88-113.

_____ (1996b) *Embattled Gods: Christianization of Igboland, 1841-1991.*Lagos/ London: Minaj Publishers.

_____ (2001) *The Scourge of the Vandals: The Nature and Control of Secret Cults in Nigerian Universities.* Nsukka, University of Nigeria Press.

_____ (1998) "The Practice of Victorious Life: Pentecostal Political theology and Practice in Nigeria, 1970-1996", *Journal of* Mission Studies, 5, 2:229-55.

Kleinman, A (1997) "Everything That Really Matters: Social Suffering, Subjectivity and the Remaking of Human Experience in a Disordering World" *Harvard Theological Review,* 90, 3:315-335.

_____ (1996)With Joan "The Appeal of Experience; The Dismay of Images: Cultural Appropriations of Suffering in Our times", *Daedalus,* 125, 1:1-24.

Laitin, D.D. (1986) *Hegemony and Culture: Politics and Religious Change Among the Yoruba* Chicago: University of Chicago Press.

Magesa, L(1997) *African Traditional Religion: The Moral Traditions of Abundant Life.* Maryknoll, NY, Orbis Books.

Oji, K. (1985)*The Action Phase of Ethical Revolution, 1991-2000.*Lagos: MKO Publishers.

Olupona, J. K. (1989) "Religious Pluralism and Civil Religion in Africa", *Dialogue & Alliance*2, 4:41-48.

_____ (1991) *Kingship, Religion and Rituals in a Nigerian Community.* Stockholm Almqvist & Wiksell International.

Oosthuizen, G. (1997) "African Environment: An Empirical Analysis", *Africa Insight,* 26, 4: 308-324.

Oseni, Z.I. (1988) "Islamic Scholars as Spiritual Healers in a Nigerian Community" In A.B. Balogun &Ade Dopamu eds. *The Place of Religion in the*

Development of Nigeria. Department of Religious Studies, University of Ilorin: 236-253.

Rambo, L.R. (1993) *Understanding Religious Conversion.* New Haven, Yale University Press.

Sanneh, L. (1996) *Piety and Power, Muslims and Christians in West Africa.* Orbis Books.

_____ (1997) *The Crown and the Turban: Muslims and West African Pluralism.* Boulder, Colorado: Westview Press.

Shorter, A. (1987) *Songs and Symbols of Initiation.* Nairobi, Cath. Higher Institute, E. Africa.

Turner, V. (1967)*The Forest of Symbols: Aspects of Ndembu Ritual.* Cornell University Press.

Usman, Y. B. (1987)*The Manipulation of Religion in Nigeria, 1977-87.*Kaduna, Vanguard Publ.

Williams, P. & Toyin Falola, (1995), *Religious Impact on the Nation State.* Aldershot, Avebury.

Wilson, M.(1957), *Ritual Kingship Among the Nyakyusa.* London, Oxford University Press.

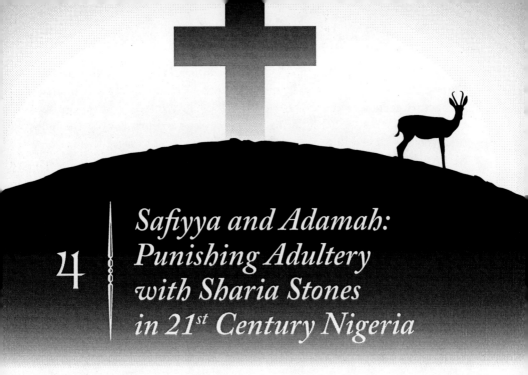

4 | Safiyya and Adamah: Punishing Adultery with Sharia Stones in 21ˢᵗ Century Nigeria

Introduction: The New Phase of Sharia Controversy in Nigeria, 1999-2002

In 1999, the Nigerian political space buzzed with activities following the return of democratic, civilian elections after years of military rule. In one of the Northern states, Zamfara, it was alleged that one of the candidates was strapped for campaign funds and creatively turned his soapbox strategy into a populist religious enterprise. He promised that, if elected into the Government House, he would provide security, amenities, and reform the state by first reforming the morals of the society through the application of the Sharia laws. It may sound as political opportunism but he struck a cord among the masses who felt that their poor conditions were as a result of the ethics of the rich who abandoned the dictates of Islam, ignored the Sharia and garnered wealth without due concern for the poor. The disinherited rural and urban poor, unemployed, as well as students of Universities and Polytechnics had nursed years of anger at their fellow Moslems, the Federal Government and Christians from the south. The chief of the Federal Government Information Unit in Gasau admitted that many families watched helplessly as their children dropped out of school and squandered their youthful lives in debauched lifestyle and armed robbery gangs. Life in the state was insecure and many saw the judgment of God whose laws as embodied in the Sharia had been abandoned. A restoration of religious imperatives of Islam would cure the moral ills of society. So, the politician's promise, in spite of his hidden or actual agenda, was the message that people wanted to hear. During periods of intense social suffering, people tend to accept solutions that are delivered with certainty and with divine insurance; messages that urge a return to things that worked in the past. Fundamentalists argued Marty and Appleby have five characteristics: against secularism; for protection of identity and way of life; with weapons selected out of tradition; against those seen as enemies to their cause; in obedience to God.[1]

There has been a tradition of socio-economic interpretation of religious insurgence in Northern Nigeria though scholars as Kukah and Ilesanmi have examined the political dimensions too.[2] Thus, it is quite possible to interpret the resurgence of the Sharia riddle in Nigerian politics by examining the socio-economic and political background of the contemporary public space. The non-religious dimension is compelling because the candidate had graduated from Ado Bayero University, Kano, in economics and was not known to belong to any fundamentalist group. He worked for various Federal Government financial parasatals before staking his fortunes on democratic politics. The return of democracy offered many opportunities that would have been impossible under dictatorial military dispensations. His reading of the times was not an isolated case. The former military President Yakubu Gowon had in 1996-7 toured the nation organising prayers for the nation. The return of religion into the modern political space was exciting as it provided a very succinct explanation of the collapse of the economy and morality. Legitimacy crises bred social insecurity as the level of social violence increased; corruption vitiated the moral fibre of communities as the competition for dwindling resources intensified. The irony is that the elite were more prone to manipulate the religious fervour in such conditions.[3] The dizzy events of 1993-1998 under General Sani Abacha, a Muslim soldier from Kano, proved both traumatic and a good example of how he and his cronies could stash away billions of dollars while the nation reeled under harsh conditions amidst the collapse of basic infrastructure. With this backdrop, Ahmad Sani Yerima Bakura's religious populism won the election as the Governor of Zamfara State through a religious interpretation of the crisis of yesteryears. He promised that the restoration of the Sharia was the cure of the malaise and the hope for the future for both his state and the rest of Islamized Northern Nigeria.

Admittedly, Sharia controversies have dogged the heels of the nation since political independence in 1960. Every Constitutional review exercise witnessed a virulent public debate over the purviews of the Sharia. The background is that in the 10th Century Islam entered the sector that became

Northern Nigeria in 1914 (when the North and the South were amalgam-ated). There is little evidence on how the sharia was enforced during the period between Usman Dan Fodio's jihad in 1804 and the British conquest in 1906. But the Sokoto Caliphate imposed nomadic Fulani hegemony on the Hausa-Habe communities, created an elaborate administrative struc-ture and encrusted orthodoxy. Colonial enterprise soon dismantled the legal structure in 1902 leaving only a rump in the Indirect Rule strategy of governance. Sharia purview was technically restricted to civil matters and personal law.[4] The Constitution of the modern nation enshrined this rump including the provision for appellate courts. All efforts to enlarge the purviews were stoutly resisted as discordant with the prevalent English Common Law; the posture that Nigeria was a secular state; the smell of Northern domination and particularity of Islam; and the fear for the safety of non-Moslems living in the Northern region. Unbeknown to many, the military dictator, General Sani Abacha had made changes in the Constitu-tion of 1999 that created loopholes for the enactment of the Sharia in the North. Yerima exploited the provision that empowered

> the House of Assembly of a State to make laws for the peace, order and good government of the State or any part thereof with respect to the following matters, that is to say: (a) any matter not included in the Executive Legislative List set out in Part 1 of the second schedule to this constitution;...(c)any other matter with respect to which it is empowered to make laws in accordance with the provisions of this Constitution (4:7)

This buttressed the section that permitted a state with Moslem majority to enact the Sharia. The Constitution sought to restrict the State Houses further by privileging the supremacy of the National Assembly whose laws shall prevail over State laws (4:5) It had an eye to the provisions on freedom of religion, association and fundamental human rights.

Thus, by 2000 all ingredients for a significant new phase of Sharia crisis were ready whether religious, political, social or constitutional. The political scene was confounded by the fact the President was a Christian southerner from a different political party so that any action of his could easily be construed as partisan, anti-Islam and anti-North; ethnicity could be added to the broth especially as he was a Yoruba. Following upon his election, Yerima delivered his promise by declaring that Zamfara state was a Sharia state. He sought the assistance of the Center for Islamic Legal Studies, Ahmadu Bello University, in Zaria to codify both the Penal Code and Criminal Procedure Code. The northern states hurriedly promulgated the sharia system so as to forestall the protests by the Federal Government.

Moreover, Zamfara State modified the efforts of yesteryears by the late Sardauna of Sokoto who had ingenuously incorporated the national penal code into an Islamic jurisprudence, applied a liberal interpretation of the penalties and strove valiantly to integrate Islamic and Western education so that his people would not be marginalized in the new dispensation.

The Zamfara codes created new sections on capital punishments prescribing death penalty for murder (*Qisasi*) and made provisions (*huddi*) on theft and adultery (*zina*) and rape that included severance of limbs and death by stoning (*rajmi*) where the penal code under the First Republic had prescribed fifty lashes. They failed to provide for adequate preconditions before such severe *huddi* could be applied. Recently, Sheikh Sidi Attahiru Ibrahim published a slim attempt, *Hasken Alku'rani da Suanah Cikin Haddodin Sharia Musulunchi (Light in the Qu'ran and Sunnah in the capital offences in the Sharia)* to correct many of the omissions in the penal codes of Zamfara and other states who copied from Zamfara including their errors.[5]

Some internal critics of the system confide that a certain jostling for influence within the Sharia drafting committees created the errors. Many politicians rely on the prayers of some *seriki* for their success in power adventure. They reward such ritual agents with appointment into Sharia committees. The half-educated religious contingent constitutes the majority in such committees and would usually thwart informed opinions of the legal professionals. Many of these frustrated professionals either resort to sycophancy to profit from the public purse or resign themselves to watching the Sharia being implemented without adequate structures. The religious fervor intimidates open dissent. Indeed, Yerima's popularity soared like the eagle's; he acquired the accolade of a jihad leader. When he arrived in the Nigerian camp in Mecca during the pilgrimage of 2001, he was cheered while the Vice President Atiku was booed as a saboteur! Other state governors came under pressure to install the Sharia or lose legitimacy; a bandwagon effect ensued as ten other northern states followed suite: Katsina, Bauchi, Niger, Jigawa, Kebbi, Kano, Gombe, Yobe, Borno and Kaduna, where the large Christian population in the south of the state resisted and matters turned into a bloody mayhem but the administration went on to impose sharia.

The Sharia controversy rocked the foundations of the Nigerian polity threatening its nascent democracy. Initially it was presumed to be only a constitutional problem but the actual application of the *huddi* aroused international concern. The nation watched in disbelief as the Sharia legal system started like a guillotine, cutting off the hand of Bello Jangedi who stole two bicycles in Zamfara. Other such punishments followed with dizzying regularity, ignoring all protests. The global community mounted an enormous pressure on the Nigerian Government to overturn such verdicts.

This paper attempts to use the case study of Safiyyatu Hussein of Tungar Tudu, Sokoto State and her beautiful daughter Adamah to reconstruct the many dimensions of this new phase of the Sharia controversy that includes capital punishment, especially stoning for adultery. The paper argues that while political and socio-economic dimensions are important, the sharia question should be examined from a wider perspective that privileges the religious dimension. It is from this dynamic epicentre that the other enriching political, socio-economic, gender and global variables make sense and simplify a riddle. Sharia discourses that begin from the non-religious considerations run the risk of grabbing the stick from the wrong end to befuddle analysis. For instance, when President Olusegun Obasanjo declared that Sharia was a political problem *manqué* that would, like a sail in a false leeward gale, lose wind the prediction was self-serving because he knew that he could not successfully contest it in the courts. He understood the constitutional provisions and dreaded the force of religion in the modern political space. It is based on long conversations with Saffiya, her lawyers especially Abdulkadir Imam Ibrahim and representatives of many local and international pressure groups. The Nigerian Ambassador in Italy and his Information Officer who were particularly beleaguered were most informative. It analyses the transcripts of the Upper and Appeal Sharia courts. Based mostly on field research, this historical reconstruction runs all the risks of doing contemporary history.

"Le cause celebre": Safiyya and Adamah

Safiyyatu Hussaini is a spare-built, dark young woman of about 35years of age who lives in a village, Tungar Tudu in Chimola District, Gwadabawa Local Government Area, Sokoto State. Two years after her divorce from Yusuf S. of Birni Kware, she developed a casual romantic relationship with a farmer and fisherman, Yakubu Abubakar. From all indications, the enticement included the occasional gifts of small amounts of money and a promise of marriage. She was not keen on the marriage offer but needed the occasional gifts because she lived in abject poverty; had custody of their four children and lived with her aged parents and a brother who is a fisherman. After four encounters, she became pregnant and delivered a beautiful daughter, Adamah; simply adorable child with aquiline features. While she was pregnant, her brother who belongs to the fanatical, pro-orthodoxy *izalatu* reported to the Sharia Implementation Committee (such committees sprouted at the prospect of encoding the Sharia) that his elder sister was pregnant! They charged her to the Lower Sharia court that quickly disclaimed any competence, realizing that it involved *zina (adultery)* and capital punishment.

On the 23rd of December, 2000, someone alerted the police at Gwad-abawa Area Command. Two policemen investigated: Corporal Aliyu Joseph (112724) is a Moslem and Joseph U.T. (113600) is a Christian. The accused were detained and charged to the Upper Sharia Court, Gwad-abawa, presided by Mohammadu Bello Sunyinnawal. They were granted bail and hearing started on 3rd July 2001.[6]

The case got intricate because of conflicting recollections of what transpired when the policemen investigated. The first two prosecution witnesses, Ibrahim (64 years old farmer) and Attahiru (45 years old farmer) from Tungar Tudu village asserted that when confronted in the presence of the policemen, both parties had admitted guilt; that the fierce argument on that day was the moot point whether they had three or four encounters. [7] But when the two policemen took the witness stand after some days, they denied that Yakubu had confessed to guilt in their presence! In court, Yakubu denied any sexual encounters with Safiyyatu and any prior confession. Much to the contrary, he asserted, "Attahiru was a friend to Abdullahi a relative of Safiyyatu and he is their neighbour."[8] He impugned their integrity by alleging that the two men colluded and were keen to implicate him falsely. He utilized the provision in the Sharia legal system that stipulated that one can only be guilty if he confessed and if four witnesses testified that they saw the offence when it was committed. Without either, Yakubu was acquitted in spite of Safiyya's insistence. Apparently, during their detention, Yakubu's wealthy uncle intervened on his behalf, educated him to deny the charges and sealed the ears of the policemen with a bribe. He was acquitted for want of evidence.

This may raise the query on how Yerima could use immoral men (Moslem and Christian) to restore viable public morality. It also raises the larger gender issue that there is an in-built patriarchal ideology that makes it easier for males to escape the stones in cases of adultery. For instance, the four witnesses must come from the East, West, North and South and must be honest men who saw the act *in situ*. A member of the Muslim Lawyers Forum joked that evidence from a hidden camera may not be accepted; spying is not permissible; it must be by word of mouth. Even if the policemen had not accepted a bribe (which is only an allegation by a lawyer), Yakubu could change his plea at any time during the procedure and withdraw his confession. This paper shall not deal adequately with the gender ideology of the Sharia. As Sanusi Lamido Sanusi would argue,

> even a cursory student of Islamic history knows that all the trappings of gender inequality present in Muslim society have socio-economic, as opposed to religious roots. The excessive restriction of women and other manifestations of male domina-

tion are no more an integral part of Islam as a religion than, say, the sanctification of the Arabic language and the tendency towards institutionalised racism which appear in some of the literature of those days. Muslim men, like men everywhere, are the last to accept that gender inequality is a social contraption rather than a religious imperative. This is natural not only because men are the ultimate beneficiaries of this inequality but also because only those who are victims of injustice tend to see it and appreciate the absurdity of attributing it to God. [9]

Eyes turned on Safiyya who had confessed. Even if she did not, her child Adamah was the witness to her guilt and death. For the Maliki school, pregnancy is a prima facie of adultery. The rest of the trial took care of technical matters: to ensure that she did not aver that her former husband was responsible. She had to repeat that she had been divorced for two years and had seen her menstrual period three times since the divorce. The provision for *izari* requires that she should be given many opportunities to make some remarks. If she changed her plea at any stage, the proceedings would change course. Instead of *izari*, the judge merely ensured that she was informed that the offence was *zina*. He did not explain it to her. The judge invited two elders to witness her confession in public.

On October, 9th, 2001, he delivered the judgment. Following the Haddith of Muwadda Imam Malik, he pronounced a judgment of *Rajmi* on the basis of adultery (*zina*); that Safiyyatu Hussaini should be *stoned to death with average stones*, according to section 129(b) of the Sharia Criminal Procedure Code of Sokoto State, *after weaning her baby*. He granted her thirty days to appeal. It was at this point that Safiyya's uncle who is a fisherman endeavoured to secure legal services. He approached Abdulkadir Imam Ibrahim of Mutunchi Law Chambers, Sokoto, who was a member of the panel that drew up the Sharia codes for the state. Other lawyers offered their services in the wake of public outcry about another "barbaric" punitive measure. Ibrahim led a team of ten lawyers to the Sharia Court of Appeal of Sokoto State on March 25th, 2002.

The nature of the public outcry is important for the case. It conferred it with a celebrity status that risked hardening the hearts of the protagonists. At the internal level, the establishment of Sharia system pitted the north against the south once more. Many southerners feared for their lives and emigration from the north started. They owned the target business centres such as hotels and drinking saloons. Violence in the crisis of religious politics and secular ideology became more endemic in Nigeria from 1980.[10] Media hype also heated up the political temperature especially as the media orchestrated what *Tell Magazine* dubbed as "*The battle for*

Safiya's life."[11] It is alleged that the southerners control the print media in Nigeria and specifically the Yoruba, the President's ethnic group. Unsavoury epithets on the Sharia by the press, therefore, rankled. People urged the Federal Government to intervene to restrain the Sharia within civil code purview and uphold human rights.

The Minister of Justice intoned that stoning will not occur in the Nigeria of 2001 to the chagrin of Moslems who alleged baiting. Yet the Government avoided a legal intervention arguing that "the only way to end the controversy over the Islamic legal code is for aggrieved persons who have their rights infringed upon, to seek redress apparently in the conventional courts;…the rights that are violated by Sharia law are vested in individuals. For instance, if someone slaps you, will government go to court for you? The rights violated has nothing to do with the state. If the Federal Government go to court against Zamfara State over Sharia law, it will be dismissed because it will be academic."[12] Others insisted that no one in the nation should suffer for an offence beyond what is allowable in other parts of the nation; that danger loomed for non-Muslims who dreaded the fearsome *huddi*. Letters to the editors were particularly picturesque as a contributor speculated that after cutting off the limbs of their people and stoning their women, the jihadists may invade the south! Another wondered that if they would sever limbs from those who stole rams, what would happen to Government officials who stole millions of dollars? Indeed, the case of a Deputy Speaker of the House in Zamfara who sold his official car to a merchant in Kano was breathing dust under the carpet.[13]

The political reading of Safiyya's case was not far behind: that Sharia was a revengeful instrument by the Northern elite to rock Obasanjo's political boat; mobilize the masses against him to test the mettle of the democratic experiment; armed with the superior voting power of the north, their agendum is to block his chances for re-election to a second term in office; and to punish him for blocking contract routes for the elite and for restructuring the administration in a manner to remove their lackeys. It was alleged that the north had dumped a deserving Igbo for Obasanjo who rewarded his patrons by reneging on his secret promises and instead turned to marginalize the north. The decision by the Arewa Consultative Forum (the mouthpiece of the northern political class) was that he must be embarrassed by casting Sharia stones in 21st century Nigeria. Obasanjo's defenders assured all that the Sharia governors were bankrupt of policies to alleviate the suffering of the poor and used the fodder of Sharia as diversionary tactics. The media warfare drove the northerners into defensive trenches. A campaign against non-Sharia politicians, professionals and intellectuals ensued. Dialogue became impossible in the din and threats.

Equally lost is the complexity that within Islam, there is an internal class warfare expressed through the popular demand for the Sharia. Its full import may not be understood but its broad statement as an instrument capable of taming the consumption habit of the rich is attractive. The irony is that the elite may equally perceive it as an instrument to control the masses in their tendency to manipulate religious feelings for political ends.

Crucial to an understanding the currents under the facts is Lamin Sanneh's argument that Islamic political theology contains an unabashed affirmation that the state's power should be used to promote religion; the *umma* should not be ruled by unbelievers. If such a ruler engages in pejorative actions, there is a Qu'ranic demand to act or voice a protest or at the least pray against such a ruler.[14] For years, Moslems have ruled Nigeria. From this perspective, a rotational Presidency that implies long periods of being ruled by others creates a psychological uncertainty; a feeling of loss of control. Installing the Sharia laws becomes a soothing act; a symbol of regaining control. It is the politics of mobilization that rejects the implications in a reconciliation system; a reassertion of orthodoxy that rejects religious mixing. Reassertion of orthodoxy after a period of mixing has a long genealogy in Islamic history as the core aspect in jihads.

A feature of the Nigerian public space is the proliferation of NGO's. The phenomenon assumed incredible proportions in the midst of legitimacy crises, state failure, massive corruption, environmental degradation and abuse of human rights. Foreign countries bypassed the corrupt state to rebuild battered civil society, fund empowerment projects and protect human rights. A plethora of NGO's proliferated in the period between 1995-1998 and were on ground to join the affray in 2000-2001: Civil Liberties Organization, Access to Justice, Committee for Defence of Human Rights, Campaign for Democracy, Women Rights Advancement and Protection Alternative, National Coalition on Violence Against Women, Women Defence Project, International Federation of Women Lawyers, National Council for Women Societies and Women Advocates Research and Documentation Centre, to name a few. All opposed the sentence of death by stoning. Twenty groups joined forces under the banner, *Safiya Must Not Die Campaign (SMDC)*. As should be expected in such matters, there were a host of agendas: some fought against executions; others against the dire implications for the womenfolk; others drew attention to the rights of the child, Adamah who would be deprived of a mother. Some asserted that the poor, illiterate and rural dwellers bore the brunt of the Sharia stones. Sharia, it has been alleged, was for the vulnerable.

The Federal Government had opposed the new status of the Sharia but this did not save it from intense international pressure. To take Italy and Spain as examples, the Nigerian Ambassador to Italy said that the embassy received two container loads of protest; the safety of the embassy was threatened with a letter bomb; internet websites opened for protesters. The strength of new technology was mobilized against Nigeria draped with a Taliban image. The ambassador said that he was summoned twice each to the offices of Foreign Affairs, Prime Minister and President. The Vatican added its voice as the Pope urged the faithful to pray for Safiyya. Naples and Rome adopted Safiyya and offered her the keys to the cities. In Spain, the embassy received a long petition with 600, 000 signatures. Nigeria was asked to uphold international protocols that it had signed. Foreign investment was threatened as the security factor was hyped and the foreign press spun gory stories. Many lost sight of paternalism since the same Europeans still cuddled with Arab sheikhs who apply the same *huddi*.

Yet it is a touching sign of the import of the global village to note the international outcry about a spare-built Hausa woman in the backwoods of Sokoto State. The Hands off Cain, St.Egidio Community, Centrodionysia and other agencies in Italy worked together to pressurize the Federal Government of Nigeria. Indeed, when the Sharia Court of Appeal, Sokoto State acquitted Safiyya, the Mayor of Rome lit up the Coliseum in celebration of her life! Given the grand size of the Coliseum, the effect could only be imagined. All parties claimed victory as the Moslems insisted that the Sharia legal system has been vindicated because its interior brims with justice and its courts perfumed with the fragrance of mercy. International organizations saluted the power of media technology as a means of mobilizing a wide array of populations for an ethical cause and matter of life. Women celebrated femocracy. The rest of Nigeria did not have much to rejoice about because the cricket still shrieked as another woman in Katsina State faced the prospect of Sharia stones after weaning her baby.[15]

The Interior and Hermeneutics of the Sharia

Sharia in the life of a Moslem

The proceedings in the Sharia Court of Appeal of Sokoto State presided by Alhaji Muhammad Bello Silame, Grand Khadi, provides an intriguing view of the interior of the Sharia legal system because appeals serve as internal, corrective critiques of any judiciary system. It gives us the insider's perspective. Sharia is the warp and weft of the Islamic faith and the core of its ethical system. Its intricacy lies in its two sources, divine and human. The divine constituent is in the Qu'ran and the Prophet's Sunnah. It contains revealed principles, exhortations and laws. The Sunnah is the elaboration and exemplifications of the content of the Qu'ran. Thus one can arrive at an ethical decision by asserting the fact that it was done so in the time of the Prophet.

The human component derives from the writings of Muslim scholars and sages. There is a certain fluidity or flexibility *(muruna)* and evolution *(tatawwur)* because it is not an inherited code that devotees merely apply. It has been possible for various communities to indigenize and craft codes to solve their problems as each seeks the best means of applying the divine aspects of the Sharia. The interior of Sharia demands that judges should contextualize rulings *(mazahib)*. A people's understanding; peculiar circumstances; and due regard to changes in human conditions and experiences give flavour to the practice of Sharia in different places. It is not a fossilized code but a dynamic process that enables ancient knowledge to be applied in a modern setting. This is what is called, *iJtihad; a human activity, prone to error and subjectivities.* Its binding nature is often limited to defined contexts though its purview embraces all of life. Sharia law can be defined as both strict and flexible because it is both based on absolute principles and yet responds to changing conditions and human experiences. It combines the seemingly incompatible twin impulses of primitivism and pragmatism; the ability to hold in tension otherworldly aspirations and this worldly shrewdness. The primitivistic impulse or the idealistic side is the determination to return to first things; to be guided solely by Allah's will in every aspect of their lives. The pragmatist is the willingness to work through social and cultural forces. This explains why it is practised differently in various cultures. For instance, no Islamic West African nation is under the uncomplimentary glare of international attention as Nigeria. None has installed the Sharia in the form that the Northern states have adopted. The rulers of Gambia explicitly rejected the argument that Sharia is the cure of public moral malaise. Sharia evokes moral principles that are eternal and resonate with Christian and secular principles.[16] The perspective here is that major problems arise when Sharia is not properly indigenised; where codes woven in some contexts are applied with inflexibility in others without local initiative.

Yet Sharia is a prescriptive divine law rather than existentialist ethics. It does not permit the relativist, liberal theology of Christians. Like the Talmud, its application is choreographed systematically through a maze of authoritative voices in an exegesis that uses the human wisdom to explicate the divine without injury to the former. This explains the frustration of the devotees at the spate of protests. As the Grand Khadi and judges of the Sharia Court of Appeal, Sokoto, argued on 25th March, 2002:

It is not allowed for a person to beg for another who has been brought before a court for the offence of theft or zina punishment. It is compulsory to punish them with Hadd punishment if they are found guilty. Even if they swear not to do it again; and they change to good people. Because the issue of Hadd, if it is before an Imam and the suspect is found guilty, this is *Allah's right*; it is not proper for a person to save another from Hadd punishment.[17]

However, all do not arrive at the same positions and therefore there are at least four major schools of Islamic jurisprudence, the *Hanafi, Shafii, Hanbali* and *Maliki*. Following the Zamfara examples, Nigerian Sharia states opted to rely heavily on the *Maliki* school that was designed in Arabia and introduced by the Almoravids. This is fraught with problems that are both ideological and too intricately legal for our concern here.

Suffice it to say that Sharia is an agent of social control that leaves the socialization process to the Qu'ran and blends the restrictive and deterrent models with punitive instruments. But this is imaged as a spiritual cleansing odyssey as obvious in the Hadith that tells the story of Maiz who went to the Prophet to confess *zina*. He requested the Prophet to *cleanse* him and knew what the cleansing process involved. Stoning on earth will give him eternal salvation in heaven. The modern man may appreciate the Prophet's response when he sent some people to inquire whether the man is sane or has a family history of insanity. The Sokoto judges believe that through an unflinching application of *Hadd*, Sharia would extol virtue (*ma'rufat*) and cleanse the society of vices *(munkarat)*. Advocates point to extirpation of prostitution, burglary, social violence and hedonistic lifestyle in Sharia states; that Sharia may be the antidote to the scourge of HIV/AIDS. The jury is still out.

This paper argues that in spite of the religious imperative to practice Sharia in the multi-religious context of Nigeria, the gap between the ideal and the practice must be recognized as well as the need for its indigenisation. The process of indigenisation includes enlightening people about the intricacies because the relationship between knowledge and ignorance is akin to that between good and evil.

Choreographing Sharia law

This backdrop gives poignancy to the strategy of Safiyyatu's lawyers in the handling the case of stoning for adultery. They took the position that the fault was not with the Sharia but in the application. They sought to show that the legal system was installed in a hurry without the basic infrastructure and that there is a lack of trained lawyers and judges. This has produced vagaries and inconsistencies in the application. For instance, in Jigawa State, the Sharia Court sentenced 50 -year old Sarumi Moham- med to death for raping a nine-year old girl while five other men were fined 5, 000 naira (fifty dollars/euros) each for raping an 11-year old girl.[18] In Niger State, the young lovers, Ahmadu Ibrahim(32 years) and Fatima Usman (30 years) were first given an option of a fine of 15, 000 naira (150 dollars/euros) each or five years imprisonment for adultery; while they were serving the prison sentence in Suleja Prison because they could not afford such an exorbitant fine, their case was revisited and changed into stoning on the grounds that the judge who fined them had applied an old code that was more lenient. The judge did not realize that in the sharia system, it is illegal to punish a single offence twice.[19] The National Chair- man of Muslim Lawyers Forum, Barrister Awwal Bida insisted that "the judge erred in law. It is wrong for a judge to try a case and review it himself. It is wrong."[20] In the case of Amina in Katsina state, two of the Appeals Court judges who confirmed the verdict of the Upper Sharia Court were unqualified, having failed the competency appraisal test in which only thirty of the eighty judges passed. Other problems include illiteracy of the masses; lack of public enlightenment about the legal system; lack of access to legal services. For instance, Safiyya did not enjoy the benefits of legal intervention until the Appeal Courts level and no one offered to pay the Law firm. Poverty and ignorance combine to make some folks vulnerable.

To explore deeper the choreography of Sharia, the appellant's counsel in Safiyya's case did not wish to pursue the gender ideology or even mention Yakubu, the man who was responsible for the pregnancy. Instead, he took the position that the end of Sharia is to explore every nook of the process for a route to save the accused from Hadd because the Qu'ran says that *"Do not kill a soul which Allah has made sacred except through the due process" (6:151); "the greatest sin is to associate something with God and to kill human beings" (Hadith of the Prophet. PBUH); "And whosoever saves a life it is as though he has saved the lives of all mankind" (5:32)* He started by attacking the manner of the arrest, arguing that in the time of the prophet, offenders came by themselves to the prophet; for instance, Maiz came four times. The counter that the prophet sent Unaisu to a female suspect to ask her if she committed *zina* and to stone her if she did, is misunderstood precisely because the lady had denied and sought punishment for those who defamed her but unfortunately for her, the man in the case confessed. [21] The Qu'ran enjoins believers, *"Do not spy on one another" (49:12); "Do not enter any house except your own homes unless you are sure of their occupant's consent" (24:27)* The concept of *Almunkar* includes gossip. Espionage on the life of individuals violates their rights to privacy. As attributed to Abu Dawud, *"When a ruler begins to search for the causes of dissatisfaction amongst his people, he spoils them."* The Prophet instructed that a person should not even enter his own house suddenly or surreptitiously. He must indicate that he is entering the house, so that he may not see his mother, sister or daughter in a condition that could be embarrassing. It is forbidden to read other people's letters. Saffiya's privacy, argued the lawyer, was violated. The judges agreed with the counsel that

> The manner in which Safiyyatu was taken to court was wrong. It is not right on a leader to send for the arrest of a suspect who is suspected to have committed zina; therefore the manner the police went to the house of Safiyyatu in order to get informa- tion to the effect that she committed zina is wrong and contrary to the principles of Islamic law.[22]

With this vantage point secured, the lawyer forayed into the prideful arena of the Sharia legal system that permits an accused to change an earlier confession and plea. He annulled the confession and argued that the child belonged to the former husband because the law understood that a hidden pregnancy (sleeping foetus) could gestate through five years. The judges agreed to the provision in the law but demurred on the matter of paternity; the other court should have investigated the matter.

The change of plea was based on the technicality that Safiyyatu did not understand the charge and the trial judge did not adequately explain to her the meaning of *zina*, an Arabic word. Safiyya is a rural, illiterate Hausa woman and obviously does not know what the foreign term meant. Her plea to a charge that she did not understand negates it. This is complicated by the fact that an allegation of *zina* must follow certain pre-requisites including ascertaining that she is a true Moslem adult, mature, not from a slave descent; that her marriage had been contracted under a strict Islamic rule and duly consummated. The law is for Muslims in a Muslim commu- nity. Not only that the trail judge did not ascertain any of these, he did not mention in the record of the trial the date, time and place that the offence was committed. He did not offer her *izari*, a number of opportunities to defend herself and even change her plea. As *coup de grace*, the competence of the Upper Sharia court was challenged. The first report is said to have been made on 23rd December 2000 but the law was not signed into effect by the Governor of Sokoto State until 25th January 2001. She cannot be punished under a non-existent law or retroactively. The Upper Sharia Court lacked competence to try her and so she was discharged; if not *de facto* but *de jure*.

The temper of the Sharia is to find all possible ways to avoid throwing stones. As the judges put the matter " where a situation gets confused with respect to Haddi punishment, you should leave the Haddi at any chance because there is no doubt that haddi punishment can be set aside by Subha"[23] An example of a *subha* in this case would be to claim that a man slept with her when she was a sleep or genuinely believed that she had a legal relationship with the man. All schools of jurisprudence will accept this plea. Even in cases of murder, *Qisasi*, the condemned can still be allowed to live if the offended family demands monetary compensation (*diya*).

Some aspects of the Appeal judgment are pertinent for understanding the interior intricacies of the Sharia process on Haddi. There is a constraint to be fair and to assist the accused to escape. The Prophet (S.A.W.) was said to be cautious in arriving at guilty verdicts; that once, during a time of famine that drove people to commit many thefts, he virtually suspended it lest a whole community will be mutilated. This explains the due care to determine who is qualified to stand trial for *zina* and to explain the meaning with homespun imagery. Illiteracy and ignorance should not be allowed to hinder the ability of the accused. The Prophet not only ignored Maiz's confession four times, he queried him whether he understood the meaning; whether he put his genital into the woman's as one puts a gourd into a well and did with her illegally what he would do with the wife legally. As mentioned earlier, *izari* is a process that must punctuate the trial at several points so as to give the accused an opportunity to extricate oneself and change a plea. Any such denial would commence the procedure all over again. Safiyya could, therefore, recant her allegation against Yakubu and give her baby to her former husband. Interestingly, Yakubu did not press a charge against her for defamation. It was as if the process was choreographed intentionally. Then was the contrived and medically preposterous notion of a hidden pregnancy that would last five years. This is based on Imam al-Darqutni's report that Imam Malik often said that "this our slave girl, the wife of Muhammad Ibn 'Ajlan, is a truthful woman. Her husband is also a truthful man. She had three pregnancies in twelve years. Each pregnancy lasted four years." Based on this Malik put the gestation period at four years. Shafii and Hanbal schools agreed; later Malik scholars modified it to five.[24] Contrary to the notion that the law was biased towards males, the judges suggested that the woman was entitled to demand that her accusers should provide four witnesses to testify that she committed *zina*. As the Qu'ran says, "Why did they not bring four witnesses of it? So as they have not brought witnesses they are liars in the sight of Allah" *(24:13)* Pregnancy is not enough evidence; there must be witnesses.

Meanwhile, the State Attorney gaped in bewilderment as the excited activities of the Sharia enforcers and Sharia vigilantes were adjudged to be *haram*. The offender is to surrender voluntarily for the stony purification. This does not negate the roles of law enforcement officers in the society but addressed coercion, spying and lack of opportunity to defend oneself; it was a declaration against arbitrary exercise of power. An undercurrent was the frustration of the Appeal Court judges with the poor quality of and inefficiency of the police, the Upper Court judge and the State Attorney. Sanyinnawal ignored the elementary rules of evidence, faltered at every step of the procedure and fatally flawed the case. They lashed out against the State Attorney accusing him of ignorance and repeated citations of the wrong Hadiths and authorities.[25] They overruled all his counter pleas except the fact the court is not obliged to advise or provide the accused with legal service. The implications for the poor and illiterate in a case of life and death are immense.

Some argue that the spate of international lobby and protest forced the Federal government to negotiate the acquittal but the judges left the impression that it was the general temper of *zina* process in Sharia legal system that was choreographed; that the sentence of *rijma* is not to be pronounced lightly. A tradition on the prophet's youngest wife, Aisha, says that she passed a night with a soldier; when she returned and was accused, she denied any sexual misdemeanour and the Prophet ordered her freedom.

Sharia Stones For Lovers

The Sharia Court of Appeal, Sokoto State, sidestepped two crucial areas: one was the rights of Adamah and the four older siblings. Admittedly, the Upper Sharia court offered that the weaning period should be over before Safiyya presents herself for execution. If she failed to come voluntarily, the community should bring her. But in actual Sharia process, if she escaped outside the boundaries of her village, no one is supposed to scout for her. In the judgment at the appeals level, Adamah was neither mentioned nor was there any discussions on how she will be brought up if her mother was stoned to death with average-sized stones. What are the rights of a child under the Sharia law?; or is this a modern sensitivity that contests the undergirding ideology of ancient legal traditions?

Equally side-stepped was the specific matter of death by stoning for adultery. Noticeably, this is not practised among African Moslems whether in the North or West. The hallmark of secularity holds sway in Moslem countries as Tunisia and Morocco whose economies have been healthier. The stony punishment has been a sore point that has brought opprobrium to Islam in 21st Century Nigeria. It deserves a revisit especially as stoning is not prescribed in the Qu'ran. Rather it is rooted in three sources: it was practised in the time of the Holy Prophet; who borrowed it from the Jews; and it is strongly advocated by the Maliki school of jurisprudence that Nigeria Islamic lawyers follow closely ignoring three other schools who oppose it. Thus, put crudely, it is rooted in the shifting sands of contested interpretations, the human dimension of the Sharia. Some have argued that the Prophet's Hadith on which it is based came after the revelation of the Qu'ran and that this explains its absence. Can Hadith abrogate a Qu'ranic provision? From another dimension: in 1955, when Nasser abolished sharia courts in Egypt, some Nigerians urged in the pages of the *Nigerian Citizen* that Nigeria should do the same because the application was too conservative and the basis of the Maliki law was syncretistic, a mixture of true Islamic ethics and European vestiges acquired in Spain.[26]

The Maliki school contend that if an unmarried woman is found pregnant without a case of proven rape, she has committed adultery and should be punished by a hundred lashes or stoned to death. However, other schools apply the discretionary, *tazir,* punishment. According to Hidya, if a woman confessed, "the maximum number of stripes in a tazir punishment is thirty nine and the minimum is three. But the judge may add a sentence of imprisonment as well. Some jurists say that the maximum is seventy–nine stripes." [27] But the Hanafi school insist on four admissions at four different court sittings. Imam Shafi'I believes that following Maiz's case so closely is pedantic. What this does not address is the Qu'ranic verse that says that "And for those of your women who are guilty of adultery, call to witness against them four witnesses from among you; so if they bear witness, confine them to the houses until death takes them away or Allah makes a way for them." (4:15) Life imprisonment in the house was the punishment. But the Qu'ran also provided in 24:2 that "the adulteress and adulterer, flog each with a hundred stripes, and let not pity for them detain you from obedience to Allah, if you believe in Allah and the last day, and let a party of Muslims witness their chastisement." The punishment of flogging is clear and the number hardly debatable. Thus, only the Ma'iz case mentions stoning. Sabiq cites Usul al-Shashi, a reputed source of Islamic jurisprudence in arguing that Ma'iz's case occurred in an early period in the history of Islam. Indeed, most of modern Muslim jurists, argues Sabiq, neither privilege that Hadith nor accept stoning as punishment.[28]

The application in Nigeria may come from the economic and cultural dependence on Saudi Arabia and Iran. International Islamic influence has used funds to nurture both radical Sunni and Shiites within Nigeria. The radicalism in the Iranian Revolution inspired many young people in the

Universities. Some years ago, the surreptitious registration of Nigeria as a member of the Organization of Islamic Communities caused a political uproar. It was seen as indicative of an intentional effort to web Nigeria into an international Islamic league. The Pakistani, Yusuf Farde, funded the Supreme Council of Islamic Affairs. The *izalatu* under Sheik Gumi had Saudi roots. From the 1970's the Saudis distributed works of anti-Western Islamists like Sayyid Quitb and Abu Ala Maududi.[29] Maududi's books and other such literature flow from the Islamic Foundation in Leicester, England. It could be argued that such foreign influences rather than an indigenous initiative has buttressed the use of Sharia stones. Several factors explain why the soil proved so fertile: a development of Islamic consciousness under radical external influences; the use of religion as a cultural signifier and identification of the other; anti-Western sentiments woven into anti-Christian sentiments in the faces of biting Structural Adjustment Programmes and the insurgence of Pentecostals into Northern Nigeria; anti-Zionist diatribe.[30] Three illustrations from 2000-2002 will suffice: when Bonkee tried a second revival meeting in Kano in 1991, after a first venture in which over a million came to hear him, Kano went ablaze as the Moslems felt that their ancient citadel had been desecrated. As Americans attacked the Talibans, Kano Moslems attacked Christian southerners as if they collaborated with Americans. When Safiyya visited Rome with Adamah and her lawyer in September 2002, to receive the key to the city, the Governor of Sokoto State blocked her exit; the Governor of Zamfara State, Yerima, announced to the faithful who had gathered in a stadium that there was a plot to convert Safiyya to Christianity; every Moslem should resist this plot. The Governor of Sokoto announced that he will write the President of Nigeria to explain how Safiyya and Adamah got their passports! [31]The Muslim Youth League was duly incensed to denounce the visit with juicy anti- Western epithets.

Obviously, they exaggerated the missionary impulse of 21st century Christianity in Europe. More cogently, their insistence on death penalty by stoning challenges the Constitutional indictment against inhuman degrading treatment of people: every individual is entitled to dignity of his person and therefore no person shall be subjected to torture or inhuman or degrading treatment" (4:34 (1) (a)) Yet the matter betrays the dilemma of pluralism in 21st Century Nigeria weaving ethnicity, religion, virulent politics and the impact of socio-economic disasters into a tapestry of multiple identities and mayhem. It is a problem that would not disappear by citation of constitutional provisions precisely because Sharia falls within the realm of Islamic religious tenets and way of life and should therefore be seen as both legal and religious. The larger issue of death penalty is like the riddle of the phoenix. As Augustine insisted, there is no private right to kill. One can only kill under the authority of God, as communicated by direct or implicit command from God, or by a legitimate ruler who carries out God's intent to restrain evil on earth. Augustine further suggests that one obeys such a command does not himself kill. He acts only as an instrument of the one who commands. His argument has been attacked but the point remains whether the Prophet (S.A.W.) had a revelation that commanded killing for adultery. Even more distressing, can anyone appeal against a divine law in a common law court?

Notes

1. Marty, M.E. and R.S.Appleby, *Fundamentalism Observed* (Chicago, University of Chicago Press, 1991).

2. Isichei, E. "The Maitatsine Rising in Nigeria, 1980-85: a revolt of the disinherited", *Journal of Religion in Africa,* 17, 3(Oct, 1987): 194-208; Hiskett, M. "The Maitatsine Riots of Kano, 1980: an assessment", *ibid.,* 209-223; Takya, J. "The Foundations of Religious Intolerance in Nigeria", *Bulletin of Ecumenical Theology,* 2, 2(1989): 31-41; Kukah, M.H. *Religion, Politics and Power in Northern Nigeria (*Ibadan, Spectrum Press, 1994); Ilesanmi, S.O. *Religious Pluralism and the Nigerian State (*Athens Ohio: Ohio University Press, 1997).

3. Usman, B.*The Manipulation of Religion in Nigeria* (Kaduna, Vanguard Press, 1987).

4. Christelow, A. "Islamic Law and Judicial Practice in Nigeria: an historical perspective"*Journal of Muslim Minority Affairs,* 22, 1 (2002): 185-204.

5. Ibrahim, S.A. *Hasken Alku'rani da Suanah Cikin Haddodin Sharia Musulunchi* (Sokoto, Futuree Business Equipment, 2001).

6. Transcript of Upper Sharia Court, Gwadabawa, Sokoto State: Case File no. USC/ GW/CR/F1/10/2001.

7. ibid., 2.

8. ibid., 4.

9. www.gamji.com/sanusi 16.htm.

10. Kalu, O.U. *Power, Poverty and Prayer: The Challenges of Poverty and Pluralism in African Christianity, 1960-1996* (Frankfurt, Peter Lang, 2000): 133-159; Falola, T.*Violence in Nigeria: The Crisis of Religious Politics and Secular Ideologies* (Rochester, Rochester University Press, 1998).

11. *Tell Magazine (Lagos, Nigeria),* vol.49, December 3rd, 2001.

12. *Guardian Newspaper (Lagos, Nigeria)* August 22nd, 2002: article no.3.

13. *Tell Magazine,* 49, 2001: 37.

14. See, Sanneh, L. *Piety and Power: Muslims and Christians in West Africa* (Maryknoll, NY, Orbis, 1996).

15. *Guradian Newspaper,* August 20th, 2002.
16. Tukur, M.M. *Leadership and Governance in Nigeria: The Relevance of Values* (London, Hodder and Stoughton, 1999).
17. Certified True Copy, *Transcripts of Sharia Court of Appeal,* Sokoto State, 25th March, 2002: 44.
18. *Guardian Newspaper,* 3rd September, 2002: 21.
19. *ibid.,* 30th August, 2002: 4.
20. *ibid., 29th August, 2002: 2.*
21. *Transcript of Sharia Court of Appeal, Sokoto State, 25/3/2002:* 45-46.
22. *ibid., 46.*
23. *ibid., 44.*
24. see, www.gamji.com/sanusi28.htm.
25. *Transcript, Sharia court of Appeal, Sokoto State, 25/3/2002:* 43-44.
26. see, the contours of the sharia debate in Paden, J.N. *Ahmadu Bello* (Zaria, Gaskiya, 1986): 206-208.
27. Waliulla, M. *Muslim Jurisprudence and the Qu'ranic Law of Crimes* (New Delhi, Taj Co. Ltd., 1986): 146, 139-42 discuss Ma'iz's case fully. See, Enayat, H. *Modern Islamic Political Thought* (London, 1982): 131.
28. Sabiq, S *Fiqh-Sunnah, Darak-Firk* (Beirut, 1973), vol. 2: 409. Information from Abdukadir Imam Ibrahim, Safiyya's lawyer.
29. *Newsweek*(Weekly Magazine, Lagos, Nigeria), 16th-22nd September, 2002: 63.
30. Laitin, D.D. *Hegemony and Culture: Politics and Religious Change Among the Yoruba (*Chicago University Press, 1988).
31. *Trumpet Newspaper,* 9th September, 2002; *Daily Trust, 9th* September, 2002. Both papers are produced in the northern sharia states of Nigeria.But see the report on the anger of the northern youths in *Vanguard Newspaper, (*Ibadan, Nigeria) 19th September, 2002.

Bibliography

Falola, T. (1998) *Violence in Nigeria: The Crisis of Religious Politics and Secular Ideologies* (Rochester: Rochester University Press).

Hiskett, M. (1987) " The Maitatsine Riots of Kano, 1980: an assessment", *Journal of Religion in Africa,* 17, 3, Oct: 209-223.

Ibrahim, S.A. (2001) *Hasken Alku'rani da Suanah Cikin Haddodin Sharia Musulunci* (Sokoto: Futures Business Equipment).

Ilesanmi, S.O. (1997) *Religious Pluralism and the Nigerian State (*Athens, Ohio: University Press).

Isichei, E. (1987) "The Maitatsine Rising in Nigeria, 1980-85: a revolt of the disinherited" *Journal of Religion in Africa,* 17, 3, Oct.: 194-208.

Kalu, O.U. (2000) *Power, Poverty and Prayer: the challenges of poverty and pluralism in African Christianity, 1960-1996.* (Frankfurt am Main: Peter Lang).

Kukah, M.H. (1994) *Religion, Politics and Power in Northern Nigeria* (Ibadan: Spectrum Press).

Ladan, M.T. (1993) " The Relationship Between Law and Morality: the Nigerian experience", *Law in Society Journal (Ahmadu Bello University),* 2 Dec.: 1-12.

Laitin, D. D. (1993) *Hegemony and Culture: Politics and Religious Change Among the Yoruba* (Chicago: University of Chicago Press).

Marty, M.E. and R.S. Appleby (1991) *Fundamentalism Observed* (Chicago: University of Chicago Press).

Mawdudi, A.A. (1976) *Human Rights in Islam (*Leicester: the Islamic Foundation).

_____ (1986) *Islamic Law and Constitution,* ed. A. Kurshid.(New Delhi: Taj Co. Ltd).

Rashid, S. ed. (1988) *Islamic Law in Nigeria: application and teaching.* (Lagos: Islamic Publication Bureau).

Sanneh, L. (1996) *Piety and Power: Muslims and Christians in West Africa* (Maryknoll, NY: Orbis).

Sabiq, S. (1973) *Fiqh-Sunnah, Darak-Fikr* (Beirut), vol. 2.

Takya, J. (1989) "The Foundations of Religious Intolerance in Nigeria", *Bulletin of Ecumenical Theology,* 2, 2: 31-41.

Tukur, M.M.(1999) *Leadership and Governance in Nigeria: The Relevance of Values* (London: Hodder and Stoughton).

Usman Bala (1987) *The Manipulation of Religion in Nigeria* (Kaduna: Vanguard Press).

Waliulla, M. (1986) *Muslim Jurisprudence and the Qu'ranic Law of Crimes* (New Delhi: Taj Co. Ltd.).

Original Manuscripts

Case no USC/GW/CR/FI/10/2001 Upper Sharia Court, Gwadabawa, Sokoto State.3rd July 2001-9th October, 2001. Translated by Abdurauf A. Shehu, 22/1/2002.

Sharia Court of Appeal of Sokoto State, Sokoto Judicial Division, 25th March, 2002. translated by Ibrahim Ladan, D.D. Litigation, High Court of Justice, Sokoto, 27th July, 2002.

Nigerian Newspapers and Magazines, 2000-2002.

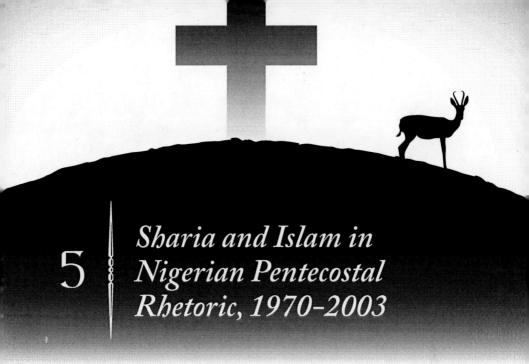

5 | Sharia and Islam in Nigerian Pentecostal Rhetoric, 1970–2003

Introduction

In 2003, Nigeria featured much in the global news. First, some women were condemned to be stoned to death with regular stones for alleged adultery. Second, there was a riot in which many were killed and churches torched in the northern parts of the country because a beauty pageant event was staged during Ramadan and an article appeared in a newspaper, *This Day*, that some thought ridiculed the Prophet.[1] The ostensible reasons were the rise of a violent face of Islam and the enactment of "sharia states" in the northern sectors of the country in 2002. The global community was aghast and protested vigorously.

This reflection will center on the implication of Pentecostal/Charismatic movement in the violent face of religious politics in Nigeria. It will firstly explain the sharia in Muslim religion and life; and historicize Islamic politics in Nigeria through four phases from its insertion to the contemporary democratic dispensation. Commentators have canvassed a number of explanations for the radicalization of Islamic politics including the competition for dwindling economic resources, response to modernity, the dilemma of pluralism in a modern African state and some include the 'clash of fundamentalisms' induced by the insurgence of Pentecostalism and charismatic forces into Islamic strongholds. They argue that this elicits the re-assertion of local identities and compel the manipulation of religion as a cultural signifier. How do the Pentecostal/ charismatic rhetoric image I slam and the sharia?

The Sharia in Islamic Religion and Life

It is germane to understand what the sharia is in Islamic life. Sharia is the wool and weft of the Islamic faith and the core of its ethical system. Its intricacy lies in its two sources, divine and human. The divine constituent is in the Qur'an and the Prophet's Sunnah. It contains revealed principles, exhortations and laws. The Sunnah is the elaboration and exemplifications of the content of the Qur'an. Thus, one can arrive at an ethical decision by asserting the fact that it was done so in the time of the Prophet.

The human component derives from the writings of Muslim scholars and sages. There is a certain fluidity or flexibility *(muruna)* and evolution *(tatawwur)* because it is not an inherited code that devotees merely apply. It has been possible for various communities to inculturate and craft codes to solve their problems as each seeks the best means of applying the divine aspects of the sharia. The interior of sharia demands that judges should contextualize rulings *(mazahib).* The flavour of the practice of the sharia in different contexts is compelled by the people's self-understanding; peculiar circumstances; changes in human conditions and experiences. It is not a fossilized code but a dynamic process that enables ancient knowledge to be applied in a modern setting. This is what is called, *itjihad,* a human activity, prone to error and subjectivities. Its binding nature is often limited to defined contexts though its purview embraces all of life. Sharia law can be defined as both strict and flexible because it is both based on absolute principles and yet responds to changing conditions and human experiences. It combines the seemingly incompatible twin impulses of primitivism and pragmatism; the ability to hold in tension otherworldly aspirations and this worldly shrewdness. The primitivistic impulse or the idealistic side is the determination to return to first things; to be guided solely by Allah's will in every aspect of their lives. The pragmatist is the willingness to work through social and cultural forces. This explains why it is practised differently in various cultures. It could be argued that sharia evokes moral principles that are eternal and resonate with Christian and secular principles. The perspective here is that major problems arise when sharia is not properly indigenised; where codes woven in some contexts are applied with inflexibility in others without local initiative.

Yet sharia is a prescriptive divine law rather than existentialist ethics. It does not permit the relativist, liberal theology of Christians. Like the Talmud, its application is choreographed systematically through a maze of authoritative voices in an exegesis that uses the human wisdom to explicate the divine without injury to the former. This explains the frustration of the devotees at the spate of protests. As the Grand Khadi and judges of the Sharia Court of Appeal, Sokoto, argued on 25th March, 2002: " It is not allowed for a person to beg for another who has been brought before a court for the offence of theft or zina punishment. It is compulsory to punish them with Hadd punishment if they are found guilty. Even if they swear not to do it again; and they change to good people. Because the issue of Hadd, if it is before an Imam and the suspect is found guilty, this is *Allah's right*; it is not proper for a person to save another from Hadd punishment."[2] However, all do not arrive at the same positions and, therefore, there are at least four major schools of Islamic jurisprudence, the Hanafi, Shafii, Hanbali and Maliki. Following the Zamfara examples, Nigerian sharia states opted to rely heavily on the Maliki School that was designed in Arabia and introduced by the Almoravids. This is fraught with problems that are both ideological and too intricately legal for our concern here.

Suffice it to say that sharia is an agent of social control that leaves the socialization process to the Qur'an and blends the restrictive and deterrent models with punitive instruments. The Sokoto judges argued that through an unflinching application of *Hadd*, Sharia would extol virtue (*ma'rufat*) and cleanse the society of vices *(munkarat)*. Advocates claim an extirpation of prostitution, burglary, social violence and hedonistic lifestyle; that sharia may even be the antidote to the scourge of HIV/AIDS. The jury is still out.

Historicizing Islamic Presence in Nigeria

In constructing a historical portrait of Islamic presence in Nigeria, periodization is crucial because the face of Islam has changed through time. Islam in Nigeria is a part of the trans-Saharan movement of the religion after it captured the Maghrib in the 7th century AD. Soon, Dyula traders followed the River Niger into trading cities such as Zaria, Kano and across to Borno-Kanem empire around the Lake Chad. Thus, by the ninth century, northern Nigeria was woven into the tapestry of Central Sudanic culture. In Kano city, there is a section called *Dandalin Turawa* where the Arabs first settled. They still maintain an identity that traces their origin to Libya. Their District Head, the *Mai Unguwar*, still recites the oral traditions of their caravan route to Kano and the distinctive architecture, cuisine and other cultural ingredients confirm Arabic origins.[3] Islam appealed to the people because of its magico-spiritual techniques through prayers and charms, social affability, the prestige of its international network and its political and military clout. Its divination process soon absorbed the indigenous techniques. A key aspect of the pre-colonial history of the region is that nine jihads or assertion of orthodoxy occurred before the turn of the 19th century. Each involved state creation as the Fulani reshaped the map of West Africa. The Uthman dan Fodio jihad that created the Sokoto Caliphate in Nigeria by 1804 was typical of the evolution of new administrative structures that followed the change of Islamic presence from quarantine through mixing to jihads.[4]

This backdrop colours *Islamic presence in the colonial setting*. The British colonial officers were intrigued by the sophistication of the emirate administrative structure of the Sokoto Caliphate that extended from northern Nigeria southward to north-eastern Yorubaland. Emirs and viziers collected revenue and dispensed justice. The harsh exploitation of the poor Habe Hausa by the elite escaped their attention. Indirect rule, compelled by lack of manpower, happily adopted the structure. The British were fascinated by the architecture, durbars and horses, the speed of the cavalry and tone of skin colour of the Fulani and concluded that this was a non-African people with a culture worthy of protection and preservation. A protectionist policy by 'Christian' Britain ensured that Islam benefited most from colonial presence. Missionaries were barred from emirates; much lobbying modified this to *"one mission, one emirate"* policy. Muslims utilized the railway and new communication facilities to trade in the south. The British, however, severely restricted sharia ethics to matters of personal law. Criminal matters rested under the purview of the new judiciary and administrative structures. Indeed, by 1958, an internal debate ensued among Moslems in the pages of the *Nigerian Citizen* newspaper that threatened the rump of the sharia. The debate ensued in the wake of the abolition of Islamic courts in Egypt by Nasser. Three positions emerged: some argued that the interpretation was too conservative and lacked the spirit of the Qur'an; others argued that it was built on a syncretistic version that emerged through Almoravid culture contact with European legal system and, therefore, not true to the Qur'an; a third urged its retention on pragmatic grounds; that while the decision in Egypt was welcome, Northern Nigeria did not possess the manpower with the legal expertise to imitate Egypt.[5]

But the early independence period between 1960 and the end of the civil war in 1970, witnessed a vigorous attempt to root an Islamic consciousness and presence in the independent state. The lightning rod was the Premier of Northern Nigeria, the Sardauna of Sokoto, a grandson of Uthman Dan Fodio, a scion of the ruling dynasty in the Caliphate. He used the state apparatus to evangelise by enticing individuals and communities with monetary reward and promotion in the civil service. A political party, Northern Peoples' Congress, was another sharp instrument in the endeavour. His goal was to unite the whole of the northern region of the country under Islam. This is the *One North* program of the period, 1960-66. The fact was that the Jihad of 1804 did not conquer all the communities in the north; many un-Isalmized ethnic groups became Christian under the evangelical missionary impulse of the Sudan United, Sudan Interior Missions and Dutch Reformed Christian Mission. The Sardauna imposed Muslim rulers on many of them and lured the elite of the Plateau and the Middle Belt zones. He initiated the use of money from Saudi Arabia to fund Islamization policies in Nigeria. Muslims felt insecure in the new amalgamation of ethnic groups called Nigeria. They had neither mineral resources as oil nor a sea- port but possessed a robust invented history and cultural pride.[6] Moreover, Islam perceives state power as central in promoting religion; thus, control of the centre of the Federal government remained a cardinal goal.

It could be surmised that oil wealth enabled Nigeria to recover from the devastating three years of civil war (1966-70). It provided the resources for reconstruction efforts. But oil boom had its dark sides. The war created a new moral context as it gave bitterness, greed and raw ethnic emotions a free space where these could be mistaken for ethnic or national varieties of patriotism. Ethnicity became the major harvest from the battlefields of the civil war while corruption ate the innards of the socio-political culture. Meanwhile, the military dictatorship controlled by Muslims and, with its unitary structure of command, vitiated the federal polity and militarised the social space. The story of Nigeria henceforth would be dominated by the virulent competition for "the national cake". It became tempting for the elite to manipulate religion and ethnicity.

Under the military dictatorship between 1970 and 1999, the internal changes within Islam could be illustrated in two time frames, between 1970-79 and 1980-98. During the leadership of Sarduana, two power nodes controlled Islamic politics, namely, the political party (NPC) and *Jamatu Nasril Islam* (Victory for Islam) that operated as the religious vanguard of the Nigerian Supreme Council for Islam, chaired by the Sultan of Sokoto, the spiritual head of the *umma*. A sufi brotherhood, Qadriyya dominated the interior of the *sunni* spirituality. But opposition was rife. On the political front, the Tiv community led the rebellion against encroaching Fulani pastoralists while the rest of the Middle Belt elite sponsored a political party, the *United Middle Belt Congress*. In the city of Kano, opponents of the Caliphate preferred the Tiyaniyya sufi order under the charismatic leadership of the Senegalese Niass and formed their own party, the *Northern Elements Progressive Union*, led by the populist Alhaji Aminu Kano.

His contention was that Uthman dan Fodio was a leader who cared for the poor but that his scions became elitist consumers who ignored the poor and were unworthy of the heritage of the jihad leader.

But in the post-civil war era, the hub of political activism shifted radically to the youths and students. In 1977, the *Moslem Students Society* (MSS) was formed; *Radiance Magazine* and *Movement for Progressive Nigeria* became the radical critics of the elite. The youth perceived a gap between Muslim realities and Islamic ideals. They alleged that the Moslem elite neither observed the *ribah* laws, nor practised *zakat* nor used their political influence to install the true Moslem ethical system, the sharia. Meanwhile, other groups such as the *izalatu* and *Wahabis* were opposed to the occult misuse of the sufi orders. They became the conservative movements for the restoration of orthodoxy. All these groups became politically radicalised and forged a social movement for political action. The trend in the literature explains the phenomenon by appeal to the socio-economic background of Nigeria that acted as the template for the religious script from the late 1970's into the 1980's.[7]. The perspective here is that the explanation scheme should include more variables and should not portray the interior of Islam as if it was monolithic.

Internal differences include the Shiite votaries patronized by Iran. The impact of international Islam in the post-Iranian revolution changed the face of youthful Islam in Nigeria. Within the radical student body emerged the *darika* and anti-*darika*. The Sunni who dominated the government persecuted the Shiites.[8] Meanwhile, the level of rural-urban migration created new negative social forces. A band of youths emerged by the late 1970's just as the oil boom turned into oil doom and coups and counter-coups betrayed the Nigerian military as armed bands of power adventurers. These were the *yan almajiris*, unemployed followers of mallams. They beg, steal and provide the personnel for riots; they serve as thugs for politicians. From the 1980's, the danger posed by the combined forces of radical students and unemployed youth deepened as the face of Islam turned violent. Consistently from 1980 to date, all manners of problems have turned into riots and burning of churches. Commissions of inquiries would deploy socio-economic analyses that argue that the softness of the state and collapse of economies have created poverty and potentials for rebellion among the unemployed.

Once, a charlatan preacher from The Republic of Niger, Mohammed Marwa, led the rioters as a pied piper; at other times, fights would break out in secondary schools, Polytechnics and Universities and envelope towns. Meanwhile, Islamic insurgence took a number of routes: some promoted Qur'anic schools and education (*islamiyya*); others sought to bridge the gap between the north and south in western education (*madrassa*); some forged deep contacts with patrons from Libya, Pakistan, Iran, Turkey, Iraq and especially Saudi Arabia. Commercial relationships, banking, membership in the highly politicised OPEC and Organisation of Islamic Countries cemented the obvious efforts to turn Nigeria into an Islamic state. The linkage of Islamic radical politics to international Arab geopolitics is a crucial dimension that explains the rhetoric, funding and strategies, especially the diatribe against real or perceived Western cultural influence and its modernity project. Islam imaged Christianity as a vestige of Western presence and the revolution in Iran as the hope for the future. At many points in time, the enactment of sharia laws would serve as the clarion call for uniting the centrifugal forces within Islam. It should be important to underscore that the politicisation of Islam and the violent tendency created a populist type of Islam that sought to control the elite even when the elite pretended to hold the reins of power.

This is important for undestanding the face of Islam in *the new democratic dispensation from 1999- to the present*. The return of democratic rule created a public space for the free pursuit of religious and political programs without fear of Secret Service harassment. It was possible for populist politicians to mobilize against the wealthy Muslims and tap into the radicalism of either students or *almajiris*. The `new breed` politicians lacked restraint, discipline and redemptive social goals.

The driving force in Islamic politics in this period focussed on the threat posed by the *rotational presidency* provision in the new Constitution that enabled a southerner to enter the Aso Rock in Abuja (where the Presidents of the country live and work). It does appear that the Muslim military leaders who built the complex hardly anticipated that a non-Muslim would ever live there. Inside Aso Rock, thereare three mosques and no Christian worship place. Even the domestic allocation of space assumes that the occupant would have at least four wives. At the back of the huge complex is a ritual space where some mallams would daily bury live rams as sacrifices to maintain the *baraka (power)* of the leader. It is public knowledge that huge amounts of public funds were spent on the definition of this ostensibly public space along explicitly Muslim lines.

In conclusion, sharia provisions had always existed in the Nigerian Constitution and in practice. Christelow argues that Emirate councils continued to implement the criminal prescriptions of the sharia under the colonial rule until the last decade of the 1950's.[9] The major shift is that the new rulers reintroduced the purview of sharia to cover criminal processes (*Huddu and Qisasi*) and invoked the punishments from the Maliki legal structure. The class factor is crucial in understanding the sharia. The masses want the sharia in the belief that it would help them in legal, social and economic matters; that sharia ethics prescribe a humane and non-exploitative relationship among social groups. Women believe that sharia laws protect the rights of women in a predominantly patriarchal culture in matters over divorce and rights to land and property.[10]

Anatomy of Islamic Politics, 1970-2003

With the historical background delineated, the politics of religion can be analysed starting from broad themes to specific discourses in the literature. First, the ecology of the religious landscape should be painted with bold strokes of the brush. In the modern political space, religion has been resilient and ignored the predictions of its demise by prophets of secularism. Second, many of the contesting religious forms have historical backgrounds that make them innately dysfunctional forces in the modern public space. They are all religions of protest; they operated separately with hostile perceptions of one another for much of the time; each is imbued with a vision and endowed with sacred texts; competing claims of uniqueness obviate fruitful contacts and the patterns of insertion and modes of appropriation belie the rhetoric of being peaceful religions. Thus, in cases of the worst forms of manifestations, devotees could claim that fervent forms are not true to core affirmations. Thus, the fundamentalists on either divide could be disowned.

Third, most of West Africa is Muslim with about 80 million devotees. A survey from 1992-1996 indicates that when ranked, West African states show a predominant level (1), second-ranking (2) and third-ranking (3) of the population as follows:

Rank	Muslim	Christian	African Traditional Religion
1	8	5	5
2	2	6	10
3	8	7	3

Out of 18 states in West Africa, most are Muslim states and primal religion is a strong force.[11] Thus, Nigerian Muslims want to act as other Muslim countries in the region. The political dimensions to OPEC, OIC (Organization of Islamic Countries) and ECOWAS (Economic Organisation of West African States) create further pressures. With a population of over 120 million, Nigeria has the largest concentration of Muslims in the region and definitely the wealthiest. Thus, there is a psychological pressure to demonstrate this character, with a perception of Christians and the state as the blocking stones. Geopolitics, therefore, explains an aspect of Muslim insurgence.

Among the privileged discourses is that contemporary Islam is challenged and compelled to respond to insurgent modernity symbolized by global cultural forces and the posture of secularity by imploding power of the state and its use of liberal ideology. These forces collide with the predominant theocratic conception of power that informs Islamic domestic and public arrangements.[12] Therefore, there is a rejection of the separation of religion and politics because Islam covers all aspects of life; it is a total way of life. Even those who move towards a notional separation only mean to say that the religious sphere is non-identical though connected with the political sphere. But state power should be used to provide the coercion that ensures religious integrity. It may not be safely assumed that Islamic political thought has been monologic. Some Muslim clerics are concerned that there should be enough distance between the crown and turban to prevent the manipulation of the sacred by political entrepreneurs. All the nuances have been canvassed as Islam struggles to respond to the challenges of modernity.[13] Fundamentalists stand out as sore thumbs because of the head-on attack on modern confidence in political ultimacy and the futility of the state. In all genres of Islamic political theology, the urge is always there to create a certain environment for the *umma* where Islamic ethics and culture predominate and to reject with violence any political arrangement that marginalizes the *umma*. The use of force in religious matters that was a core aspect of pre-modern European culture is still hale and hearty in Nigeria.[14] Within the democratic dispensation in contemporary Nigeria, Muslims have the confidence that the time has come to boldly create a vibrant Islamic cultural space. In doing so, they deploy anti-Western diatribe based on new forms of literature produced by the Muslim diaspora in the West. The measure, provenance and message of this genre of literature invite study.

For some social analysts, the radicalisation of Islamic politics brings to the fore the dilemma of pluralism. What happens to non-Muslims living under the sharia?[15] There was a widely discussed case of a southerner Igbo, Livinus Obi who was flogged by 100 Muslim youth on the night of 30th December 2000 outside his home for drinking beer.[16] In a contested political space, less time is spent on cultivating dialogue.

Charismatic-Pentecostal Insurgence, 1970-2003

The argument in this paper is that the explosion of Pentecostal/charismatic spirituality among Christians only *partially* explains the militancy in contemporary Islam imaged as the response to insurgent forms of Christianity that have challenged an assured sacred space. All over Africa, a new form of charismatic movement appeared in the 1970's. Unlike the earlier prophetic movements, young "puritan preachers" led the new movement. By the next decade of the 1980's, the movement proliferated; global cultural factors mediated by American prosperity and tele -evangelistic ministries became important. In the 1990's the indigenous factor regained pre-eminence as the Intercessors for Africa re-emphasized a holiness ethic and turned the focus to nationalist ideology and God's grand designs for the continent and the black race.[17] Two things happened: young people threatened mainline churches and were forced out by the late 1970's. These founded Pentecostal churches and indulged in anti-establishment diatribes. But soon, the mainline churches were compelled to stop the haemorrhage with encapsulating strategies that created religious space for the charismatic young people and women and thereby became increasingly charismatized. The political ideology of Nigerian mainline churches gradually abandoned the doctrine of the two kingdoms and became engaged in reshaping the political terrain.

Equally crucial is the fact that from the mid-1970's, charismatic Christianity flooded the northern Nigeria, after the civil war.[18] This period of rapid expansion coincided with the rise of youthful radical Islam. University students from the south who went for National Youth Service Corps in the north, established vigorous evangelical programs that differed from the muted, accomodationist, quarantined forms of Christian presence symbolized by the mission churches located in enclaves known as 'strangers' quarters'. It is argued that in about **ten** ways, charismatic Pentecostal forces reshaped Christian–Muslim relationship. Their invigorated evangelical strategy that privileged the conversion of Muslims re-memorialized the temper of old evangelicalism that inspired the 'Sudan parties' in the 19th century.[19] Along with his was a deliberate high profiling of Muslim converts. Such people, like Pastor Shaba Adams an Islamic scholar who converted in the late 1970's, were paraded as keynote speakers in many public conventions and outreaches. Some converted Muslim clerics such as Pastor El-Isa Buba confessed that they had led armed bands of young men to kill Christians. Meanwhile, Pentecostal churches proliferated and competed among themselves by developing evangelical tours that linked ancient Muslim spaces to international Pentecostal cultural forces. Evangelical ministries in the West were excited with the revitalization of dreams of cross-cultural mission. The 2000AD and Beyond Project, for instance, plunged into the opportunities for converting Muslims and funded a number of the projects. Typical was Reinhard Bonnke's outreach in Kano city where over a million people filled the Race Course every night for a week. He dispatched vans to gather lame people from the streets and many were healed. It was such blatant proselytising among Muslims that provoked opposition when arrangements started in 1991 for a repeat performance. The Moslem rioters claimed that the walls of the ancient city were desecrated with Christian posters; that the venue should be changed. In anger, they burnt churches.

A number of major changes occurred within the Christian churches during this time frame. By the end of the 1970's, the bulwark of resistance against Pentecostal forces collapsed. The charismatization of the mainline churches provided new resources for Pentecostal evangelism. Thus, many southern businessmen and lay Christians rose to the challenge of rebuilding the burnt churches. The demographic character of Pentecostalism changed as the upper middle class comprising of professionals joined the charismatic band. Both the critical mass and quality and wealth of membership would be important in its public profile. The youthful character and appeal to the upward mobile sector of the population meant that it attracted females and young people who constituted the core demography of membership of all types of churches. By quirk of historical conjuncture, as each church was still negotiating its brand of encapsulation strategy, the Islamic political radicalism intensified.

Meanwhile, Christians challenged Islamic monopoly of power. This is exemplified in the constitutional battle to enshrine the sharia. At the Constitutional Drafting Committee of 1979, Moslem delegates sought to broaden the purview of the sharia by insisting that Sharia Courts of Appeal should be established outside the northern region into every part of the country. Eighty-three of them staged a walk-out against the body that refused to accede to the demand. The tactics backfired because the churches became even more unified in its opposition to Islam. Charismatic influence flowed into the leadership of Christian Association of Nigeria that was formed in the late 1970's as a new ecumenical venture by Christians of all hues to checkmate the *Jamatu Nasril Islam* and Supreme Council for Islam. This venture became a radical political pressure group. Enwerem dubbed this trend as "a dangerous awakening."[20]

An interesting aspect of the new religious landscape was the emergence of highly visible Christian spaces in northern regions of Nigeria. In every northern city, space is divided between the ancient sites and strangers' quarters on the outskirts called, *Sabon Gari*. As the commercial power of the southerners developed, these areas bore distinct southern, Christian identity that charismatic groups constructed as redeemed spaces or archetypal Goshen. In Kaduna, for instance, the Christian habitat situated across the river from the ancient city that was a part of Central Sudan in the medieval period, is known as 'New Jerusalem'. Somini Sengupta's report for *New York Times*, points to the power of identity and otherness embedded in that name and how it conjured negative responses from Muslims.[21] Many worship centres dotted the interstices between bustling shops and industries. This profile attracted Muslim hostile attention as if Christians had seized holy land for infidel activities. In Bauchi town, for instance, the local officials decided to relocate all churches on one site on the outskirts of the town as if to quarantine them. Muslims who had been protected from Christian proselytes by colonial officers in yesteryears were aghast at the boldness of Christian entrepreneurs.

Another index of the hostile environment is the rise of an intense rivalry over the appropriation of modern media as propaganda. Muslims countered the charismatic insurgence by imitating the propagation techniques of the Christians that employed radio, TV, tracts and cassettes. The attraction of the media for the Pentecostal groups has become a major area of research.[22] Muslim vendors invaded the motor parks and public places with cassettes blaring Muslim songs and sermons. The *da'wah* call compelled Islamic evangelism to surge from the mosques into the public space. The geography of religious expression became important in understanding the new face of religion in Nigeria. Competition in the religious market intensified. This explains the easy resort to violence. A typical incident occurred in a motor park in Kano. In 2001, Moslem young men claimed that a Christian driver reversed his lorry onto a bench; the Qur'an on it fell down and that the tyres went over the holy book! He was lynched.

As mentioned earlier, the jihad did not cover all communities and Muslim rulers had been imposed on many of such communities. The minority ethnic groups that were missionalized by the old evangelical groups (such as the Sudan United Mission, Sudan Interior Mission, Dutch Reformed Christian Mission) started to assert their autonomy, recover years of battered identity and reject the politics of cultural domination and exclusion. They recruited Christianity as the cultural signifier and mark of identity just as their opponents employed Islam. A number of issues became the flash points such as, chieftaincy matters, pilgrimages, equal allocation of time and space in state-owned media, and the share of political offices. They revisited the imposed concept *One North* and insisted that no longer shall Muslim leaders govern them. In the case of Zango Kataf, a violent encounter ensued as the Muslim Hausa rulers balked at the cultural renaissance.

Another sore point is that the Federal Government of Nigeria participates and sponsors Islamic pilgrims to Mecca. It set up a Pilgrims Board and sends an official delegation. At a certain point in time about 50, 000 people went on the hajj in one year. Saudi Arabia has since forced a reduction of such large numbers. The pilgrims enjoyed subsidized foreign currency exchange; many could afford to engage in trade and other profitable non-religious activities. Christians insisted that they should be sponsored to go on pilgrimage to Jerusalem and Rome. In Nigeria, those who perform the hajj are called *Alhaji / Alhaja*. Christian pilgrims started to write *JP* or Jerusalem Pilgrim after their names! Roman Catholic and Anglican patrons started a lucrative trade in bottles of water from Jordan and crucifixes that have been blessed by being placed on the marbles stones in the holy sites on Mount Olive and Holy Sepulchre in Jerusalem.

The environment became volatile because the youths in schools became the vanguard. Conflicts boiled over in many Secondary schools, Polytechnics and Universities. At the tertiary levels, elections into Students Union positions took the character of religious battles. The unemployed, artisan apprentices, houseboys and street urchins supplied the fodders for these battles. A certain theology among the Christians that could be dubbed as the "*third slap doctrine*" sustained the new determination to avenge violent attacks: it was argued that when the Bible encouraged them to turn their cheeks, it provided for only two slaps. But after the second slap, the Bible went silent and, therefore, one could avenge on the basis of the silence. There shall be no comment on the exegesis. Suffice it that many Christians decided that they would defend themselves under attack.

The Bondwoman : Demonization of Islam in Pentecostal Theology

It should be emphasized that the charismatic and Pentecostal groups demonized Islam in their theology and practices: first, the *bondwoman* concept was used to critique the state and the dominance of Moslems in the governance of the country. It was pointed out that the Book of Ecclesiastes said that it was a strange sight when

> Folly is set in great dignity, and the rich sit in low places.
> I have seen servants upon horses and princes walking as servants. (10: 6-7)

So, years of Muslim control of the governance must be unnatural; it was time for Christians to regain their lost saddle. They are the children of a rich potentate and should sit in the high places and ride on horses. A second strand of the motif treated Ishmael as outside the covenant and Islam as the illegitimate religion of the bondwoman. As Ishmael's descendants constituted a threat to the children of Isaac, so does Islam constitute a threat to the Christians. This particular threat was a punishment because of lack of faith, in that Ishmael was born out of the impatience that tried to help God. This perspective was the standard fare of 19th century evangelical missionary era in spite of E.W Smith's attempt to rescue Islam from hostile perceptions.[23] A survey of the favourite sermons among Pentecostals confirms the centrality of this political theme.

Third, from here, the doctrinal assault would climb to what Moslems would regard as blasphemous heights querying who Allah was. Allah, it was claimed, was one of the 360 gods in the Ka'abah in pre-Islamic period of Arabia and survived the reorganization of this temple after Mohammed's victory because his father was the priest of that particular deity before he died. Pentecostal rhetoric condemns the idolatry in Islamic divination, magic, charms, amulets, sufi rituals and potions including the water from washing the Qur'anic tablet. Pentecostal cosmology demonizes the core symbols such as the moon, star and the rituals of power in Islam. Pentecostal cosmology is constructed with a three-dimensional perception of heaven: the highest heaven or the third heaven is where God dwells though it is agreed that the 'heavens of heavens' cannot contain him. The second heaven below is where Satan and his cohorts were demoted after the unsuccessful rebellion. From there, they control the first heaven where the constellation system is located-the sun, moon, stars-Orion, Pleiades, Arcturus and Mazzaroth (Job 38: 31-32) The principalities and powers in the second heaven use the powers located in the constellations in the first heaven to control the destinies of individuals and communities. Early morning calls from the minaret are imaged as invocations to the princes of the air that control the second heaven and as incantations for tapping power from the first heaven for controlling the destinies of cities and the nation. Such prayers are political actions in the struggle for the soul of the nation. They urge Christians to counter the powerful pronouncements instead of "being at ease in Zion." All night vigils or tarrying on prayer-mountains and the practice of early morning shouts serve as viable rebuttals in the competition for controlling the air space and destiny of Nigeria.

Fourth, the demonization of Islam in Pentecostal rhetoric and practice move ineluctably into the international political arena. Crucial is the concept of Christian Zionism. A favourite text is David's high profiling and construction of Jerusalem as the Lord's delight and premier cultic centre. He encouraged all to

> Pray for the peace of Jerusalem:
> They shall prosper that love thee;
> Peace be within thy walls: and prosperity... (Psalm 121: 6-7)

Pentecostals pray for the well-being of Jerusalem and support Israel. At the religious level, this yields blessings. But this politics of difference contests international Islam. Christian Zionism takes different shapes and dynamics in different contexts. In Nigeria, there are indigenous cultural roots: many ethnic groups trace their origins to Hebraic sources. Johnson's *History of the Yoruba* of south-western Nigeria did so in the 19th century; G.T. Basden's *Niger Ibos* repeated this for the Igbo of the south-east in 1937.[24] Scholars and missionaries have pointed to the attraction of the Old Testament to Africans. The myths of origin utilize the resonance in cultural, ritual and cultic symbolic forms between Hebrew and Nigerian ethnic groups. Christians start from the self-perception as the New Israel and tap into the rich symbolic and cultural resources. The ideology moves from here to the African renaissance discourse in political analysis that reconstructs Africa's destiny by rejecting the discourses on "new realism" and "African pessimism" propagated by Western scholars; it rejects the pejorative Hamitic theory that alleges a curse on Ham's descendants. Much to the contrary, the Bible did not say that Noah cursed Ham. Africans are not descendants of Canaan. Africans or black people tap into the ancestry of the early Jewish patriarchs because Abraham and Moses married black women. Many Pentecostals watch videos and read the books by John Hagee's ministry that unabashedly supports Israel and the magazine produced by a Zionist group, *Israel My Glory*. It should be stressed that this ideology is not sourced from America but rather is validated and reinforced by the American sources. In the politics of Independence, Yoruba and Igbo states patronized Israel contractors and agriculturalists in developing the new regions.

Within this perspective, Pentecostals image the introduction of the sharia as a component of an insiduous project to Islamize Nigeria and declare the Maghrib as Arab instead of being a part of Africa. They recapture the force of the passage in Psalm 68: 31 that inspired "Ethiopianism" and African religious and cultural nationalism in the 19th century to weave a black theology of engagement.

Pentecostal rhetoric is built on a conspiracy theory that Muslims have completed a grand design to make Africa a Muslim continent by 2005. This was the key concern of the 7th International Ministers and Christian Leadership Conference and Prayer Retreat at Port Harcourt in 2003. Speakers "exposed" how Ghaddafi, the President of Libya has used money to trap African leaders and how Muslims are setting up Islamic schools and buying up property in the continent. Key target countries are Nigeria, Ghana, Kenya, South Africa and Zimbabwe. In the report, it is alleged that a "world renowned missionary to Muslims, Dr Bahjat Bataresh exposed the details of the plot."[25] The economic dimension to Pentecostal rhetoric is that the sharia project in Nigeria affected southern business very badly. The irony is that these businessmen control the sale of alcohol, hotel, entertainment and tourist business. However, the sharia threatens the southerners as the alkali court judges might be biased against stranger elements.

Muslims perceive the Christians as supporters of the provision that Nigeria is a secular state, an idea that is Western. The Christians employ enough liberal arsenal to support the state on the issue of secularity understood as partial separation. They do not see the concept as in any way diminishing God's control over history. However, Christian political theology remains ambiguous. A major element is that Christians in Nigeria have moved rapidly from political apathy into a theology of engagement. Pentecostals critique the state but appears ready to work with it if given the opportunity. The Intercessors for Africa, for instance, has developed the concept of land deliverance to reclaim lost covenant opportunities for the nation and to claim command position to work with God in the end times.[26] Its new program, dubbed as SALT, has joined the fight against corruption by holding leadership workshops for civil servants and top government functionaries. The theology has many strands borrowed from many sources but all conclude that there is a responsibility to improve the moral basis for leadership. Some argue that saints should go into politics because when the righteous are in authority, the people will rejoice. Some pastors have transformed pulpits into soapboxes urging Pentecostal congregations to register as a voting block, and many pastors attract the patronage of the political class asking for either prayers or votes of the congregations. The Pentecostal Fellowship of Nigeria, Lagos Branch, announced that four million of their members registered during the Voters' Registration exercise in 2002 and would vote for people who will carry out the social welfare agenda of the fellowship.[27]

In conclusion, faced with a new political landscape, religious politics in Nigeria has changed significantly. Islam has used the sharia as the lightning rod of their politics; a rallying cry. Christian resurgence through charismatism has enabled the mainline churches to become keenly aware of Islamic efforts to capture the public space. When a Muslim military leader surreptitiously registered Nigeria as a member of the Organisation of Islamic Countries in 1986, the uproar mobilized by Christian Association of Nigeria forced the withdrawal.[28] The insurgence has inspired Muslim violence. This has raised the old question whether religion is a dysfunctional force in the modern public space especially when politicised.

The discourse on dialogue has failed to move beyond theory to practice because there is often a failure to accept plurality in the worldview and cultural backgrounds of communities. Certain theological strands within the world religions reinforce the rejection of pluralism especially when combined with a streak of conservatism. Few accept the possibility to be rooted in one's belief system and be open to others. This explains the privileging of violence as a means of coercing others in spite of the claims to Abrahamic roots and shared moral concepts. Both Muslims and Pentecostals mine the resources of the worldview in constructing their theologies and in contesting for the control of the public space. Both face the dilemma of implementing a religious law and ethics in a contemporary modern state. Multi-culturalism may be more feasible in worldviews that delimit religion to the periphery. Thus, global cultural influences such as purveyed by NGOs that emanate from enlightenment worldview may not always assist. It may be argued that Islam and Pentecostalism are influenced by external forces and are vulnerable to fundamentalist voices.[29] Global information technology creates multiple centres of conflict as the events in one centre are brought vividly home in other centres. Muslims in Kano could burn churches because they watch on television the American attack on the Talibans in Afghanistan. Indeed, as the world protested over the sharia stones in punishing adultery (*zina*) and the key of Rome was given to a woman who committed *zina*, Muslims perceived incitement and frustration because these actions ridiculed Islamic ethics as barbaric. Global processes induce the intensification of local identities. Equally, the religious conflict in Nigeria is home-grown in response to declining resources and softness of the state. Sharia is a complex matter and the Nigerian Pentecostals would need to develop a concept of dialogue for the sake of a stable public space. The conjuncture of radical impulses in time (1970-80), space (northern Nigeria) and context (among the youths) within Islam and Christianity turned religious politics in Nigeria into a shark-infested water.

Notes

1. www.ngrguardiannews.com/news/article21.

2. Certified True Copy, Transcript of Sharia Court of Appeal, Sokoto State, 25/3/2002: 44.

3. See, www.mtrustonline.com/dailytrust/feature162003.htm.

4. Murray Last, *The Sokoto Caliphate* (London, Longmans, 1967); Mervyn Hiskett, *The Development of Islam in West Africa* (London, Longmans, 1984); Ross Dunn, *The Adventures of Ibn Battutta* (Berkeley, University of California Press, 1986).

5. John Paden, *Ahmadu Bello* (Zaria: Gaskiya Press, 1986): 205-206.

6. John Paden, *Religion and Political Authority in Kano* (Berkeley, University of California Press, 1973).

7. Allen Christelow, "Religious Protest and Dissent in Northern Nigeria", *Journal of the Institute of Muslim Minority Affairs, 6, 2 (1985): 375-393;* Paul Lubeck, "Islamic Protest Under Semi-industrial Capitalism", *Africa*, 55, 4 (1986): 369-397; E. Isichei, "The Maitasine Rising in Nigeria, 1980-1985: a revolt of the disinherited", *Journal of Religion in Africa*.17, 3 (Oct.1987): 194-208; M.Hiskett, "The Maitatsine Riots of Kano, 1980: an assessment", *ibid.*, : 209-223; J.Takya "The Foundations of Religious Intolerance in Nigeria", *Bulletin of Ecumenical Research*, 2, 2 (!989): 31-41.

8. www.oneworld.org/euconflict/sfp/part2/245.

9. A. Christelow, "Islamic law and judicial practice in Nigeria: an historical perspective", *Journal of Muslim Minority Affairs*, 22, 1 (2002): 185-204.

10. Ghazali Bashri, *Nigeria and Sharia* (Leicester, The Islamic Foundation, 1994); see also www.gamji.com/sharia-conf.htm and www.sharia2001.nmonline.net.

11. O.U.Kalu, "Themes in West African Church History at the Edge of the 21st Century." *Missionalia*, 30, 2 (August, 2002): 235-264. see p.237; Charlotte and Frederick Quinn, *Pride, Faith and Fear: Islam in Sub-Saharan Africa* (Oxford: Oxford University Press, 2003): 3-32.

12. John O. Hunwick, *Sharia in Songhay: the replies of al-Maghili to the questions of Askia al-hajj Muhammad.* (Oxford, Oxford University Press, 1985).

13. Lamin Sanneh, *Piety and Power: Muslims and Christians in West Africa* (Orbis, 1996).

14. Toyin Falola, *Violence in Nigeria: The crisis of religious politics and secular ideologies.* (Rochester, Rochester University Press, 1998).

15. A.R.Doi *Non-Muslim Under Sharia* (Lahore, Kazi Publications, 1990). It grew out of a lecture he gave at Ahmadu Bello University, Zaria.

16. *New Nigerian Newspaper,* 8th January, 2001.

17. O.U.Kalu, *Power, Poverty and Prayer* (Peter Lang, 2000): ch. 5.

18. M.A.Ojo, "Growth of Charismatic Movements in Northern Nigeria" Seminar on Contextualization of Christianity in Nigeria, Obafemi Awolowo University, Ife, 1989.

19. Typical of this temper is Ethel Miller, *The truth about Muhammed* (Minna, The Niger Press, 1926) The author was the sister of the peppery medical doctor, Walter Miller, who contested the British protection of Islam and onslaught against Christian missions.

20. I.M.Enwerem, *A Dangerous Awakening: Politicization of Religion in Nigeria* (Ibadan, IFRA, 1995); M.H. Kukah, *Religion, Politics and Power in Northern Nigeria* (Ibadan, Spectrum Press, 1994); S.O.Ilesanmi, *Religious Pluralism and Nigerian State* (Athens OH: Ohio University Press, 1997).

21. Somini Sengupta, "Piety and politics sunder a riot-torn Nigerian city" *New York Times*, Friday, 21st February, 2003.

22. Rosalind Hackett, "Charismatic/Pentecostal Appropriation of Media Technologies in Nigeria and Ghana", *Journal of Religion in Africa*, 28, 3 (1998): 258-277.

23. Andrew F. Walls, "Africa as the theatre of Christian engagement with Islam in the nineteenth century", *Journal of Religion in Africa*, 29, 2 (1999): 155-174.

24. See a discussion of Johnson's *History* in J.D.Y. Peel, *Religious encounter and the making of the Yoruba* (Bloomington, IN, University of Indiana Press, 2000): 304-309; G.T. Basden, *Niger Ibos* (rep. London, Frank Cass, 1966), chapt. 21.

25. www.nigeriachristiannews@yahoogroups.com 3rd February, 2003.

26. Emeka Nwankpa, *Redeeming the Land* (Achimota, African Christian Publishers, 1994); Steve Okitika, *The Battle for nations: the ministry of interceding for our nation* (Lagos, Moinab Ltd., 1996); O.U. Kalu. "The Practice of Victorious Life: Pentecostal Political Theology in Nigeria, 1970-1996", *Mission: Jnl. of Mission Studies*, (University of Ottawa, Canada), 5, 2 (1998): 229-255.

27. www.ngrguradiannews. com /news/article23.

28. See *New Nigerian Newspaper*, no.6812. Tuesday, February 6th, 1986: 1.

29. Paul Gifford, *The New Crusaders* (London, Pluto Press, 1991).

6   *The Big Drum for A Warrior: Osofo Jeremiah Wright and African American Re-Engagement of Africa*

The Sound of the Big Drum

In my village that is located in southeastern Nigeria, there is a hut near the market square. It is cordoned off with yellow palm fronds signifying that it is a sacred space. It houses a very big drum standing five feet high and about four feet long. An expert drummer, who must come from a priestly family, enters the hut only on special occasions. He must be very competent in the indigenous knowledge, folklore of the people and possess the capacity to speak with the drum idiom. During the New Yam or harvest festival, he would perform certain sacrifices to the ancestors and deities of the land before entering the hut to render an annual address analyzing the key currents in the community's life during the past year. He would start with the praise names and heroic achievements of our forefathers, recount the meaning behind the events of the year and connect the past to the present as if to say that history has meaning. He weds knowledge to a sustaining ideology. The only other time that the man enters the hut is when the village honors or caps a hero, a visionary, and an achiever who has upheld the salient values of the community and could pass for a role model. This is because the big drum tradition is an aspect of the social control model of the community. The big drum serves as a tool in the reward social control system. The Igbo community is very achievement-oriented and uses the imagery of a warrior to celebrate achievers. I believe that the image of a warrior is very apt for *Osofo* Jeremiah Wright, a man who has doggedly, against all odds, used the resources garnered from his parents and teachers to fight for the black person's cause. If we were in my village, the flutist would have joined the big drum, and using its broader sonic range, accompanied the big drum in a call-and response mode to usher *Osofo* Jeremiah Wright into the village square.

Let me point out another key aspect of the big drum: it celebrates people but does not indulge in hagiography. The big drum is said to have the "tongue of the tiger," at once sharp and focused on the truth. It does not sing light praises but interprets. It is a form of performed history that teaches and inspires through story telling. This is what has saved this tradition from abuse. It heralds only true warriors. This tradition could be found among various ethnic groups in West Africa. Among the Yoruba of southwestern Nigeria, the *oriki* tradition performed the task of choreographed history. It does not merely perform the story of the past, it includes a discourse on the significance of history and how other performers have handled the story. Indeed, the performers, *arokin*, often emphasize how they inherited the tradition and have faithfully maintained it. In some ways, they resemble the *griots* among the Mande of Senegal, Mali and Guinea, also known as *belen Tigui*, respected wise men with deep knowledge of the course and meaning behind events. But the big drummer in my village is more critical; he resembles the performer whom the Ikwerre of the Niger Delta describe as having the *python's eyes* noted for its penetrating and embracing vision.

I have performed the initial sacrifices through research and interviews and wish to climb into the hut and beat the big drum for a warrior. Being a historian by training and coming from the ruling family, *Umueze Ekeuke of Ohafia Udumeze,* I have the audacity to do so. I wish to begin by saying why *Osofo* Jeremiah Wright is a worthy village warrior whose visionary ministry through the years deserves the attention and praises of the village community. I will start by describing the breadth of his particular ministry of re-engaging Africa—a vision that is not fully shared; a vision that has been ridiculed by those who have absorbed the white image of a dark continent and who feel that the imperatives of assimilation compel the need to distance themselves from the savagery of Africa. I hear that some people complained about the pastor's dashiki instead of proper suits as may become a pastor of an important, city congregation. But, once the pastor embraced the vision, he pursued it passionately and achieved much with great creativity. But I will probe his motives, strategy and rhetoric and finally locate his dreams and achievements within the larger framework and scholarship of African American evangelization of Africa-a theme that runs like a creeping plant throughout African American church history. It is this fact that informs the sub-title that he is re-engaging and not creating the African American engagement of Africa that was very vibrant in the 19th century before the impetus waned. Commentators have canvassed explanations. The fact remains that before any white missionary organization was formed, African Americans were already evangelizing Africa, often aided by blacks from the Caribbean. [1] They produced the Creole class that evangelized West Africa, established commercial enterprises and served as civil servants and advocates of education and liberation. The significance of *Osofo* Wright is his role in the renaissance of a theme that suffered disaster along the pathway of black history. We have come to celebrate how *Osofo* Jeremiah Wright's social –activist theology produced a black church's practical mission to engage the public space and to respond to the black person's challenges of identity, poverty and social justice globally. More cogently, he is concerned about a particular challenge called *CWB*—being a *Christian While Black*, in the United States and abroad.[2]

The Hunter Warrior and the Bush Pig

My village is nestled on a tributary of the Cross river. The fertile soil yields rich harvests of yams, rice, cassava and okro. The biggest challenge is the seasonal ravages by hordes of wild bush pigs. From a certain perspective, *Osofo* Jeremiah Wright's mission resembles the task of a hunter warrior who decides to confront the bush pig and to respond to the challenge that destroys the village community's farms, food security and causes hunger and poverty in the midst of a rich ecosystem. There is a close resemblance between bush pigs and foreign exploitation of Africa. My village celebrates the hunter who kills the bush pig. After the big drum welcomes the hunter to the village square, a masquerade dance will begin that re-enacts the hunter's ordeals while confronting the bush pig. The staccato music and vigorous disorderly dance choreographs the encounter in which the prospect of victory remains precarious until the pig is dead. The dance is simply named after the bush pig, *atu*.

The enormity of the challenge is because of the nature of bush pigs. Bush pigs terrorize villages and could wipe out a community's food security in one fell swoop. A village's farmland often resembles a disastrous battlefield after the visit of bush pigs. Bush pigs go in hordes and would uproot yams and cassava and trample down corns/ maize, beans and okro. The animal is big and endowed with vicious horns. Its skin is so thick that the pellets from den guns could hardly penetrate. A bush pig gets angry if fired upon and would charge viciously towards the gun man instead of running away! The bush pig treats a den gun like a Chinese- made toy from Walt Mart. Often, the hunter would throw away the gun and climb onto a tree. Even there, safety may not be assured because the cunning animal would excrete his faeces, urinate on it, mix it with his tails and would fling the concoction onto the hunter. This concoction burns and itches and could force the hunter to scratch his body, loose his grip and fall at the unmerciful big feet of the waiting bush pig. A brave warrior-hunter who killed a bush pig, therefore, deserved the full eight-day celebration! Africa's contemporary bush pigs are agents of globalization and multinational corporations. The wars in Liberia, Sierra Leone and eastern Congo are diamond and mineral wars. The World Bank and IMF have extended the cords of structural adjustment programs throughout Africa to exploit the resources and collect spurious debts. Beneath the macro-economic numbers is massive poverty as darkness has hit Africa at noontide. Who will rescue us from the menace or join us in the hunt for the bush pigs?

In early June, 2006, Pastor Wright received a letter from a Congolese immigrant. He introduced himself and went straight to the point:

> I am from the Democratic Republic of Congo. Thank you so much for all that you are doing to make people aware of what is going on in Africa. Every time I attend service at Trinity, I feel as if I am back home. I find it admirable that you embrace Africa and encourage your congregation to do the same. It is for this reason that I thought I should write to you to express my concern about the conflict that is taking place in the Congo. Four million Congolese have perished since the start of a civil war in 1998. I am pleading with you to put pressure on the US government to end this monstrous atrocity. [3]

He enclosed a detailed documentation that proves that the war in Congo was over control of minerals: gold, diamond, niobium, cobalt, uranium, copper and especially coltan(*columbium tantalite*) that is key to the manufacture of mobile phones. DRC holds 80% of the world's coltan reserve, more than 60% of the world's cobalt and the world's largest supplier of high grade copper. The father of the current American president is a director in Barrick Gold (which is a client of Andrew Young's Goodworks International lobbying firm), one of the competing American companies that supply arms to insurgents. Other past premiers of Canada as well as the immediate past president of the United States have connections with some of the companies involved in the Congo. The televangelist Pat Robertson's *Operation Blessing* is a front for his diamond mining interests in the Congo, according to two pilots who fly supplies to the mines under the guise of flying relief supplies. Indeed, an airport that was touted in his TV program as being constructed for aid relief was actually for freighting equipments and supplies to the diamond mine. Permit me to point to some other aspects of this letter that deserve note: the writer pointed to the worship life of TUCC that brings joy to African visitors—my humble self included—and that reinforces the feeling of ebony kinship. But the writer implies that underneath the worship is the pastor's clear objective to reconnect African Americans to an African heritage and roots, not in a romantic manner but to recover lost knowledge and to practice a different kind of mission that shares, partners and passionately participates in the joys, fears and hopes of the people. Worship serves as an instrument for building a beloved community that is empowered to dare to respond to the outside world with fidelity.

We will like to know why Africa is central in the vision because another letter from National Council of African Women, North Chicago Branch, asked for financial support in a mercy mission to Maseno Hospital in Kenya because, says the writer,

> We know that you are a pacesetter and leader in your service for Africa. It will be one of the greatest honors for you to come to encourage us as we embark upon this momentous foreign service journey.

The encomium about being a leader in African matters can better be understood from a letter that pastor got from a lady who said that the son went to Ghana and died there. The lady wrote Pastor Wright on February 8th, 2006 to help her get her son's body back to the United States because "I am unfamiliar with how to handle this type of situation and any assistance you could render would be most appreciated." In fact, the distraught lady thought that Ghana was in South Africa. The Chicago community knows about the connection between this church and Africa and yet the church has not taken one single television advertisement! The cumulative impact of silent deeds is being felt.

Still another letter came from West Africa when a diasporic group, the Ga Dangme Foundation, Chicago, wrote Pastor Wright enthusing about the special relationship between the Foundation and TUCC. As they said, "We sincerely appreciate your very generous offer…No one could have been more generous than you in your support of the GDF." The Ga Dangme in the homeland honored Pastor Wright with a chieftaincy title as the Chief of Community Development and the Chicago diaspora performed a colorful durbar in this sanctuary after the installation. But the more successful enterprise in Ghana is the Computer School in Saltpond where TUCC is working with the Saltpond Redevelopment Institute founded in 1986 by an indigene, Dr Andrew Agen Davis, MD. At Saltpond, *Osofo* Wright's handprint is literally etched in concrete to show the people's appreciation. The records show that the school graduated 77 students between the years 2002-2005; that many of the students are now self employed and have opened their own cyber cafes while others have gone for further technical training abroad or gained admission into local universities. The project builds the human resources of local churches because a number of the students are nuns and pastors. I believe that the Saltpond project worked because of an underlying ideology. I point to this fact because many people who go on mission to Africa develop a savior mentality and tell the people what they need. In these projects, Pastor Wright works with indigenous people to help them perform better. As one document put it,

> we do not simply go to a country and do that which we think should be done. Instead, we go only where local Christians invite us and we do that which we have been asked to do with them. Funds are handled locally. Projects and types of mission are determined by partners. (Memo: November 14th, 2004)

My favorite letters came from young girls, students of the Liberty Educational Foundation (Vocational Training) at Koforidua in the eastern region of Ghana. Coming from a small village that is plagued by youth unemployment and the prospects of wasted generations, you can understand how these brief hand-written letters to Pastor Wright moved me to tears. Each enclosed her picture, a measure of accountability by the school officials who also included a receipt for the scholarship money received. Doris used a formal letter-writing technique entitling her missive as "Letter of Appreciation" and surged forth,

> I was extremely happy when it was announced that you have decided to sponsor my education. I am therefore writing to say a big thank you to you all. I appreciate your gesture and promise to learn hard.

Another young girl, 19-year old Lydia wrote,

> "I am one of the lucky recipients of your scholarship scheme. I wish to say how grateful I am to you and your congregation for coming to solve my educational problem for me."

Felicia spoke in the same vein:

> "I wish to write this letter to thank you from the bottom of my heart for deciding to come to my aid with a scholarship. I shall work hard to merit the award."

The matron of the school prophesied into the future of the enterprise:

> "The Lord has really worked through you to bring light and hope into the lives of thousands who will be benefiting from the universal goal we have set and intend to achieve."[4]

I could read you more letters because TUCC under *Osofo* Jeremiah Wright engaged in world-wide, co-operative ventures to study, affirm, reconnect and serve black peoples all over the globe. It contributes to Steve Biko Institute, Bahia. The name evokes memories of Pastor Wright's role in the anti-apartheid struggle. Two comments here: the first is that African American direct political engagement with the liberation of Africa would run from Max Yergan's Council of African Affairs founded in 1937, through the American Negro Leadership Conference of Africa and the African Liberation Support Committee of the 1960s to the mobilization against apartheid in South Africa in the 1980s.[5] Second, an awesome event connects *Osofo* Wright with South African apartheid struggle. One Sunday morning, eight governors from South Africa came to worship at TUCC. After the welcome and clapping, the pastor invited any of one of them who wished to say a few words. One stood up and in an emotive but steady tone recounted how he was imprisoned with Mandela; how hopeless the conditions were but how they heard about a church in Chicago that flew a banner calling for their freedom. He said that many of them rejoiced to know that in a far –distant land, some people cared so deeply. The prisoners wistfully promised that if they ever got out from Robin Island, they would visit and thank that church. Many did not survive but that, on behalf of himself and his dead prison inmates, he came to thank the church. Then, he launched into an indigenous African liturgy-often heard at ancestral shrines when the intermediary between human beings and the deities would invoke the spirits of those who are not present by calling out their names. Names are powerful metonyms. He named each dead person with the refrain, "he thanks you." As he went through a list of names in a deliberate measure, both the pastor and the congregation burst into tears. The living and the dead re-united at the altar to show that they are grateful for the care of a black church during the dark, hopeless days. Such a history of advocacy connected TUCC with the Africa Action group in Washington.

Within the larger denomination, TUCC partners with Global Outreach International and participated in crafting a proposal within the Cluster Six group "to research the needs of Africans and how African American UCC Churches can act in a united manner to respond to those identified needs." TUCC co-operates with Church World Service on projects in Kenya and Angola focused on hunger and poverty alleviation.

In August 2005, five people from Illinois Conference of United Church of Christ traveled to Angola to forge partnership with Congregational Church of Angola. A note of interest is that TUCC prepared its own agenda built on learning more and recovering the fact that one of the first three missionaries sent by the American Board of Commissioners for Foreign Mission in1880 was an African American; and in 1922 an African American Galangue Mission was established supported by the American Missionary Association. TUCC assists many Chicago-based agencies to effectively engage in poverty alleviation and social justice causes. For instance, in June, 2006, the Third World Benevolent, a sub-committee of the Africa Mission Committee of TUCC, reviewed some applications for assistance from organizations engaged in Africa: Friends of Sheltered Children in Kenya (FOSCIK) that sponsors orphanages, caters for the destitute, abused and abandoned children in Kenya; The South Africa Ubuntu Project that partners with Pastor Sylvester Cele in HIV/AIDS project in Durban; the National Council of African Women; and the Terry Support and Youth Residence in Kenya and others. It funded between 50% to 100% of the requests. While supporting a health intervention project through the Ubuntu Project, TUCC saved the Inanda Seminary in the same Kwazulu-Natal region of South Africa from closing its doors. This school was founded by the UCC denomination in the 1880s as a high school for the training of black girls. In recent times, funding was discontinued leaving the task to the alumnae of the institution. Matters got so bad that the school could no longer pay salaries and was about to close. Providentially, *Osofo* Wright and a delegation from TUCC were visiting. He spent $100,000 to rescue the school from closing down permanently and has since then served as a partner to both Inanda and another school in Guguletu.

The vision embraces all black peoples and seeks to affirm that we are all one like the jingle in South African television that would mellifluously ring out: *"Si-mu-nye-ee, we are all one!"* Therefore, TUCC has engaged in a number of exchange contacts: they hosted black visitors from Brazil led by Marlene Moreira da Silva, President of the Institute of Theological Studies at Bahia to discuss the intersection of race, gender, and religion among African descended indigenes of Brazil. They have undertaken trips to Brazil and saw first hand the poverty and human rights problems of black people. A touching letter came from Father Athaylton Belo (Father Tata) about alleviation projects such as the Casa do Menor project located in S. Joao de Meriti. He emphasized the need to mobilize black lawyers to work on black civil rights cases. As he described the fate of youths roaming hopelessly around the streets, he broke down: (sic)

> Dr Jeremiah, I am sorry so much if I am boring you with those points; but please, remember that I am in a country which black people as you know are very poor in general. I have been working a such long time with black people. And I came from a poor family as well. I think that I am a leader and I do know that I need more and more for to be a good black leader in Brazil and I am not ashame in Jesus Christ to ask your help in yours experience no just in case of money, in your spirituality also. God knows everything! He knows everything! He knows my heart! I do believe so! Any advise, any help would be very good to me. God bless you, thanks very much for your friendship and love in Jesus for me and to Brazil! [6]

He promised to improve on his English. *Osofo* Wright sent a gentle comforting and affirming reply, telling him that it was important to ask for co-operation and assistance, that he himself will like to improve on his Portuguese and raised questions to determine how much will be required to pursue the Casa do Menor project. Dr Jeremiah Wright's forte and legacy is this capacity to feel other people's pain of humiliation; this capacity to empathize, this capacity to respond to the individual and offer a hand that lifts up those pushed down into the miry pit by systemic social injustice.

A similar area of engagement with Africa diaspora is in Colombia. TUCC has hosted a group from Colombia where displaced, deprived and miseducated black people are suffering. The project started in November 2005 when Ms Zulia Mena, the first Afro-Colombian Congress woman (1994-1998) visited Chicago to raise black consciousness on the plight of her people. During Zulia Mena's term in the congress. she successfully secured the legalization of Afrocentric education. She got the government to implement the provisions envisioned in the 1991 constitutional reform. Just at the same time, a violent and brutal assault was mounted against the Afro-Colombians to forcibly displace them and acquire their land. In 1997 the Rio Sucio massacre killed hundreds and displaced thousands because some multinational corporations wanted hardwood; pharmaceutical companies wanted biodiversified ecology for the fauna; and oil companies wanted an opportunity to explore. Colombian government's military operated with paramilitary units(just as in Darfur) to secure land for mega projects such as highways, new ports, palm plantations and tourist havens. The bush pig has struck again!

The response was to initiate an exchange educational program comprising of a partnership between Colombian schools of Palenque and Villa Espanan in Quibdo, Choco and Chicago schools comprising of Barbara Sizemore Charter Middle School, Betty Shabazz International Charter School and DuSable Leadership Charter School. The goal was to acknowledge the communities' basic needs for education and medical supplies. The next step was to ascertain the real dimension of the bush pig's destructive invasion. It was decided to send a fact finding reconnaissance team, followed by sponsoring Spanish-speaking Afro-Colombians to train in alternative Afrocentric education and cultural models that could bring social change utilizing the unique perspective and knowledge of Afro-Colombian culture. The plight of the youth who were the targets of the genocide was acute. Another phase would include visits by the Chicago schools to Colombian schools: De San Basilio En La Costa Atlantica (Palenque), Obapo (Quibdo, Choco) and Luis Gonzalo Perea. It was hoped that a regular exchange program would follow annually to achieve optimal effect through material, educational, morale-building, spiritual and ideological tools. The program is successfully moving into a pan-North American phase scheduled for Summer, 2008 when delegates from United States, Colombia, Haiti, Brazil and Panama will gather in Colombia in the International Education Summit Conference of Africans in the Western Hemisphere under the theme, *One Voice, One Vision and Shared Solution.* As described by Aris White,

> this empowering historical event will provide Africans in the diaspora a sacred space to share experiences of the challenges and solutions that have mobilized us to triumph through adversity, human rights abuses and marginalization or to the deletion of contributions/ influence of our ancestors…Our immediate goal is to develop explicit strategies to strengthen, advance and promote our legacies and consciousness.

These are brief examples of the diasporic breadth, commitment, vision and passion of *Osofo* Jeremiah Wright in advocacy, cultural education and learning, networking, poverty alleviation, community building, mobilization and re-envisioning. As the Ghanaian lady put it, the Lord has really worked through him to bring light and hope to many.

The Dance of the Warrior-Hunter: Motives, Strategy and Rhetoric

But the drummer in the hut looks beneath actions to question the hero's motives because philanthropy often hides infected motives. Motives clothe strategies. Many have spoken about the man, his theology and preaching. The drummer dares to probe the warrior hunter's ego. At the climax of the celebration, the drummer would start a praise music for the warrior. The flutist joins to lure the hero to dance into the square and answer the drummer's call. But there is a snare in the drummer's call: he wants to know the man inside the fancy costume. He wants to know whether the celebrant would caparison to the beat of the drum with the footwork of a self-centered person. I can now see him moving forward and suddenly, to the cheer of the crowd, *Osofo* responds with self-assurance and bold confidence but steps out like a man conscious of the fate of the folk rather than the pride of the solo entrepreneur. Pastor Wright always works within the community and strives to leave a legacy for the community. When the Kwame Nkrumah Charter School was to be named, a grateful board wanted to name it after him but Pastor Wright demurred and nudged the board towards an Africanist who was educated in Lincoln University and whose dreams bore the imprints of DuBois and Padmore's legacy. He sacrificed self-promotion so as to inscribe a legacy from a core black heritage. Some shoulders shrugged in bewilderment.

Certain inspirational forces drive the man's activities. His upbringing and a certain Igbo sense of duality: life and values of the country folk/ life and values of educated town folk; a Christianity painted in white colors, culture and racism/ the reality of Christ, his ministry and his gospel; white education/ the scholarship of Leo Hansberry and the study of the African American spirituals. How does one achieve balance and engage suffering? This iron in the soul was compounded by the black allure to Islam as if it was the true religion of blacks and the misrepresentation of Christianity as a white race's religion—without realizing that the African cultural and geographical matrices remain central to the Bible and the gospel; that most of the Western world joined Christianity later but domesticated, honed and clothed Christianity as a tribal religion. Meanwhile, various branches of the African race have absorbed the white image and caricatures. These images have wiped out vestiges of black ancestral homeland ties. *Osofo* Wright's motives are to deconstruct the identity crisis, confront the bush pig and wipe out the stereotypes. These could be achieved through a new form of education because, he said, "I cannot love me if I am looking at myself through the colonizer's lenses. I must leave a legacy that enables people to realize and deconstruct miseducation."[7]

At the background some white scholars jeered: Dinesh D'Souza's polemic *Illiberal Education* (1991), Allan Bloom's *Closing of the American Mind* (1987), Robert Hughes, *Culture of Complaint* (1993), Mary Lefkowitz, *Not Out of Africa* (1996) and Stephen Howe, *Afrocentrism: Mythical Pasts, and Imagined Homes* (1998)[8] These yelled against the eruption of ethnicity, wildly polemical separatism, tendency to fabricate myths about the past and insurgent nationalism. They jeered at Afrocentrism for looking to a romantic past, mythical reconstruction of yesterday to find some understanding of the cultural basis of today's racial and class challenges.

The issues of identity, pluralism and faith commitment are central to the footsteps of the celebrant's dance. Identity is built on *ubuntu* meaning that self-worth is moored to knowing, connecting, touching, feeling and affirming the larger black race in Africa and Africa diaspora. The goal is to engage Africa and Africa diaspora with mind, body and heart; learning, touching, physically experiencing and acting towards its well-being by responding to the contemporary challenges. African American children and adults can successfully negotiate the culture wars in American pluralistic environment by anchoring in African and African diasporic cultural roots as well in the experiences of being in contemporary America. This is a creative ideology that has been opposed but re-articulated with a difference. *Osofo* Wright argues that the first principle is to engage Africa realizing that there are many cultures in a big continent. One must avoid a romantic journey and avoid the safari mentality. The first imperative is to study the context. The second is to engage the contemporary problems and to do so without fanfare, exhibitionism or television glare but to engage it with humility akin to the Greek *metanoia* or repentance. The third is to avoid the "uplift" idea, the philanthropic, messianic mentality. When one experiences another culture without these blockages, stereotypes vanish; and that person can tell others about the enduring experiences. The word will spread and counter the misinformation that has gathered like a moss through the years. For instance, in the Caribbean ministry, he argued that a person who goes to the resorts in the Caribbeans may never know anything about the people and the ebony connection to the people. Much to the contrary, the holiday-maker will continue to harbor the negative images created by colonial overlords. But this racial divide can close by identifying Caribbean immigrants, standing by them, understanding and appreciating Caribbean culture and thereby nurturing a new perspective. For instance, many African Americans notice a linguistic difference between themselves and the Caribbean native speakers without realizing that if one used the five characteristics of language (pragmatics, semantics, syntax, grammar and phonics) that both are speaking from the same language group in spite of differences in certain notes and pronunciation of certain letters. He argues persuasively that cultural retention from Africa throughout the diaspora is extensive in language, music, dance and culture. The lack of Africentric cultural education created the illusion against cultural retention.

Fourth, he believes in touching the lives of individuals because making a difference in someone's life can be powerful. Put differently, while some emphasize proclamation (Greek *exercomai*) as the missionary tool for liberation, *Osofo* Wright privileges witness (Greek *marturomai*) as a force that liberates and transforms ways of thinking, promotes human dignity and develops healthy solidarity among people. His motive has been to decolonize cultural education through developing the life of the mind by reading neglected African and African American authors. Group study tours, sojourns for longer periods, lectures from indigenous resource persons, various dimensions of culture sharing and exchanges are his favorite strategies for decolonizing the minds of all Africans, at home and in the diaspora. His perspective on cultural education resonates with the words of William Hooper Councill, President of the Agricultural and Mechanical College for Negroes, Normal, Alabama in his *Lamp of Wisdom* (1898:5):

> I hope that by the light of this little Lamp of Wisdom the world may see more clearly the merits of the Negro and accord him a man's chance in the race of life and that the Negro himself may take fresh courage and press forward to grander achievements.[9]

The Libation For The Ancestors:
The Religious Roots of Re-engagement

Why does he go back to Africa for strength to fight the black person's battle? I tell you one compelling reason. When a child is born, the umbilical cord is put in a calabash and some herbs are spread on it. As the calabash is being buried, libations and incantations are used to dedicate the child to the land. My people believe that the effects of the ritual follow the individual to the end of life; that the feet will always carry the individual back to the land where the umbilical cord is buried. *Osofo* Jeremiah Wright's feet always carried him back to the legacy left by the parents. The first was to respect and pursue the life of the mind. The second was to serve the Lord and God's people. But he had questions to settle before entering the ministry and read voraciously to seek for answers. His mind and feet went back to the origins of Christianity, especially Africa in the Bible and in early consolidation of the Jesus movement. Thus, there are religious reasons for his quest. This reminds me of what happens after the warrior-hunter's dance. The elders would step out, offer libatory drinks to the ancestors (who must be getting quite thirsty in the tropical heat). They recount what they are doing and what the hero has achieved and begin a religious explanation of the deeper meaning of the day's celebration. Certain deep questions are crucial for the Africans. As Lamin Sanneh, the Gambian professor at Yale, asked: *whose religion is Christianity anywhere?* How does the black person recover an enabling, living faith that can sustain and give meaning to the journey called life? Will the black church turn its back on Africa in the face of the opposition from many leaders of the black church, especially those who disdain the life of the mind?

It must be restated that *Osofo* Wright works from the inside-outwards, from the problems in the black community and church outwards to the black diaspora, and for the benefit of all. Engaging Africa is a way of responding to the problems at home. In 1995 he published a collection of his sermons, *African Who Shaped Our Faith*.[10] It combines exquisite homilectics with Africentric scholarship. He examined how a lie has been told often enough to become deeply ingrained in the black person's psyche that Christianity is a white religion and Jesus was a Caucasian male. Race, color and Christianity combined to emasculate black interest and engendered a psychological self-rejection in the black child. As he intoned, "God gave me the burden for getting African American men back into the church" inspired by "great princes of the pulpits" like Dr Johnny Youngblood, Dr Frank Reid and Dr Robert Franklin.[11] He argued that s the "original civilizing information" that influenced Europeans came from Africa; that most of the people in both Old and New Testaments are people of African descent; and that the three major world religions evolved from among the descendants of black people. Africa may not be mentioned in the Bible but the Bible describes important African kingdoms in the ancient world; so, there is evidence of the African presence in the Bible because of the geographical and cultural purviews of the Africa plate, "the land of Ham" at that time. He concluded that there is enough in the African stories to give the African American children enough positive self-esteem to last through a life time; or as Martin Bernal would say, the political purpose for writing *Black Athena* was to lessen European cultural arrogance!

Since Wright's book is a collection of sermon, it touched upon but did not delve into the scholarly debates as Edwin M. Yamauchi and others did. Let me summarize the intellectual strands that are important in this deconstruction/reconstruction process. The Bible has been used to support racism understood as the negative definition of the other through a hierarchy of races. But racialism, the belief in the distinctive characters of different racial groups, can be deployed as an antidote. In 2006, Colin Kidd, *The Forging of Races, Race and Scripture in the Protestant Atlantic World, 1600-2000* insisted that the Bible itself is color-blind with regard to racial difference, tending towards monogenism with the benign capacity to render racial otherness as a type of cousinage or remote kinship; that racism was grounded in the pseudo-scientific scholarship of the 19th century; and that triumphant elements of Western culture have clung stubbornly to some ancient texts as the last word on human relations.[12] Black scholarship has revisited the havoc wreaked by translators, the false assertions about the curse of Ham, the boundaries of Africa, the achievements of early African kingdoms of Egypt, Nubia and Ethiopia, the stolen legacy by Greeks, Africa's contribution to the formation and consolidation of the Jesus movement when it moved its center from Jerusalem to the Graeco-Roman world and the role of Alexandria and Carthage in early Christian apologetics.[13] The key issues are whether Egyptians were Africans, black, and shared a continuous community with Cushites and those living south of the Sahara. Another discourse examines the impact of this legacy on African American sense of identity, attachment to Christianity and imperative for Pan African racial identity. This runs into the debate about the degree of African retention in African American culture and religion. The politics of assimilation often derailed the academic component of the debate. To cut the chase, *Osofo* Wright has followed the literature closely and believes that Africans were key players in the origins of the Bible and the formation and spread of Christianity. Study visits to different parts of Africa would enable the African Americans to recover this heritage. He dismisses those who argue against cultural retentions as Merchants of Venice scholars.

Contemporary literature tends to support him. For instance, in 1969, John Mbiti, the Kenyan New Testament scholar concluded that "historically Christianity is very much an African religion." Keith Burton, *The Blessing of Africa: The Bible and African Christianity* (2006) set two goals: to review the role of the land of Ham in the history of Christianity and to join "the growing battery of research that aims to set the record straight" about the myth of the Curse of Ham. In the same year, David M. Goldberg's *The Curse of Ham: Race and Slavery in Early Judaism, Christianity and Islam* approached the theme from history of ideas, reconstructing the history of early Jewish, Christian and Muslim interpretations of Noah's curse on Canaan as the rationalization for slavery.[14] Goldberg explained when and how myths and misrepresentations about color and race originated and the important sources of anti-black racism. Burton's is a historical reconstruction of the role of biblical Africa and its people in the growth of Christianity from its Canaanite origins to the contemporary period. The first task, he said, is to identify the geography of biblical Africa and the locations of the sons of Ham: Canaan, Misrayim, Cush and Put. The emphasis is the geography and not ethnicity because the land of Ham was inhabited by people of different shades, facial features and hair texture. Locating Misrayim in the Maghrib, Canaan in the Middle East, Cush in the horn of Africa, Burton located Put in sub-Saharan Africa, equating it with the ancient Punt below Ethiopia. He argues that the lack of genealogy and sparse reference in the Bible are balanced by shared Bantu linguistic similarities to make a case for a common heritage. Second, he uses a clear typology to showcase the African personalities- political, spouses and con-cubines, citizens, friends of Israel and believers in the Messiah. This sets the background for a third theme, the openness of Africans to receiving the message of salvation in the Messiah. He argues that there was a prevalence of the culture of the Bible among disparate tribes in sub-Saharan Africa as evidence of their exposure to the Bible before slavery. Burton's location of Put is significant from two angles: because many African American writers will identify with Egypt but use the "degradation hypothesis" to explain the culture of south Saharan Africa; and because many West African com-munities claim a connection with Egypt, Nile or Israel.

The significance of all these is that *Osofo* Wright arrives at his praxis from a biblical perspective. This is Christian Africentrism defined as an emphasis on shared African origins among all black people, taking pride in those origins and an interest in African history and culture and in those aspects that have survived in the New World cultures and a belief that that Eurocentric bias has blocked and distorted the knowledge of Afri-cans about their cultures and roots in the Biblical stories and making of Christianity. Within this broad definition there are many strands: cultural romanticist, secular ideological, academic/ analytic advocacy, Freeman-sonry, and Christian. He believes that the path to recovering the lost legacy must start by building a Spirit-filled congregation, solidly rooted in the Bible. This means the deliberate cultivation of a mature, black Christian congregation from which faith emits and realizes all the original meaning and adhesion to Christ and his gospel; a congregation that takes Jesus seriously enough to risk in acts of love; and a congregation that cultivates the life of the mind. He firstly strengthens the fiber of the ecclesial com-munity and imbues it with a new zeal and renewal in the Spirit so that it can meet the challenges of the new realities. Since blacks shaped our faith, we should know, affirm this heritage and follow the implications to the full. Thus, in engaging Africa and the African diaspora, Pastor Wright works through two committees of the church: the Caribbean Committee and the Africa Ministry. Their engagement must be centered around the ten principles of his vision that the TUCC congregation must be a loving, Spirit-filled community committed to adoration, salvation, reconciliation, liberation, restoration, economic parity, biblical education, cultural education, commitment to Africa and the historical education of Africa people in diaspora. The ministries are funded from tithes, God's holy money from the store house of the Lord that should be used to continue the Lord's ministry of reconciliation. This engenders a spirit of stewardship, commitment and passion. It saves the congregation from being a project-oriented community without a sustainable spirituality.

When the Drummer Staggers Home

Towards evening, the drummer beats the last praise to the village and to the warrior and starts the slow walk home—slow because he has been drinking a fair quantity of gin which the village chiefs and the appreciative audience delivered to the drum- hut. As people stroll back home, like those on the road to Emmaus, they recount what they have just experienced. How does one paint *Osofo* Wright on the broad canvass of African American engagement of Africa? That canvass reflects one of the ironies of history, especially the role that black people who had been brutally taken away from their homes played in the evangelization of the African homelands. It was as if by an inexplicable providential force, the slave trade that had vitiated the missionary impulse between 1500 and 1800 yielded the resources for counteracting its effects on Africa. Yet because Europeans dominated the story-telling about the expansion of Christianity into non-Western worlds, the roles of non-Western actors remained in the dark. Cornel West and Eddie Glaude explain the background as thus:

> African Americans found in the Christian gospel as it was preached during the great revivals, liberating possibilities in their personal experiences of conversion, in the family resemblance of evangelical worship services of an African past, and in a vocabulary that enabled the slave to escape the psychic effects of slavery. They were no longer extensions of a white master's will. Instead, many Christian slaves came to see themselves as unique-even chosen- with a different moral sense about them, capable of distinguishing intuitively the wrongness of slavery and racial discrimination and the rightness of their common complaint, because of their distinctive relationship to God.[15]

There are three dimensions of the problem: first (and without prejudice to the contours of the debate on African retentions in African American spirituality), that the Christianity that some slaves had absorbed in the motherland from early Christianity and the Portuguese was synthesized with ingredients of African indigenous religions, cultures and Islam to generate a very charismatic spirituality that characterized African American Christianity. Second, that spirituality was garnished with evocative symbolism and rhetoric drawn from the Bible. [16] For instance, the 19th century Ethiopian movement imaged African American evangelization of Africa as *the return of the exiles*. Perhaps no one noted how it jarred prominently against the reclaiming of the heritage of Egypt. Third, that spirituality empowered African Americans' involvement in the evangelization of Africa right from the eighteenth century as a way of responding to the system in the United States after emancipation. Lamin Sanneh, *Abolitionists Abroad* has reconstructed the period adequately.[17]

Briefly, therefore, one could trace four phases of African American missionary engagement of Africa:

i.   The early contacts by African Americans who were inspired by evangelical spirituality and the Higher Life movement in the 18th century.

ii. The nationalist ideology of redeeming Africa through religion which was strong from the 19th through mid 20th century. This served as the clarion call of the Ethiopian movement, catalyzed the flowering of black missionary enterprises as a sequel to emancipation and back-to-Africa movement, and became a core aspect of African Pentecostalism in the 20th century. Various advocates articulated the different strands of the stirring ideology. The churches founded by Ethiopianists in southern Africa served as the channel for the vertical growth of Pentecostalism at the turn of the century. The African American presence was most conspicuous in Sierra-Leone, Gold Coast, Nigeria, Cameroon, Fernando Po, Congo, South Africa, Zimbabwe, Egypt and Ethiopia.[18]

iii. The African American Pentecostal engagement with Africa at the turn of the century could be illustrated with the Azusa Street connection, 1906-1910, the missionary achievements of United Pentecostal Council of the Assemblies of God (UPCAG with no connection to AOG Springfield), and the activities of female missionaries from the Church of God in Christ in Liberia during the period 1920-1950.

iv. The tensile strength of the black missionary enterprise buckled through decades. Massive re-engagement was renewed in the late 1970s as could be seen by the influence of James Cone on black liberation theology in southern Africa in the late 1970s. It bloomed in the 1980s.

Gyraud Wilmore explains the withdrawal:

> But with the struggle against virtual genocide in an era of racial hatred and violence at home, together with the distractions of the First World War and Great Depression, black church support of missions gradually declined and much was left in disarray that had been so auspiciously begun during the last quarter of the nineteenth century.[19]

Curtis J.Evans points more clearly to assimilation politics. Within the internal adjustment processes in the face of American culture wars, the process of racial identification gyrated: the 'negro' became the beautiful 'black' and finally an African American with identifiable roots. The quest to reconnect with mother Africa blossomed again with the dominant imagery of Joseph's fate in the Bible. As Bishop Charles Blake of COGIC, West Angeles, put it:

> From my teenage years, I have loved Africa, and I have sought to connect with my African heritage. I was blessed to begin visiting Africa in the 1980s and have done so annually since that time. In 1998, Rev Eugene Rivers and his congregation in Boston submitted to my Episcopal oversight. His activist aspirations to mitigate suffering in Africa were contagious. I joined him in founding the Pan African Charismatic Evangelical Congress in the year 2000... addressing the HIV/AIDS pandemic...We provide financial support, supplies and equipments, best practices consultation, and we employ a comprehensive approach to orphan care, incorporating principles developed by UNICEF and UNAIDS...We cannot allow 40 million children in Africa to live, suffer and die without all the help we can give them. If not us, who? If not now, when? If not there, where?

He argued that the motivation for promoting a broad scale African American awareness of plight of Africa and for the mobilization of a movement as intense and comprehensive as the civil rights movement was because

> Blacks were also sold into slavery, many times by our brothers in Africa. Like Joseph, our forefathers endured many trials, much humiliations and suffering. But Joseph held to his dreams... Through a series of supernatural and providential events Joseph was blessed by God to become the vice-president of Egypt. We through a series of phenomenal and supernatural events have by God's grace come to success and power in this land of our captivity...Joseph realized that this blessed promotion had taken place so that he could fulfill his God-given destiny of reaching back to those same brothers who sold him into slavery and save them from starvation and death.[20]

The new missionaries represented themselves as Black Joseph. In a similar vein, Rev LaVerne Hanes Stevens formed the *Joseph Project* in Tyrone Georgia after an emotional visit to Ghana in 2001.[21] The project promotes group visits by churches to different parts of Africa, especially West Africa. The visits are like therapeutic corporate ministries of sustaining, healing and reconciling. Many hope to reconcile with the progenies of those who sold slaves and thereby restore dignity. Each rhetorical image was loaded with the ambivalent relationship to the motherland. Scholarship leaned into the winds. From 1982 a number of studies recaptured the story of the intense period of black missionary enterprise in Africa. As Sylvia Jacobs explained the attraction,

Afro-Americans' historical identification with the continent of Africa is increasingly being seen as one aspect of their survival in the United States. Moreover, their responses to the events occurring on the continent demonstrate a continuing interest in the fate of the homeland. Recently, black Americans and Africans have come to accept the fact that their lives and histories have been intricately linked. Thus, we see a reaffirmation of this kinship bond by Afro-Americans and a concern for a rediscovery of their deep ties to Africa. [22]

Typology of Contemporary African American Engagement of Africa

What is the character of contemporary African American engagement? There are eight identifiable patterns of contemporary African American engagement of Africa:

i. Old denominations such as COGIC, AOG, AMEC, AME Zion, have retained missionary presence. Some, as COGIC, claim a measure of growth mostly in southern and central Africa. But the charismatic landscape has changed significantly in Africa.

ii. Some African American mega ministries have opened branches in Africa, for instance, T.D. Jake's Potter House.

iii. Others invite African pastors to international retreats and pulpit exchanges. The magazine *Charisma* contains many spread pages that advertise conferences and that show the African American pastors who invite Africans to minister.

iv. Many super evangelists such as Juanita Bynum undertake evangelistic crusades in Africa that draw large crowds.

v. Others, such as Bishop W.R. Portee of Southside Christian Palace Church, Los Angeles, California, combine huge evangelistic crusades with poverty alleviation projects. His wife uses the Wailing Wall organization as a mode of access to womenfolk. He testifies that God told him about the importance of Africa in the end times and especially Nigeria. This resonates with the type of prophecies given by Intercessors for Africa, Nigeria prayer House. Portee has, therefore, invested millions of dollars on evangelistic electronic equipments and buses for large crusades and rural evangelism. He has teamed up with some Nigerian bishops whom he ordained to do "apostolic visitations" and crusades in southwestern Nigeria. He appears regularly on TV One (Chicago) preaching and canvassing for contributions.

vi. A number of the Black Joseph projects function as NGOs, sourcing funds from government and the public. This is exemplified by Bishop Blake's *Save Africa's* Children *Fund/Pan African Children's Fund*. This may hinder the capacity to speak prophetically about the government's foreign policy in Africa. African compatriots learn from these how to cuddle towards politicians for patronage. Internally, such projects compete virulently. Bishop Blake said that he was saddened by the negative effects of rivalry. In his address to the Interfaith Summit (quoted earlier), he admonished:

> I believe that it was John Maxwell who said, it takes teamwork to make a dream work. We must respect the actualities and potentials of every participant. We must work together to maximize our collective impact. We are much better working together with respect, than we are apart.

A sub-variety comprises of churches like Apostolic Church, Chicago, led by Bishop Brazier that does not engage directly with

African churches but gives hundreds of thousands of dollars yearly to NGOs like World Vision and other trusted agencies operating in South Africa and Kenya.

vii. Many African American churches organize visits to Africa. They come bearing gifts, sponsoring small projects or with a team of medical professionals. Some are focused, learning and sharing short-term missions such as led by Dr J. Wright of TUCC, Chicago. Some work with local churches and empower them to perform better. But others are safari missionary excursions that run the risk of functioning without adequate knowledge of the mission field resulting in wrong strategies and failed endeavors.[23] The missionary should learn, take from the people and give something to the people in a dialogical manner and without the rescuer mentality. Philanthropy has hidden paternalistic traps. Quite often rural communities have benefited from these interactions.

viii. Many African American churches engage in leadership development whereby they network with African pastors, grant them academic degrees and ordain them as bishops under the American jurisdiction. Some create Houses of Bishops empowered to ordain bishops in various African nations.

In conclusion, *Osofo* Jeremiah Wright neither emphasizes the return of the exiles rhetoric in the Ethiopianism movement nor the Joseph imagery of the post-1980 African American engagement of Africa. He endeavors to strike a balance between spiritual connection and intellectual curiosity. He puts the foot on learning, reconnecting, researching and sharing. He emphasizes his intent to touch individuals and provide help without fanfare and rhetoric. Above all, he strives to expose a middle class black congregation to its rich cultural heritage that has been maligned through the centuries. His holistic understanding of mission needs to be emphasized: first, it is characterized by the quality of being, saying and doing in community and for community of black folks. Second, it starts by building and nurturing a *koinonia* through worship and Bible study, teaching and preaching so that it embodies the presence of the reign of God in community. Third, from the black community at home it flows to all black people in Africa and in diaspora responding to the challenges of global issues of social justice and transforming social despair with hope. He perceives mission as a reciprocal activity between Africa and African diasporic communities. Finally, he perceives education as a powerful tool of witnessing and proclaiming human liberation. For these, I beat the big drum for a brave warrior and hunter who has saved many communities from the ravages of the bush pigs. I beat the big drum for *Nii Afotey Oblum II, the Noyaa Mantse of Katamanso.*

Notes

1. Waibinte Wariboko, *Ruined by Race: Afro-Caribbean Missionaries and the Evangelization of Southern Nigeria, 1895-1925* (Trenton, NJ: Africa World Press, 2007); J.H. Kopytoff, *A Preface to Modern Nigeria: The Sierra- Leonians in Yorubaland, 1830-1890* (Madison, WI: University of Wisconsin Press, 1965).

2. Glen Usry and Craig S. Keener, *Black Man's Religion: Can Christianity Be Afrocentric?* (Downers grove, IL: IVP Academic, 1996).

3. TUCC, File: Africa Ministry.

4. Ibid.

5. Bernard Makhosezwe Magubane, *The Ties That Bind: African-American Consciousness of Africa (*Trenton, NJ: Africa World Press, 1987) and George M. Fredrickson, *Black Liberation: A Comparative History of Black Ideologies in the United States and South Africa* (New York: OUP, 1995) trace the connections.

6. TUCC, File: Africa Ministry, dated Rio de Janeiro, December, 14th, 2004.

7. See, Carter G. Woodson, *The Mis-Education of the Negro* (Washington, DC, 1933); TUCC: Taped Interview with Rev Dr Jeremiah Wright, January 7th, 2008.

8. Dinesh D'Souza's polemic *Illiberal Education* (New York, 1991), Allan Bloom's *Closing of the American Mind* (New York, 1987), Robert Hughes, *Culture of Complaint* (New York, 1993), Mary Lefkowitz, *Not Out of Africa* (New York, 1996) and Stephen Howe, *Afrocentrism: Mythical Pasts, and Imagined Homes* (London: Verso, 1998).

9. William H. Council, *Lamp of Wisdom* (Nashville, TN, 1898), 5.

10. J. Wright, *African Who Shaped Our Faith.* (Chicago: Urban Ministries, 1995).

11. *ibid.*, 210-211.

12. Colin Kidd, *The Forging of Races, Race and Scripture in the Protestant Atlantic World, 1600-2000* (Cambridge University Press, 2006).

13. See map 5 and Rodney S. Sadler, "The Place and Role of Africa and African Imagery in the Bible" In Brian G. Blount *et als* eds., *True to Our Native Land: African American New Testament Commentary* (Minneapolis, MN: Fortress, 2007:23-30; Ogbu U Kalu, *African Christianity: An African Story.* (Trenton, NJ., Africa World Press, 2007); E.M. Yamauchi, *Africa and the Bible (*Grand Rapids, MI: Baker Academics, 2004).

14. Keith Burton, *The Blessing of Africa: The Bible and African Christianity* (Downers Grove, IL: IVP, 2006); David M. Goldberg's *The Curse of Ham: Race and Slavery in Early Judaism, Christianity and Islam* (Princeton University Press, 2006).

15. Cornel West and Eddie S. Glaude (eds) *African American Religious Thought: An Anthology* (Loiusville, Ky: Westminster John Knox Press, 2003), xx.

16. On the debate, see, Albert Robeateau, "The Death of the Gods", *ibid.*, 239-284; Theophus H. Smith, "Exodus" *ibid.*, 301-337; Joseph R. Coan, "Redemption of Africa: The vital impulse of Black American Overseas Missionaries", *Journal of the Interdenominational Theological Center*, 1, 2 (Spring 1974):27-37.

17. Lamin Sanneh, *Abolitionists Abroad* (Harvard University Press, 1999).

18. See details in Ogbu U Kalu, "Ethiopianism in African Christianity" *Christianity in Africa: An African Story* ed Ogbu U Kalu (Trenton, NJ: Africa World Press, 2007), chapter 10;William E. Phipps, *William Sheppard: African American Livingstone* (Louisville, Ky, Geneva Press, 2002); P. Kennedy, *Black Livingstone: A True Tale of Adventure in the 19th Century Congo* (New York, Viking, 2002).

19. Gyraud S. Wilmore, "Black Americans I Mission: Setting the Records Straight", *International Bulletin of Missionary Research*, 10, 3 (July, 1986), 100; Curtis J. Evans, "Urbanization and the End of Black churches in the Modern World." *Church History*, 76, 4 (December, 2007):799-822.

20. Bishop Charles E. Blake, Sr, "Address to Faith based Solutions to Social Issues: Interfaith Summit on Africa", 19th July, 2006. See enclosure in *From Faith to Action: A Resource for Faith-Based Groups*(Santa Cruz, CA: Firelight Foundation, 2006).

21. Her story is told in *Charisma* July 2007, 23.

22. Sylvia Jacobs, ed. *Black Americans and the Missionary Movement in Africa* (Westport, Conn., Greenwood Press, 1982), xi; see bibliographical essay, pp.229-237; W.L Williams, *Black Americans and the Evangelization of Africa, 1877-1900* Madison, University of Wisconsin Press, 1982).

23. This came out strongly during my interview in Accra in June 2007 with Bishop Victor L. Powell and a team from Rhema Word International Ministries, Albany, Georgia.

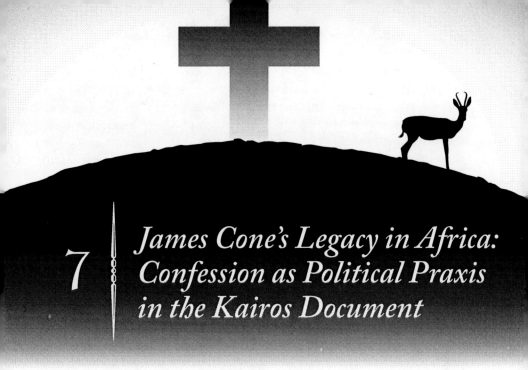

7 | James Cone's Legacy in Africa: Confession as Political Praxis in the Kairos Document

Introduction:
The Prophet, The Watchman and The Madman

This reflection sets out to achieve three goals: the key is to show the legacy of James Cone from a global perspective, specifically his contributions to the development of African theology. The second is the irony that Cone was influenced by Karl Barth's Barmen declaration in his response to the outrage against blacks in the United States in the violent late 1960s. This dimension has escaped scholarly attention. Thirdly, both Cone and the Barmen declaration influenced South African theologians who scripted the Kairos Document. Each party contextualized the use of the strategy; but for all, confession served as a form of political praxis.

In the ministry of the church, it is understood that there are many ways of expressing the core of the gospel and sharing its resources with people. Simply, one may preach or proclaim it from the roof-top; teach its cardinal principles or witness to others about its salvific power. The Greek words are rich and specific about each variety of expression. Confessions resemble the witness act and challenge those who say that they belong to Christ to live like him. From this perspective, a confession is what Christians should do at all times; all life is confession and it is one of the marks of a church. There is a mandate to testify to the faith once delivered to the saints in and out of season. Yet there are moments when the people of God in a place declare about the quality and character of their lifestyle. It is said that the tiger does not sing about its tigritude but in Christian pilgrimage, the pilgrims are often forced to blow their trumpets and declare their identity rather loudly not because the trumpets may rust from disuse but to avoid mistaken identity and to arouse those who are at ease in Zion. This process draws from the prophetic tradition that goes beyond prediction of time- space events to discerning the interior realities of manifest events. It is like looking into the seeds of the present time to say which seed will grow and which will not; or, with a change of imagery, discerning what is *going on* beneath what is *happening*. The prophetic capacity is a gift as the Holy Spirit empowers and opens the eyes of God's servants to see beneath events. The prophet could go further and become a watchman, perched on the security tower of a community to warn them of the approach and devices (stratagems or wiles) of the enemy. The prophet both tells the people about the mind of God and warns of impending dangers. The tasks are performed with no concern for personal physical risk because of a compelling mandate, a fire in the bones, to ensure that no one is lost because the person was not warned. If the people heard but chose to ignore a warning, God will excuse the responsibility of the watchman. Like a courier, the prophet speaks God's word to the people and the people's concerns to God. The tradition combines the tasks of prophesying, keeping the daily watch, and interceding under the power of the Holy Spirit.

Throughout the story of Christianity, there have been moments when the leaders have woken to their prophetic and watchman roles especially when boars raid the vineyard or political rulers, as madmen, seize the priest's role and wield the sacred rod in the temple. In such moments of crisis, leaders invoke God to ensure that the legitimate rod should bud. But the problem is hardly that simple precisely because the boundaries of the sacred roles of princes have been contested through time with biblical authority lined up behind both sides of the fence.

The churches in Germany witnessed such a crisis moment in1933/4 when the Weimar Republic collapsed under the weight of military defeat, the disease of the democratic liberalism and the resurgence of National Socialism. The nature of the challenge must be spelled out clearly precisely because it was not about the freedom of worship as many foreigners concluded in their efforts to support the beleaguered churches of Germany. During a visit to Britain, Karl Barth strained to correct the impression and specify the type of action that could aid the brethren in Germany:

> The fight is not about the freedom, but about the necessary bondage of the conscience; and not about the freedom, but about the substance of the church, ie. about the preservation, rediscovery and authentication of the true Christian faith. (it. Clements, 1986: 15-24)

He insisted that German Christians did not require material aid or protest letters addressed to the state; rather, their urgent need was for Christians in foreign lands to join them in affirming a common confession in the midst of the intervention of the German Reich to repackage Christianity. The Anglo-Saxon audience must have been puzzled. How can a confession adequately serve as a tool of protest?

The Watchman and the People: Confession as Being, Doing and Saying

Christians have used different types of confessions in expressing beliefs and rituals such as the baptismal, doxological, confession of guilt and drawing the boundaries of doctrinal belief. Most people may be more familiar with the doctrinal forms used in settling disputes about matters of belief. These became increasingly familiar in the intra-mural warfare within the scions of the Reformation. However, *situational confessions* are slightly different and serve as instruments for crisis moments; as a re-definition of the relation between the Christian confession and political reality; a composite image of the *being, saying and doing* of the body of Christ in such times. They speak to localized crisis situations and, therefore, betray four characteristics: they react and respond to a situation or context; they are embedded in a specific ecclesial structure; advocate a certain activity, and boldly distinguish between the legitimate and illegitimate forces operating underneath manifest events.

In the Barmen Declaration of 1934, a synod of some German Evangelical Churches met to react to the dangerous secular and ecclesial contexts in which many evangelical churches, mission boards, academy, prominent theologians and missiologists supported the National Socialist cause; used biblical and theological resources to legitimize the regime; supported the re-organization of the church structures; aided the state creation of a Reich church (*Reichskirche*) with a bishop; tolerated the Aryan clause and anti-Semitist diatribe of the regime; and aligned missionary policies of *volkschirche* with a tribalist ideology based on blood, soil, racial purity and national destiny. The Lutheran mission of Neuendettelsau, Bavaria, for instance, was so deeply 'Nazified' that they made their mission candidates to join the Brown Shirts. There was a widespread conviction within the missionary bodies that Nazism would aid missions to achieve their goals, and the ideology would reunite mission with churches, an idea that the doyen of European missiology, Gustav Warneck harped upon. The anti-liberal and anti-communist invectives equally appealed. The nature of this collusion became more apparent when in 1993 Werner Ustorf discovered the Minute Books of the Council and Federation of German Protestant Missions, 1924-1949. The secretary, Walter Freytag (1899-1959) had left them with his personal secretary, Frau Ursula Ebert, with instructions to keep them private.(Ustorf, 1997: 63-82)

Robert P. Ericksen has tried to show how incredibly a welter of respect-able intellectuals such as Gerhard Kittel, Paul Althaus and Emmanuel Hirsch provided the ideological prop for Hitler whom he describes as "a political answer to a very difficult question". (1985) Most intriguing in this trio was Paul Althaus who lacked the opportunism of Kittel and the acerbic character of Hirsch. Regarded as the gentleman intellectual by col-leagues, he nevertheless turned his immense resources to promote National Socialism. His reading of the background to the groundswell support for Hitler deserves attention.

> As a Christian church, we bestow no political card. But in knowledge of the mandate of the state, we may express our thanks to God and our joyful preparedness when we see a state which after a time of depletion and paralysis has broken through to a new knowledge of sovereign authority, of service to the life of the volk, of responsibility for freedom, legitimacy, and justice of volkisch existence. We may express our thankful-ness and joyful readiness for that which manifests a will for the genuine brotherhood of blood brothers in our new order of the volk...We Christians know ourselves bound by God's will to the promotion of National Socialism, so that all members and ranks of the volk will be ready for service and sacrifice to one another. (cit. Ericksen, 1985: 86)

The collusion of the German churches with the socialist forces started shortly before Hitler came to power when The Faith Movement of German Christians organized and brewed a theology in which the gospel was interpreted with a lens inscribed with a racially construed manifest destiny. In July 1933, Hitler could easily sign an order based on an agree-ment with the leaders of the regional churches to create a national German Protestant Church. Thus, the harmonization of throne and altar, father-land and church, gospel and patriotism created both a crisis moment and embedded an ecclesial structure that violated the inner core of the presence of the kingdom of God in the communities.

Some leaders responded: Martin Niemoller founded the Pastors' Emergency League in September and mobilized the Confessional Synod of the German Evangelical Church at Barmen, May 29-31, 1934, to respond and advocate a specific activity in rebuttal and at a great risk. It was not a matter of religious freedom precisely because the churches were not restrained from worshipping. Much to the contrary, it is reported that the Baptists told their British counterpart that they had never been freer as under the Reich; the Free Church communities welcomed Hitler's accession to power as guaranteeing security and privileges and the Vatican signed a concordat with the Nazis. Thus, the situational confession at Barmen was designed to respond to challenges from two directions; externally, from the state and more cogently from the Christian communities that allowed nationalist allegiance to contest their Christian commitment. The core concern was how a church responds in a crisis moment when the dominant culture essays to overawe the gospel's affirmations and destroy the unity of the Christian community. The protest group that converged at Barmen rejected the collusion with the state. It sought to declare that certain modes of action and attitudes were incompatible and irreconcilable with Christian convictions. Dismayed that believers were on both sides of the conflict, it sought to focus on an action that would recreate the unity of faith rather than the union of the churches; give the churches a definite profile; and a clear, prophetic voice "in their decisions in church politics" (art.6).

The strategy is germane. First, Barmen conferees did not contest the creation of a national church but claimed to be the church. It imaged the contemporary union church as illegitimate, based on a false understanding of the source, role and dynamics of church governance. Second, they intentionally seized the high ground from which to make the voice of the church heard; that high ground was the freedom and power of the word. They shared Bonhoeffer's insistence in his lecture, "Protestantism Without Reformation" that *the essential freedom of the church is not a gift of the world to the church, but the freedom of the Word of God itself to gain a hearing.*" (In Robertson, 1965: 104) As article six of Bremen Declaration intoned, "the word of God is not fettered." It has its own power and freedom and life span that extends into the eschaton. Third, they focused on the affirmation of the inner core of the Christian faith as the location of the identity of God's people. The process or action in proclaiming these truths (*doing* and *saying*) reinforces *being*. Thus, they employed the model of a doctrinal confession in six theses. Fourth, they avoided a direct confrontation with the state but focused on the church's response to the matters of identity, task and life-style, source of authority and 'the bounds of either sword', as John Milton put it. Defensive drivers are usually advised to avoid the glare of oncoming vehicles and focus on the centerline of the road. This is what the leaders at Bremen did.

Talkin' and Testifyin': Barmen, Cone and Black Power

They insisted that their goal was to explain the current situation. This declaration or explanation combined the prophet's role to stand on the word of God and stubbornly declare it, with the watchman's role to warn against obvious dangers of cankerworms in the body of Christ. As Jeremiah Wright's contribution on "underground theology' in *Black Faith and Public Talk* put the matter, it brings to the surface the power of a hidden "underground theology" that pulsates beneath the hard surface of the institutional structure. (Hopkins, 1999: 96-102) Thus, the common style in all the six theses would begin with a biblical passage; followed by a thesis or appropriation of the text; and a counterpoint that serves as anti-thesis or exposure of an incipient false teaching. The structure placed theology at the center of political ethics and pursued an ecumenical response or common confession amidst corrosive circumstances. Intriguingly, it employed a prescriptive ethical norm that was Biblical, unabashedly Christo-centric and quite typical of Karl Barth who sole-authored the declaration. However, commentators have rooted some of the theses into the soil of earlier confessions such as the Heidelberg Catechism, Second Helvetic Confession, Dusseldorf Theses (1934) and Ten Theses of Bern of 1528. He did not ignore the heritage of the community but built upon it and upon the uniqueness of Christ. (Dowey, 1968: 255-6)

There is a sense in my madness that starts a reflection on Professor James Cone's legacy in Africa from such a far distance. On a closer look the distance is not that far because (i) the intention here is to examine the impact of Professor Cone's prophetic theological ethics, especially how he influenced the rise of black liberation theology in South Africa and the Kairos Document. (ii) It is argued that Professor Cone was much enamored with Barth's theology of the word: proclaimed, written and revealed, the role that Barth assigned to the church as a bulwark against the authoritarian and repressive state, and his trenchant Christology. He selected from him and other white theologians to make his point. As he himself confessed,

> I am embarrassed by the extent of my captivation by white concepts. And I realize that I am still partly enslaved by them.

The struggle to overcome this enslavement has been a constant struggle in my intellectual development. That is why I will always indebted to my black colleagues for assisting me in this endeavor. (Cone, 2004: 77)

(iii) Black Consciousness Theology in South Africa used the Barmen confessional strategy as a model of political praxis after the scorching Soweto crisis. While the format was Barthian, the content was, would you say Conish? This is because the condition in South Africa in 1986 was similar to the conditions in the United States in 1968.

People have responded to Cone's political theology in various ways. His book, *My Soul Looks Back* is a touching response that shows that he is always prepared to be challenged, to learn and to pursue the goal with an intense passion. He advocates the highest level of academic rigor and dialogue for black scholarship. He insists that the black church must become the agent for liberating the black poor; therefore, it is vulnerable to criticisms from its theologians; and the theologians must equally be open to the mutual criticisms from the black church because

> Black theology must be a church discipline, true to itself only when validated in the context of people struggling for the freedom of the oppressed. Its chief task is to help the church to be faithful to the task of preaching and living the liberating gospel of Jesus Christ in the world today. (Cone, 2004: 77)

Doing black theology is not an academic enterprise but is a matter of life and death. Professor Cone's prophetic ministry was born in the summer heat of untoward events, and has retained the fiery mark of urgency, a task for the Gideon Company, a process that is always re-tooling, constantly searching for institutional and human agencies that could carry the task to its fulfillment. As Cornel West said in his contribution to *Black Faith and Public Talk*, one should consider Cone's cry from the heart in the context of

> the corpses of young black folk...(and) 329 uprisings in 257 cities between 1964-1969. After 212 uprisings on the night that the bullets went through the precious body of Martin Luther King Jnr., America can no longer deny the fact that either it comes to terms with the vicious legacy of white supremacy, or the curtain will fall on the precious experiment in democracy called America. (Hopkins, 1999: 12-13)

Like Karl Barth's endeavor in the Barmen Declaration, it was a brand of crisis theology. Black theology was the theological arm to black power seeking to relate the black struggle for freedom to the biblical claim regarding the justice of God. Black power itself was the political challenge to the non-violence preached by Martin Luther King. It was built on the Bible as the core and the Christocentric-driven theology nicknamed, "Jesusology," that captured black Christian imagination and flowed profusely into preaching understood as the work of the Spirit.(Cone, 2004: 81) Blackness was the context, the reason for the oppression by whites, and the question is whether theology could serve as a tool of liberation of the black person from white oppression.

Cone met the ethical challenge by rejecting white theology as biased tribal reading of the Bible and reflection, and reaffirming a certain understanding of God: God's *love* must be understood from the perspective of His partiality and love for the *poor*. God manifested His divine *freedom* by creating human beings in His own image(*imago Dei*). God demonstrated His *justice, righteousness*, and *salvation* by entering into the depths of humanity's pain and oppression to liberate them from demonic forces or structures of racism and forces of domination. His *kingdom* stands for poor people's hope and empowers them to organize and achieve their liberation in human history. The *cross* and *resurrection* become channels of liberation from the material bondage crafted by principalities and powers. *Heaven* is the ultimate destination of a new beginning without an end, a place of rest after a well-fought fight here on earth.

Within this perspective, *reconciliation* could only be achieved by firstly achieving the freedom of the poor. The victims set the conditions. Perhaps, the oppressors might change and become reconciled to oppressed blacks. Before the white man removes his boot from the face of the fallen black person, there could be no meaningful discussion about reconciliation. As Dwight Hopkins summarized the matter in his *Introducing Black Theology of Liberation*, the foundations of black theology between 1966-1980 were: slave religion, reinterpretation of the Bible, the broad political and cultural currents within the civil rights and black power movements, a new method of doing theology, and conversations with and insights from the decolonization experiences of black peoples and movements in the southern hemisphere. (1999) This stark summary has deliberately highlighted the key aspects of Cone's theology that attracted Africans. Theology is not heuristic but the reflections by human beings about the relationship of God to human beings and the world of nature. It's God-talk in human situations.

Black Man, You Are On Your Own!: Cone and Kairos Document in Africa

James Cone had a long empowering conversation with African and Third World Theologians in Accra in December, 1977. It was a very defining encounter in the refining of his theology. He faced the difficult assertion by some African theologians that black theology was different from African theology. He faced the double consciousness of having African and American roots, and the universal claim of common faith in Christ. He was confronted by the insistence by some as Professor John Mbiti that African theology must emerge from the written, oral and symbolic production of the people of God. The debate was somewhat misunderstood and it should be useful to summarize Mbiti's theological positions.

John Mbiti, a Kenyan scholar, pioneered the articulation of African Theology. In his doctoral dissertation at Cambridge University in 1963, he used the concept of eschatology to expose the underlying task of African theology. He distinguished between the layers of what the New Testament taught, what missionaries conveyed to the Akamba people, how the Kikamba conceptualized life after death in their indigenous worldview, and, therefore, how they decoded missionary teachings, by appropriating some elements and reconfiguring these through the prism of their worldview. In culture contacts, despite the efforts by hegemonic forces to implant certain doctrines, hearers appropriate the gospel from their worldviews. The gospel is an eternal gift of God but Christianity is an indigenized structure. The bearers brought the gospel repackaged with western culture and enlightenment worldview. They privileged literacy, and communicated in various European vernaculars to people who emphasized orality, narrative theology, maximum participation in liturgy, inclusion of visions, dreams, and a relationship between body and mind manifested through healing and prayer. The question is: what did the hearers hear and say about the relationship of God to human beings and the world of nature? This is theology or God-talk.

Mbiti refused to castigate missionaries while rejecting the denigration of indigenous religions and cultures. He argued that the sources of doing theology comprise of the Bible as the source of divine revelation, the indigenous worldviews, religions, cultures, oral reflections by the people of God, the existential forces in their environments, the heritage of Christian traditions and the presence of other religious faiths. African Christianity results from the encounter of the gospel with these factors. Crucial is Mbiti's conclusion that African religions and cultures embody a preparation for the gospel because Christ is in every culture and judges all cultures. African Christianity is a continuum with dimensions of African religions such as the celebration of life and corporate sense of existence. God is one and has been known and worshipped in various ways by African peoples before the missionaries arrived. This explains the wide areas of resonance between African and Biblical worldviews: a charismatic perception of reality; three dimensional perception of space; the dynamic relations of "here and now" to the "not yet" period; the power in the blood, name, and words; the reality of miracles and supernatural interventions in daily lives. All these are and many more serve as pathways for inculturation. However, there are differences. The African perceives time as an event (*kairos*); life flows in a cyclical fashion from birth through death to reincarnation. The New Testament perceives time as abstract (*kronos*) that moves in a linear fashion from the past through the present to the future. Mbiti's conception of the future in African thought has elicited much debate. The African's fascination with the Bible indicates a cultural appreciation of the similar contents of its world. The high level of cultural resonance explains the Hamitic theories of origin found among many Bantoid-speaking African people. Some claim to be the lost tribe of Israel!

Mbiti, therefore, studied African religions and cultures (focusing on shared elements), concepts of God, prayers, love and marriage and the use of the Bible. Combined with his vernacular poems and anthropological studies, he rehabilitated Africa's rich cultural heritage and religious consciousness, and brought them into Christian theology, and thereby removed the veil of strangeness of the gospel among African communities. He showed that prayers, libations, sacrifices, dance music, rites of passage, festivals were means of weaving covenants with the Supreme Being, spirits and ancestors and to ward off evil. He showed how these could be redirected towards God in a conversation process. The task of communication was the church's major task. A key instrument is the translation of the Bible into the vernacular. Vernacularization removes the slur from indigenous cultures. It means that God is not partial to any race of people. Indeed, Africans have tended to emphasize the pneumatic resources of the gospel because of their charismatic worldview. Mbiti, therefore, paid attention to the creative liturgy and theology of African Indigenous churches. Employing a phenomenological approach, he sidesteps the typologies developed by anthropologists.

Mibiti recognized that the core of gospel-culture encounter is the role of Christ. Other scholars canvassed the notion of Christ as ancestor. Mbiti argued that Christ answers the search for meaning and wholeness in every culture including African religious life. Christ completes the sacralization of the whole of life that removes the veil between the sacred and the profane. In Africa, the human world is a mirror of the spirit world. He is the crowning completion of all quests, the brilliance of the flickering light in world religions. Other scholars have tried to image the face of Jesus in Africa as a chief, king, ancestor and guest. These imageries fail to capture the full Jesus. Mbiti focused on Christ's meaning and lordship over life, reconciling the whole of creation to God. He has worked on eco-theology in Africa.

Mbiti's theology made an enormous impact in African academy and church life. He interpreted Africa to the universal church and academy. As an evangelical Anglican priest, his concern was the communication of the Bible in Africa. However, he lacked a strong political theology as espoused by the liberation theologians. This left the impression, as John Parratt has harped upon, that there are two genres of African theology, the cultural and political. (Parratt, 1995: 1-24)

Cone dealt with the contextualization problem by reclaiming his African origins. He balanced the cultural and political concerns of theology and concluded that "there is some sense in which the black world is one," with "inextricably bound" future and common historical option. Economic and political domination, racism, oppression compel solidarity and recovery of our history to achieve liberation. He refused to abandon the social context of theology. As he argued,

> without the indigenization of theology, liberation theology's claim to be derived from and accountable to oppressed peoples is a farce. Indigenization opens the door for the people's creative participation in the interpretation of the Gospel for their life situation. But indigenization without liberation limits a given theological expression to the particularity of its cultural context. It fails to recognize the universal dimension of the gospel and the global context of theology. (Appiah-Kubi and Torres, 1979: 178, 184)

Cone elicited much support from an avalanche of African theologians. It must be asserted that it was from his influence *rather than from Latin America* that liberation theology gained enormous reputation in Africa. His impact was particularly felt in Southern Africa because, when other regions of the continent were hoisting their new flags, learning new national anthems, and celebrating political independence, repressive regimes bared their fangs in the southern region. In West Africa, for instance, the major theological task was the search for an indigenous theology relevant to African culture. But in South Africa, Cone's first publications created a political wave and reanimated a desultory political terrain. It reshaped the political discourse because the harsh state reaction against protests groups after Shaperville scorched the political terrain. The old brigade of African freedom advocates were imprisoned, exiled or driven underground.

Ironically, the establishment of black universities and homelands backfired as a new band of urban, educated detribalized students came to the fore. They rejected the homelands and the repressive apartheid regime, and found the new theology as a clear articulation of their anger and hopes. These young people were mostly brought up in black townships as Soweto, Umlazi, New Brighton and Langa. They had studied at the recently founded black ethnic universities of Zululand, the North, Durban-Westville, Western Cape and Fort Hare. Across denominational and ethnic divides, they started debates on black theology, and reinvented the sedate organizations such as the University Christian Movement and the Students' Christian Movement into radical black activist groups. The new wine broke the old wine skin and shredded the students' unions. New leadership emerged such as Steve Biko. This is briefly the background of the Black Consciousness Movement. Their battle cry was simply put: *black man, you are on your own!* They lost the innocence that the white man could do anything good for the black man. They struggled and debated on how best to appropriate the insight to fit their condition, and ground the new theology into the primal ethical values as kinship, community, identity, and *ubuntu*. When they published the *Essays in Black Theology* in 1971, the government heard the message loud and clear and banned the book and exiled Basil Moore, the secretary of UMC. (Moore, 1973) Allan Boesak (who took copious notes at the Accra conference when Cone and Mbiti debated the relationship between black and African theologies) explained in *Farewell to Innocence* that for these young men,

> *Black Consciousness* may be described as the awareness of black people that their humanity is constituted by their blackness. It means that black people are no longer ashamed that they are black, that they have a black history and a black culture distinct from the history and culture of white people. It means that blacks are determined to be judged no longer by, and to adhere no longer to white values. It is an attitude, a way of life. Viewed thus, Black Consciousness is an integral part of Black Power. But *Black Power* is also a clear critique of and a force of fundamental change in systems and patterns in society which oppress or which give rise to the oppression of black people. *Black theology* is the reflection of black Christians on the situation in which they live and on their struggle for liberation. (Boesak, 1977: 1)

The farewell message, like the separation period in a ritual of pass[...] deliberately quoted *in extenso* to demonstrate the impact of Cone'[...] on the young people as they bade farewell to innocence. Their position was not derivative; rather, they deeply decoded what their black brother from across the great lake said. Indeed, Boesak adopted the idea from Rollo May's concept of pseudo- innocence that keeps a black person from realizing the power of bondage by racist structures on one's whole being. He argued that he was brought up within a Dutch Reformed tradition in which they swore by Abram Kuyper. Then he gained a new consciousness of who he really is. He realized that he lived in a structure governed by "pigmentocracy;" and that the task is both to liberate the gospel from misuse by whites and to address the existential situation. It is a situational theology.

Archbishop Desmond Tutu insisted that liberation theology was not an academic matter because

> it issues out of the crucible of human suffering and anguish. It happens because people cry out, 'Oh God, how long. And of liberation theology is a sense really a theodicy. It seeks to justify God and the ways of God to a downtrodden and perplexed people. (in Appiah-Kubi and Torres, 1979: 163)

He was writing soon after the murder of Steve Biko and acknowledged that the theology was inspired by the experience and spirituals of Americans.(ibid.164) Like Cone, Tutu declared in 1977 that

> we are engaged in something too urgent to wait for the approbation of the West or those who would blindly follow western standards of acceptability and play western games using western rules.

Much to the contrary,

> other theologies are challenged to become more truly incarnational by being concerned for the whole person, body and soul. They are called upon to glory in their inbuilt obsolescence, not to cry out for permanence and a validity that properly belongs only to Gospel of Jesus Christ. (ibid., 168)

Then the calabash of blood broke on their heads as the Soweto riots challenged the renaissance of black political hopes. A feverish response followed as a number of Christians worked together through several months to declare the mind of the people of God on the political situation in 1986.

The *Kairos Document* x-rayed the apartheid system that was established in 1948 and became most brutal from the 1960's. Both the Shaperville uprising in 1960 and the Soweto riots in 1986 indicate that the regime faced equally unrelenting challenges. Some Christians under the umbrella of the Southern Africa Council of Churches were moved by the example of the Germans in 1934 to speak prophetically against the antics of the mad rulers and the unfaithfulness of some churches. They were not the whole church because the three branches of the Dutch Reformed churches (NGK, NHK, GK) supported apartheid from similar reasons as the 'German Christians' who supported Hitler. They deployed covenant theology, natural theology, race, blood, soil and the history of the Boers in South Africa. In Pretoria, they constructed a huge monument that inscribed on granite a certain view of history about the suffering people's great, exilic trek to a land that God gave them. The divine duty was to drive away all the inferior races and occupy till Christ returns. The academy especially at Stellenbosch provided the intellectual arsenal for separate development of the races. The cursory proof-texting in their use of the Bible was betrayed in a debate on the Scripture and Apartheid that raged in the pages of the NGK's *Die Kerkbode*. Professor P.V. Pistorius (1907-1972) of the University of Pretoria attacked his colleague, B.J. Marais who in 1948 dared to suggest that there was not a line in the Scriptures to buttress the church's support for apartheid:

> I read: 'Honour your father and mother.' For that reason I practice colour apartheid because the inheritance of my fathers and mothers would disappear in colour mixing. 'You shall not commit murder'. I read, and because I know that colour mixing will lead to the death of our volk and Western civilization here in South Africa, I practise apartheid. (Hofmeyr et als, 2001: 22)

The white Pentecostals accepted it with a strong apolitical theology to the point of using the support of the American Right to legitimate the regime. (Gifford, 1991) When Frank Chikane, a minister of the Apostolic Faith Mission, joined the SAAC in its protests against apartheid, the church defrocked him. The Baptists used a doctrine of the separation of church and state to urge their members away from political engagement. The African Independent Churches encouraged their people to avoid the political terrain like the plague and created ritual havens where the wounds of the system could be healed.(Anderson, 2003) A wider band of Christians such as the Anglicans and Catholics remained ambivalent. John de Gruchy stated the matter rather crisply:

neither the Roman Catholic Church nor the various Lutheran
synods have been in the forefront of the struggle against racism
in South Africa until fairly recently. (1979: 97)

He explained the dilemma of the Catholics as well as the revolt of the black
priests. Only a few Christians opposed the system. Collaboration, withdrawal, ambivalence and opposition fragmented Christian responses to the
state. Thus, South Africa shared similar challenges as Germany; challenges
that emanated from both the state and within the Christian family. They
shared the same dilemma as the black churches in the United States that
frustrated Cone into a severe criticism of the black church until he feared
that the whites might steal the thunder for a desperately heinous activity.

The *Kairos Document* came like an uncomfortable sound of the ram's
horn. It was neither the first confession nor would it be the last but came
at a particular point in the story of apartheid and with a unique style. As an
antecedent, in 1979, the *Broederkrig*, a group of non-white ministers and
evangelists of Dutch Reformed churches, founded in 1974, used a five-
point confession that sounded like a re-harsh of Bremen to bear witness
to the liberating acts of God who stands on the side of the oppressed. As
some articles declared their goal:

> 2. To take seriously the prophetic mission of the church where
> the oppressive structures and laws in Southern Africa are con-
> cerned and furthermore: the priestly mission, where the victims
> of the un-Christian policy and practices of these countries are
> concerned, including the fearful oppressors themselves...3. To
> let the Kingship of Christ triumph over the ideology of apart-
> heid... (see, articles in Vischer, 1982: 20-22)

It made little impact on the public space.

Indeed, John W. de Gruchy has argued that between Cottlesoe
Consultation in 1960 to the Rustenburg National Conference of church
leaders (November, 5-9 1990), many efforts were made to discuss the
moral implications of the legitimization of the apartheid system on the
basis of the Scriptures because internal dissent was slowly brewing: some
church leaders wanted the argument from necessity to replace the biblical
ones while a few dared to swim against the currents by declaring apartheid
as unbiblical. (1991: 21-34) As the Dutch churches retreated from ecumenical endeavors after 1960, internal opposition, however weak sprouted.
Beyers Naude started the Christian Institute that issued *The Message to the
People of South Africa* (1968). The World Council of Churches between
1966-68 took a more radical route to combat racism by supporting the

churches in South Africa that opposed the regime. By 1970's the African Enterprise appeared on the scene with more radical goals. The emergence of liberation theology in the late 1970's inspired many in South Africa and elicited more radical options. Two routes faced the churches, reform or revolution. Thus, the appearance of the Kairos document signaled the rise of younger opposition that was highly critical not only of the NGK and its doctrine of apartheid but the reformist, liberal English-speaking churches and other members of Southern Africa Council of Churches who had been preaching peace, reconciliation and reform. As Allan Boesak intoned during the WCC General Assembly, Vancouver, in the summer of 1983, *there cannot be peace without justice!*

After Soweto crisis, there was a rejection of cheap reconciliation. The stakes were raised as the landscape changed. The black political spectrum shattered: the non-violent ideology of the United Democratic Front (UDC) no longer spoke for many. Equally contested was the universal visions of Z.K. Matthews and Albert Luthuli representing the ANC. More people inclined towards the anti-white position of Robert Sobukwe (one of those arrested in the aftermath of Shaperville) and his Pan African Congress (PAC) as well as the black liberation theology of Steve Biko and his Black Consciousness Movement (BCM) that focused on the violent reaction of Jesus to the oppressors who trafficked at the expense of the poor. It may be argued that Tutu's *sword in the ploughshare policy* and his march to Parliament in 1988 represented Barmen more faithfully even as the spectrum shifted to more revolutionary prescriptions. (Kalu, 2000: 99-100) The similarity between Martin Luther King's position and the violent criticism of the Black Power could not be lost upon the readers.

Thus, while similarities existed with Barmen, many discontinuities are palpable: the Barmen Document was authored by a single person and used a doctrinal confessional style. The Kairos Document was written by a group and signed by a large number of Christians from different churches. They bridged over ethnic consciousness that hampered the efforts of the older generation, and the denominational gullies that missionaries dug. The contents resonated more with Cone's idea than with Marxist purists. It may not have the theological clarity or succinctness of Barmen but it theologized more elaborately and contained a deep social analysis of the state. It used a liberation theological model to engage in a trenchant description and critique of the contemporary regime. Its real title stressed a *"theological comment on the political crisis in South Africa"*. It was a situational confession whose four cardinal aspects were: first, a critique of state theology that misused Paul in its tendency to brand all opposition as communist. The illusion was that South Africa was the bastion of Western democracy against Communism. During the cold war, American foreign policy bankrolled the myth. Second, it attacked the church theology of the ambivalent group that employed middle axiom to preach reconciliation. The document invited them to distinguish between mere quarrels and conflicts in the household of faith from structural injustice.

This required the examination of the concept of justice because an unjust political dispensation deserved a radical response and total dismantling, not reformation. Third, the context recalls the preference for the poor, marginalized and oppressed in the ministry of Jesus. Fourth, it combined a contextual or prophetic theology with searching questions about life in South Africa. It interpreted Scriptures for those conditions in profoundly new ways. Later, Jurgen Moltmann in his *The Way of Jesus* validated the Kairos Document's approach when he argued that the role of Christian political theology was to interpret the dangerous memory of the messianic message of Christ within the conditions of contemporary society in order to free human beings practically from the coercions of society and to prepare the way for the eschatological freedom of the new humanity. (1990: 102)

But in 1986, many white liberals accepted the social analysis of the Kairos Document but dreaded the revolutionary option and its alleged empowerment of the leftists. Violence increased as other geopolitical forces gathered to thwart the confidence of the apartheid state. Soon, the pillars of apartheid buckled as more critical voices emerged from university professors who wrote joint appeals to the state. Even the conscience of lay Christians stirred. But it was the black force, roused by the Kairos Document that countered apartheid. Many died at the twilight of victory just as Bonhoeffer. But the interest here is how Cone's prophetic speaking inspired blacks and whites in South Africa who appropriated its resources for their own context and adapted them to suit their own situation.

Some people considered the Kairos Document as a protest that signaled the prophetic, non-violent posture against a violent, mad structure as untenable. They read it as a document that inspired resistance. The *being* and *saying* of the church as defined by the protesters should compel the basis of *doing* a different type of political action that went beyond the ambiguous protests by the English churches. The South African case study shows how Christians all over the world will continue to hear both Cone's theology and the Barmen model of using confession as political praxis. Each context would appropriate its resources in different ways for decision-making in troubled times. This is what contextual method of doing theology is all about.

Bibliography

Anderson, Allan (2003) "Pentecostals and Apartheid in South Africa During Ninety Years, 1908-1998," http: /www.pctii.org/cyberj/Anderson.html.

Appiah-Kubi, Kofi and Sergio Torres eds (1979) *Africa Theology Enroute* (Maryknoll, NY: Orbis, 1979).

Clements, Keith W. (1968) "Bonhoeffer, Bremen and Anglo- Saxon Individualism" *Journal of Theology for Southern Africa(JTSA)*, 54, (March): 15-24.

Cone, James H. (2004) *My Soul Looks Back* (Maryknoll, NY: Orbis).

Dowey, Edward A. (1968) *A Commentary on the Confession of 1967 and An Introduction to the Book of Confessions* (Philadelphia, The Westminster Press).

Ericksen, Robert P. (1985) *Theologies Under Hitler* (Yale University Press).

Flett, John (2003) "From Jerusalem to Oxford: Mission as the Foundation and Goal of Ecumenical Social Thought" *International Bulletin of Missionary Research*, 27, 1: 17-20.

De Gruchy J, W. (1979)*The Church Struggle in South Africa* (Grand Rapids, Eerdmans).

_____ (1995) *Christianity and Democracy* (Cambridge University Press).

_____ (1991) "From Cottesloe to Rustenburg and Beyond", *JTSA*, 74: 21-34.

Gifford, Paul (1991) *The New Crusaders* (London Pluto Press).

Harvey, B. trans. *Guiding Principles of the German Christian Church Movement (National Church Movement) in Thurigen.*

Hofmeyr, J.W. et als eds.(2001)*1948+50 Years: Theology, Apartheid and Church* (University of Pretoria, IMER Publications).

Hopkins, Dwight, (1999) *Introducing black theology of liberation* (Maryknoll, NY: Orbis).

_____ (1999) *Black Faith and Public Talk: critical essays on James H. Cone's Black Theology and Black Power* (Orbis).

Huber, Wolfang (1991) "The Barmen Declaration and the Kairos Document on Relationship Between Confession and Politics", *JTSA*, 75: 48-60.

Kalu, O.U. (2000) *Power, Poverty and Prayer: The Challenges of Poverty and Pluralism in African Christianity, 1960-1996* (Frankfurt, Peter Lang).

_____ (2003) "Remembering South Africa: Kairos Document, Religious Commitment and National Identity" World Mission Institute Workshop, Chicago, April 22nd -23rd.

Moltmann, Jurgen (1990) *The Way of Jesus: Christology in Messianic Dimensions* (London: SCM Press).

Moore, B. (1973) *Black Theology: the South African Voice* (London: C. Hurst).

Parratt, John (1995) *Reinventing Christianity: African Theology* Today (Grand Rapids, Eerdmans).

Robertson, E.H., ed., (1965) *No Rusty Sword* (London, Collins).

Rohls, Jan (1998) *Reformed Confessions: Theology from Zurich to Barmen* (Louisville, Westminster John Knox).

Smith, Graeme (1997) "Be of Good Cheer": Christian Mission Confronts Social Disintegration in the 1937 Oxford Conference" In Lynne Price et als eds *Mission Matters* (Frankfurt, Peter Lang): 49-62.

Ustorf, Werner (1997) "The Documents that Re-appeared: The Minute books of the Council and Federation of German Protestant Missions, 1924-1949" *Mission Matters*: 63-82.

Vischer, Lukas ed. (1982) *Reformed Witness Today: a collection of Confessions and Statements of Faith Issues by Reformed Churches* (Bern: Evangelische Arbeitsstelle Oukumene Schweiz).

The Constitution of the Presbyterian Church (USA): Part 1: Book of Confessions. General Assembly, Louisville, Ky., 1983: 801-828.

Part II

RELIGION, CULTURE, AND SOCIAL ENGAGEMENT

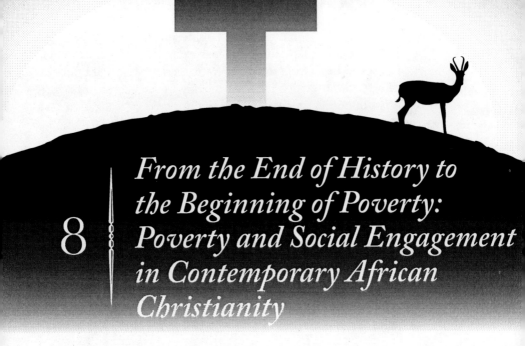

8 From the End of History to the Beginning of Poverty: Poverty and Social Engagement in Contemporary African Christianity

Historiography: After 1989

When Francis Fukuyama declared the end of history in 1989 because of the fall of Communist Russia, he actually surmised the end of virulent ideological contests and the victory of capitalism and liberal democracy. He intoned that the impact of 1989 was not just political but unleashed cultural, technological and economic forces that reshaped the globe; that big business will pacify the clash of cultures; that the world will move together as it builds the bodies through which we can trust each other more; that trust will emanate from shared cultural values and shared interests. He further argued that beyond theories, basic self-interest is the basis of modern economic interdependence; that in a market-dominated world, the primary human interaction is competition, not support and solidarity. He virtually prophesied that the new world order and its asymmetrical power relations will intensify the scourge of poverty among the weaker communities such as Africa. Stronger economies will create an osmotic pull engendering massive emigration or brain drain. At the root of the high level of emigration from Africa are the failures of the new states. The key question is how the trends affected religious groups. Did the impact of globalization enervate the capacity to creatively engage the challenges in the public space? This reflection argues that the after-effects of 1989 could best be understood from the long view of the patterns of Christian engagement of the public space from the era of political independence (in the 1960s) to the end of the millennium. This may explain why the brief public visibility of the churches during the democratization process that followed the second liberation of Africa faded as quickly as the flower under the scorching sun. But one thing was gained, namely, a gradual realization that purely economic approaches to the African dilemma could not suffice. As Vinay Samuel, Executive Director, International Fellowship of Evangelical Mission Theologians, summarized a consultation between the World Bank and the Council of Anglican Provinces of Africa in 2001, the bank has now realized that economy and finance do not hold all the answers and that any viable option must recover the role of the transcendence and the contribution of churches. He also argued that Africa's failure was based on loss of world markets, bad governance and population growth; that the churches have a major part to play in the solution because of size and geographical spread, by the fact that in most developing countries, religious leaders are close to the poor and are among the most trusted representatives. Faith communities offer health services, education and shelter to the vulnerable and spiritual ties are crucial in conflict transformation. The church's presence is crucial by being where the poor are, by bringing dignity to the poor, by bringing local relevance—being there when the "briefcase" NGOs are gone, and by bringing a moral vision. "No moral vision can shape society without a transcendent reference point; people want society to be shaped by a moral vision—not just by economic, social and political constructiveness." [12] The church has among its intangible assets the capacity to imbue the poor with hope, a necessary ingredient in human survival. It has some core competencies, theological resources such as a theology of holistic mission, infrastructure and global network or social capital. Thus, the challenge is to examine the role of African churches in their responses to the African states mired in Africa's pathology. A poet characterized the postcolonial context as "*we on us*" because the process of decolonization or passive revolution left the burden of governance in the hands of indigenous leaders both in church and state.

However, one must hasten to differentiate the process of decolonization in church and state precisely because they took different routes and covered different time frames. The declaration of *uhuru* in the state did not mean that missionaries packed up and left. Much to the contrary, they presumed that they showed greater accountability and moral responsibility towards the indigenes and proved more acceptable than the colonial administrations. A three-pronged attack woke them rudely from the illusion: nationalists attacked from the right flank, indigenizers from the center, and charismatic youths from the left. It could be argued that the decolonization of the church in Africa was not completed until 1975. Thus, the General Assembly of the World Council of Churches in Nairobi in that year was more than symbolic. It was a confirmation of what the Pope said in Uganda a few years earlier that an *African Christianity* had emerged that had an identifiable character. African Christianity had come of age. Thus, the key question would be this: after the whites left the coconut in African hands, what did Africans do with both the gospel (the semen) and Christianity (the shell or institution)? To what extent did they creatively engage the social space or respond to the scourge of poverty that catalyzed legitimacy crises and social instability? The decolonized African Christianity was confronted by the challenges of the environment, consisting of both the vestiges of missionary structures (mental and structural) and the politics of independence as the new states sought to oust the church from the control of education and social welfare services.

The historiographical assumptions must be made clear. African church history in this period explores the ways that Africans experienced the core message of the gospel, appropriated and deployed its resources in responding to the challenges that confronted the communities and how their interventions empowered people who have been made vulnerable by the forces in the new dispensation. Did the churches serve as tools of hope amidst the challenges of state building? It is a different type of history that explores the impact of the gospel rather than just the institutional church on the daily lives of communities and yet reflects on the relationship of those communities to the larger society.

Sometimes social scientists treat the church just as any other institution in the society and proceed to examine its function in the socio-economic arena. Commentators misrepresent the nature of the church and make wrong demands from the church. From a theological perspective, we define the church less as an institution but as a people, a community of those who have been called out from their former lives into a new relationship with Christ. Institutional structures serve to organize but the story is about people who are inside the institutional canopy, who are mandated to share and proclaim the reign of God over the whole inhabited earth, to continue what God had started in the career of the man, Jesus. This reign is perceived in concrete terms as God's love that is a gift to be received and shared with the neighbor. The people are to be the signs, witnesses, representatives of this large design to reconcile peoples and establish a new era of peace and justice. It is an ethical community. So, its story should be about its faithfulness in living out the faith affirmations or the lack of it. They should not just "talk the faith" but "walk the faith." A church of any variety could only be known by the style of its *being, saying* and *doing*. These are the marks that determine the community's identity, the yardstick by which its faithfulness could be measured and the stuff with which its story could be told. The church's responsibility for the public space is rooted in its core identity and connection with the reign of God. This contests the implications of ideals such as the secularity of the public space, its separation from religious and moral imperatives, the dichotomy between the things of Caesar and the things of Christ or the boundaries between the "two kingdoms." The Christian relationship to the secular world remains complex and riddled with ambiguities but the church is called to be a prophetic voice in the market place. This is crucial in a worldview where there is no line of division between the profane and sacred. Sociological analysis must be attentive to the theological self-understanding by the church.

There is a certain embedded element of bias in the story of the church. A new way of re-telling the story in the wake of *uhuru* is to recover the experiences of the people who are exposed to the reign of God. This is faithful to both the Hebrew and Greek terminologies that differentiated between the institution of assemblage and the people who have assembled. It is a story of both the gospel bearers and the receptors and the changes that occurred through a new relationship. This church historiography privileges African agency as they reclaim their voice and their story and use the gospel to rebuild their battered image and endangered environment. History could be an ideological tool for oppression or liberation. As active agents, African Christians inculturated the gospel in a number of ways and creatively wove a tapestry that was unique. Ironically, this historiography confers enormous responsibilities on African Christians: it demands commitment and accountability to gospel mandates. It is a historiography that enables us to interrogate how the churches responded to the challenges in the African ecosystem.

Within this period, Africa was traumatized and plagued with legitimacy crises, dictatorship, coups and counter-coups, civil wars, and the emergence of soft states that were either prebendary or praetorian. The environment was scorched by economic collapse, massive poverty, and environmental degradation. It is impossible to tell the story of the churches beyond the impact of these untoward forces. It was a period when globalization became the dominant ideology that shaped trans-national relationships: political, economic and cultural. The collapse of the Soviet Union ended the cold war and heralded the triumph of the globalization process and the reinforcement of local identities.

The Earth Groaned:
The Context of African Political Economy

Attention must be drawn to the importance of ecological ethics in doing church history because human beings live and are sustained on the earth; their stewardly relationship to the earth or the lack of it may determine the level of poverty or wealth. Human story ineluctably must include the story of the earth as a shared space with sentient and non-sentient beings. The religious affirmation of God's creation of the whole inhabited earth compels a sensitive response and obligation. Salvation story includes the redemption of a groaning earth. Churches are to witness and nurture salient eco ethics because this explains the scourge of poverty. Africans are inheritors of an indigenous worldview that sacralized nature; a repertoire of indigenous knowledge nurtured salient eco ethics. From this perspective, Christian values resonate in African indigenous value systems. Yet some African cultural practices were intimate enemies of the ecology. Churches are under mandate to deploy the resources of the gospel as instruments for challenging the states to be responsible, and to engineer eco ethics that cure the non-salutary practices.

Ideally, the reflection should explore the character of these matters of governance, economy, religion and ecological challenges and explore the contours of the responses by different types of Christian presence: the mainline churches, the new charismatic Christianity, and the rising crescendo of feminist theology. But the constraints of space may permit only some of the broad agenda. Ecological and feminist concerns will be given more airing in a future outing.

Doing history demands attention to periodization or mapping of time. The story line appears to break between 1960–1989 and 1990–1996 when the Second Liberation of Africa from home-grown dictators consolidated. The last half decade of the millennium from 1996–2000 was characterized as the period of African Renaissance. The collapse of apartheid in South Africa and the accession to power by a number of younger leaders in Ghana, Uganda, Namibia, Botswana and the Republic of Benin raised the hope that the enigma of African pathology could be solved; enigma because there is no doubt about the wealth, beauty and human resources in the continent; enigma because no one could explain why the land spews out its educated manpower while hordes of foreigners instigate "mineral resources wars." Certain key features of the African context in the period under review are the numerical explosion of Christianity, the massive growth of other competing religious traditions, a highly pluralistic public space and the globalism characterised by cultural, economic and technological forces. Poverty resulted from failed policies and the impact of global economic forces. Competition for scarce resources intensified ethnic and religious competition.

In the early 1990s Adrian Hastings, a consummate historian, theologian and social activist intoned that

> Black Africa is today totally inconceivable apart from the presence of Christianity, a presence which a couple of generations ago could still be unreasonably dismissed as fundamentally marginal and a mere subsidiary aspect of colonialism.[3]

Kwame Bediako cast his mind back to the Edinburgh Conference of 1910 and traced the contours of this element of surprise in the transformation of African Christianity. He declared that African Christianity has now acquired a greater consciousness of her African identity and character. The greater challenge for the future is how to be of service to Africa as she voyages into the political realm of the 21st Century. [4] Not only that 'new dimensions' have emerged in African Christian spirituality as Paul Gifford said, but that the roles of Christian leaders in the contemporary political crises have enlarged tremendously. Both Bediako and Gifford list the cases of Togo, Benin, Ghana, Liberia in West Africa, Kenya, Uganda, Tanzania and Madagascar in East Africa, Zaire, Malawi and Zambia in Central Africa and South Africa as examples.

Indeed, the March 1996 election in the Republic of Benin is a good case in point. Without resort to mono-causal analysis, there is little doubt that the religious factor was the crucial element. Ironically, Soglo, a former World Bank economist, came to power with the support of the church during "the second liberation of Africa." The Roman Catholic Archbishop of Cotonou brokered the constitutional crises in the effort to throw off the Marxist military dictator, Kerekou. Once in power, Soglo shifted allegiance to vodoo priests. It should be noted that the majority of his countrymen bow to traditional gods and the python is the controlling spirit. Dahomey means 'in the belly of the python'. Roman Catholics are the next in numerical strength followed by United Methodists, *Aladura* (African Independent Churches) and Pentecostal/Evangelicals in that order. Soglo declared vodoo as the national religion, and installed a vodoo national holiday. He decorated the capital city, Cotonou, with sculptured vodoo symbols. Meanwhile, vodoo priests practised their sacrifices in the glare of the national television and blared their confident support for Soglo in the proposed national election. During the first balloting, they appeared prophetic as Soglo led the pack. But there was no clear majority and two of the candidates dropped off. Soglo and Kerekou now squared in a run-off.

The Christians became alarmed. Meanwhile, it was alleged that Kerekou had become born-again under the ministry of an Assemblies of God pastor. He showed his new-fangled allegiance in statements and actions even in his northern native home. Christian groups of all hues undertook long-drawn fasting and praying all over the nation in support of Kerekou. They turned out in large numbers to vote. Tension mounted so much that while the results were awaited, pandemonium enveloped the capital city. On March 23rd, 1996 as two thieves were pursued through the Dantokpa market—the largest market in West Africa—people fled surmising that the army was about to take over and save Soglo from an imminent defeat. The chaos spread into the city and a garbled version reached the hinterland. It was rumoured that the Roman Catholic Archbishop of Cotonou had fled the country. Churches filled through the night to ask God to intervene on behalf of his Christian people. Early on the Sunday morning, March 25th, the television announced that Kerekou had won. Sunday services turned into Thanksgiving Victory dances in the churches. The atmosphere was electric as people imagined the victory of the Christian God over the vodoo python.

The example of the Republic of Benin draws attention to certain salient factors: there has been a pulsating criticism that the church in Africa has, for the most part, failed to produce an adequate theology and institutional force to oppose the encroaching power of the state or to deal with the problem of poverty at its source; that it has danced around the tail of the python, repairing the havoc caused by the tail while gamely avoiding the head; that the *Aladura* were not politically-conscientized and that the matter has grown worse with the implosion of Pentecostalism.

This chapter poses the problem by examining the role of religion in the public space, the resilience of religion as it is mixes with ethnicity in the politics of new states and the emergence of competing new voices in the public square energized by liberal democracy. The new political dispensation has enlarged the public political space. Competitors easily resort to violence so as to attract attention or get their ways. Probing into the interior of Christianity, it shows that the mainline churches often remain elitist and, therefore, the pronouncements of church leaders and institutional organizations should be re-examined. But political theology should be about people's God-talk about the meaning of Christ in the midst of human conditions. As Ruth Marshall argued, more attention should be paid to the huge body of believers and to popular forms of Christian beliefs and practices. Moreover, changes in the religious landscape such as the rise of charismatic/Pentecostal movements since the early 1970s have great political import. They have created a new Christian culture that is seeping rapidly into the mainline churches through the charismatic movement. The scholarship on charismatic politics has shifted from the emphasis on externality and American influence and allegation of a conservative political ideology. Recent literature such as by Donald Miller and Tetsunao Yamamori contends that there is a discernible new face of Christian social engagement by a progressive wing of global Pentecostalism. At issue is how Christians understand and respond to secular power. Lamin Sanneh has in both his *Power and Piety* and *Crown and the Turban* (1996, 1997) drew attention to the deeper level of Islamic understanding of the political uses of power.[5]

Poverty is the dominant theme in African studies, especially its growth in spite of the growth of Christianity. Poverty surely means many things to different people and comes in types but even the most ardent theorist must be astonished at the increasing pauperization of African communities especially after 1989. The choice of poverty as the overarching conceptual scheme arises from many factors: it was the primary concern of Jesus. It also occupied the attention of the modernization discourse in the 1960s. The goal was to cure the underdevelopment of African countries or what Dennis Goulet calls 'vulnerability' in his book *The Cruel Choice*. This captures the failure of many low-income countries to maximally tap their resources, meet their development goals and consequently suffered elite domination and increased pauperization.[6] In the 1970s the discourse shifted from development to liberation, proffering social revolution as an alternative recourse. After 1989, Western powers insisted upon democratization as the path out of poverty; but it, too, was vitiated by a corrupt political culture. As a pundit observed, democracy does not work on an empty stomach. All constitutional arrangements fall at the beck of "money bags," creating a gap between transitions and consolidation of democratic governance. Between the years 1985–1995, political scientists moved from Afropessimism that described the poor conditions of Africa to New Realism that virtually declared the malaise as incurable. The perception here supplies the religious dimension to the failure of the post-1989 democratization process.

It argues that at the root of underdevelopment is an ethical factor, namely, the emphasis on the modern market and the modern state. People in the Third World had great hopes that once they were freed from the colonial yoke, they would have a great future with better human conditions. However, international economy colluded with unwholesome internal factors to create a dependency syndrome. This politics of economic stagnation has internal explanations but is for the most part externally induced. It could best be explored through the pages of World Bank Reports. The reason is simply that the World Bank and the twin sister, International Monetary Fund, are the vanguards of the Western liberal economics that devised the modernization theory for newly-independent African countries, designed to move them into mass-consumption societies, following W.W. Rostow's five-stages. Colonial governments, that were undemocratic, posited neo-democratic structures in the process of decolonization and expected these to succeed with no experience and with nation-states made up by tribes and tongues who were brought together, each in a daze and without any patriotic twitch. The new capitalist economy paid little attention to the base resources because cold-war ideology was supreme. Poor leadership and corruption took their tolls; meanwhile, the mobilisation theory which wiped out countervailing, indigenous power nodes only led to the growth of the state under the one party system and dictators who were called *fathers of the nations*. Praetorian and prebendary state structures proliferated between 1965–1990. All practised *the politics of the belly*.[7] Other forces in the backdrop include increased ethnic rivalry in the midst of dwindling resources, the resurgence of fundamentalist Islam with emphasis on territoriality and the competition for the control of the political space by charismatic Christianity.

Thereafter, the World Bank Report (1994), *Adjustment in Africa: Reforms, Results and the_Road Ahead*, reviewed the development trajectory for Africa in the post-Cold War years, and imposed the Structural adjustment Program. However, the social cost and economic decline of countries that implemented the Structural Adjustment Programme (SAP) became staggering. The SAP is designed to take over the economies of debtor nations and run them in such a way that IMF could collect for the Club of Rome.[8]

Perhaps we should compare this with two earlier reports such as *Accelerated_Development in Sub-Sahara* (1981) and *Sub-Saharan Africa: from Crisis to Sustainable_Growth* (1989). The impression is that the crisis in Africa has been intractable. For instance, the 1981 report identified two problems, namely, the implosion of the state and the centrality of political factors in the rapidly declining conditions in Africa. The wisdom was to pare down the role of the state and encourage right policies and practices. By 1989 the catalogue was worse: predatory, static policies stifled entrepreneurship and investment; instability was caused by incompetent and unpredictable management of public sector and failed legal systems; meanwhile, environmental degradation and abuse of human rights followed. The 1994 report, therefore, recommended a number of ideological shifts. It prescribed the need to redirect and rebuild the capacity of African states towards good governance. This is measured by the degree of accountability, transparency and openness in decision-making, rule of law and efficient public management. Political and economic liberation should dovetail, be undertaken simultaneously, and be perceived as mutually supportive. This is in tune with the ideology of the Second Liberation, consequent upon the fall of Communism and the triumph of liberal capitalism and the divinity of the market.

The World Bank offered Africa the model of *East Asian Miracles* (World Bank, 1993) without considering the differences in socio-cultural and value systems. Besides, East Asia was built on the state as the key agent, an interventionist state which literally selected the sectors for control. [9] To deal with disastrous micro-economic fall-out, NGO's proliferated as agents of poverty alleviation programs, designed to sedate the poor masses while the IMF recovered her debts. The model is to bypass the corrupt state and carry the global market message to the grassroots. Equally crucial is the fact that Africa is on the receiving end of the dark sides of globalisation: the debilitating impact on the poor nations exercised by the globalisation of the economy, the policies of the international financial institutions, the unequal distribution of the new technologies of communication and production and the investment of foreign capital for greater profit without concern for human and environmental consequences. As institutionally weak partners in global economy and cultural interaction, the poor nations inevitably experience economic decline and cultural uncertainty and slide more deeply into debt. Offers of debt relief either did not cut deep enough or were not balanced with trade opportunities and access to Western capital markets.

Power and Poverty: The State and Society During the Second Liberation of Africa

Commentators note the complexity in a typology of states in Africa. For instance, in 1960, nearly all the African countries modelled their constitutions on the example of former colonial powers—Westminster or the Republic. The exceptions are the Arab and Islamic countries of North Africa—Egypt, Libya, Tunisia, Algeria and Morocco –, which deployed the *sharia* except for Tunisia. Soon after independence many structures changed beyond recognition towards an authoritarian presidential system. In others, one-party systems emerged directed towards African Socialism, or geared to Marxism-Leninism with tightly "democratic centralist" structure. In another large number of states, military groups swept away the constitution or intervened frequently enough to create praetorian conditions. Only in a few cases did the original constitutional framework remain as semi-competitive or polyarchic systems. Of 26 polyarchies at the beginning of the 1960's only six turned out to be reasonably functioning and stable in 1980 (Botswana, Gambia, Kenya, Lesotho, Mauritius and Senegal). Of the socialist states, four turned out relatively stable (Guinea, Congo/Brazzaville, Tanzania, Zambia). The relatively stable authoritarian states included Ivory Coast, Gabon, Malawi and Swaziland. By contrast, 22 countries had a military government in 1980 which meanwhile, following several changes in government, also included praetorian states such as Nigeria and Uganda.

In the wake of the collapse of the Soviet Union in the 1980's, a second liberation (after liberation from colonialism) started. As to be expected, World Bank and IMF turned the liberation from home dictators into a political conditionality for funds. As Mitterand declared his support at La Baule in 1990, "conferences" started in Africa to oust dictators. Some lost, others manipulated the votes (Cameroon and Togo), Mobotu held tight, the military used subterfuge to survive in Nigeria, democratization produced war in Somalia and Rwanda while others changed stripe as in Ghana. With the new wind, old political theories were blown off the rampart. The modernization theory of Lipset and Apter that considered mobilization and one-party structures as the most viable option became discredited. The dependency theory of Lowenthal that ignored the force of internal political conditions became flawed especially in states comprising of major regional, cultural and ethnic divisions within them. [10]

Meanwhile, new ideologies jostled: the secularist against the non-secularist; theocratic and otherwise, and yet there is no African state which ignores the religious factor or is anti-religious in principle. A core character in the evolution of African states is that the rise of the monopolistic state (which Lamin Sanneh dubs a *theological state*) [11] has gone *pari passu* with both the diminution of civil or human rights as well as economic decline. Musa I.M. Abutudu explains this by appeal to the tendency towards the formation of a predatory elite. The state, through development plans, patronage, expenditure, employment, illegitimate accumulation of public wealth and alliance with multi-nationals or metropolitan bourgeoisie create and further the long-term interest of a dominating class. Thereafter, the apparatus of state is deployed to consolidate the class, the regime and the personal survival of the ruling group. The ruler privatises the state and runs it as it was his farm. This is the prebendal state. Leadership is the core problem in governance.

Andreas Thimm restated the relationship between human rights and economic development by arguing that it is precisely the guarantee of political and civil rights that has released those social energies, and lent the process of economic development an incomparable dynamism that translated into high social standards. Broader socio-economic development is not a prerequisite of democracy but a consequence of active economic and political participation by large sections of the population. Empirical data show that it is not true that large-scale state control and denial of rights could mobilize national energies into economic growth. Indeed, corruption has ruined the reputation of the military or praetorian states where rulers govern the states as if they were military barracks. Africa must develop institutional capacity for democratic governance as a means of economic survival. [12] Ali Mazrui has drawn attention to the tension between the evolution of the modern state and society in Africa that has accentuated the inability of the state to respond adequately to the needs of the society. Africa, he argues, consists of ancient societies and new states. Tensions between the societal age and state youthfulness are at the core of Africa's political maladjustment. [13]

Another malaise is the force of emergent values in the political culture. For instance, in Africa, primal religious beliefs and practices are a manifest and unquestioned parts of ordinary life. They weld decisive bonds and influences on most people's lives—village, kinship, the local shrine, oral passing on of the learning of the elders. But as the social scale enlarges, a clear chasm develops between a small elite and vast mass of the people according to wealth, status, and education.[14] Soon, emergent values arise from urban contexts, nurtured in new trading and industrial networks, civil society such as the trade union organizations, and media. As rapid social change reconfigures the economic and cultural foundations of the society, three interpenetrating publics emerge—the primal, the Western, and the emergent. Three value systems follow apace and the elite meander through the publics in an unconscionable manner. Thus, someone could steal from the western public or civil service and receive a chieftaincy accolade in the primal public though the offender must have broken the salient value of the primal public. The dominance of emergent values signifies the collapse of the primal solidarities and social control models that sustained the world we have lost. What does the church do in the midst of the growing power of the new emergent values? As Anyang Nyong'o articulated the task,

> The success of democracy in Africa will greatly depend on political and social engineering, the organization of political parties, and the deliberate creation of a democratic ethos that will *tame the state* as well as *civilize political actors*.[15]

Untamed predatory state structures and unrestrained and uncivilized political actors create a political culture that is incapable of utilizing the enormous resources of the continent to save the people from poverty.

Prayer and Poverty:
Christianity and the Bowls of the Poor

In reflecting on the pattern of the churches' response to the challenges of the growth of state power and the bowls of the poor, we must first examine the character of the presence of the church in Africa. There are enormous regional differences ranging from predominantly Muslim North through the heavily Christianized southern and central sector and a divided western Africa. In West Africa, a combination of Islam and traditional religion affected Christian presence. In a 1990 survey of West Africa, Muslims had the majority in Niger, Guinea, Mali, Guinea-Bissau, Gambia and Senegal. They are a large force in Nigeria. Traditional religion held a major sway in Benin, Togo, Cote D'Ivoire and Guinea-Bissau. It also held second place to Islam in Guinea, Mali and Senegal. [16]

Generally, missiometric surveys show that Christianity has grown tremendously in the last decade in Africa. Even in areas of alternative challenge, the percentage of growth has been phenomenal. Guinea is perhaps a good example of what has happened to the fallow grounds of Africa. Between 1919 and 1952, only the Christian and Missionary Alliance, the Roman Catholic Church, and a small Anglican group in Conakry were allowed to operate. Gradually, other groups came in. But in 1967 the Roman Catholic Archbishop of Guinea was implicated in a coup plot and the anvil fell on Christianity till Sekou Toure died in 1984. The new government opened the door to missions declaring complete freedom of religion and an open society as in Cote d'Ivoire. They saw that the restrictions, repressions and Marxist socialism produced economic disasters. Guinea in 1984 was a ruined country; its spirit had been broken. Since then, the missions have poured into the gap. Thus, the second liberation wind tended to favour Christianity when the moral bankruptcy of its enemies was betrayed in broad daylight.

But as Adrian Hastings has argued, the relationship between church and state in Africa is complicated by the fact of overlap as each claims some form of absolute loyalty over the same people. Christians appear to belong to two cities on the earth and have woven various theologies for survival. For instance, churches in apartheid South Africa produced self-serving theological emphases.[17] It has become necessary therefore, to restate the theological foundations for the Christian participation in the politics of poverty alleviation. As Karl Barth intoned, a democratic conception of the state is a justifiable expansion of the thought of the New Testament, and Bonhoeffer concurred. We shall not, however, pursue this line of argument. [18]

Rather, the take-off here is Paul Gifford's assertion that "the most significant development within African Christianity during the decade (1980's/1990's) was the mushrooming of new churches". The Pentecostals (outside) and charismatics (inside) have forced changes on the society, mainline churches and the African Indigenous Churches. He measures their growth by numbers, by the strength of missionary personnel and by their funds. He concludes that while Roman Catholics have grown and remain a formidable force, Pentecostals have grown more rapidly and at the expense of both mainline churches and the African Indigenous Churches. He adduces five reasons: governments' efforts to co-opt mainline churches, the elitist "Big Man" model of leadership, NGO-ization of churches by funding agents in a bid to avoid corrupt regimes, weak theology and problems of identity as faith churches thrive on faith gospel of health and wealth and a certain understanding of spirits in the African environment. A new Christian culture has emerged. The barriers between Pentecostals and evangelicals have collapsed and many members of African Instituted Churches are joining the Pentecostals' bandwagon as their non-denominational ecclesiology creates a new form of polity.

Since the Ghana Evangelism Committee conducted two in-depth surveys, Gifford uses the statistics to illustrate what is certainly a worldwide trend.[19] The question is, what is the impact of this trend on a) the state and b) the African societies characterized by high population growth, most of whom are in the rural areas, illiterate and increasingly impoverished? In many parts of Africa the largest sector of the population are children, youth and females. Before then, it should be necessary to state that the mainline churches are responding to the Pentecostal challenge, the implosion of state power and pauperization of the society in a robust manner. Paul Gifford, for instance, acknowledged in the *New Crusader* that the bulk of social service in Southern Africa is borne by the mainline churches rather than by the fundamentalist right-wing groups—the target of his contribution. They have allied more closely with NGOs whose activities in Africa have increased in the midst of natural disaster, wars and epidemics such as HIV/AIDs and spinal meningitis. Indeed, the racialization of WCC posture on justice and peace has meant an increased role for member churches.

But as Adrian Hastings argued in his *African Christianity*, (1979), there are certain factors which determine the impact of the church on the state, namely, the size and ecclesiastical organization, the spread of and quality of adherents, the pattern of colonial church-state relations precisely because post-independence relations tend to be part of a continuation or in part, a reversal of what went before. He includes the theological emphasis, for example, other worldliness, the attitude towards other churches and religions and the overall character of world-wide relationship. If, for instance, a church is big, such as the Roman Catholic Church, it may be difficult for the state to ignore her. Proscription may only occur in crisis periods. Possible patterns of relationship may exist: the state may clearly co-operate by showing a willingness to share work in definite fields; it may grant special status to the church as both watch where one tries to retain ultimate control. These patterns exist in different states in Africa based on varied local conditions. In all situations, the state listens to the voice of the church based on the level of democratic culture in which the government could admit public opposition.

In the polyarchies and praetorian states of Africa, the churches apparently enjoy a larger capacity to express their views. An example is a booklet entitled, *Christian Council Response to Ghana's Search for a New Democratic System* (1990). The Chairman, Rt. Rev. D.A. Koranterg observed that there are three reasons for the publication. Among these, it was to thank God that "we in Ghana now enjoy a climate in which we are able to discuss freely the political future of this country and share the official contribution made to the National Defence Council Government". This was innocuous and did not involve a challenge over human rights or social policies. Indeed, it concentrated on political structure. A clearer image of church-state relations in Ghana appears in J.S. Pobee's *Religion and Politics in Ghana* (1991). But even in a praetorian state such as Nigeria, the voice of the church is strong. Indeed, The Christian Association of Nigeria operates as a civil society as she harnesses the energies of those who are discriminated against because of tribe and religion.[20] The situation in South Africa is a different model of Christian presence in a distraught society. There is a unique quality in which a cardinal theological concept is placed at the centre of the political road to recovery. I have dubbed it *Simunye Theology*, an effort to achieve unity through repentance. This is what the Truth and Reconciliation Commission, a seventeen-member group led by Archbishop Desmond Tutu and Dr. Alex Boraine stands for. One may argue that this was made possible by the fact that about 70% of South Africans attend church. The matter is more complex.

At the background are certain facts: anti-apartheid battle was borne by young people. Younger than Steve Biko was a host of conscientized youth. Their future then is now their present laden with such expectations. Young whites, on the other hand, wonder why their teeth should be set on edge because the fathers ate sour grapes. They are even more disquieted because the political ranks of their fathers have been broken between diehards and liberals. The blacks are not united as the *Inkatha*, representing Zululand, an old society feels awkward in a young state. Moreover, the implementation of affirmative action has created a black middle class that has deserted the homelands. Resentment is brewing. And yet a certain haunting tune punctuates television programmes: "Si-mu-ny-e-e, we are one"! It is a Zulu word breathing the hope for the future, anxious for the return of love for one nation. But can people sweep the past under the carpet? The government, therefore, set up the Truth and Reconciliation Commission comprising of eminent churchmen, theologians and laypeople to provide a forum for aggrieved people to talk openly about the brutality that they suffered from white and black. The catharsis or self-purging process should lead people to forgive and become reconciled. The theological underpinning is immense. However, criticisms abound—does it re-open old wounds? provide possibilities for prosecution and justice? Or, would it serve as a sanctuary for those who brutalized others? Is it an African way of achieving reconciliation? The Nigerian experiment of the same strategy with the Oputa Panel under President Olusegun Obasanjo equally proved inconclusive.

In South Africa, the General Synodical Commission of the Dutch Reformed Church made several public statements critical of the TRC : suspecting its capacity to be impartial; alleging that it could prove to be another Nuremberg; and arguing the danger of bringing a theological principle into the centre of legal governance. Happily, on 10th February, 1996, in a letter published in the official weekly of the DRC, *Die Kerkbode*, forty nine ministers signed a challenge to the DRC to be more openly and constructively supportive of TRC.[21] The ministers were compelled by the spirit of the Kairos Document of 1985 which inspired the Rustenburg Declaration of November 1990, when 230 representatives, 97 denominations and 40 church associations declared that a culture of violence was rooted in the years of inequalities and that another Kairos, a decisive moment had arrived full of opportunities but, like a minefield, littered with dangers. The articulation of ethics of reconciliation which has become a part of state policy provides a unique contribution from South Africa.[22] In spite of the failures and collusion of yesteryears, these churches have a major contribution by providing a model for conflict transformation.

Beauty For Ashes?:
The Question Mark for Pentecostals

It is easily acknowledged that African appropriation of the gospel has privileged the charismatic or pneumatic resources because they responded from a charismatic indigenous worldview. In the 1920's the *Zionists, Roho* or *Aladura* as they were labelled in various regions of Africa reshaped the religious landscape and contested the monopoly of the mainline churches. The implication for the public space was not as creative. From the 1970s a new Christianity imploded. The impact of the rise of Pentecostal/charismatic wind on the socio-economic and political problem of poverty has been fraught with controversy. Some allege that the Pentecostals promote privatized piety and neglect the social structures of injustice; that the social and political theology of Pentecostals appears obscure. On the contrary, the mainline churches produced the political class in their schools and have deliberately sought to get their people into government or conferred knighthood titles on those who hold power and thereby turned them into *defensores fidei.* Their synods have published declaratory positions on socio-economic policies and, in some cases, they have operated more effectively as civil societies.

Much of the diatribe focuses on the diagnosis of African pathology: whether it stems from only political and socio-economic or from moral and spiritual forces? The Pentecostal view of history is that societies live in the middle of the whirlwind of the Holy Spirit that is the driving force of human history—not the acts of men. The solution is to link the power of the Spirit to the idea and practice of liberation arguing that, anyone who claims to have received the Holy Spirit must of necessity identify with and involve oneself in the people's struggle. This is because Jesus declared that He was indwelt by the Spirit of the Lord during his ministry of preaching the good news to the *poor*, setting the *prisoners* free, giving sight to the *blind*, releasing the *oppressed* and *bruised* and proclaiming the acceptable year of the God's favour. Christ, therefore, engaged in *pneumatic reasoning* that responded to the vulnerable of the earth with compassion and mercy. This is set against the *instrumental* reasoning of the secular state that exploits others as instruments to achieve ends. As Paul Felton would argue, charismatic emphasis is attitudinal, urging a change of life style that contests the pervasive egoism of secular society.[23]

The new Christianity offers an alternative religious space for creating a new community that combines the reconstruction of personhood and inner life with social action perceived as the outgrowth of that new community. Ruth Marshall, working with Nigerian data, concluded that,

> The Pentecostals or "born agains" are the most dynamic group of Christians in Nigeria today precisely because they engage with this contemporary situation and the history that has brought it into being. This movement gathers its force not in spite of the failures of the church in the past but precisely because of them. The history ... is the failure to construct a redemptive and empowering theology, a Christian identity and practice which

could have helped alleviate (pauperization) ... This failure is indissolubly linked to the failure of the post-colonial state to redeem its promises of democracy and development while at the same time allowing a few to enjoy the fruits of modernity to an obscene extent".[24]

Thus, Pentecostal political theology has moved firstly from rebuilding the bruised self-perception of the individual to secondly, empowering him with new hope and confidence to thirdly assisting him to garner the rich promises of the gospel and fourthly enabling him to reclaim, redeem and liberate the *land*. The "land" includes the economic, the social and the political (local and international). The shift from the individual to the public realm is achieved with peculiar symbols of pneumatic reasoning. As Paul Gifford argued, "unless the attitude of the mass of the population are changed, political action will inevitably reflect the values which Christians are called upon to challenge in their fidelity to the gospel".[25]

Some use historical, cultural and religious discourses to examine the rise of Pentecostalism in Africa especially after 1970. But others deploy the instrumentalist discourse, arguing that the economic woes and political instability in Africa catalyzed an increase in Christian activities and radical religious responses. The irony is that Pentecostalism becomes a *balm in Gilead*, a "fit" into indigenous spirituality because people want the new Christianity to do for them what the old religion did. This spirituality responds to the indigenous explanations for misfortunes that have survived in the modern urban space or emergent culture. Thus, there is concern for health and healing, demonic oppression, witchcraft activities and the scourge of poverty. People want release from the untoward conditions through prophecy and word of knowledge. Tabona Shoko of the University of Zimbabwe contends that the concern for health and well-being was so crucial in the goals of traditional religion that it has remained central in Africa's new Christianity.[26]

In the midst of hopelessness, Pentecostal preaching has offered hope and new life in Christ which empowers the individual to face difficulties. The pre-requisite is a new ethic that assists self-integration. The individual moves out of the wreckages of the past into a new life. It is a psycho-spiritual journey. The individual gains access to a concerned and caring community. The worldview is an ordered moral universe that makes sense of chaos. Even more interesting is that Pentecostal world-view accepts indigenous world-view, an "alive universe" in which demonic forces siege human life. However, the matter of Pentecostal reconstruction of African world-view is a large one, especially the relationship with inculturation theology.[27]

Is the Pentecostal fellowship a breeding ground in democratic practice? Both Ruth Marshall and Paul Gifford point in different directions but acknowledge that the egalitarian, youthful atmosphere does not preclude the fact that the pastor-founder who had the vision wields control. But intermediate roles abound within the system to create a new ecclesiology and healing religious space. The core issue is that they provide hope which is the best antidote to hopelessness and poverty. The will to arise is the beginning of poverty alleviation. This underlies the instrumentalist analyses that the new community offers institutional support in matters of health, education, and employment. A number of Pentecostal churches have founded universities. Efficacious prayers provide therapy and empowerment as the believer forays into a hostile world. It nurtures viable work ethics as the condition for progress. It is believed that holy life and honest work ethic should yield material and professional dividends, especially if one *gives* back to the "store-house of the Lord" in tithes and offerings. The guiding principle is that sowing and reaping elicit prosperity.

The new community is built on stable family ethics as the core of both church and nation. These buttress marital fidelity, mutual respect, sharing of responsibilities and stress on the nuclear family. Young women find opportunities for dignified living. The argument is that personal ethics enhance citizenship quality. Indeed, the key problem of many African states is that of good leadership and governance. Pentecostal ethics draw on the biblical resources for nurturing both. As Chinua Achebe said in *The Trouble With Nigeria*, the lack of leaders with moral stability has been the bane of the nation. Pentecostals fulfil the moral need which secular states have tried unsuccessfully to achieve through many anti-corruption programs.

From here Pentecostal political theology has forayed wider. At the deep end, it has tackled the after-effect of racism and slavery as evident in Mensa Otabil's *Beyond the Rivers of Ethiopia*. [28] By inheriting the mantles of Camus, Fanon, Manoni and Nkrumah, and the battle cry of Ethiopianism movement of yesteryears, the spiritual dimension to the black person's dilemma is re-imagined through the lenses of a liberating gospel. Theirs is a lived political theology. It may be weak in theory and bowdlerized by some of the preachers. Indeed, some argue that the emphasis on prosperity and wealth diminish personal responsibility and induce a weak political response that fails to challenge the structures of injustice; that Pentecostals spend more on media and self-promotion than on fighting injustice. Pentecostalism is a movement; there are many emphases; there are differences in various regions of Africa.

Post 1989 Theological Trend:
Intercession as Political Praxis

The most closely argued political theology has come from the 'Intercessors for Africa'. This group of professionals—lawyers, engineers, architects, computer scientists—emphasize land deliverance through intercession. Their theology starts with the land and the authority of power holders. Repenting about the idolatry of ancestral past, releasing the land and rulers back to God should set the stage for rebuilding the economy and politics of African communities. They argue that the land is controlled by ancestral spirits and other gods through elders, rulers and those with priestly authority who re-energise ancient covenants through festivals. Parents transmit, through blood, spiritual powers into their progenitors. These spiritual acts determine the events and fortunes of individuals and generations. They argue that both indigenous religions and the gospel attest that things that are seen are made of things that are unseen. Until these covenants are broken, the altars dismantled, and spiritual gates conquered, one cannot be redeemed or delivered from these destructive forces to enjoy the prosperity offered by God. As long as the legal authority given to these spirits is not withdrawn, they would continue to make demands, visiting the debts of the fathers upon their generations. Thus, hindrances, stumbling blocks to development are explained as demands by covenanting deities. This is the basis for deliverance ministries. The diagnosis makes sense within the idiom of the canon.

This is true for the individuals as it is for the nation. This causality scheme proceeds to explain the fortunes of the nations with the covenants and the idolatries committed by past and present leaders of the nation. It is alleged that to gain power, some of them tapped unwholesome spiritual powers, committed murder, and ruled corruptly. Their actions exposed their nations to the wrath of God. The Pentecostals counterbalance this sad scenario with reminders of God's good design, counsel and purpose for the African continent. They urge members to stand as watchmen and intercessors for their nations and to pray down the will of God, the only sure solution for the malaise afflicting their nations of the continent. At a prayer conference, Steve Okitika, an engineer, meticulously catalogued all the prophecies given on Nigeria between the years 1973–1993, to show the contours of the divine counsel. Thus, in the midst of the socio-economic crises, he interpreted the economic woes of the present as a consequence of the idolatry of the fathers and leaders, and assured the audience of God's design to liberate. As Emeka Nwankpa's *Redeeming the Land* (1995) argues, economic constraints force emigration and brain drain as the polluted land spews out her people. This analysis has influenced Third Wave theology in the United States. It is a hermeneutic for *prophetic praying* and *strategic warfare* because the ministry of Jesus, focusing on the poor, captives, bruised, blind and such vulnerable people was a veritable warfare.

Within this scheme, a running commentary against rulers is carried on. It may not require marching to the capital or taking a paid advert in the newspapers. Rather, the battle is carried on the knees. They argue that bad rulers are demonised, and should be removed from office through the protracted fasting, vigils and prayers by the saints. Believers are urged to be politically sensitive by "praying down the will of God" for their nations and for Africa. Here, three things are crucial: the kingdom of God interweaves into the present aeon. Beyond mere prayers for rulers, believers take spiritual authority over the structures of society and the men who create them and bend both to the will of God. Reading the signs of the time restates the enduring sovereign will of God in the midst of chaotic movements.

The criticism against Pentecostal political praxis could be misplaced because some political activities are more covert than overt. Allegations that some Pentecostals legitimize despots by citing Duncan Williams/ Rawlings, Yongi Cho/Moi relationships could be equally misplaced. It may reflect on the growing power of Pentecostal culture that attracts politicians. David Maxwell shows that when Mugabe's government failed in their attack on Ezekiel Guti's Zimbabwe Assemblies of God Africa, Mugabe rallied to openly support the church. In a riveting example of the political hybridity that emerged, Maxwell described how "Mugabe lifted his hands to become momentarily a charismatic Christian, gave his testimony at prayer breakfast and appropriated the language of moral and spiritual renewal to replace the discredited rhetoric of Marxism-Leninism and engagement with economic liberalisation and structural adjustment."[29] Pentecostals believe that a ruler, as any human being, willing to hear the gospel and willing to attend an outreach, and be exposed to the cleansing power of the Word and Prayer, is better than one who holds his retreats on the seashore communing with marine spirits. Stephen Ellis and Gerrie ter Haar in *Worlds of Power* illustrate how African leaders resort to indigenous and oriental mystical religions to sustain their power and legitimacy.[30] In the post-1989 Africa, Protestants have abandoned the old doctrine of the Two Kingdoms and shifted to the politics of engagement. The forms of engagement range from spiritual warfare and emergency relief to political activism. For instance, in Nigeria, Pentecostals have been the bulwark of the ecumenical body, Christian Association of Nigeria, and engaged in an enormous relief work in Liberia and Sierra Leone. In recent times, many Pentecostal groups have prayed their people into state houses as governors.

They have also designed City Projects in which certain urban centres are targeted and the immoral qualities of the rulers of the city taken as "prayer point". Sanitizing the undisciplined cultures of large urban areas has been a viable political task. The SALT project was crafted in 1999 to retrain civil servants and leaders in the moral uses of power. It may be argued that charismatic /Pentecostal spirituality under-propped the ideology of African Renaissance that followed the end of apartheid in South Africa.

Pentecostalism is a broad movement. Many studies have focused on the faith healing and prosperity genres. This is partial. Others have devoted energy to the abuses by mercenary prophets. This category exists in all religious forms. There is a need to re-understand the achievement of Pentecostal political theology: at the theoretical level, it runs roughshod of the old debate in Christian ethics between individual and social ethics. It destroys the dichotomy of two kingdoms. Rather, it affirms that saved individuals make worthy citizens and those who wish to rule the public must first rule their homes well. This explains attention to the private lives of public political actors. Without ignoring charitable institutions, Pentecostals have attacked pauperization at the root. The liberation of people must perforce move from individual and spiritual levels to the social/structural / systemic and manifest levels. This is the politics of subversion. Their goal is to replace beauty for ashes that rulers in contemporary Africa have rubbed on the faces of their people. Finally, Pentecostal fellowships constitute a new ecumenical dimension in African Christianity that eschews ethnicity, and enlarges the space for women. In some African countries as in South Africa and Nigeria, they have succeeded in mobilizing people to become more politically aware and to relate their Christian faith to issues of social justice.

Conclusion: Prophetic Voice and Humane Marketplace in Post 1989 World

In conclusion, this reflection has tried to show that liberal democracy that was the song and dance in 1989 has enlarged the public space, liberalized media but also intensified competition and even catalyzed violence. The process has compelled Christians in Africa to become more engaged in issues of social justice. Many mainline churches have taken the cue from their foreign metropolises. While the Roman Catholic Church has been particularly creative, legitimacy crisis has created new opportunities for the churches. Pentecostalism has a progressive wing that has gone beyond personal conversion to hone a muscular political theology of engagement. A broader understanding of the purviews of political theology would enable us to see that the reified distinction between privatised religiosity and attack on systemic evils may not exist in their life experiences. They do not perceive the problem with Africa as the lack of policies. The problem is with the ethics of power. Corruption and poor leadership destroy even the best policies. Corrupt seed breed corrupt trees. This perception is not new but now argued with a strong biblical force. Equally interesting is that while the diatribe on World Bank and IMF is rife, attention is turned inwards to a moral critique of African failure. Our leaders have poured ashes on our faces by creating the blockages that prevent the resources of the nation from trickling down. The World Bank policies may have aided macro-economic growth but failed to tackle micro-economic growth. In recent times, commentators have blamed the failures of Africa on poor leadership instead of pointing to the activities of outsiders. As Jean N. Nayinzira, leader of the Hutu Christian Democratic Party (PCD) put the matter,

> It was this notion of impunity that rotted our society. The (corrupt *Akaza*) were allowed to function with impunity. They were nervous about power-sharing. The idea of impunity must be purged from Rwanda society and throughout Africa if we are ever to have peace and some measure of prosperity.

The socio-economic structures of contemporary Africa have challenged the churches to re-imagine the patterns of their political engagement. The theology and the power for confronting dictators may still be weak, but many voices including the feminist voices have countered the collusion of yesteryears. As a proverb puts the matter, cattle are born with ears, they grow horns later. Globalisation as a description of an emergent asymmetrical power relationship has deepened the economic and social woes of Africa, and compelled a certain articulation and praxis in Christian response to political stagnation and poverty. Happily, the collapse of the hybris of modernity has produced a re-religionization process. Churches bring faith inspired motivations and ethics in seeking for new answers to endemic problems such as poverty. Redefining the role of faith in development is the beginning of wisdom.

Notes

1. V. Samuel, "The World Bank and the Churches: Reflections at the Outset of a New Partnership", in: D. Belshaw/R. Calderisi/Ch. Sugden (Eds.), *Faith Development: Partnership between the World Bank and the Churches of Africa* (Oxford: Regnum Books, 2001, 237–243).

2. A. Hastings, "Christianity in Africa", in: URSULA King (Ed.), *Turning Points in Religious Studies* (Edinburgh: T&T Clark, 1990, 208).

3. K. Bediako, *Christianity in Africa* (Edinburgh 1995), 235.

4. D. E. Miller/T. Yamamori, *Global Pentecostalism: The New Face of Christian Social Engagement* (Berkeley 2007); P. Gifford, *New Dimensions in African Christianity* (Nairobi 1992); idem, "Some Recent Developments in African Christianity" (*African Affairs* 93, 373, Oct. 1994, 513–534); idem, (Ed.), *The Christian Churches and the Democratization of Africa* (Leiden 1995); idem, *Ghana's New Christianity* (Bloomington 2004); L. Vanderaa, *A Survey for Christian Reformed World Missions and Churches in West Africa* (CRWM) (Grand Rapids, Michigan, May 1991), 1–8 gives the %ages of various religions:

Religions	1983	1990
Christians	22 %	28 %
Catholics	16.5	20.1
Protestants	1.8	2.5*
Evangelicals	1.0	1.5
African Indigenous	2.0	2.5
African Traditional	64.0	56.0
Muslims	14.0	16.0

* United Methodist 73, 000 out of 109, 700 Protestants

See also: R. Marshall, "God is Not a Democrat: Pentecostalism and Democratisation in Nigeria", in: P. Gifford (Ed.) *Christian Churches*, 239–260, see p. 240f; L. Sanneh, *Piety and Power: Muslims and Christians in Africa* (Maryknoll, NY: Orbis Books, 1996).

5. D. Goulet, The Cruel Choice: A New Concept in the Theory of Development (New York 1973).

6. J. de Santa Ana (Ed.) *The Political Economy of the Holy Spirit* (Geneva 1990) pursues these points further. J.F. Bayart, *The State in Africa: The Politics of the Belly* (London 1993).

7. See: *The Nigerian Guardian Newspaper* (Lagos), Jan. 22, 1996, 16; *Economics* 49/50, 1994 is devoted to the issue of poverty; *Canadian Journal of African Studies* 25, Feb. 1995 devotes six essays on World Bank Reports.

8. E. Hutchful, "Smoke and Mirrors: World Bank's Social Dimension of Adjustment Programme" (*Review of African of Political Economy* 62, 1994, 569–584).

9. D. Berg-Schlosser, "Democratization in Africa—Conditions and Prospects" (*Law and State* 52, 1995, 37–57).

10. M.I.M. Abutudu, *The State, Civil Society and the Democratization Process in Nigeria* (CODESRIA Monograph 1/95, January, 1995).

11. A. Thimm, "Development, Human Rights and Democracy" (*Law and State* 52, 1995): 89–101; "The UN Report: Unauthorized Copy of What Abacha

is Hiding" (*Tempo: A Nigerian Magazine*, 6, No.21, 30 May 1996). A team of UN Human Rights officials visited Nigeria on 29 March, 1996 and reported on 13 May, 1996. Signed by John P. Pace, V.A. Mailimath and Atsi Kofi Amega.; C.B.E. Botombele, "Democracy for all: A Universal Desire or A Threat to the Survival and Development of Mankind?" (*Law and State* 49/50, 1994, 1–14); L. Diamond, "The Second Liberation" *Africa Report* 37, No. 6, (1992), 41.

12. A. Mazrui, "Social Engineering for the 21st Century: An African Perspective" (Kaduna, Nigeria, *New Nigerian Newspaper*, October, 14–15, 1994):3-6.

13. A. Hastings, "Between Politics and Prayer", in: Idem, *A History of African Christianity, 1950–1975* (Cambridge, 1979, Chap. 5); Idem, "A Typology of Church-State Relations", in: Idem, *The Faces of God: Reflections on Church and Society* (Maryknoll, NY: Orbis Books, 1976, Chap.5); Idem, "The Churches and Democracy: Reviewing a Relationship", in: P. Gifford (Ed.), *Christian Churches*, 36–46.

14. P. A. Nyong'o, *Thirty Years of Independence in Africa: The Lost Decades* (Harare 1992).

15. L. Vanderaa, *A Survey for Christian Reformed World Missions and Churches in West Africa* (Grand Rapids, Michigan: Christian Reformed World Mission, May 1991): 1–8.

16. J. W. De Gruchy, "Theological Reflections on the Task of the Church in the Democratization of Africa", in: P. Gifford (Ed.), *Christian Churches*, (Leiden: E.J.Brill, 2005, 47 ff.).

17. J.W. Hofmeyr/ S. du Toit/ C.J.J. Froneman (Eds.) *Perspective on Kairos* (Kaapstad 1987); P. Gifford, *The New Crusaders* (London 1991).

18. P. Gifford, "Some Recent Development in African Christianity" (*African Affairs* 93, 1994, 513–534); Idem, "Ghana's Charismatic Churches" (*Journal of Religion in Africa* 24, 3, 1994, 241–265); see also: G. ter Haar, "Standing Up for Jesus: A Survey of New Developments is Christianity in Ghana" (*Exchange*, 23, 3, Dec. 1994, 229–239).

19. J. S. Pobee, *Religion and Politics in Ghana* (Accra 1991).

20. E. de Villiers, "The Challenge to the Afrikaans Churches" (University of Pretoria, Faculty of Theology, Ms, May, 1996). I am grateful to Prof. de Villiers for a stimulating discussion in May 1996 in Pretoria.

21. P. Walshe, "Christianity and Democratization in South Africa", in: P. Gifford (Ed.) *Christian Churches*, 1995:74-94.

22. P. Felton, "Towards a Charismatic Social Theology", *Theological Renewal*, 8, (1987): 29-43.

23. See also: G.L. Thompson, "Ministering to the Oppressed: Change, Power and Faith in Some of the Independent Charismatic Churches in Durban during the 1900s" (MA, History, University of Natal 1995).

24. R. Marshall, "God is not a Democrat", in: P. Gifford (Ed.), *Christian Churches*, 246.

25. T. Shoko, *Karanga Indigenous Religion In Zimbabwe: Health and Well-Being* (Aldershot, UK: 2007).

26. P. R. Clifford, "Involvement in Struggle for a Just Society" (*Mission Studies* 1, 1984, 26–33). See: Intercessors for Africa, *Biblical strategies for dealing with the desolation of Africa*. A Publication of Intercessors for Africa (Lagos 2002). I have dealt more fully with this in O. U. Kalu, *African Pentecostalism: An Introduction* (New York: Oxford University Press, 2008).

27. O. U. Kalu, "Unconquered Spiritual Gates: Inculturation Theology in Africa Revisited" (*Jnl of Inculturation Theology* 1, 1, 1994, 25–37); Idem, "Preserving a Worldview: Pentecostalism in the African Map of the Universe" (*Pneuma* 24, 2, 2002, 110–137); Idem, "Pentecostal and Charismatic Reshaping of the African Religious Landscape in the 1990's (*Mission Studies* [Journal of IAMS] 20, 1, 39, 2003, 84–111).

28. D. Maxwell, *African Gifts of the Spirit: Pentecostalism and the Rise of a Zimbabwean Transnational Religious Movement* (Oxford 2006, 146–148; see p. 148).

29. S. Ellis/G. ter Haar, *Religious Thought and Political Practice in Africa* (New York 2004); O. U. Kalu, "Harsh Flutes: The Religious Dimension of Legitimacy Crisis in Nigeria, 1993–1998", in: T. Falola (Ed.), *Nigeria In the Twentieth Century* (Durham, NC 2002, 667–685).

9 | *Poverty and its Alleviation in Colonial Nigeria*

Introduction

A number of concerns inform this reflection: first, the new millennium has started in Nigeria, as in most countries of Africa, with the scourge of poverty; at once harsh and with an unrelenting force, increasing the pauperization of communities. Ravaging poverty scorches other forms of cultural production and destroys the image of its populace. This reality spurs scholarly reflection because social intellectuals must perforce beam inquiries on matters of great social concerns. Knowledge must lead to commitment and provide solutions to deep problems. Incidentally, the attractive characteristic of the muscular intellectual output of early Europe was that it was notably achieved amidst unspeakable violence, famine, plague, and destruction. Second, social history has often been dominated by the activities of the elite and policies of rulers. In the designation of a period of African history as the colonial, the allure to the doings of colonial masters may diminish the proper focus on the indigenous people whose life stories should be the proper concern of their history. The French *Annales* school led by Marc Bloch and Lucien Febvre drew attention to the great import of the history of everyday life; a history that moves into the infrapolitical zone to reconstruct the lives of common people, the *sans culottes*. Third and further informing this reflection is the heightened awareness of the contribution of indigenous knowledge in appraising modern solutions to social problems. One of the resources of postmodernism is the reappropriation of discarded worldviews; this trend enables the search for new insights to intractable contemporary problems from the debris of ancient theories of knowledge. In the postcolonial period, when some African leaders sought new developmental strategies, they resorted to what was dubbed as African socialism in an effort to harness the resources of indigenous knowledge for new solutions. As Julius Nyerere argued, in African primal culture, "nobody starved, either for food or of human dignity, because he lacked personal wealth; he could depend on the wealth possessed by the community of which he was a member. That was socialism." Dame Lucy Mair had said a similar thing in 1944 when urging that colonial the social welfare policy should center in towns instead of worrying about rural communities: "There is no problem of delinquency in a village where the authority of chiefs or elders is respected and therefore effective, no unemployment or destitution where everyone draws his living from the land."[1]

This portrait of primal culture may beg the question whether traditional African societies lacked both class differentiation and poor people but highlighted the potentials of primal knowledge as a clue to modern solutions. This invites the search for viable exits from African primal vision, worldviews, and cultural practices. What manner of social ethics and resource allocation prevented or alleviated the scourge of abject levels of poverty? Nyerere did more: he rooted the modern faces of poverty in Africa in the colonial experience and alleged that alleviation strategies, dubbed as development projects, had failed; that there was need for a radical paradigm shift. Fourth, scholars have followed him to draw a connection between colonialism and poverty. It is admitted that the colonial phase was a short time frame in the lives of many communities, extending through less than a lifetime, but its transformative impact was tremendous as it reshaped socioeconomic, political, religious, and moral foundations of communities. As Toyin Falola and J. Ahazuem would argue, using the underdevelopment model, the colonial project exploited and transformed the Nigerian peasants into producers of raw materials for the benefit of Lebanese traders and European exporters. This commercialization of agriculture partially explains the implosion of poverty. B. Onimode specified how the production of cash crops incorporated the rural peasants into the imperial economy and diminished their food security.[2]

Within this perspective, a revisit to the world of the ordinary Nigerian in colonial times might provide clues about the changing faces of poverty: its perception, causes, and alleviation strategies that were tried in the past. The question could be raised whether these strategies hold any clues for our embattled communities. Obviously, various panaceas and enormous financial resources have not sufficed; rather, they have created an open predicament. Moreover, global processes ensure that the definition of poverty and its alleviation strategies are provided by external change agents that operate from differing worldviews. Could it be that the wrong medicine is being dispensed to people who diagnose their maladies differently? Put the matter differently: do the World Bank and the average Nigerian understand poverty in the same way?. When Britain ruled the waves, was there a shared perception of poverty and its alleviation that was dubbed as development? Whose reality prevailed? Yet the force of global or external processes must be balanced with an understanding of internal factors in profiling poverty and its alleviation. As Keith Hart pointed out, analysts of West African political economy and agriculture often gloss over the massive impediments to growth that originate from local and social conditions.[3]

The world of the Nigerian in the so-called colonial era was predominantly rural and agricultural, with strong traditional socioeconomic, political, and religious moorings. However, nascent urbanization and its emergent culture that Fela Ransome-Kuti dubbed as *shakara culture* (neither traditional nor Western) captured the attention of the new rulers to the disparaging neglect of the rural areas. To reconstruct the perception of poverty and its alleviation, a case study of Igbo rural communities will be employed. This is because of the vast ecological and cultural differentiations among Nigerian peoples, though certain aspects of the worldviews were shared. The context was suffused in each place by the contest between "three publics", namely, the indigenous worldview, emergent culture, and Western alternatives. This has been the staple diet of the novels of early Nigerian writers and bears little repetition here. The core of the argument is that poverty is as much a cultural fact as it is economic and its meaning is embedded in the language and culture of the people. Culture itself is hewn from the rock of the people's coping mechanisms in the face of certain ecological challenges. Culture is not heuristic but is produced as communities seek to eke a sustainable existence from the ecosystem that they inhabit. A meaningful discussion of poverty must be specific about the cultural context. The faces of poverty varied among the Hausa in the savannah grassland of Nigeria, among the Yoruba of the forested southwest, the Igbo of the southeast and the Efik of the Cross River. The historian must perforce reconstruct the profiles of such communities within a time perspective. The effort here will be more modest than a comparative perspective.

Poverty in Primal Communities: Perception and Causes

Language is more than the outer skin of cultures; it betrays its heart-beat. When the white men ruled Nigeria, the people expressed their understanding of the increasing levels of poverty in their indigenous vernaculars that betrayed the meaning and typology of the unsavory condition. Explanations of causes and strategies for alleviation took their roots from the meaning and typology. For instance, the Yoruba of southwestern Nigeria had words such as *osise, otosi, oluponju, aimi, ifeni, alagbe* and *madekoso.* The Hausa knew of the *matsiyat* (destitutes), *kutare* (lepers), *guragu* (cripples), *makafi* (blind), *kusanti* (deformed), *mahankata* (mentally ill), and generally, the *talakawa* (poor people). Each word gave a different cameo of indigenous perception and a close analysis of these would provide a composite picture. From the innards of the culture, it may mean that a beggar acting from a religious, cultic mandate may be an ascetic rather than a poor man. Thus, studies of poverty have been bedeviled by the lack of consensus about its meaning because of varied cultural perceptions. Whose reality is to be used? What level of deprivation could be perceived as subsistence insecurity? Other factors combine to confuse. There is the *spatial factor* because of a difference between urban and rural contexts. Though urbanity preceded the colonial time frame, the new urban centers were different kettles of fish and created a new face of poverty. Recognition of *time factor* emphasizes that the hunger gap that occurs in African societies immediately after the planting season till harvest time is not perceived as poverty among the indigenous people. Such a *conjunctural/relative* type of poverty differs from *structural* types that bite more deeply into the roots of a community's life, threatening the food security and health-care system of the community. Moreover, most studies tend to approach poverty as an economic fact rather than a moral, ethical matter. Using static numerical indices, they miss the historical perspective that images societies as living, evolving structures whose internal contradictions continuously produce new forms of poverty and wealth and new perceptions of the problem.

The argument here is that a viable analysis should mine indigenous language and knowledge and profile poverty from strong cultural and historical perspectives. Typology and periodization are essential in understanding poverty. Among the Igbo of southern Nigeria, persistent lack of material things was denoted as *ubiam.* But, in fact, this may just mean that the person does not produce enough to exchange for other things that the individual needs. The person has some things but needs other resources to fulfill social obligations. The deficit model operates by emphasizing lack and need. *Ubiam* may refer to conjuctural poverty. A more sustained, structural, generic lack will be denoted as *ogbenye*. A very acute form is the inability to feed oneself. This is described as a condition where one's mouth is covered with ashes, *ogbenye onu ntu*. Why ashes? Possibly, the person does not have enough firewood and must continue to blow into the hearth to keep the little coal aflame. Or, could not marry and has to make the cooking fire for himself. It may just refer to the connection between food and the ashes of the hearth. But it is abject poverty; structural lack or need. *Ogbenye*, however, does not always refer to lack of material things but more often includes lack of kinship support, relations, family network, and social security. A proverb says that any one who lacks a kinship group would more likely lose a case (*Onye enwere ummunna, ikpe mara ya*). There is an enormous risk if one was absent from where yams are being roasted in an open fire set up in the village square; one's yam might be removed from the fire by another person. There would be no one to speak on his behalf in an egalitarian context. This is perhaps the source of the anecdote that, as a missionary described to a group of villagers the tortures that Jews meted out to Jesus, an old man queried whether Jesus did not have a kin group and concluded that if they did not rise up in revenge, he must have been a bad man! A materially wealthy person could still be referred to as a poor person by the village folk. In Northern Igbo dialect, the person would be referred to as *nwagenye*. This is quite different from *Ogbenye ntu* that may also arise from the lack of kinship support group who could provide for their relation's lack of food. Indigenous knowledge constructed the family and community as the key determinants of poverty or its absence. This may raise the moral dimensions about individual responsibility; whether the person has failed to hold his own end of the rope in the family dynamics or whether the extended family failed in their moral obligations to the poor person. Implicit here is that the socialization process inculcates the knowledge and skills required for sustainable living in a particular ecosystem. Poverty, therefore, goes beyond the lack of material things to include the lack of knowledge and skill that enhance participation in socioeconomic and political life of the community. Poverty is a combination of the lack of material things, knowledge, skill, dignity, sense of well-being, political voice, and the social support system or family. It is the lack of power to be truly human; the lack of the "moral foundations of abundant life." [4]

Beyond the perception of poverty as relational, the meaning was deduced from the accepted value of the community, described as *nka na nzere*, long life and dignity. A person who lived with good health and fulfilled social obligations would be perceived as rich, *ogaranya*. Such a dignified person would show it by taking traditional titles to indicate the hierarchy of local prominence. Thus, a scantily-clad man, with a rope tied on his ankle, a stool in one hand, and an *ofo* stick on the other, may appear to an outsider as a poor man but in fact is an *ozo* titled man, a fully achieved person. He sits in the hut of power and his tongue is said to be as sharp as that of the tiger; that is, he is morally transparent and will judge righteous judgment and speak the truth without concern for whose horse is gored. In primal communities, the family, age grades, and community confer certain obligations on the individual. In an achievement-oriented society, premium is put on the performance of those responsibilities. This is dignity, and the pursuit of a dignified living is the path to abundance. Failure is perceived as poverty because it diminishes the person; robs the person of political voice in the market square, among the age grade, and in the gender relations within the society. Women may taunt the person as *ofeke* or *okokporo*, sporting a pair of scrotum. The person's freedom and basic human rights may be violated by his inability to marry unless the person's kin group responds to the challenge and, in common parlance, "provides the person with a wife and a mat"; that is, to pay the bride price and provide him with shelter. A person is not regarded as poor as long he has people behind him. Status can change based on achievement or ascription or adequate alleviation of lack.

Within such a value system, there was a great tendency to taunt and label people who failed to attain social obligations. For instance, if a person could not afford to join secret societies, he would be labeled as *ikpo* and forced to hide indoors with women and children during the ritual curfew. Constraints of space would hinder the exploration of the negative aspects of traditional life such as oppressive and dehumanizing patterns of power relations, institutionalized injustice, social violence, the politics of exclusion and cultural mores that encrusted fear and vulnerability. For instance, festivals were periods of high consumption that exposed sex and wealth differentiations, and some forms of masquerades set out to humiliate and terrorize the uninitiated. Life in traditional communities was not a romantic revelry under the moonlight. Much to the contrary, certain social control models intimidated the poor, infirm, disabled and the stranger. Yet a tradition of humane living was encrusted within a restrictive social control model that employed satiric songs, dances, gossip, and a peer-group joking relationship to restrain the wealthy from preying on the less fortunate. Power in all its pomp must be exercised with moderation.

The faces of poverty could be further probed by examining the causes. Land and food security are connected. In most of Igboland, land is held both by extended families and by community. At planting seasons, the holders of any parcel of land designated by the elders for cultivation would allocate farm portions to all members of the family and to nonmembers who would be required to pay fees; the accrued income would be shared among family members. A rotational farming/shifting cultivation system ensured that some people's lands would be declared as fallow while other family and communal lands would be farmed. Bush burning may have harmed soil nutrients but rotation gave respite to agricultural land and enhanced productivity. Ecological factors and farming may, however, have affected food security. Communities inhabiting harsh terrains and infertile land would suffer from low yields unless they planted the right crops in the right places. African communities generally did little to conserve their natural resources and did not replant used forest resources. They expected the gods to replenish the earth.[5] Indeed, it has been pointed out that the introduction of cassava saved many West African communities from a breakdown in food security. Some have, therefore, argued that poverty was endemic to the African context because of the threatened ecological balance in tropical temperatures; that shifting agriculture demands an immense availability of land that could not be sustained in the face of population explosion; tropical diseases affected animal production and protein intake; subsistence production limited the required surplus for responding to natural disasters and increased food demand; that many communities had thin, infertile soil. All these may have caused structural poverty.[6] Many rebuttals point to the fact that these jeremiads do not describe specific contexts and historical periods. Subsistence agriculture served until other external change agents degraded the environment, encroached on agricultural land and changed the mode of production. There was no lack of technological inventions: big hoes were developed to aid the cultivation of heavy clay soil; new forms of traps for hunting; nets for fishing; creative devices for preservation of corn, okro, cassava, and other sustenance required for the *unwu* period (after planting season). Agricultural cycle followed the contours of the natural seasons. Inaccessibility to land and labor should certainly cause poverty but this may occur when natural disasters (famine, drought, flood) war, death, and infirmity reduced the individual's capacity to farm. Intergroup relations sometimes resulted in wars, which in turn disrupted trade and exchange systems. Wars could cause conjuctural poverty and yield a harvest of orphans and widows. Attitudes toward orphans and widows were embedded in social norms.

On this point, John Iliffe's canvas needs to be repainted.[7] Igbo people tended to fear orphaned children whose parents died of illnesses or inexplicable diseases but not by war. This arose from the belief that *Ogbanje* children were supposed to come from the spirit world to haunt parents. People would be afraid to take in such children after the parents died.

Similarly, twins were considered unnatural and, in the patriarchal ideology, the mothers were the ones ostracized with the children. At the root of poverty in primal communities was a combination of individual failure and power relations. Until the colonial project changed the economic structure, patriarchy engendered the feminization of poverty. This is the intriguing argument in D. U. Iyam's *Broken Hoe*, that reconstructs the social history and cultural reconfiguration in Biase of southeastern Nigeria.[8] An illustration is the treatment of widows. Widowhood practice in Igboland has generated a spate of literature as a part of resurgent gender studies. Responses to widows differed in many culture areas of Igboland. They were either looked after by their original families or children, or remarried within the husband's family in a ritual called *nkuchi*. A widow without children was buried in her natal home. The threat to a widow was the tendency for the husband's relations to treat her as if she killed the husband by witchcraft and to seize all the deceased's property. When indigenous family ties weakened, the fate of the widow became more harrowing. But as long as the tensile strength of communal ethos held, the widow was not unduly exposed to poverty.

Other social norms may cause poverty; for instance, domestic slavery that may arise from war, outright sale, or pawning. A family may pawn a member as collateral for a debt. This change of status from *amadi* to *ohu* conferred a stigma that stuck through the generations. *Ohu* or slave status evoked discrimination and denial of means of production, social status, human rights, and political freedom. Another type of slavery with a religious undertone was the *osu* caste system, referring to people who were sacrificed to deities. Male ones serve in the precincts of the shrine and female ones were like temple prostitutes. People do not marry from this caste and they cease to belong to any families. More examples abound to show that poverty could be caused by ecological, economic, social, and religious norms. In a worldview that was suffused with religion and where socioeconomic and political processes were sacralized, religious causes for poverty were supreme. Indeed, it was believed that the failure of individuals to produce and reproduce could come from curses, ancestral spirits, witchcraft, and sorcery. An unstable woman would be declared as being troubled by an *ogwugwu* spirit, connected with marine spirit. Diviners would try to liberate the hapless one; often they would declare that the woman was married to a spirit husband residing in the water and would need to be divorced before she could function normally in the human world. They would demand an expensive catalogue of sacrificial items that deepened the poverty of the votary. Bareness was a serious matter because it contested a core value to preserve one's name: *ahamefula*, (may my name not be lost*)*. Those who offend their ancestors may find their life paths blocked. Hateful neighbors may use sorcery to cause ill health. Causality was always explained by an appeal to spiritual sources. This is why the levels of witchcraft accusations betrayed the degree of social disharmony. At such times, the chiefs invited a strong medicine man from a neighboring village to dispense detection potions that would ferret out sorcerers. At other times, litigating individuals made pilgrimage to powerful deities such as *Ogbunorie* of Umuneoha or *Kamalu* of Ngwanyieke for arbitration. At the turn of the 1900s, the Aro slave traders established a fake arbitration divinity called *Ibin Ukpabi*. They sold the votaries into slavery by pretending that the deity had 'eaten' the culprits. Intensive efforts to destroy the groves by the colonial officers between 1912-1925 failed.[9] Certain inexplicable diseases such as smallpox and leprosy evoked ostracism from the frightened communities who acted in selfpreservation and from an ideology that put a premium on group survival as higher than the individual's. *Ekpenta* (the Igbo word for leprosy) was dreaded as an infectious disease caused by the spirits and from poisoning. Extended family structures proved incapable of responding to the challenge. Gradually leprosy communities sprouted in the forests and the number of such clusters in Igboland left the impression of a dreadful level of poverty in the hinterland.[10]

As Iliffe's poverty register derived from missionary records shows, infirmity was a major cause of poverty. This may lead to a discussion on health and health-care delivery in colonial Nigeria. Suffice it to say that traditional methods remained dominant in the colonial era, especially in the rural areas, and the limitations made health issues a major concern embedded in taboos, and cultic and herbal practices. The wide range of indigenous pharmacopoeia is nonetheless intriguing. Therapy was diagnosed through divination and incantation. The register of therapeutic practices included herbalism, massage, hydrotherapy, pasting, blood letting/cupping, heat treatment, and faith healing. The traditional methods of treating hemorrhage and fracture have been integrated into modern medicine. Health was perceived as both the absence of disease as well as peace with the worlds of humans, nature, and spirits. Dissonance with this three dimensional perception of reality might trigger illhealth, both physical and psychological. An inescapable feature of indigenous life raises the moral question about people's sensitivity to the sufferings of others. The ridicule and harsh responses to people who were mad, deformed, or suffering from elephantiasis or incurable sores (possibly as a result of diabetes) indicate a poor level of sensitivity. The society laughed at the weak. The stranger suffered exclusion until the person was, as a proselyte, engrafted into the cultural norms.

Certain conclusions emerge from the Igbo case study: there are about eight subculture theatres within Igboland; some subculture areas are patrilineal and others matrilineal in inheritance. Each inheritance pattern creates situations that could induce vulnerability or serve as a social safety net. Land scarcity and population pressure is more visible in the central and northwestern sectors of Igboland, and this determines the profile of poverty in such places. Early contact with Europeans intensified the formation of towns and exposed certain subcultures to a sustained assault on indigenous mores and created the types of poverty that missionary records described in the nineteenth century. For instance, take the incidence of begging. It was more common in Northern Nigeria where it was sustained by Islamic religious values but it would carry a stigma in any Igbo culture theatre. Oluada Equuiano could declare in the eighteenth century that the Igbo had no beggars, not even ascetic, religious types as found among the Yoruba.[11] The Igbo had few large towns and nothing resembling the case as among the Yoruba. Towns developed from market centers, ritual centers, and communication nodal points. Thus, during the colonial period, more towns would develop from railroad junctions, new road systems, and administrative centers. Until this reconfiguration, communal values remained strong among the segmentary political structures. Igbo relationships with their neighbors did not yield to the internecine wars as among the inhabitants of the Niger-Benue river conflux or among the Yoruba groups; the incidence of slavery remained manageable until the trans Atlantic slave trade provoked slave raiding and kidnapping in the interior. It has also been shown that abolition created a surplus of slaves in the interior and the incidence of cultic blood sacrifices increased in the regions that could not utilize the surplus slaves in plantation farming. Indeed, a tradition of absorbing slaves into families started. In other cases, as among the Nkanu group of villages, slave villages that had been founded and used as buffers grew, rich as successful farmers and challenged the master villages by the mid -1920s.[12] Conjunctural poverty was more prevalent; structural poverty became more pronounced as the indigenous structures came under pressure with the insertion of colonial policies. Cash nexus replaced trade by barter system; consumption habits changed, creating new forms of need, social obligations, and vulnerability. Initially, poverty was less a matter of material things and more a matter of relationship, dignity, power, and moral stability. The faces of poverty changed. But before dealing with the new forms, the alleviation strategies will be instructive for mining indigenous knowledge.

Poverty Alleviation in Primal Communities:
Moral, Cultural and Community Imperatives

The Igbo people say that *"onye kwe, chi ya ekwe"* (when one affirms, the personal god will confirm). *Chi* is the personal spirit that a person inherits and that determines fate and destiny in life pilgrimage. But it is not a fatalistic perception of the world. This saying appears to locate poverty or its absence in human agency; the individual's willpower and the strength of the right hand that is represented by the icon, *ikenga*. A combined interaction between divine and human agencies enables an individual to achieve and escape poverty. The gods and the individual are blamed. Often the person's relationship with the *chi* is queried: did the person inherit a bad *chi* or failed to give kola nuts to the *chi?* Poverty alleviation, therefore, involved ritualized stabilization of relationships between the human and divine. The restoration of moral order ensures that human activities succeed and evil is warded off. Things that are seen are made of things that are unseen. Alleviation is not merely achieved by an intensification of human activities but by first restraining the capacity of negative moral forces from ruining human projects. The worldview is a precarious one in which evil forces essay to thwart salient human endeavors. Moral balance is of the essence; attention must be paid to purity and danger. When moral order is abused, poverty will enter the domains of individuals, family and community.

Basic also are the roles of the family, nuclear and extended, in poverty alleviation. The extended family comprised *umunna* or *umudi* (father's family), *umunne* (mother's family) and *umuada* (the married daughters of a family). In communities with a patrilocal residence, the father's kindred may inhabit an identifiable space or compound or ward and could offer mutual aid to members. *Ugwo*, borrowing, was more prevalent in this close-knit blood relationship. People could borrow clothes for festival occasions. It was joked that a person with borrowed clothes does not dance with freedom and exuberance because the owner may be watching with concern. *Usury* was practiced and people put up family land as collateral for loans. The rates might not have been high but the responsibility of the kindred to borrow for the welfare of a member was a core value. A family might even sell land to defray the medical costs of a member or pay for funeral expenses. Funeral costs were the responsibility of the firstborn son (*di okpala)* and the *umunna* patrilineage assisted by the other siblings. The mother's kindred might have been dispersed but still had roles in providing a social security network for the individual. In communities with a matrilineal inheritance pattern, the *umunne* played the primary role in cases of infirmity, death, and conjunctural poverty. *Umuada* usually would confront a brother who was disgracing the family with a lifestyle of laziness, drunkenness, sexual immorality, or moral failings that magnetized poverty. In the same manner, they would confront his wives for failing to look after their brother. They had a strong voice in their natal homes. Beyond the boundaries of the family, other social groups such as the age grade and the village community had immense responsibilities. Sometimes an age grade could assist members with labor for cultivating their farms or erecting houses. Some age grades had an inner group who used a system of *isusu*, contribution, as a means of accumulating money for personal projects that required a reasonable amount of money. This strategy would become the basis for cooperative societies. Accounts of Nigerian recaptives in Sierra Leone indicate that they exported and practiced this homegrown strategy into foreign lands. They called them the Big Companies and Little Companies.[13] Community and communal ethos provided a solidarity network proffering rewards and responsibilities. Food security and safety were the responsibilities of the entire community. The elders made the rules for economic activities following the due decision-making processes of the communities. The people were involved in determining the strategies for ensuring their food security. They understood their ecosystem so well that their proverbs and myths were suffused with imageries from the world of animals and nature. Nyerere and Kaunda referred to this communal ethos as the moral foundation of African socialism; Kaunda found resonance in Christian social ethics and, therefore, christened his own design as Christian humanism. Chinua Achebe's novel *Things Fall Apart* is built around the struggle to adjust indigenous ethics to a new worldview introduced by the colonial project, a worldview that encrusted individualism. In that unequal contest, the embattled ancestral fence that had protected the community gradually fell apart. Other scholars have canvassed a resilient perspective. The jury is still out.

In the nuclear family, the gender factor is supreme as the woman's ingenuity could sustain the family, especially during the hunger gap. She gathered firewood, assisted by her daughters; sourced for berries and food seasoning from the forest; grew vegetables in farms and gardens, and cultivated root crops as cassava and coco yams. Here again, the socialization model enabled young people to know their ecology, its resources and challenges, and gain a higher level of sustainability. Those in forest regions taught their young to farm, set traps, and hunt; their hunters could smell animals from far distances. Riverine people ensured rich harvesting techniques of marine resources. Indigenous knowledge is rich with minutiae of surviving strategies in each ecosystem. Alleviation strategies built on cursory studies by consultants that ignore the rich reservoir of indigenous knowledge of the ecosystem must fail. There was a division of labor as the men harvested palm trees, tapped wine, and cultivated yams. Some men engaged in long distance trade while the women dominated the eight-day markets. Women took responsibility for feeding the entire family. In some villages, if a man collapsed in public because of hunger, his wives would be severely fined and accused of a plan to kill the man. However, an economic revolution was in process because as women engaged in cash crop economy, it gave them more economic power with vast social consequences. Some women became richer than men. The impulse of the womenfolk to produce and reproduce and sustain their families bred the dominant market women of the future. Polygyny that was supported with the argument that it provided labor for farms was attacked; matters worsened when the children went off to schools and disdained farm labor. Many anthropological studies are shifting again, from strident ideological feminism to reconstruct the domestic and market roots of feminine power found in contemporary Africa.[14] Indeed, Lugard pointed with respect to the rising power of women when the system that he built was stung by their organized rebellion in 1929. Writing the preface to Sylvia Leith Ross' *African Women,* Lugard rejected the portrait of the invisible woman and contended that the African woman is "ambitious, courageous, self-reliant, hardworking and independent...she claims full equality with the opposite sex and would seem indeed to be the dominant partner."[15]

Another alleviation strategy was through apprenticeship, a system that people found to be better than pawning. Artisans had apprentices who were freely offered by families that wanted to provide for their members. Differently termed as *uzu* (among Cross River /Eastern Igbo) and *ife mmadu* (among the Northern Igbo), the system enabled the wealthy to aid the poor because the wealthy were not supposed to muzzle the ox that tilled the field. In the future, apprenticeship to teachers, traders and artisans assisted many children of the poor to acquire education and develop coping skills in a new colonial economy. Young people paid their way through service. Marriage linkages were another form of survival technique because the Ohafia Igbo say that " *ogo wu ifu ikwu*" (a son - in-law is a leader in the wife's natal family). A wealthy in-law could be an asset; intergroup and village marriages cemented alliances.

In summary, community, culture, and family engendered salient ethics and served as structural agencies that staved off poverty except those types caused by natural and spiritual forces. This may suggest that neighborhood associations, village community development agencies, and other types of civil societies, whether based on ethnicity or beyond ethnic boundaries, could serve as poverty alleviation agencies because they possessed organic roots and bonds that ensured viability. From this perspective, ethnicity, that has been vilified as tribalism and as a dysfunctional force in the modern public space, may have its uses in designing poverty alleviation strategies.[16] The artificial character of NGO's and impersonal government agencies cause development failure. As an aside, those were the clay feet of Ujaama projects that moved from organic conceptions to artificial implementation strategies.

Colonialism as Antistructure: Embattled Values and New Vistas

Colonialism was a system of overrule that comprised new colonial administrative machinery, a judiciary, and economic order, all sanctified with a monotheistic religion that was imbued with civilized values. It was an antistructure that sought to embed a new moral economy designed to remodel the cultures it encountered in its own image. It was built on a racial ideology that perceived the Western enlightenment worldview as truly capable of enlightening other dark cultures. It sought to reconfigure both the mindset of its victims as well as the features of their everyday life. Much of its character has been subjected to criticism and bears little repetition. Suffice to say that the moral economy model makes it possible to examine how agents respond to dominant structures by either loyalty, voice or exit. The story of colonial encounters in Nigeria is replete with examples of the three responses in the face of the insurgent alternatives. Development failures in contemporary Nigeria can be traced to many of the unresolved aspects of colonial hegemony and the clash of worldviews; the failure of poverty alleviation strategies emanate more from privileging the neocolonial models than from a congenital African pathology.

But first, it must be stressed again that the colonial period was brief in many parts of Nigeria. For instance, the British presence in Igboland was less significant before the Aro Expedition of 1901 that brought the new reality into the hinterland. Thereafter, colonial hegemony consolidated amidst the flares of primary forms of resistance until the First World War created a depletion of manpower necessary for a truly imperial rule. Much of the colonial achievements occurred in the interwar years that witnessed the Great Depression and more poignantly after the Second World War. The aftermath of that war fueled political nationalism as the indigenous elite gave voice against the yaws of colonialism; threatened to exit and forced a headlong decolonization. It would be dangerous, however, to view decolonization as anything better than a passive revolution; that is, when those who wield power find the conditions untenable and devise new means by creating indigenous surrogates who hold power on the former rulers' behalf. These gloved hands stick out from behind the throne to direct what has been termed as neocolonialism. This brief periodization argues that the force and style of colonial presence ebbed and flowed based on counter forces of global geopolitics. Thus, colonial perception and response to poverty varied in the periods between 1900-14, 1914-45, and thereafter.

The greatest achievement of colonialism was to create a new context that, in turn, created a new face of poverty. It transformed the geography by the creation of urban centers. Rural-urban migration and population shifts bred an emergent public and culture that was neither primal nor fully Western. Wole Soyinka's *Interpreters* and Cyprian Ekwensi's *Jagua Nana* give us glimpses into this raucous context. Market economy followed suit as the growth of urban markets and nascent industrialization lured migrant laborers. Merchant houses and government offices needed clerks. Urbanity in this period went beyond the population size of inhabitants to include semi-industrial capitalism, job differentiation, and an improved infrastructure. The colonial powers emphasized the building of roads, rail, and the use of waterways. Each project created new towns. The presence of the government paraphernalia enhanced the status of towns. For instance, when the seat of government moved from Calabar to Enugu in 1906, the status of Enugu changed dramatically as the infrastructure improved. But its importance was further enhanced by the discovery of bitumen coal in 1909 and the construction of the Southern Railroad from Enugu to Port Harcourt between 1913 and 1916. Workers surged to the two new towns. At Enugu, the whites lived in the government reserved area, the indigenous middle level clerks lived in Ogui and Asata wards, while the coal miners lived at Iva Valley and Coal Camp with a crowded body of petty traders and artisans. Meanwhile, towns along the railroad such as Aba, Umuahia, Uzuakoli and Afikpo became important. Many towns remained semi-urban. Yet urban slums sprouted because less attention was paid to the crowded habitats of the indigenous folks. Meanwhile, the new economy raised the problems of employment/unemployment and a new class of laboring poor emerged who earned meager wages. Antisocial consequences followed as the politics of urban penury intensified. The long story of Nigerian currencies started. By 1926, taxes were introduced, to the consternation of many. Dependence on wages for sustainability replaced the reliance on land. Youth bulge in urban demography created the problem of delinquency. Thus, the Human Development Indices measured by the problems of water, food, shelter, employment, lack of voice, and loss of dignity, arose from the social and cultural changes induced by urbanity and new modes of production.

Official economic policy focused on agricultural cash crops. In some places, scientific agriculture, plantation economy, experimental farms, and new food crops were introduced. The towns were the centers of exchange and this export- driven economy fed on rural production and thereby transformed it. Chima Korieh and Olatunji Ojo have pursued some aspects of the cash crop economy and its dire impact on the macroeconomic pattern in colonial Nigeria and its gender implications.[17] Two major concerns here are, first, the impact of the new economic pull that put pressure on rural subsistence societies and, second, the new social values generated by urban life that threatened old social control models without yielding a sustainable alternative. Embattled traditional structures failed to buffer people from the new faces of poverty. Admittedly 'villagization' of the modern space followed as the people carried their village ethics into the towns. Village organizations, town unions, community development associations, thrift clubs, enabled people to thrive in the colonial economy. Some times, a few people from the same village would form a friendship club (*otu ndi enyi*) based on trust, and contributed monthly to pool resources and mobilize enough capital for one of their members in a business endeavor. The survival strategies of Nigerians in the new colonial economy will make a fascinating study. But new aspects and allures created habits that countered the village norms. Imitation of white people called "kolo mentality" (a form of loyalty response to colonialism); new consumption habits; and the disdain for rural ethics crept in. The gathering of people from many cultures and subcultures created a new context, an open society. Education became the greatest instrument for attacking primal values and the social control system and the installation of a colonial counterculture. That was the space allocated to missions. But in every society town air appears to give people new freedoms and anonymity. It provided opportunities for the accumulation of wealth without the obligations of succoring the poor.

From its inception, colonial ideology was built on replacing the slave trade with legitimate trade. The focus was on the production of cash crops such as cocoa, groundnuts, cotton, palm oil and kernel as raw materials for European factories. Every district officer supplied a table of cash crop production in the quarterly, half-yearly, and annual reports to the provincial commissioner who, in turn, attached a longer table in the report to the Lieutenant Governor. In Igboland, palm oil and kernel dominated the concern of these reports. The local producers sold to middlemen who itinerated through villages of the Palm Belt or carried their products to markets, some far and others near. The Cross River/Eastern Igbo communities, for instance, ferried their kegs of palm oil and bags of palm kernel by canoes along the Uduma River and Enyong Creek to large towns as Itu and through the Cross River to Calabar. In exchange, they bought European goods such as cloth, helmets, hats, mirrors, guns, swords, machetes, handkerchiefs, ivory bangles, walking sticks and shirts. These articles became means of wealth and social differentiations among rural peasants. To show off their new wealth, the achieved women performed a particular dance with mirrors that were framed in carved wood and tied with colorful handkerchiefs. They would flash the mirror in the sun so that the poor people could watch the reflection of the sun with admiration. Social differentiation intensified in the rural sector as consumption habits changed and palettes for foreign goods sharpened. The focus on cash crops diminished the concern for subsistence agriculture; rural-urban migration drained the labor supply of village communities. Increasingly, some villages lacked able-bodied young people to farm. Some of these insisted on being hired to work for older relations and kindred. Markets also became more important not only as fora for exchange but as social occasions. The status of women changed in the new economy as many of them became traders; this contested the real authority of male leaders whose income diminished. Men held authority while women had the power. Those who lived in towns, educated young people, and female traders contested the authority of village elders; some overtly, others covertly. These social and cultural changes, generational opposition, new values and insertion of a new worldview created new forms of poverty and attacked the alleviation strategies, values, and agencies that worked in primal societies.

The new context that the colonial regime created is important for understanding its responses to poverty. Before 1914, colonial officers showed little concern about poverty. They left the matter to indigenous communities, missionaries, and local philanthropists. As Lucy Mair argued, indigenous structures and values had the capacity to respond to poverty. When the population of towns continued to grow and the incidence of urban poor became visible, the response focused on towns to the neglect of the rural environment. The colonial regime applied conceptions of poor based on conditions in Britain, and resorted to correction institutional solutions. As John Iliffe concluded,

> In British colonies, government made little provision for the poor before the Second World War. Officials believed that African families and communities looked after their needy members and that any supplementary care could best be given by missionaries. Government provided general services: increasing control of famine; free but limited public health services; legislation against abuses; rudimentary urban sanitation and

control of working conditions. District Officers generally had small discretionary funds to relieve distress."[18]

Conditions after the First World War had drawn attention to the problem and the Great Depression exacerbated matters. Even then, poverty was misconceived only in terms of the disabled: sick, dying, deaf, blind, leprous, truant, or physically incapacitated. Missionary strategy was based on the use of charitable institutions and schools as a means of evangelization. Thus, missionary groups competed among themselves to establish industrial institutions for acquisition of skills, hospitals, dispensaries, primary schools, homes for the destitute, leprosaria, and motherless babies homes. They paid much attention to the rescue of twins, the training of girls, and care of the sick. In a few cases, missions engaged in creating wealth such as their role in cocoa production in Western Nigeria. The greatest achievement of missions remained in the field of education. Government aided schools because they produced clerks and hospitals. Mission education remained at the primary level for a long time in many parts of Nigeria. There were few secondary schools until the 1940s. In Igboland, for example, the first secondary school was the Dennis Memorial Grammar School, founded at Onitsha in 1925 by the Anglicans with money raised from among the Igbo. In the explosion of such schools by indigenous entrepreneurs, both the rival mission bodies and government joined the affray between 1924-45. Perhaps, social Catholicism and social gospel among Protestants inspired the intervention of missions but rivalry and evangelical strategy determined the pace and direction of alleviation interventions. Some missions achieved more in certain areas than others. For instance, the Presbyterians and Methodists left indelible imprints on the fight against leprosy. The Salvation Army focused on urban welfare intervention. Roman Catholic leadership in the medical and educational apostolates remains incontrovertible. Increasingly, the government intervened to control the quality, curricula, and location of schools. Grants-in-aid, based on reports of education inspectors became an instrument of pressure.

Secular institutional charity followed the poor laws and institutional format of Britain. Initially, the government established welfare officers and institutions to handle cases of juvenile delinquency, the disabled (blind, cripples, insane), and beggars. These services remained rudimentary until after the Second World War. Government encouraged indigenous philanthropists to assist. In the mid 1930s, secular charity institutions such as the Red Cross (founded in 1863) gained access to the colonies in Kenya, Ghana, and Nigeria. Others would follow as late as the last decade of the colonial period. By this time, the concept of social welfare was challenged because of its narrow purview in urban areas while the majority of the populace lived in the rural hinterland. It was also felt that intervention should focus on community development or prevention. In the Eastern Nigeria of the late 1950s, mobilization of rural labor for government projects was achieved with a propaganda machine that sent mobile film units into villages to show a film entitled, "Planning for Prosperity." It showed happy Udi villagers working on new roads; others constructing a rural dispensary; contented coal miners waving their pickaxes; and students of University College, Ibadan, in academic gowns, relaxing on the steps of the library (when they should have been inside poring over tomes). Meanwhile, predatory sanitary inspectors roamed through village markets collecting bribes from hapless traders. Once in a while a stampede would ensue as the sanitary inspectors were sighted. Unscrupulous people called "Umu DC" (district commissioners' children), usually fair complexioned and sporting paper and pen, would impersonate government officials to add to the vulnerability of rural dwellers. There was difficulty in integrating welfare practices with indigenous poverty alleviation strategies; official policy and practices remained inchoate. State, religious, and secular agencies often moved in different directions. The great irony was that the government recognized the tensile strength of indigenous knowledge and practices but failed to tap the resources.

Quite damning was the failure to relate poverty to environmental protection. Indigenous ideology sacralized the world of nature and contained wholesome ecological ethics, in spite of the lack of an ethic of replenishment. But the development theory that dominated colonial ideology privileged the exploitation of natural resources for foreign markets and degraded the environment. Aggregative indices computed the wealth of the colonies by their export capacity and consumer potential. The neglect of the ecological health of Nigeria was related to racial ideology. In those places where mosquitoes barred settler white communities, such neglect was brutal while much care was lavished in Central and Southern Africa. The dominant theory in African sociopolitical analysis, dubbed as "Afro-pessimism, " leaves the impression that there is no strategy for African problems that could suffice or adequately confront the scourge of poverty; that the lack of leadership as well as other debilitating factors have combined to doom the continent. A shift to a more hopeful model, namely, an African renaissance, enhances a social analysis that sees potential in indigenous knowledge; that a part of the African problem is rooted in the exploitative ideology of colonialism.[19]

In conclusion, the past has uses for the present. This reflection on the colonial period of Nigerian history shows that postcolonial regimes in Africa inherited the lack of concern for the poor and the environment. Modernization theories of the 1960s focused on using Western indices in mapping developmental strategies. The object was to "catch up" with the West or to repackage the continent in the Western image. Black skins wore white masks. Those theories collapsed before they could clamber up to the takeoff stage. The proto-Marxist "under-development" theories that followed in the 1970s proved better at criticism than prescription. African nations that turned Marxist watched their economies collapse. In the cold war, both pro-Western and pro-Eastern nations fell into the debt trap. Ideological vanguards turned into dictators, and slogans about the masses rang hollow. Pessimists dominated the 1980s as if to throw in the towel. The second liberation of Africa from dictators in the 1990s has been built with the slogan of democracy following the collapse of Communism. But this may ring hollow again unless there is a renaissance of spirit in the new millennium that is moored on the symbols of transcendence in African indigenous knowledge. Thus, lessons in poverty alleviation strategies from the colonial period are many: African countries must wake up to the scourge of poverty. Sustainable projects must perforce be woven into the contours of the geography and geology of communities (that is, their ecology and life development paths) and culture. To tap the salvatory aspects of indigenous knowledge, there must be an in-depth understanding of the ecological resources of our communities; that is, how the people coped and what traumatized the coping mechanisms. This will recover the value of culture, ethnicity, organic agencies, and civil society in alleviation strategies. It will recover the moral dimension to poverty and restore those communal ethics and social control models that created the tradition of humane living. It must be reaffirmed that life is sacred and that poverty is the single force that is eroding the dignity of the Nigerian. It is the source of the drain on the country's human resources. Above all, it requires the mobilization of the resources of entire communities, including the power of the youth and women. This will challenge gender ideologies. The past holds much that is good but also contains limitations. Cognizant of the dynamic nature of culture, every community will need to engage in social engineering that embeds new ethics that follow the grooves of the old. This is traditionalization, a model that argues that the domestication of change agents can best be achieved by working from the grassroots and a concern for the theology of life.

Notes

1. Julius K. Nyerere, "Ujaama-the basis of African Socialism" In his *Freedom and Unity* (Dar es Salaam, 1966): 164; Lucy P. Mair, *Welfare in the British Colonies* (London, 1944): 109-10.

2. T. Falola (ed) *Britain and Nigeria: Exploitation or Development?* (London: Zed, 1987):80-90; see, B. Onimode, *Imperialism and Underdevelopment in Nigeria: The Dialectics of Mass Poverty* (London: Zed, 1982).

3. Keith Hart, *The Political Economy of West African Agriculture* (Cambridge University Press, 1982).

4. Laurenti Magesa, *African Traditional Religion: The Moral Foundations of Abundant Life* (Maryknoll, NY: Orbis, 1997).

5. Ogbu U. Kalu, "The Gods Are To Blame: Religion, Worldview and Light Ecological Footprints in Africa", *Africana Marbugensia* (University of Marburg), 32, 1/2 (1999):3-26.

6. R.W. July, *A History of the African People* (New York: Charles Scribner, 1970):570.

7. John Iliffe, *The African Poor: a history* (Cambridge University Press, 1987): 88-94.

8. D. U. Iyam, *Broken Hoe: Cultural Reconfiguration in Biase, Southern Nigeria* (Chicago University Press, 1995):2-7.

9. Ogbu U. Kalu, "Missionaries, Colonial Government and Secret Societies in South Eastern Igboland", *Journal of the Historical Society of Nigeria*, 9, 1 (1977): 75-90.

10. For a study of Presbyterian leprosarial work, see Ogbu U. Kalu, *A Century and Half of Presbyterian Witness in Nigeria, 1846-1996 (*Enugu: Presbyterian Church Publication, 1996): 193-219.

11. John Iliffe, "Poverty in Nineteenth-Century Yorubaland", *Journal of African History*, 25 (1984):43-57.

12. Carolyn Brown, "Testing the Boundaries of Marginality: Twentieth Century Slavery and Emancipation Struggle in Nkanu, Northern Igboland, 1920-1929", *Journal of African History*, 37, 1 (1997):51-80. See, Ogbu U. Kalu, *Embattled Gods: Christianization of Igboland, 1841-1991*, (Lagos/London: Minaj Publishers, 1996), chapter 5.

13. See, Jean H. Kopytoff, *A Preface to Modern Nigeria* (Madison: University of Wisconsin Press, 1964).

14. Jane L. Parpart (ed), *Women and Development in Africa* (New York: University of America Press, 1980); Ify Amadiume, *Reinventing Africa: Matriarchy, Religion and Culture* (London: Zed, 1997).

15. Sylvia Leith Ross, *African Women: A Study of the Ibo of Nigeria*, (London: Routledge, 1939), foreword.

16. The argument has been pursued at greater length in Ogbu Larry U. Kalu, "Religion, Ethnicity and Development in Africa," In N. Onwu (ed) *Reform-*

ing the Reformed Tradition: African Presbyterianism in the 21ˢᵗ Century (Enugu: Presbyterian Church Publications, 2001): 54-84.

17. See, Adebayo Oyebade (ed) *The Transformation of Nigeria: Essays in Honor of Toyin Falola* (Trenton, NJ: Africa World Press, 2002):223-260;383-404.

18. Iliffe, *The African Poor*, 200.

19. See, Ogbu U. Kalu, *Power, Poverty and Prayer: The Challenges of Poverty and Pluralism in African Christianity, 1960-1996* (Frankfurt am Main: Peter Lang, 2000), chapters 2 and 3.

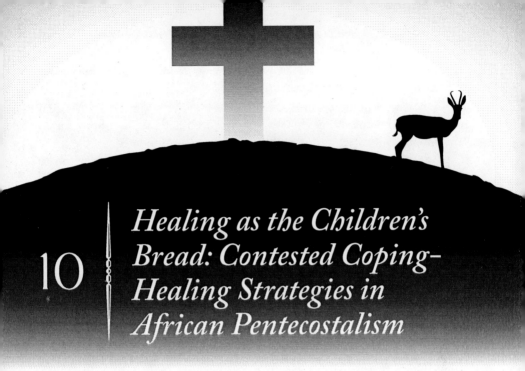

10 | Healing as the Children's Bread: Contested Coping-Healing Strategies in African Pentecostalism

Introduction:
Science, Indigenous Religion and Faith Healing

Jesus said it: the power to be healthy is as easily available to believers as the children's bread. Indeed, the word for health and salvation in Greek is the same: *soteria*. But the simplicity of the statement becomes the problem for human beings and is often the point of contention with Pentecostal theology for which the Bible is paradigmatic. There are various levels of the contestation against global Pentecostal concept and practice of healing and specifically in African Pentecostalism. First is the "scientific" attitude of medical practitioners towards indigenous or alternative medicine and towards faith healing. Admittedly there is a plurality of voices within the opposition based on the faith affirmation of individuals, shifts in theory of knowledge and developments in medical science and technology. Medical attitude operates from a naturalistic worldview and pursues a defined goal: germ theory, prevention and cure of disease through surgery and medical preparations or drugs. Following natural laws and organic theories, there is hardly any place for a belief in a supernatural force that could intervene to stop the operation of the laws that govern the structures and functions of the human body. As modern medical establishment became more organized and discovered effective drugs, therapies and technologies two contradictory trends emerged: the willingness to explore and affirm alternative healing techniques and the increased attack on divine healing, especially as paraded by virtuoso televangelists.[1]

The second dimension is the attitude manifested by disciplines that emerged from enlightenment worldview, when natural philosophy metamorphosed into science in the 18th century and consolidated the theory of knowledge as the world advanced from the achievements of Newton to Einstein's. Psychologists and psychiatrists have experimented on the explanation and translation of the processes in indigenous healing and in faith healing from "scientific" perspectives and idiom. They join neuroscientists to puzzle how the brain informs the mind and body or conveys the impact of religious rituals such as laying of hands or anointing with oil. They explore the relationship between the psyche and the body and study the process of interaction. For instance, theories in psychotherapy argue that spirit possession is merely an outward manifestation of something deeper; and that neurotic sickness is developed in order to correct psychic balance. This fuels the argument that faith healing is merely a psycho-therapeutic device; that some people have been hurt by traumatic experiences they have undergone when no healing occurred; that faith healing or coping healing phenomenon is an emotional and psychological manipulation and could easily derail into a money-making racket.

A third dimension is the intra-mural debate within the religious realm. Some Christians contest the religious healing within non-Christian faiths as emanating from unwholesome spirits. Among the Christians, some operate from the enlightenment worldview to reject faith healing. Theological opponents wonder whether there is no place for redemptive suffering. This raises the problem of theodicy, providence and God's connection to suffering: if God is loving and all powerful, why does he not eliminate human suffering? Theologies of various hues have grappled with this: Calvin accepted the notion that God causes everything as could be seen in the story of Job. A modern mind finds this difficult and would rather imagine suffering love as the character of God. From the rational deism that preceded Enlightenment worldview, a theory of rational theodicy made the Christian concept of providence unintelligible before process theology disenchanted theology, limited God within the boundaries of human freedom and rejected any possibility of a divine intervention that ignores the laws of nature. Stanley Hauerwas, *God, Medicine and Suffering* aptly summarizes centuries of Protestant apologetics and concludes that there is no universal theodicy even in the Bible and none of the theories will suffice; that the task of the church is to be a community of care towards the sufferer.[2] But theories about theodicy have a sociological base. In North America, opposition to faith cure or divine healing could be traced from the early opposition to the holiness movement and the Pentecostal movement that contested mainline Christianity with a charismatic spirituality. It is said that when John G. Lake returned home to America from South Africa in 1913, he gathered a number of doctors to examine those whom he cured by faith and thereby squelched the wild rumors percolating around his healing ministry.

In Africa, health and healing is a very important aspect of religious life and explains the rapid growth of both African Instituted Churches during the inter-war years and charismatic Pentecostal movements that grew rapidly from the 1970s. Healing is the heartbeat of the liturgy and the entire religious life of many growing religious movements in the continent. It brings the community of suffering together; it ushers supernatural power into the gathered community and enables all to glow together in its warmth. It releases the energy for participatory worship that integrates the body, spirit and soul.

I watched the healing of a deaf and dumb boy in a Pentecostal gathering that met in a school house in Monrovia, Liberia. Apparently, most of the congregation knew the boy. The dancing and praise worship took over the rest of the service. The din was so loud that the neighborhood gathered and instead of complaining about the ruined peace on a Sunday afternoon, joined in the celebration. Stuart C. Bate intoned that in South Africa, mainline churches have declined by 25% while coping-healing churches have grown by 23% and that these churches constitute "one of the most visible phenomena in South African Christianity today."[3]

This paper is about the contestation between science and signs and wonders, especially about the theme of health and healing. For the sake of clarity, it focuses on health and healing in African Pentecostalism: the conception, theology, practice of faith healing and the diatribe from scientific perspectives. The paper engages the debate around faith healing from a combination of religious and cultural discourses arguing that much of the contestation arises from a clash of worldviews. It explores what the Pentecostal churches mean by health and healing. The pulsating questions are: what are the sources and boundaries of Pentecostal understanding of health and healing? Is healing cure? Can healing occur without physical cure? Can healing always occur? Are the claims sustainable or faked? Who can heal? Are Pentecostals against modern scientific medicine?

To begin with the last question: some churches are remnants of the old naked faith movement. For instance, some Pentecostal churches in West Africa have the historical roots in the Faith Tabernacle whose pamphlets came through the mail boats from Philadelphia during the inter-war years. They emphasized divine healing without resort to modern medical facilities, thereby accentuating the contestation about religious and modern scientific worldviews. But most Pentecostal churches perceive both as being complementary. In more recent times, some commentators aver that the popularity of divine healing arises from the poverty in the Third World communities that are plagued by the collapse of health care delivery system. Others insist that the use of instruments such as olive oil, water, incense, candles and indigenous symbols such as pigeons and foodstuff (drawn from Levitical laws in the Bible) heightens the possibility of manipulation and emotional control in the healing process. Diagnosis through dreams, visions, ritual cleansing, confinement to prayer houses, faith homes, waterfronts and secluded places increases the level of vulnerability for the afflicted.

Thus, in the African context, the battle about healing rages on four fronts: modernity project subsumes all the scientific arguments and disdain against indigenous religions, cultures and religious-oriented healing practices. Missionary Christianity, operating with an ideology of "scientific racism," underscored the opposition to indigenous spirituality. But within the Christian camp, theologians war against charismatic faith healers and Pentecostals demonize African Instituted Churches. To pursue the debate within the Christian fold, the theme of healing is connected to the larger theme of power, signs and wonders, and betrays the great divide between the Christianity in the northern globe and the emergent dominant Christianity in the southern globe. Christian theologians in the northern globe contest the Biblical validity of faith healing either by subscribing to cessationist theology which claims that the *charismata* have ceased to operate or by simply disputing miracles. Others argue that African Christians subscribe to the validity of demonic spiritual forces and appeal to these in the explanation of causality. In the northern globe, those operating with modern scientific worldview regard the appeal to demons and the practice of divine healing as obscurantist. Healing, therefore, draws attention to the use of the Bible in southern Christianity and the relationship between Christian practices and indigenous worldviews, cultures and healing practices. Intones Phillip Jenkins,

> For many African and Asian Christians, familiarity with the New Testament world extends to their understanding of evil and sickness. As in the early church, much of global south Christianity today is a healing religion par excellence, with a strong belief in the objective existence of evil, and a willingness to accept the reality of demons and the diabolical. Biblical texts and passages that the south makes central are seen by many northern churches as marginal, symbolic or purely historical in nature.[4]

Are the Africans indulging in pre-scientific and pre-modern worldview? Paul G. Hiebert's book, *Transforming Worldviews* suggests revisiting the biblical and indigenous worldviews. The question is, therefore, how Africans appropriate the gospel from their own worldviews and about hermeneutics. As Walter Wink has argued in his *Naming the Powers: The Language of Power in the New Testament,* the language of power dominates the pages of the Bible and especially the ministry of Jesus. Ironically, the internal debate within African Christianity is precisely about the relationship of African and Biblical worldviews. African Pentecostals demonize the African Instituted Churches by condemning the dosage of indigenous rituals, symbols and instruments in the healing practices. [5]

Healing in an African Culture and Indigenous Worldview

The contention here is that both the Pentecostals and the AICs share the same conception of health and healing, operate with the same map of the universe, derive the concept from the indigenous African cosmologies, and use Christian resources to answer questions raised within the interiors of those cosmologies. Both have developed a cultural ideology that shifted prominently from inherited missionary cultural ideology and linked the gospel to indigenous worlds and idioms. A good example is a study by Tabona Shoko of the University of Zimbabwe. This is a phenomenological case study of the ethnography and religion of his own people, the Karanga communities located near Mberengwa district of Zimbabwe's Shona ethnic group. Despite the limit of the scope that could constrain any large conclusion about the rest of the continent, his contentions could be easily replicated. Shoko examines the pragmatic nature of an indigenous religion in which health and healing are central, and analyzes how the Karanga explain the causes of affliction, diagnose and treat illnesses and social ruptures and the wide range of pharmacopeia in the indigenous knowledge. The concept of health, diagnosis and treatment are linked to how the ancestors and the host of spirits that abound in the universe protect, empower, and revitalize the physical, social, and spiritual well-being of the community. Rooted in indigenous worldview, the Karanaga notion of health and explanation of illness include the broad gamut of social relationships, connection to the world of nature, sensitivity to social control models, rites of passage and the community's relationship to totems and ancestral spirits (*vadzimu*). This is a volatile dimension because the spiritual forces are often capricious. For instance, the ancestral spirits (*midzimu*) provide health and wealth as well as drought, plague, and misfortune. Karanga indigenous knowledge provides various explanations for diverse diseases and prescribes medicine and rituals of healing. Rituals are as important as the herbs precisely because it is the ritual that animate the herbs and ensure efficacy. Indeed, among the Igbo of southeastern Nigeria, there is a difference between, *dibia afa*, the diviner who prognosticates about human destiny and *dibia ogwu*, the herbalist or healer who listens to the spirits as they direct the footsteps to herbs.

Since Mberengwa is an area with low, erratic rainfall and frequent droughts, a powerful *Mwari* cult provides identity, fertility, rainmaking, and oracular functions. The key ones that feature in the healing and deliverance rites are *mashavi* alien spirits, *ngozi* angry spirits, *mhodoro* lion spirit, and witchcraft spirits such as *zvidhoma* and *zvitokorochi*, and ghosts such as *magoritoto*, *bvuri*, and *zvipoko*. Since disease is believed to be caused by spirit possession, witchcraft, and sorcery, as well as socio-moral and natural causes, Shoko describes how each force operates and discusses how the ritual antidote is diagnosed through spirit possession, dice, calabash, and dreams. It should be noted that the people do not discount natural causes of affliction. Moreover, healing is rightly presented in broad terms, involving the due observance of the rites of passage, communal rites for protecting the land, rain-making and appeasing offended spirits and human beings. Health is restored by ingesting curative herbs, exorcism, implanting powerful medicinal into human bodies, extracting objects, and other preventive and protective rituals of purity. Healing is beyond cure to include the restoration of the human, moral and psychic order through rituals of appeasement, propitiation and restitution.

Shoko uses a case study of an African Instituted Church, *St Elijah Chikoro Chomweya*, to argue that the indigenous perception of health and healing practices have persisted into contemporary Christian forms. In Karanga, the *n'anga* is still a key local personality. The major conclusion is that the African Instituted Churches source their conception of healing and healing processes from the traditional healing culture and practice. He demonstrates how the AICs imitate the *n'anga's* use of herbs, divination, and exorcism. With a detailed ethnography attentive to gender and political structure, he traces the changes catalyzed by colonialism and modernity. But he emphasizes the resilience of indigenous culture in the modern public space.

Shoko supports Bate's linkages between indigenous healing practices and charismatic Christian spirituality by arguing that in this region of Zimbabwe, the mainline mission churches, the Lutherans and Roman Catholics hardly prospered. The two churches opened hospitals and schools and supported the war of liberation but failed to attract loyalty. The Karanga preferred the African Instituted Churches (AICs), especially Bishop Samuel Mutendi's Zion Christian Church and the African Apostolic Church of Johane Marange. Schism may be rife among them but they accept the validity of the indigenous worldview in their explanation of and response to illness. Shoko argues that in a symbiotic relationship, Christianity in Karanga is an extension of the pervasive indigenous religion. [6] David Maxwell in *African Gifts of the Spirit* shows that in Zimbabwe, early Pentecostalism resembled both indigenous witchcraft eradication agents and the AICs. The early Apostolic Faith Mission pastors wore long beards, dressed like the Vastopori priests and indulged in a new wave of witchcraft cleansing in rural communities. Charismatic Christian evangelization clashed prominently with an equally charismatic indigenous worldview.[7]

Amandla: Spirituality, Deliverance and Healing in African Pentecostalism

Anatomy of the Theological Diatribe Against Pentecostalism

A closer look betrays that often the debates about healing, science, theology and indigenous worldviews are like dialogues among the deaf where people talk past one another or deliberately emphasize one of the many aspects of health and healing: concept of healing and wellbeing, type, cause (etiology), diagnosis, therapeutic method, physical cure of suffering and other forms of social healing. Let us begin by examining the theological debate within the Christian community, especially the diatribe against Pentecostalism. Before prevention, healing and cure, what causes illness and suffering? Many Western theologians are irked by the fact that African Pentecostals ascribe all causes of suffering to evil forces and to supernatural powers. As said earlier, this is not correct because many Pentecostals privilege natural causes, are attentive to matters of hygiene, adopt the modern scientific germ theory and accept personal responsibility. But they also operate with a worldview that places a causal connection between purity and danger, between personal sin, the sins of ancestors or 'iniquities of the fathers' and the health of an individual, family and community. Critics aver that privileging sin as cause turns the victim into an escapegoat and evades personal responsibility. Pentecostals counter that the Old Testament, Jewish and early Christian communities accepted the moral roots of affliction and the connection between ancestors and the fortunes of their progenitors; that Job's friends asked him whether rushes (reeds) can grow where there is no marsh because they believed that when the fathers eat sour grapes, the children's teeth will be set on edge. Sin opens the gates for the invasion of dis-ease.

Walter Hollenweger, however, admits that the challenge posed by Pentecostalism to contemporary Christianity is the recovery of the perception of the church as a healing community.[8] He represents the middle road that does not deny divine healing but insists that while it is true that God's faithfulness and promise to heal are eternal, God has the freedom to choose how, when and whether to act. Therefore, the causal connection to sin is *expressis verbis* rejected by the gospel; that there are healthy sinners and sick saints. Critics from the mainline churches reject the claim that faith automatically leads to health or unbelief to sickness or that faith is a condition for healing. Pentecostal healers, they allege, may unjustly judge the victims, indulge in self-salvation, parade the illusion of control over evil, collude with witch finders to usurp the role of God and strengthen people's fear of witches and belief in magic. Hollenweger, therefore, admonished Pentecostal virtuoso healers against propaganda or trumpeting of healing success because this confuses success with blessing and failure with curse. Healing should occur in a worshipping community and incorporated into liturgy.

Diagnosis and Healing Process

The question remains about diagnostic method, agency of health-care delivery and method of healing. For instance, can all believers heal? Pentecostals respond that though healing is available in the Cross, everyone does not have that special charisma to heal. Gifts differ. The core of African Pentecostal diagnosis and healing method is the emphasis on spirituality, deliverance and healing. Among Pentecostals, healing is supremely interwoven with the activities of the Holy Spirit. In South Africa, the Christian concept of *Amandla* in Zulu language signifies the authority and power of the Holy Spirit over all types of oppression. It evokes the extra power and graces through which the Holy Spirit diagnoses, heals and revitalizes. God's Spirit is a vitalizing energy, a flowing and outpouring of power. It is virtually presumed that if a person is connected to, swims in, and is constantly renewed by the flowing power, the person will prosper and be in health. Pentecostal pneumatology emphasizes a supernatural reality; that what is seen is made of what is not seen; that there is a spiritual dimension to all of life. The linkage is the power in the word of God. Faith (whether of the patient or others) is not merely believing but acting on what the word of God says; every word is true and possible; therefore, if anyone acts on the Word of God, the promises will manifest in the physical realm. This is essential for the healing process and has more weight than the words or reports of medical doctors. It becomes a question about whose report should be believed in matters of life and death!

Pentecostal theology of health and healing uses the examples by Jesus and the apostles to demonstrate the explanation of causality, different styles of diagnoses and healing/therapeutic methods. Christians are called to imitate Christ. People are given the gifts (charismata) for the benefit of the whole community. From this perspective, gifts of word of knowledge (discernment), tongues and prophecy are diagnostic tools. The power gifts of faith and healing are the transformative vehicles for what God, who created the human beings, wants to do. In African Pentecostal scholarship, the healing camps that have sprouted all over the continent as communities of suffering attract attention connected to their practices, Biblical basis and relationship with indigenous religious practices. Admittedly, malpractice could seep into the system but they are inculturating paths. Sometimes healing occurs under television glare in an environment that looks too commercialized to be edifying. Two key aspects must be noted: in the Pentecostal theology of health and healing, healing is not simply physical cure. It is also recognized that coping-healing practices are mediated by worldviews, cultures, symbolic systems and healing myths. Laurenti Magesa aptly captures this:

> If the instinctive cultural impulse of most Africans leads to the belief that being community or in community is healthy, then it also implies that any lack of community harmony is 'dis-ease.' Specifically, lack of physical health is often understood to be symptomatic of a lack of spiritual, emotional or moral health; it is physically and spiritually harmful to the society and the individual concerned.[9]

Within this perception, sickness could be physical, psychological, socio-economical and political. Health is achieved through reconciliation among human beings and by restoring the integrity of creation. Social scientists acknowledge many salient features of indigenous healing methods; anthropologists have argued that the level of witchcraft accusations in a community signifies the level of discord or unhealthy social relations; that witchcraft offered a release of tension within certain types of African social structures. In many African communities, a "walking corpse" is someone who is alive and physically well but is living in conflict with family, neighbors or community. It resonates with the characterization of Zacchaeus: he was wealthy and physically well but he was morally deficient or short as the Greek word, *helikia* suggests. He did not have much character and was despised by the community. The text used the word, *zeteios* to say that he was a seeker, someone who was materially wealthy and showed all the trappings of external wholeness but was in fact empty in the inside and needing help. He was everything less than what his name, *ZaKaI* (pure, innocent) might suggest. He was healed through a ritual of restitution, restoration and commensality.

Similarly, unhealthy environmental ethics not only cause poverty but become a disease that requires healing. The African Instituted Churches in Zimbabwe have grasped the ecological theme. They celebrate a tree planting eucharist as a healing, reconciling process. The first part of this ritual of regeneration consists of dancing around a heap of seedlings designated for planting. They invoke *Mwari*, God, as the Lord of all creation. Instead of a remote God, he was immanent and fully present. Then, the liturgy shifts to a simulation of the ritual of baptism in a stream. This is used to emphasize conversion, repentance and washing away of sins. Sins are imaged as the operation of forces that bedevil social harmony and well-being. Disharmony is attributed to the operation of witches (*varoyi*). At the tree-planting eucharist, there is an insistence on public confession for ecological sin imaged as witchcraft (ecological *varoyi*). Ecological degradation is represented as the breakdown of moral order which, in turn, spirals into the breakdown of the economy. Those who chopped down trees without replanting them are like witches; and so were those who ploughed on the banks of rivers causing the rivers to silt. In some cases, night vigils of confession were adopted. For African Indigenous Churches (AICs) who regard "crossing river Jordan" in baptism as crucial, the eucharistic re-enactment required a commitment to help restore creation as a part of God's plan, as a sign of genuine conversion and repentance in recognition of the gifts of God's grace. Finally, unrepentant ecological *varoyi* are cast out by Spirit-filled prophets in the same way as the mediums used to detect wizard-traitors at secret *pungwe* meetings during the war for liberation.[10]

From a different perspective, the chopped trees were imaged as the dead who were murdered and whose ghosts, *ngozi*, were crying for appeasement. When a vengeful spirit possessed anyone, the person would become an agent who did terrible things. So insensitivity to the environment could be construed as a form of *ngozi* possession. The eucharistic confession and sacrifices begged the spirit to go away and have rest. After deliverance and cleansing, the Holy Spirit was invoked as the life-giver, fountain of life, and healer to renew the community and bless the trees. The sacrality of the land and the ancestor-guardians were confirmed by sprinkling of holy water. As the congregation surges out to plant trees, one could hear the voice of the officiating priest saying,

> Mwari saw the devastation of the land. So he called his envoys to shoulder the task of deliverance. Come ye messengers of Mwari, come ... We are now the deliverers of the stricken land.[11]

This marked a significant shift from the attitude of fatalism found in many peasant societies which watched helplessly as the biodiversity disappeared.

The confession liturgy is particularly evocative:

> Look at the stagnant water
> where all the trees were felled
> Without trees the water-holes mourn
> without trees the gullies form
> For, the tree-roots to hold the soil are gone!
>
> I, the human being
> your closest friend
> have committed a serious offence
> as ngozi, the vengeful spirit
> I destroyed you, our friends.
> So, the seedlings brought here today
> are the "bodies" mutumbu of restoration
> a sacrifice to appease
> the vengeful spirit
> We plant these seedlings today
> as admission of guilt
> laying the ngozi to rest
> Strengthening our bonds with you
> our tree friends of the heart.
>
> Indeed, there were forests
> abundance of rain
> But in our ignorance and greed
> we left the land naked
> Like a person in shame
> our country is shy
> in its nakedness.[12]

This prayer and ritual show how Africans transform their relationship with nature into a more organic and healthy form.

The language of health in many African communities connects health to life and harmony. It is not built around the germ theory. For instance, from the 1990s and the rise of a strong intercessory ministry, African Pentecostals perform rituals to redeem the land. Land deliverance and healing of nations operate from the same prophetic linkage of human wellbeing to ecological ethics. The ritual of land deliverance is sometimes subtle and avoids overt iconoclasm. Believers can "walk" around shrines because they are regarded as hostile, polluted grounds. They, therefore, command the demonic spirits to leave. They believe that poverty is caused by polluting the land through idolatry or yielding the land to spirits that are hostile to God. Pollution destroys or compromises the security and well-being of the community. Disease, drought, famine and other natural disasters could follow. The cure is to *expel* the evil spirits and to *restore* the land to the creator. Deliverance is beyond exorcism. Sometimes, during emotional crusades, those with authority over the land and affairs of the community will be asked to confess the iniquities of the fathers which are being visited upon their progenies and to hand over the land to the authority of Jesus. As the chief choreographs restoration, this symbolic action will ensure prosperity for all the people. In these ways, the born again brethren in Africa bring a spiritual solution to the socio-economic issues of the day, taking the context, the worldview and the ecology of the communities and bringing them within the gospel mandate. Of course, the religious explanation of causality is the point of contention. Some scientists distinguish between organic and psychosomatic diseases and reject the capacity of faith healing to effect permanent organic healing. Demons, ancestors and dreams are translated in modern, western idioms.

Pentecostal healing practice emphasizes the power of the Holy Spirit by a liturgy that invites the Holy Spirit either through singing, dancing, intense prayer, tarrying and fasting. Healing is often preceded by reading the word and helping the patient to read or hear the word as a foundation for faith. It is believed that God gave believers certain powerful instruments, namely, the Word, the Name and blood of Jesus and the power of the Holy Spirit. Healing liturgy is designed to promote the manifestation of these powerful sources. Altar calls, power services on weekdays, pilgrimages, retreats and prayer camps provide the locations for the powers to manifest. Specific methods are followed to ensure integrity in the healing process: spiritual mapping examines the doors and gates through which sin and disease entered. Covenant tracking excavates the various covenanting rituals in indigenous culture with which the person /s may have been entangled. It surveys the religious history of the patient/s just as medical doctors explore medical histories. Prayer walk cleans the environment. Deliverance consists of exorcism and in-filling with the Holy Spirit.

Unfortunately, some Pentecostal preachers and their followers put a premium on healing as physical cure. When this does not happen or people relapse, spiritual and credibility crises follow. By confining the practice of healing to physical cure, they have thereby lured opponents to debate the authenticity of such claims, the possibility of malpractice and fraud. However, discussions of suffering often fail to explain the source and type-is it suffering from wrong choices, life style, and accident, or in the course of promoting the gospel? Suffering cannot be romanticized. Indeed, some Pentecostal groups draw a distinction between healing and divine health which is imaged as a healthy life derived from a close spiritual walk with God. He sustains the health of those engaged in His service. Healing is about liberation from all that dehumanizes; it is the restoration of life. As Jacques Matthey said in his summary of a consultation organized by the World Council of Churches in Accra, Ghana:

> to experience healing is not just to experience freedom from sickness and illness, or problems and suffering. Healing is a sign of what the Old Testament calls "shalom" (peace, salvation) as the establishment or restoration of right and reconciled relationships, now and at the end of time.[13]

Pentecostal theology is constructed on the plank that healing is the *sign* and *witness* that the reign of God is among God's people; that the power of God to heal is as easily available to God's people as parents demonstrate the obligation to put bread on the children's table. It is also rooted in the Greek New Testament use of *asthenos* and its opposite *asthenes*, weakness and strength. In the healing pericope in James 5:14-18, weakness refers to various types-emotional, physical, economic, sin, death, spiritual and powerlessness. James describes the healing process with rich restorative words as *sozo (save), egerin (raise)* and *iaomai(heal)*. Sickness includes more than physical illness and healing is greater than curing.

In Africa, colonialism nearly eroded the holistic connection between the spiritual and physical aspects of healing. But cultural nationalism has created a resurgence of indigenous knowledge and healing practices. Ironically, the global north has become critical and disenchanted with modern chemical-based medicine. Perhaps postmodernity or development within science itself may have raised doubts whether the chemicals do more harm than good. There is a present danger in an over-reliance on modern medical practices and its use of chemicals as if there is a technology for overcoming death. The debate between scientific and theological perception of Indigenous religions and the new Christianity in the Third World may hold prospects for our understanding and practice of healing. A number of religious trends such as the growth of eastern religions and developments in healing practices have combined with the rediscovery of the power of nature among avid environmentalists to propose a return to herbs and natural cures and to alternative medicine. Scientists recognize the value in indigenous knowledge and pharmacopeias. The indigenous herbalist and diviner are now given due recognition by governments and health officials.

Pharmacognosy has won a new lease on life though the question remains whether herbs retain efficacy without indigenous religious rituals.

In the two last parts of this paper, it is, therefore argued that the direction for African Pentecostal scholarship on health and healing is to examine three crucial dimensions, namely, the connection between Pentecostal concept of health and healing to the concept of salvation and poverty; Pentecostal hermeneutics; and the liturgy of healing especially music and dance. In some churches, healing rituals occur during intense music and dance. We shall consider the first two and preserve the third for another outing.

Nkwa: Salvation and Healing in African Pentecostal Theology

The concept of salvation in Pentecostal theology has attracted attention but the tendency was to explore it from the pulsating prosperity gospel.[14] Salvation is a military term signifying liberation from an inimical and life threatening situation, and being set free to live an authentic life. Asamoah-Gyadu defines it as suggesting two fundamental emphases in Pentecostal soteriology: conversion and transformation through empowerment. African Pentecostals teach a doctrine of sequential three fold conversion: believers move from "leprous anointing" (repentance from sin and initial acceptance of Christ), to "priestly anointing" (spirit baptism, sealed and seated with Christ and manifestation of the charismatic gifts of the Spirit) to "kingly anointing" (or capacity to engage in a power encounter with forces of darkness). While a few teach total sanctification, the majority acknowledge that sanctification is a process that yields more and more fruits of the Spirit. The debate about tongues as an initial evidence exists but does not rage as widely as in the western world. Born again Christians are encouraged to "covet" the gift less as evidence but more as an instrument for effective prayer that avails much. It is said to be the language of the angels that confuses Satan. It becomes one of the weapons in the warfare imagery of both salvation and the security of a Christian life. It could, therefore, be used to detect and defeat an oppressive demon.

The gift of tongues can be received either by laying of hands or by the power in the word of the pastor who will ask people at the altar to open their mouths, start saying something loudly without worrying about what they are saying. People have claimed that suddenly the speech motor will change. Each stage is followed by testimonies to acknowledge that the encounter with Christ has transformed the person from the inside, liberated from the power of evil ways of life, and empowered with the capacity to live a Godly life. Repentance and bridge-burning acts demonstrated by answering the altar call become the signs that conversion has occurred. In this scenario, Spirit baptism starts a deeper level of commitment that increases the sanctification and the accession to spiritual gifts. It is suggested that many people accept Christ but do not progress to the level of "kingly anointing." Without this endurance, believers backslide and become cold Christians and bench-warmers. Pentecostal diatribe against the established churches is that they fail to empower believers. Asamoah-Gyadu puts it aptly, when outsiders see the exuberant aspects of Pentecostal behavior, they lose sight of Pentecostal central affirmation that the experience of the Holy Spirit transforms human life.[15] It confers divine health.

There are three emphases here: salvation means to be liberated, as if in a warfare, from evil forces and sinful habits. They imagine and objectify the persistence of the sinful drive as being external and from a personality called Satan who hinders and essays to destroy the ability of a Christian to run a good race or live a healthy life. Salvation manifests in the transformation of material, physical and psychic well-being. In traditional religion such objectification existed. Witchcraft provided the idiom for articulating it. A person could be born as a witch and may not even know it, as if possessed. The person could be liberated through a ritual process. This is different from sorcery when a person deliberately acquires the capacity for hurting others through charms and medicine. Sorcery uses a method of tactile contacts in exercising the capacity. Either way, there is a force out there that confers the power to harm others. Individuals resort to acquire antidotes and to gain a countervailing power that enables one to progress or enhance life force, maintain psychic equilibrium, and resist those who may wish to harm or diminish one's coping capacity. Africans cultural idiom provided a pathway to resignify that unspecified power as Satan by utilizing the missionary, biblical language and symbol. Todd Vanden Berg demonstrates this by using the example of the Logunda community in central Nigeria to show how the indigenous concept of evil is reconfigured through a process of "grounded integration, " rooted in the traditional beliefs about evil.[16] Personal responsibility and personal sin are never denied but healing is both communal and from the interaction with spiritual power. Peace, personal and communal integrity are restored through religious rituals that tap supernatural power.

Francis Young captures this in his study of salvation in the New Testament:

> Salvation...is God's rescue operation, re-creation, the restoration of a wholeness which involves transformation into 'Christs, ' into bearers of the divine image.[17]

A theology of healing, therefore, emerges from covenant theology, the concept of salvation and the atoning death of Christ. Kinsgsley Larbi has deployed the etymology of the concept of wholeness among the Akan to underscore the resonance with the biblical view. African anthropology emphasizes vitality of life and abundant life as the chief goals for daily living. These are the ends of every religious ritual: to preserve, enhance, and protect life. Abundant life among the Akan resonates with the Hebrew concept of *shalom*, denoting total wholeness that is physical, psychological, spiritual and social. For the African, it describes peace with God, the gods, ancestors, fellow human beings (family and community) and the world of nature. Natural forces co-operate by yielding their increase.

Many African communities share this understanding that health and prosperity are not material but reflect inner peace, satisfaction or contentment and maintenance of social networks. The Igbo of southeastern Nigeria have a proverb that says that anyone who does not possess the support from a kinship group is a vulnerable human being. When a missionary waxed vivid about how Jesus was tortured and beaten, a chief inquired about the response of his kin group because if they permitted the horrendous punishment without fighting back, Jesus must have been a bad man!

The Akan of Ghana use the concept of *Nkwa* to denote abundant life. *Nkwa*, says Larbi, includes the enjoyment of *ahonyade*, possessions, prosperity, that is wealth, riches including children. It also embodies *asomdwei*, a life of peace and tranquility, especially peace with God, the spirits, kinsfolk and neighbors. These are the contents of liturgies and concerns expressed in libations. As far back as 1974, Christian Gaba's *Sacred Scripture of an African People, the Anlo* dealt more elaborately with this. The quest for wholeness includes health, prosperity, fertility, security, dignity, community and the capacity to resist the forces that could thwart a person's *nkwa*. Such forces could be external and supernatural: *abayifo* (witches), *akaberekyerefo* (sorcerers), *asummantufo* (charmers and bad medicine men) and *awudifo* (wicked ones). It could also emanate from internal, moral faults or from polluting the land through criminal acts, misdemeanors, and flouting of prohibitions. Offences against spiritual forces have consequences that manifest in hardship and afflictions in the physical realm. People consult ritual agents who diagnose the cause and offer the process for ritual cleansing, propitiation and restoration. The agents acknowledge that they act on behalf of *Nkwagyefo* (in common parlance, *agyenkwa*), the one who saves, protects and preserves life. This strand of indigenous knowledge opens the pathway for inculturating the Jesus figure as one who rescues from danger, redeems and delivers. Mercy Amba Oduyoye says that

> The *Agyenkwa* means the one who rescues, who holds your life
> in safety, takes you out of a life-denying situation and places you
> in a life affirming one. The Rescuer plucks you from a dehuman-
> izing ambience and places you in a position where you can grow
> toward authentic humanity. The *Agyenkwa* gives you back your
> life in all its fullness.[18]

Jean and John Comaroffs in *Modernity and Its Malcontents* [19] point
the data from libations to a different direction-as responses to modernity
and the desire to access the resources of globalization. African Pentecostal theology of salvation, when properly exegeted, is rich in its capacity to
re-imagine the gospel from indigenous idiom. Pentecostal theology does
not encourage people to fold their arms and wait for manna to drop from
the skies; rather, poverty alleviation strategy in indigenous communities
was more nuanced. The Igbo people say that *"onye kwe, chi ya ekwe"* (when
one affirms, the personal god will confirm). *Chi* is the personal spirit that
a person inherits and that determines fate and destiny in life pilgrimage.
This proverb locates poverty and affliction in both supernatural and human
agency. The individual's will power and the strength of the right hand that
is represented by the icon, *ikenga* and the person's attention to moral dimensions of life can yield an escape. Often the person's relationship with the
chi is queried: did the person inherit a bad *chi* or failed to give kola nut to
the *chi?* Poverty alleviation, therefore, involved ritualized stabilization of
relationships between the human being, the divine, and the world of nature.

Restoration of moral order ensures that human activities succeed and
evil is warded off. Things that are seen are made of things that are unseen.
Alleviation is not merely achieved by intensification of human activities
but by first restraining the capacity of negative moral forces from ruining
human projects. When moral order is abused, the gates will be opened
for poverty and affliction to enter the domains of individuals, family and
community.[20] Therefore, Pentecostals provide the power of Jesus as the
agyenkwa who rescues. This is the solution that people seek in the healing
camps, prayer houses and "power services."[21]

The Word, Pentecostal Hermeneutics
and Healing in Africa

Most opponents are concerned about Biblicism, fundamentalism and
uncritical literalism among the Pentecostals in the southern globe. Pentecostals claim that they boldly, tenaciously and rightly divide the word.
But their critics have a different "systematic" manner of dividing the word.

For instance, in the hermeneutical task, certain features are required of the practioners : reading the text carefully (descriptive task), placing the text in canonical context (the synthetic task), relating the text to our situation through a certain mode of appropriation and through appeal to other authorities, and finally engaging the pragmatic task of living the text. Many theological enterprises tend to differ on the appropriation level and some tend to put the foot heavily on the pragmatic task. For Pentecostals, it is as if the pain of the human condition is too excruciating to indulge in involuted exegesis. Philosophical niceties appear as luxury. The lens used in dividing or interpreting the word would betray the interpreter's attitude to the Bible as canon, the place of tradition, the Trinity and other sources for reconstructing reality. Pentecostal "bumper-sticker" hermeneutical method has attracted much debate, because as a car sticker proclaimed, "This is the Word of God, I believe it and that is final". They bring a new approach which circumvents the crises in the art of interpreting the Bible which has changed with shifts in theory of knowledge. Enlightenment and liberalism, fundamentalism and evangelical neo-orthodoxy, each has left imprints. Pinnock has delineated the differences in hermeneutic principles of these groups. [22] Even within the Pentecostal movement the hermenutical practice has changed. In early Pentecostalism, the Bible was the word of God and understood at its face value. The operative principle of interpretation was the conviction that exegesis is best when it is as rigidly literal as credibility can stand. The horizons of the past and present were fused with a pragmatic hermeneutical leap. Allegorization eased appropriation of the text and preaching was spontaneous but not relegated to professional clergy.

The participation of the congregation in the liturgy does not wane during the hearing of the word. Rather, the congregation participates in responses as the sermon reaches for an immediate experience for the listeners. The altar call becomes the climax. Admittedly, modern Pentecostalism is more open to studied and non-literal exegesis but the temper remains much the same. The truth must be fulfilled in life experiences. The language of God in African Pentecostal liturgy buttresses this fact. They explore the language which communities use in addressing their sustaining divinities, ancestors and the Supreme Being and use these to describe God and Christ, showing that the Godhead is superior to all the powers available in the people's map of their universe. The reconstructed world is brought home to individual lives and circumstances by applying a "bumper sticker" hermeneutics or "experiential literalism". Cheryl B. Johns said that Pentecostal hermeneutics is praxis- oriented with experience and Scripture being maintained in a dialectical relationship. The Holy Spirit maintains the ongoing relationship. Lived faith is the result of the knowledge of the

Scriptures.[23] The emphases are on the experiential, relational, emotional, oral faith, immediacy of the text and a freedom to interpret and appropriate the multiple meanings of the biblical texts. By a pneumatic illumination, it recognizes a spiritual kinship between the authors and readers and ongoing continuity with the New Testament church. Personal and corporate experiences are woven into the hermeneutical task. This is the dialogical role of experience.

There is an emphasis on the narrative texts. As the reader gives authority to narrative sections of the biblical text, the text becomes a part of the person. Steve Land calls Pentecostal view of the Scripture as "Spirit-Word" and Cheryl Johns describes this approach as "knowing in active relationship." Johns has, therefore, developed a four-part process by which the study of the text becomes a means of conscientization: the Christian story serves as a source of critique for the present; then, there is a movement from present praxis to the story, bringing its own consciousness and needs to the appropriation of the story; the dialectic between the vision which arises out of the meaning of the story and our present praxis and finally, movement from present praxis to vision with the future being shaped by our appropriation. As W. Iser, *Acting of Reading* would say, reading the bible is not just a cognitive experience but an affective one. The text requires a reader to complete the circuit of communication. Pentecostals put revelation before the cognitive. Ears itch for new "piping hot revelation" which the Holy Spirit just gave to the pastor. They practice hermeneutics of trust or fidelity instead of the hermeneutics of suspicion characteristic of liberal theology.

Years ago, Schleiermacher drew a distinction between "masculine reading" of Scriptures which analyses the original meaning keeping at a historical and critical distance, and a "feminine reading" dominated by a creative intuition and immediacy with the text in our present. Pentecostal hermeneutic is feminine, eschatological, organic and helps the audience to recognize the signs of the times and to discern what God is doing in today's world. This becomes empowerment for a "counterworld imagination." The danger could be an eclectic reading ignoring the descriptive and synthetic levels of reading the text. In some cases a misappropriation or misuse of scripture may occur in the hands of an ill-trained leader. Indeed, there is a move within the camp to systemize Pentecostal theology. For instance, a preacher used Is.45:11 - "Ask me of things to come concerning my sons, and concerning the work of my hands command ye me" - as an authority to teach that believers could *command* by faith that situations like threatening rain, should stop. There are many examples of incautious Pentecostal exegesis in circulation creating an air of popular religiosity. This does not detract from the benefits of a new conscientizing empowering hermeneutic that brings the gospel home. Believers are encouraged to command diseases out of their bodies.

S.A. Ellington has explained the pattern of Pentecostal approach to the doctrine about the Scriptures. He says that Pentecostals understand and utilize doctrines in a fundamentally different way from those traditions which are more thoroughly grounded in rationalist models of considering the question of authority of the Scriptures. "For Pentecostals, doctrine is not essentially generative in function but rather descriptive," used to verbalize lived experience. "Beliefs are not derived from understanding but arise from intense experiences of encountering God." This knowing in relationship precedes articulation of experiences in normative doctrinal ways. As Brueggemann put it, "it is enough to acknowledge, be awed and delighted" in the assertion that all that exists is wrought by the extravagant generosity of God. The word is embodied in the community and, therefore, the text is read eschatologically as the intrusion of the kingdom of God into the present and as empowerment in living out its promises.[24]

To illustrate how the hermeneutic is given wing by the homiletics, we take the pericope in Luke 13:10-17 where Jesus healed the crippled woman. An African Pentecostal preacher would firstly describe the sad fate of the woman until everyone would recognize a similar case in the neighborhood and village. There may be an interlude with a plaintive song from a traditional dirge or folk-tale. Then, the entry of Jesus into the context would be portrayed in such vivid colors that each person would feel the awesome presence. The past is given life in the present. The healing occurs as the whole congregation stands to sing that "in the word of God, there is power; in the name of Jesus, every knee shall bow". Other victory choruses would follow before the coup de main in verse 16. Jesus calls the woman, "the daughter of Abraham", that is, one in whose body the promise of God and enduring covenant was powerfully at work. Her social context had constructed her otherwise - cripple, ugly, dysfunctional and worthless. For years, she accepted the verdict for life. Jesus renames her and imbues her with an imagination of being much different. She accepts the counter-verdict, "stood up straight and began to praise God." Jesus roots himself in the enduring covenant of God and refuses manifest givens, and voices a different reality that is borne on the countertext in Genesis. Pentecostal hermeneutics surfs the counterverdicts of God and use these to conscientize the people of God in the midst of life's debilitating contexts.

Answering the altar call is like a degradation ritual which ensures that they can now act differently and perceive the world very differently. The homiletics craft language in a transformative manner so that the believer would begin to speak differently and soon, through biographical testimonies, share and validate the religious belief system being advocated. The process of turning text into oral and experiential models is a recovery of what the Bible originally had been. Pentecostal hermeneutics provides an altered view of self - identity-change, bridge burning, and cognitive restructuring.

The hermeneutics underscore the Pentecostal emphasis on the power of the Word. Both in the Bible and in indigenous religions, words have power and could be deployed in resisting forces which could lead one to backslide, in reversing curses, in deliverance and in claiming the things which the Lord's hands have made. Good health is high on the list because " by His stripes we are healed." This is why it is important for the "brethren" to arrive for Bible studies and Sunday worship with notebooks so as to take down the message or "revelations" which should be applied during the week for victory. This is the practice of victorious living. Everyone is urged to be an overcomer and "demon destroyer." Preachers reproduce teaching tapes and videos and believers are encouraged to read devotional literature instead of "jezebelian" or secular novels. Ministries produce house magazines which are full of teachings. This is a far cry from the liberal critical tendency to discount the speech of God as mere rhetoric and "metaphor."

In conclusion, the contest between modern science and the African Pentecostal concept of health, healing and healing practices arise from a clash of worldviews, use of the Bible and hermeneutics. But the gulf is narrowing because Pentecostals are not averse to the resources of modern medicine but are ready to discount medical reports in the quest for divine intervention. Emphasis on experience instead of rational philosophy buttresses the conviction. Post modernity has cast doubt on the certitude in the sciences. Fraught with uncertainty about the claims of the enlightenment worldview, many scientists are engaging indigenous worldviews and religious sources for alternative healing technology. Scholarship could contribute by analyzing the basis for African Pentecostal concepts that are sourced from both the gospel and indigenous worldviews.

Notes

1. Nancy A. Hardesty, *Faith Cure: Divine Healing in the Holiness and Pentecostal Movements* (Peabody, MA: Hendrickson Publishers, 2003).

2. Stanley Hauerwas, *God, Medicine and Suffering* (Grand Rapids, MI: Eerdmans, 1990).

3. Stuart C. Bate, *Inculturation and Healing: Coping-Healing in South African Christianity* (Pietermaritzburgh: Cluster Publications, 1995), 15.

4. Philip Jenkins, *The New Faces of Christianity: Believing the Bible in the Global South* (New York: Oxford University Press, 2006), 98.

5. Paul G. Hiebert, *Transforming Worldviews: An Anthropological Understanding of How People Change* (Grand Rapids, MI: Baker Books, 2008); Walter Wink, *Naming the Powers: The Language of Power in the New Testament* (Philadelphia, PA: Fortress, 1984);Ogbu U Kalu, "Estranged Bedfellows: The Demonization of the Aladura in African Pentecostal Rhetoric" *Missionalia*, 28, 2/3 (August/November, 2000):121-142; Ogbu Kalu, *African Pentecostalism: An Introduction* (New York: Oxford University Press, 2008):65-83.

6. Tabona Shoko, *Karanga Indigenous Religion in Zimbabwe* (Aldershot, UK, and Burlington, Vt.: Ashgate, 2007); Evan M. Zuesse, *Ritual Cosmos: The Sanctification of Life in African Religions* (Athens, OH: Ohio University Press, 1979).

7. David Maxwell, *African Gifts of the Spirit: Pentecostalism and the Rise of a Zimbawean Transnational Religious Movement* (Oxford, James Currey, 2006):52-57

8. W.J. Hollenweger, "Healing Through Prayer: Superstition or Forgotten Christian Tradition?" *Theology*, 92, 747 (1989):166-174; see p. 173.

9. Laurenti Magesa, *Anatomy of Inculturation: Transforming the Church in Africa* (Maryknoll, NY: Orbis, 2004), 81; Stuart C.Bate, *Inculturation and Healing: Coping-Healing in South African Christianity* (Pietermaritzburg: Cluster Publications, 1995) is a plea for a holistic approach to coping-healing among the churches. He shows the strengths and weaknesses among the AICs and Pentecostals in South Africa.

10. M. L. Daneel, "African Independent Churches Face Challenge of Environmental Ethics," *Missionalia* 21, no. 3 (1993).

11. Ibid: 318.

12. Daneel, "African Independent Churches Face Challenge of Environmental Ethics," 326. [It should be noted that the economic and political collapse of Zimbabwe in the past few years has destroyed the tree-planting movement referenced in this article, though many chiefs and AIC prophets in rural areas are eager for its restoration.]

13. "Divine Healing, Pentecostalism and Mission, " *International Review of Mission*, 93, 370/371 (July/October, 2004), 407. The entire issue of the journal is rich with articles by prominent scholars on the subject. The Lutheran also held a conference: Ingo Wulfhorst, ed., *Ancestors, Spirits and Healing in Africa and Asia: A Challenge to the Church* (LWF: Geneva, 2005); Stanley Hauerwas, *God, Medicine and Suffering* (Grand Rapids, MI: Eerdmans, 1990).

14. E. Kingsley Larbi, "The Nature of Continuity and Discontinuity of Ghanaian Pentecostal Concept of Salvation in African Cosmology", *Asian Journal of Pentecostal Studies*, 5, 1 (2002):99-119; Asamoah-Gyadu, *African Charismatics* (2005): chapt.7-"Salvation as Prosperity."

15. Ibid., 141.

16. T.M.V. Berg, "Culture, Christianity and Witchcraft in a West African Context" in *The Changing Face of Christianity*, eds. Lamin Sanneh and Joel Carpenter (New York:OUP, 2005):45-62.

17. cit. Asamoah-Gyadu, *African Charismatics*, 143.

18. Mercy Amba Oduyoye, *Hearing and Knowing* (Maryknoll, NY: Orbis Books, 1986), 98; Christian Gaba, *The Sacred Scriptures of an African People* (New York: NOK Publishers, 1974).

19. Jean and John Comarroff, *Modernity and It Malcontents: Ritual and Power in Postcolonial Africa* (Chicago: University of Chicago Press, 1993); Opoku Onyinah, "Contemporary Witchdemonology in Africa", *International Review of Mission*, 93, 370/371 (July/October, 2004):330-345.

20. For further discussion, see, Ogbu U. Kalu, "Poverty in pre-colonial and colonial West Africa: perception, causes and alleviation" in *Themes in West Africa's History* ed. Emmanuel K. Akyeampong (Oxford: James Currey, 2006):163-185.

21. Cit. Donald McGravan, *Crucial Issues in Mission Tomorrow* (Chicago: Moody Press, 1972), 132.

22. K.J. Archer, "Pentecostal Hermeneutics: Retrospect and Prospect," *Journal of Pentecostal Theology*, 8 (1996): 63-81; S.A. Ellington, "Pentecostalism and the Authority of Scripture," *Journal of Pentecostal Theology*, 9 (1996):16-38; H.M Ervin, "Hermeneutics: A Pentecostal Option," *Pneuma*, 3, 2 (Fall, 1981); W. Iser, *The Act of Reading* (Baltimore: John Hopkins University Press, 1978); C.H. Pinnock, "The Work of the Holy Spirit in Hermeneutics," *Journal of Pentecostal Theology*, 2 (April.1993):3-23.

23. Cheryl B. Johns, *Pentecostal Formation* (Sheffield: Academic Press, 1993), 86; Steve Land, *Pentecostal Spirituality: A Passion for The Kingdom* (Sheffield, UK: Sheffield Academic Press, 1993): chapters 1, 4.

24. W. Brueggemann, *Texts Under Negotiation: The Bible and Postmodern Imagination* (Philadelphia: Fortress Press, 1993), 29; J.D. Johns, "Pentecostalism and Postmodern Worldview," *Journal of Pentecostal Theology*, 7 (1995):73-96.

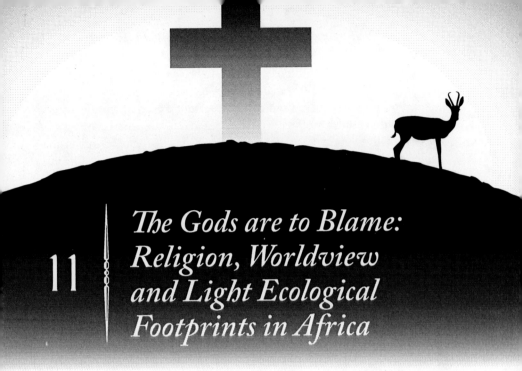

11 | *The Gods are to Blame: Religion, Worldview and Light Ecological Footprints in Africa*

The Gods are to Blame: The Problem with Religious Cosmologies

I come from South-Eastern Nigeria and more specifically from the Eastern sub-culture zone of Igboland but teach and live in a University located in the Northern zone. In the mid-1970's, the Government gave us a boon by tarring a road which enormously shortened the circuitous route which was my only way home. But within two decades, that short-cut has been split in five places by huge erosion gullies. One of these is within a densely- populated village. In the cluster habitat structure, modern buildings dot the road, away from the maddening crowded village. The erosion gully is now about ten yards from some of the 'ultra-modern' buildings erected by indigenes who have made their fortunes in the urban centers. Prestige, wealth and shelter are all rolled into one in these edifices. The erosion threat becomes more significant. Much more is at stake as these structures are perceived as evidence of 'development' and pride of the communities.

As I gaped into this particular gully which threatened the pride of the people, swallowing the electric pole and wanting more, I noticed that some iron crosses have been planted on the edges of the erosion gully as if to restrain the demons which were attacking the well-being of the community. One may immediately think of the drama of King Canute's puny effort to restrain the tumultuous path of the waves. But King Canute was parading human, kingly power. Those iron crosses symbolized something more potent, indeed, supernatural. They represent a certain worldview and different understanding of reality. They removed the matter of erosion gullies from the mundane plane and from whatever the scientists may consider as the causes of erosion. The gods are to blame. Those gods who did not want the abundant life for the community essayed to erode the community's pride and the symbols of its development. Remember that the things which are seen are made of the things which are not seen. With these iron crosses a battle was joined in the spiritual realm. The elastic nature of indigenous cosmology enables the recruitment of new forces inherent in the symbol of the cross. The Christian symbol is now rooted in primal world view and Christianity becomes an extension of primal religion. That is another matter. For now, erosion is a religious matter perceived with a primal cultural hermeneutic.

But our concern is not about erosions but about the ambivalence in the sacralized worldview or religious cosmology and the implications for conservation of ecological resources or *making light footprints on our part of the planet.* Crucial to indigenous traditions is a religious cosmology with an awareness of the integral and whole relationship of symbolical and material life. Ritual practices of the cosmological ideas which undergird society cannot be separated from daily round of subsistence practices. Remarkable intimacies with bio-regions are often believed to be the sources of sacred revelation and ritual practices which instill the collective memories of people and their survival. By sacralizing nature, indigenous worldviews purvey an ideology which is at once more eco-sensitive, eco-musical and devoid of the harsh flutes of those who see nature as a challenge to be conquered, exploited and ruled. As Peter Dunne said in a *New York Times* editorial, "the environment is not a competing interest; it is the playing field on which all other interests intersect". Theirs is an eco-centric worldview which binds humans and the rest of nature with the same umbilical cord.

This can be illustrated with an incident which occurred when the Anambra State government in Eastern Nigeria attempted to solve the scorching low food supply due to the breakdown of the agricultural industry. With World Bank loan, they acquired irrigation pumps. But in the attempt to install these, a certain community, called Amanuke, impeded those digging the irrigation trenches. They argued that the trenches desecrated their ancestral shrines. When their ancestors migrated from the Northern flood plain of the River Niger, they consecrated shrines for their ancestral gods in that forest. These gods preserve the community. Rural developers admonished them that firstly, they were denuding their forest resources; secondly, irrigation would assist them to utilize a smaller land acreage, crop three times in a year and produce more. One old chief looked quite unimpressed and countered that if the gods wanted them to crop three times, they would have spurted water from the ground. Ancestral gods are very caring. A number of factors were at play: the planners ignored the worldview and the in-put of the community at their peril. Land politics jostled with this. If the government built the irrigation contrapment, they might easily claim the ownership of the land through the Land Use Decree and the community would become tenant farmers in their own land. For our purposes, the worldview of the people aided the conservation of the biodiversity. This effort is achieved by the symbiotic relationship of people to land. The zoned shrine area is enfolded with a sacred canopy. This process is soon challenged by the pressure of resource management to respond to the scourges of poverty and depletion of food supply. The inner core of the ideology of traditional societies emerges as the gods are looked upon to replenish or sustain the viability of the soil. In this case, the community cared less about the depletion of the forest resources but rather looked up to the gods to bring water out of the ground to replenish the earth. They also invested enormous religious ardor to preserve the shrine. This calls attention to the importance of shrines in studying the conservation of fauna and flora. But the interest here is the irony, call it ambivalence which is our point of departure.

In spite of the sacralization or because of it, there is often a lack of an ideology of preservation, conservation and replacement. The gods are to blame when resources are depleted, when the un-replenished soil yield brown and stunted corn. The gods are to blame when environmentally- degrading practices scorch bio-diversity and wipe out sustainability. Admittedly, much diversity exists among the worldviews which are imaged as indigenous, untrammeled by the rationalistic, industrial ethics. The focus here will be Africa.

How can African societies escape from the crippling ambivalence to develop an ethic of conservation and walk lightly on their share of the planet in the face of encroaching Western industrial ethics and the decimation of traditional values and norms? How could the ethics of restraint, maintenance, limit to greed, selective consumption, regeneration of replaceable resources be crafted into the sacralized worldview? This is the burden of this paper. It is suggested that there may be a danger in the romanticization of indigenous worldviews despite the nuggets in traditional knowledge. From a broader perspective, humans have been acting ruthlessly on the environment long before Western industrial culture quickened the pace. Cultural engineering or worldview transformation is the only exit. Cultural engineering is predicated on Einstein's dictum that "the significant problems we face cannot be solved at the same level of thinking we were at when we created them". In other words, insanity is doing the same thing over and over again and expecting a different result. Assuming that worldview is the theory and ethos the practice, cultural engineering aims at changing the ethics in cultural practices. This could be achieved by mining indigenous knowledge to highlight those salient elements which are most eco-sensitive or eco-centric, and if necessary legitimate them through rituals as means of preserving the environment for the future generation. Culture will still serve as an anchor because the engineering will utilize the contours of the cultural terrain. This is called, *traditionalization*, when tradition is set on wheels, gestating new forms and serving as the instrument for domesticating new change- agents. In this process of globecalization, the particularity of culture is enhanced by contact with global values.

This paper shall do three things: (a) mine African worldview and indigenous knowledge to demonstrate how primal values—religious and cultural—enhance conservation of the environment; (b) explore how non-sustainable values are ironically embedded in the worldview and cultural practices; and finally, (c) delineate values which aid conservation and explore how to reconstruct and transform primal worldviews so as to prioritize these salient values. This involves changing the mind-set of society, guiding and motivating socio-cultural frameworks to move on a sustainable path.

It is certainly a tall order as it urges a paradigm shift in the relationship of humans to environment and each other. It explores such concepts as sufficiency, efficiency, productivity, non-material ways, qualitative development and such-like. It is based on the urgent concern that Africa has lost much of its biodiversity out of ignorance, the lack of a culture of conservation and the heedless, misconstrued notion of development. These internal forces have been exercabated by external change-agents.

The Sacred Egg: Anatomy of Worldview

Primal cultures are underpinned by worldviews which serve as reservoirs of indigenous knowledge. They are stored in proverbs and folk myths. Myths of origin abound, explaining how the world came into existence. One of these imagine the world as a sacred egg, at once fragile, enfolding and nurturing. Its sacred origin imbues it with a sacral order which, when understood and followed, would ensure a miracle as this seemingly fragile frame has the capacity to sustain so many and so much activity. We shall return to this precarious vision anon(Kalu, 1978 a).

From such myths people begin to construct how and why things are the way they are. Explanation aids prediction of space-time events and this, in turn, enables control. Myths of origin are, therefore, the vehicles of worldviews and differ among the ethnic groups who inhabit West Africa. A common structure underlies all of them and they share a deep-level meaning. Each is couched in religious, numinous terms: creation was the act of a Supreme Being utilizing the services of subaltern gods. The divine origin confers a sacred shroud on the created beings and social order.

People, therefore, construct a moral order, with a certain rhythm, to explain, predict and control space-time events in their ecosystem. A wise student defined worldview as how people view their world. It is a mental construct which empowers action and endows both rhythm and meaning to life processes. It is the foundation of customs, social norms and law. Worldviews are embedded in the people's experience and, then, expressed or re-enacted in their cultures. This can be illustrated with one cultural feature, namely, masquerades. These are very important in the rituals, festivals, aesthetics and plastic arts. Masquerades of semi-savannah, grassland communities tend to be clothed in dry grass. Some look like moving bundles of grass. Among the forest-zone dwellers, the masquerades leap out of the bushes as followers caparison with leaves and branches. In the Owu Festival of riverine communities of the Niger Delta, the masquerades arrive in canoes with masks depicting various kinds of fishes. The community would dance to the waterfront, welcome them with a chorus into the village and the celebration would begin. At dusk, they are led back to the beach; as they paddle off, the people would wave and cry for the departing ancestors. That is the crux of the cultural form: the masquerades are ancestors; they are the gods as guests to the human world. With their arrival, the seen and the unseen worlds meet; the living and the living-dead re-unite even if for a brief period. The Owu cultural form is a celebration of a certain worldview explaining the moral order.

The environment poses a challenge and the community constructs a world view which unravels the riddle of the universe. It must address and reflect the specific nature of the challenge by probing their inner experience. People forge culture in the encounter with and effort to tame their environment and harness her resources for the nurture of that community. Worldviews underpin the culture. As culture is the powerful expression of the creativity of the human spirit, the engine that moves civilization and the substance of history, worldview is the hermeneutic, "the cultural lens through which human experience is viewed" (Kraft, 1995: 20).

Various anthropologists have sought to capture the nuances of world-view: some call it "mind- world" and explore the differences between western and non-western mind-worlds. The ethnologist, Edward Sapir, termed it "the unconscious patterning of behavior in society...the way a people characteristically look outward on the universe". He noted that patterns of thought, attitude towards life, conceptions of time, a mental picture of what ought to be, a people's understanding of their relationship to unseen things and to the order of things, and their view of self and others-all these are included in a people's worldview. He might be inelegant in the attempt to be comprehensive (Mandelbaum, 1958: 548)

Paul G. Hiebert (1985: 46) organizes the content of worldview into three categories--cognitive, affective and evaluative. These refer to the abstract ideas, inter-personal structures and ethical values. Charles Kraft(1989: 20, 182) underscores the place of values in a worldview as "the culturally structured assumptions, values and commitments underlying a people's perception of reality". They are "deep-level bases from which people generate surface-level behavior". Therefore, concludes Marguerite Kraft(1995: 21), worldviews

> Affect how people perceive self, the in-group to which they belong, outsiders, nature around them and non-human world... (and) makes it possible for people to feel comfortable in their environment....Worldview is a picture of what is and ought to be, and it provides the motivation for behavior and gives meaning to the environment.

It is, indeed, as John Grim puts it, "a story of the world which informs all aspects of life among a people, giving subsistence practice, artistic creation, ritual play and military endeavor a significant content"(Tucker +Grim, 1993: 42).Like the rest of culture, it can be unconsciously learned but deliberately transmitted. It could become encrusted into customs safe in the womb-like warmth of the sacred egg. But, however resistant to the battering waves of change, the crusts chip away as the process of reconfiguration and reconstruction begin.

In the effort to demonstrate the relationship between African and Western scientific thought pattern, Robin Horton insisted that worldview is like theory-building and, therefore, a "quest for the unity underlying apparent diversity; for the simplicity underlying apparent complexity and for order underlying disorder; for the regularity underlying apparent anomaly "(Horton, 1993). It does more as it brings into causal relationship wider vistas of reality and everyday life. He demonstrated with Kalabari worldview showing that the fears and hopes and religious ardor of the

Kalabari could easily be understood by a close look at three basic kinds of forces: ancestors, heroes and water-spirits. Appreciating the idiom of their "mystical "thinking may not only solve the riddle of "primitive mentality" which bothered Levy-Bruhl but explain the factors at the mental matrix of the community which aid them to survive in their ecosystem. They could link events in the visible, tangible (natural effects) to their antecedents in the same world(natural causes).

Are world view constructs fantasy? Meyer Fortes in his study of the theories of the individual and his relationship to society among the Tallensi (Ghana) demurs. He takes the "multiple soul" beliefs of the Tallensi and places them in the everyday thought and behavior as a Westerner would link psychological imperatives and sociological imperatives (Fortes, 1949; 1959).The activities of gods and spirits celebrated in rituals and festivals play out in the social space much of the concerns of daily living. This is what Peter Berger calls the "cosmization of the social world"(1967).As he adds, "such a cosmos, as the ultimate ground and validation of human nomoi, need not necessarily be sacred".

It is also palpable that both culture and worldview are not static. Indeed, some have surmised the existence of three publics in African social analysis: the primal setting where the gods of our fathers hold sway, the intrusive Western public and the emergent public forged in the exegesis of the latter. It is neither African nor European. Fela Ransome-Kuti, the Afro-jazz maestro, characterizes the emergent public as "*shakara*". In his album, "*Authority Stealing*" he explores the moral implications of these cultural shifts, satirizing the *noveaux riches* who would steal money from the western public and dance to the big drum in the indigenous public. The incursion of emergent culture into the primary sector erodes her salient values without an adequate replacement, creating tension and indiscipline. These people perceive the western public as other than theirs and practice there values which cannot be tolerated in the primary public. There is a certain sense of moral anomie. The trouble arises when the same people assume leadership roles in their villages; they become bearers of unwholesome values which like virus destroy the traditional value systems. The palate for American junk culture among the youths in the emergent public puts an enervating pressure on traditional institutions. The impact of new worldviews within indigenous cultures constitutes one aspect of the task of this paper. The broader goal is, as J.B. Callicott(1993) put it,

> The revival and deliberate construction of environmental ethics from the raw materials of indigenous, traditional and contemporary cultures.(Tucker and Grim, 1993: 32)

Anthill in the Marsh:
The African's Perception of the world

It has been argued that underneath the varieties of cultures in Africa is a core worldview structure. Admittedly within a culture there could be many interlocking worldviews. Details may vary even within an ethnic group. Crucial are the concepts of Time and Space. Mircea Eliade (1959) has argued that among traditional societies there is a predominant construction of the concept of time around the movement of the agricultural season. Time is cyclical, moving from planting to harvest, followed by a repeat of the eternal cycle. The myth of eternal return is woven with this fabric. Life follows the pattern of nature, moving from birth, through accession to various stages, rights and duties, symbolized by membership in one sodality or the other, till death. Matters do not end there; a new stage of living would begin as the personality soul of the individual begins a journey through the Spirit World until reincarnation.

To fill up the details more: rites of passage celebrate the various stages of life. At birth, the out-dooring ceremony only not provides an opportunity to declare who has returned to the family, it covenants the individual to the land, the community. Eight days earlier, the child's umbilical cord would have been put in a calabash and sprinkled with herbs and after some pronouncements, buried under a tree at the back of the house. The child is rooted to the land with which it shares an everlasting bond. Through open and secret societies, the community would teach the child the salient values and coping mechanisms for harnessing nurture from the ecosystem. In the *isi ji* ceremony among the Afikpo-Edda culture complex, adolescent boys are initiated by sending them off to the bush to fend for themselves without parental aid for weeks. They live off the resources of the ecosystem which are regarded as sufficient for all their needs. They are initiated into the secrets of the natural and symbiotic relationship between them and nature (Ottenberg, 1971). Among the Biase, Ejagham and Igbo groups on the banks of the Cross River, the *akang* secret society serves the same function and the initiation ceremony is similar. The *poro* which enjoys wide provenance in West Africa contains elements affirming an identical ecological ideology.

The relationship between the child and the ecosystem is reinforced by the creation myth. In spite of variations, the account in the Ifa corpus appears in most: the Supreme Being who delegated some gods to create the earth, gave one of them the task of forming the body from clay. But he himself breathed the soul into human beings. Still another deity was chosen by the unborn child as the guardian of its destiny. The Igbo call this guardian, *chi*. The Yoruba refer to this as *Ori*. As an Ifa verse puts it,

> *Ori*, I salute you.
> *Ori*, nicknamed *atete niran*.
> He who first blesses a man before any other *orisa*
> No divinity blesses a man without the consent of his *Ori*.
> *Ori*, I salute you.
> You allow children to be born alive.
> A person whose sacrifices are accepted by his *Ori* should rejoice.
> (Abimbola, 1994: 112)

At a certain point, the individual accedes to decision- making roles and when death comes, the unity of the seen and unseen worlds become clear in the funerary rites. J. S. Mbiti in his *African Religion and Philosophy* (1969), Christian Gaba (1974) in his analysis of the sacred songs and prayers of Anlo People(Ghana) have emphasized that the human world is a replica of the spirit world. This explains the ritual of burying a slave alive so that he can continue to serve the achieved person through the journey. For one, people retain the status they had in the human world and secondly, passage through the spirit world is referred to as a journey. The return is reincarnation, reserved for those who lived honest lives and did not die from inexplicable diseases or from lightning--a punishment from the gods for a secret offence. As an Ifa *odu* or verse puts it, "all the good things of life that a man has, if he lacks good character, they belong to someone else". The person will not be able to join his earthly family to enjoy the legacy. Even as the personality soul sojourns in the ancestral world, he remains a part of his family, endowed with spiritual powers to aid them more. In all these, *kinship, spatial and biographical relations* are webbed in sacred network invoking powerful loyalty and attachment.

To focus more on the core structure of this cosmology with its predominantly religious character, the various names for God reflect His presence in response to the challenges of the ecosystem. Jan Platvoet has argued that a major trait of African indigenous religions is environmental and cultural concerns; they "differ markedly after the specific economic use which a society makes of the food resources of its environment for its livelihood"(1996: 52). As Tumai Nyajeka has argued with data from among the Shona, the shape of a circle can be said to accurately symbolize the nature of the world, defying the search for a beginning and an end and a hierarchical structure. Life is an organic web. The living and the dead are united; the spiritual and the manifest worlds flow together in a circle. (In Ruether, 1996: 135). The Dogon griot, Ogotemmeli, has left a powerful impression of the age-graded cosmology of the Dogon of Mali with elaborate close relationship shared with ancestors, land and animals (Griaule, 1975).

Though there are three dimensions of space, the sky, earth (land and water) and the ancestral worlds, all are united. Thus, R.S. Rattray in 1927 described the Ashanti world as "an alive universe". The spiritualization of space has led some to conjecture that Africans have a binary concept of space, namely, the human and the spirit world. But libations are no thrown into the air. Indeed, the sky was once very near to the earth. When women who were pounding meals constantly hit the sky with their pestles, the Supreme God lifted the sky a little higher out of their way. Aetiological myths soon yield to historical consciousness in the pursuit of the unity of the cosmos by imbuing each space with powerful forces. The sky gods, usually male, manifest as Sun, Lightning, Thunder and such-like. Among them is the moon in full beauty, female and inspiring aesthetics, creativity, giving her own light that evokes songs and dances. Otherwise, the sky gods serve as judges, oracles and arbiters. People swear by them. The Sun carries sacrifices above and mediates blessings.

The earth consists of land and water. It is said that after the gods finished creation, forming land out the anthill in the marsh, they stayed back inhabiting various features of the earth--mountains, rocks, rivers and streams. Land is the heart of the matter. It is under the guardianship of the Earth Goddess whose shrine is prominent in many communities. In many communities, large tracts of land were preserved for the ancestral shrine of a founding father and the earth deity. Even in the face of modernization, these are the last pieces of land to be touched and they contain the autochthonous fauna of many ecosystems. Intimate relationship with land is often betrayed in the names that are given to children. People are named, *Hill, High Hill, Our Hill, Rock, River, Deep Sea* and so on. The Mbari Museum in South-Eastern Nigeria is, perhaps, the most elaborate in West Africa. She nurtures the communities with her fertility. However, she is more revered in subculture theaters with high population density and acute land shortage or endowed with significant land features. Ojo (1966: 150) draws attention to the fact that some communities regard hills as their protectors and revere them. People in savannah zones tend to use the hills as shrines for sending messages to the Creator through the Sun. Land is so sacred that people swear by her and her powerful allure is the source of "tribalism" in politics.

Trees are often reverenced as imbued with spirits. Massive trunks and buttresses attract religious ardor, such as silk cotton (*Eriodendron orientale*), iroko (*Chlorophora excelsa*), boabab *(Andansonia digitata)* in deciduous forest areas. It is believed that the *Newboldia Laevis*(akoko) is inhabited by mischievous spirits which come as babies but soon return to the spirit world, breaking the hearts of families. Satin wood is found to be useful and inhabited by a munificent spirit. *The Cordia Milleni* is good for making drums and must be inhabited by a musical-minded spirit. Abnormal trees attract dreadful reverence, for instance, a palm tree with seven trunks or with sixteen branches. At Gbarnga, Liberia, a trunk from which the community had harvested firewood suddenly rose again with life inspite of the marks of the axe. They cordoned it off with palm fronds as sacred. Such trees are used as both personal and praise names.

Usually there are some specific trees on the road to a village that are alleged to be protectors standing at the gates of communities. Such trees are linked to trees in the market squares. Shrubs or trees in the market are sacred and communal sacrifices are made at their feet for the well-being of the entire community and to attract the patronage of neighboring villages to that market. Market days are sacred and farming activities are forbidden. Age grades are assigned to sweep and clean the market square; meanwhile taboos hedge the market square as the abode of benevolent spirits. Fighting and stealing are heinous crimes. Production, exchange and distribution are sacralized. G.H. Jones quipped about the West African(1936: 19) that "the towering vegetation silently growing and overwhelming his huts and cultivation, shutting him in, must have filled him with a sense of awe and impotence and fear." Little did he realize that the worldview served for conservation ethics to ensure the sustenance and protection of land.

Just as the marketplace was sacred, so was the farmland. Contact with her was hedged with taboos supervised by various deities under the Earth goddess; for instance:

i.   Communities must perform fertility rituals before land distribution begins.

ii. People must wait for everyone to commence bush clearing before setting fires.

iii. Harvesting may not start until the yams at the fertility deity's shrine have been harvested.

iv   There is a prohibition against processing certain kinds of food in the village. Cassava processing should be done outside the village and by the river--possibly for hygienic and health reasons so as to remove the cyanide acid properly and protect goats from eating these harmful chemicals.

v. Sexual intercourse in the bush, especially farmland is severely prohibited--for one it may be illicit and it is an abomination committed on the face of the Earth goddess.

vi. Fighting and especially threatening someone with a farm implement is prohibited.

vii. No one goes to the farm to fetch firewood on a market day--this avoids the temptation to steal in a farmland.

viii. The Yam god kills those who steal from other people's barns or from agricultural products heaped on the roadside.

ix. To harvest another person's hunting trap or fish trap will incur the wrath of the patron deity who may use the good services of the thunder or lightning.

These taboos and many more ensure an orderly utilization of the resources of nature and connect social ethics with ecological ethics. But much of the control is left to the gods. The Yam deity, for instance, indicates, through a diviner the areas of the farmland to be farmed each year. Crop rotation which preserves the soil through fallow is given sacred sanction.

Many animals are protected in a similar manner. Some communities regard the monkey as the abode of the ancestors; others as the abode of dead twins. In drier parts of tropical Africa, vultures are reincarnated ancestors; pythons and many other animals are totem and cannot be killed. The Igbo along with many other groups recognize that spirits operate in the human world through the following animals, birds and fishes:

i. AIR: birds--owl, crow, vulture, bat
   insects--fly, bee, soldier ant

ii LAND: lower animals--lizard, tortoise, chameleon, snake
   Higher animals--rat, monkey, dog, cat, leopard, lion, tiger, chicken
   Man

iii MARINE: crocodile, water snake
   Fish: electric fish, gold fish.

Jackson (1986) discussed the attitude to elephants among the Kuranko of the Sierra Leone where some people claim that they can turn into elephants to revenge on their enemies. J. McGregor (1989) has argued that certain religious ideas served as instruments of wildlife conservation in Southern Africa. The interesting aspect is that the category of sacred animals is selected from the three dimensions of space, further imbuing the whole universe with sacred quality. However, ritual killing of strong animals so as to acquire their spirit and power did occur. Equally interesting is the attitude towards domestic animals: one is forbidden from killing a pregnant goat or disturbing a sheep or a goat during parturition. In some villages, such animals should be tethered and their droppings used for manure in the garden.

The Earth deity is so sacred that she is regarded as the guardian of morality: inter-personal offences are perceived as pollution of her sanctity, secrecy and covenanting bonds are sealed by swearing by her. In decision-making processes, matters are sealed by knocking the staff of authority on the ground. She and the ancestors unite in creating a theory of obligation in communities where there is no secular theory of obligation. Ancestors are buried in her womb and libations are used to placate and invoke their intervention into human affairs. In certain communities, the chief would occasionally perform a ceremony in which he inquires through the priest of Earth deity whether he still enjoys her support. This evaluation exercise keeps the ethics of power from becoming oppressive. Ancestors and the Earth deity are crucial in the social control models--in socialization, restriction, punishment and reward (Kalu, 1993: 109-131).

A close taxonomy of deities would show that some communities perceive their waters as daughters of the Earth deity. Spirits inhabit water and rivers which run through long courses have shrines installed at various spots. Ifi Amadiume(1988) has provided a rich cameo of this. Marine spirits are female and give wealth, fertility, beauty and political influence. They inspire musicians and balladeers. Several marine cults feature in ethnographic studies of this region and bear little repetition. Elaborate festivals are held in honor of rivers which are the protectors of communities. Springs are also hedged with taboos and sacrifices so as to ensure that they do not dry up and that drought does not plague the people.(Kalu, 1991a)

In a research project entitled, "Gods of our fathers: a taxonomy of Igbo deities"(1991-2), we have experimented with a methodology for studying worldview, focusing on the names, gender, nature, function, provenance sacrifice and gender of the priest of each deity. The deities were distributed according to sub culture theaters. Using a sample of 615 deities, it was possible to show the organic nature of the worldview and how the emphases in each culture-area are related to the predominant ecological challenges. For instance, though the Earth deity is said to be so important, she is paid less elaborate attention by riverine communities. The culture areas prioritized the seven archetypes according to their needs: oracular, earth, nature. water, guardian/patron, ancestral and spirit force (Kalu, 1991b; 1996). It is expected that a similar pattern would be true for the wider African environment. Some communities engaged in long distance trade and therefore risked their worldview to wider perspectives. In others, secret societies predominated as the guardians of indigenous knowledge. Thus, while some developed pictographic writing, the severe ambits of secrecy prevented the skill from developing (Kalu, 1978b).

In African communities, there is an emphasis on tapping spiritual forces to aid coping ability. It is a quest for the mystery and revelatory knowledge locked in the innards of the universe. If through shamanistic rituals such knowledge was unlocked, humans will live a more abundant life. But this life force could be used for anti-social purposes, too. The prevalence of this quest for *muntu* (Tempels) or *pan-vitalism* (Asante, 1985: 289-293) is because existence is precarious. In one liturgy, the votary gives oblation to both the munificent and the malevolent gods, saying that *he came to the world and found them at loggerhead. He is ignorant of the cause but would rather be left out of the controversy.* This is easier said than done. According to Ifa texts, the Yoruba believe that there are two pantheons of gods who compete for the domination of the universe. The good gods number 400 and the hostile ones are 200. Between them and the Supreme Being is *Eshu*, a capricious deity who can aid or harm depending on the sacrifice given. It is a cosmos in which the good gods want to bless while the evil ones would thwart personal and societal goals. This precarious vision induces an ethic of stewardship, caution and attention to the unity of all creation. The world is a sacred egg; humans weave covenants with the good gods so as to ward off the machinations of the evil gods.

A covenantal understanding of this worldview is crucial. Festivals are sacred moments for re-energizing and renewal of the covenants with the gods in the sky, land, water and ancestral world. Olupona(1991) has examined the political implications in the use of festivals to legitimate the sacralized political order. Taboos hedge the bounds of behavior while the boundary of the sacred and the profane collapses. "By the sacred, " says Peter Berger,

> is meant here a quality of mysterious and awesome power, other than man and yet related to him, which is believed to reside in certain objects of experience. This quality may be attributed to natural or artificial objects, to animals or to men...The sacred cosmos is confronted by man as an immensely powerful reality other than himself. Yet this reality addresses itself to him and locates his life in an ultimately meaningful order (1967: 24).

Since this order was created from the anthill in the marsh, darkness ever threatens. Nature is at once a nurturer and yet mysterious, wild, uncontrollable and unpredictable. Human beings are hardly the masters. Eleanor Rae (1994) pursues the implications of this for gender ideology.

This order requires salient moral values for her maintenance. Ifa corpus which is found in many parts of West Africa including Nigeria, Benin, Togo and especially among the Yoruba, Fon, Igbo, Edo, Ewe teaches a number of these including hard work, self-help good character and maintenance of nature through sacrifice. "Sacrifice is the weapon that brings about resolution and tranquility in a universe in which conflict is the order of the day".(Abimbola, 1994: 106) Ifa teaches deep reverence for nature. Thus, libations, spells, incantations and chants are used as modes of communication. When a herbalist sets out for the forest, he pours libation to the patron deity and, inside the forest, he uses chants and incantation to arouse the healing herbs to draw attention to themselves. He calls them by their secret names and they respond. Efficacy of pharmacopoeia is achieved through ritual. They are addressed as human beings. For instance, the mountain is addressed as

> The old immortal man on top of a locust bean tree: if the locust bean tree does not fall down, the fat old man will not descend therefrom. Good health and immortality are the attributes of the mountain."(Abimbola, op. Cit.: 115)

Nyajeka (in Ruether, 1996: 138) concludes that among the Shona, the cosmology is non-anthropocentric "but at the same time celebrates as unique the experience of being human in the universe."

In Africa, much of the religious ardor is spent on environmental matters because as Sara Mvududu shows with data from Zimbabwe, environmental changes tend to have severe effects on families: deafforestation vitiates the energy supply, drought and soil degradation ruin the food sources and there are no synthetic alternatives as in the West.(in Ruether, 1996: 143-160) Patterns of spirituality preserve fragile and vulnerable elements in human-nature relationship. *As the old priestess said, the world is like an egg which can easily break; and, if it does, we are ruined; therefore we regularly give eggs to the gods in sacrifice so that they may remember and gently preserve us.*

African worldview is saturated with symbols, myths, religious rites and reflection. It shares much with other religious cosmologies. According to Rassmussen (In Tucker & Grim, 1994: 177), religious cosmologies may not do what science does but have distinct advantages: the mythic language emerges from the deepest experience; they trade in ultimates-ultimate origins, destiny, meaning and values; they rest at the foundation of cultural structures as well as their pinnacle as the reflection of the totality of things; they show their faces in the most common forms of art and language and promise not only meaning but survival power, deliverance, healing and well-being. In them are embedded deep knowledge, wisdom and experience such as engender hope.

The Intimate Enemy:
Ambivalent Eco-Ethics in African Cosmology

In spite of the sacralization of the ecology the question still remains whether primal cultures of Africa promoted healthy ecological ethics. How do beliefs and ideology influence resource management? D.U. Iyam captures the contemporary backdrop when he points to three trends:

i. the capacity of indigenous practices to manage rural social organization has been overwhelmed by the demands of new cultural elements generated from within and out side the society; .
ii. the resulting reconfiguration of indigenous institutions renders them less effective for communal management;
iii. consequently, a weakened array of cultural conventions and institutions have become minimally able to influence rural socio-economic relations and have created disadvantageous conditions for economic growth.(1995: 2)

The internal source of the weakening process could be related to the fact that primal cultures *ab initio* contained ambivalent ethics and, therefore, responded to the challenges of nature in a vulnerable manner. Vulnerability is the inability to control one's response to challenges. Does veneration constitute stewardship? Veneration as a coping mechanism is a vulnerable response especially when it is not supplemented with resource management. There was little of the ethic of replenishment. The tendency was to tap the resources of nature but leave it to the gods to replenish the earth. The approach here will be to illustrate with some examples of non-salient practices and, then, explore the theoretical or worldview contradictions and return to praxis.

The dominant attitude was that nature was out there to be used. For instance, if one wanted to use a satin wood, one would go to the tree with a pot of palm oil and entice the spirit inhabiting the tree to come down for a meal. During the interval the tricky man would fell the tree. But there was no cult of tree planting. Population pressure and intensification of land use were met by abandonment or resettlement. Thus, new settlements grew up in farmlands--these are usually identifiable by their names that would indicate that they are new outgrowths of old settlements. G.D. Stone (1996) has, therefore, contrasted between the "yeoman" and the "entrepreneurial" attitudes towards land use.

On the whole, African spirituality celebrates an intimacy with the natural world and the intrinsic value of a religious culture. There is a constant search for harmonious relationship with nature and awareness that nature carries hidden knowledge. The response was awe. Awe led to sacralization; a consciousness of the divine determined the pattern of space-time events. But a closer analysis of sacralization would show that it lacked the depth of the sense of the numinous in Native American Indian perception of reality or the systemization into life-patterns found among the religious traditions of the East. Indeed, when the West woke up to the impending disaster in the abuse of nature, they did not turn to Africa; rather, from the 1960's they turned to Eastern religions for an alternative insight and eco-ethics. Admittedly, even China that is suffused with Confucian and Taoist eco-centric wisdom is devastated by environmental abuse. Did this come from external change agents especially in the encounter with the West? Not necessarily. The argument here is that we should search each cosmology for the ambivalence of bearing hostile seeds or capacity to be an intimate enemy to the ecosystem.

The problem lies in the intrinsic nature of sacralization. It recognizes the aura in an object and runs away from a close contact, reserving it as holy and totally 'the other'. Consecration encourages subject-object encounter. Nature is perceived as the other, the hostile and capricious tool of the gods. The relationship is not with nature but with the deity whose force or presence imbues the natural form-rock, tree, river and so on. The direction is *human-divine rather than human-nature-divine interconnectedness*. So, the African manipulates the services of the good gods to ward off the machinations of the evil ones. The transactional model of intermediary spirits, the cynosure of religious ardor, distracts from the holism in which the Supreme Being is lord over the universe. Soon the notion of *deus remotus* crept in. This is different from the pattern of intimacy found in the Native Indian notion of unity in the communion of all things and kinship with all of nature. It has little of the serene mind-self in Buddhism that cuts the cord of craving, greed and anxiety though proverbs against greed abound in African wisdom corpus. It is different from the relationship between the Hindu and some holy rivers; for instance, the cosmic body notion that the world emanated from the navel of a goddess, the rivers become the natural forms of the goddess so that people could drink the water for purifying, taking energy into the body and such-like. In Africa, consecration tends to zone certain areas which are hedged with taboos (boundaries of behavior). These are preserved for the gods or ancestors and not because the world of nature has basic rights to exist. Consequences include exploitation of un-zoned areas and underutilization of the total resource capacity in the zoned areas.(Asante, 291).The general tendency is towards exploitation of nature rather than the altruistic emphasis on restoration. Nature serves humans rather than humans serving nature. Humans do not feel the pain of nature or hear the groan. The pursuit of the concepts of fate and destiny betrays a certain precarious vision of human life in which the deities dominate. A village can be dedicated to a deity and bear the praise name of that deity. The well-being and the preservation of the resources of the community are left to that deity and the ancestors to control on behalf of the community. The power of a deity could be tapped in a materialistic manner; the gods are not loved for themselves but for what they can give. Thus, a votary informed a shrine that if it fails to perform, the path to its grove will be overgrown with grass. The depth of the unity between humans and nature is such that the impact of this mode of sacralization does not aid values such as maintenance, replacement, restraint, regeneration, selective con-sumption, sufficiency and efficiency. It has no power to restrain the radical confrontation and interference of the human with the biological cycles and other life- systems of the planet.

The ambivalence in the worldview produced destructive eco-ethics. There was little concern for conservation and preservation in farming, hunting and fishing. For instance, a fisherman would not put back a fin-gerling into the water to spawn. Domestic animals were cared for as means of wealth rather than for any religious reasons. It was left to the gods to replenish crucial biodiversity. For instance, among the Gbaya of the Cam-eroons, *sor* is a small tree which botanists call, *Anona Senegalensis*. It has a dozen ritual uses: constructing a new village, resolving hostilities, rec-onciliation between villages, cleansing from guilt, initiation, blessing the quest for food, cooling witchcraft and breaking the strength of a dangerous person. T.G. Christensen in *An African Tree of Life (1990)* has documented this significant plant and yet the villagers who depend so much on it make scant effort to preserve it!

Changing land-holding patterns in response to population growth has affected farming practices. In many places, the predominant communal and kin-based holding pattern is giving way to individual ownership. Pres-sure on land use for human needs and reduction of arable and fallowed acreage have forced encroachment into dedicated shrine lands. Pollution has decimated natural resources because of the lack of maintenance culture. As rivers silt, communities watch helplessly. As people exploit nature for human survival, there is neither concern for depleting resources nor is there a measure for replenishing the denuded earth. The totem animal in one community is another's food. A sensitivity towards non-sentient forms and towards harmful insects and animals is a litmus test of the perception of nature in any culture as it betrays whether that culture accords nature an intrinsic value, interconnected with every living being. In Africa, does each form of nature possess a special place in life? Much to the contrary, as fauna which are crucial for human health disappear, healers travel longer distances into the bush as if the gods beckoned them further into the womb of the forest. It could be argued that only the low-level of technology prevented a more devastating human-ecology encounter. The weakening of traditional modes of control of economic activities only heightened a tendency that already existed. This is not to deny that much of the changes have been caused by the insurgence of external change-agents.

Muchakata, the enchanted tree clothing the earth

Among the Shona communities of Zimbabwe, *Muchakata* is the cork tree that is not to be felled; an enchanted tree that clothes the earth (*kufukidza nyika*). It is our symbol for reflecting on the models of worldview transformation for eco-care. The Global Forum Conference, Moscow, 1990, acknowledged that religious teaching, example and leadership are powerfully able to influence personal conduct and commitment. M. Evelyn Tucker has therefore, argued that to recognize that indigenous peoples around the globe have enormous resources to offer in the search for a functional environmental spirituality and ethics is not to suggest that they have never exploited land or resources. It does say that the consciousness of the spirit presence within nature rather than simply beyond nature is particularly high in these traditions. Thus, inspite of the ambivalence, religious cosmologies have historical and cultural importance. She makes the points that:

(a) a major aspect of the environmental crisis is in some sense religious. The exhaustion of nature's resources is leaving the human community also drained in terms of spiritual energies for discerning a viable path in the midst of a trajectory careening towards self-destruction;

(b) both consciously and unconsciously our attitudes toward nature have been formed by religious worldview and ethics;

(c) the recovery of the sense of respect, awe or creation mystique in nature is the first step towards a pro-active program for conserving bio-diversity;

(d) in this process of re-thinking human-earth relations, religions themselves are being significantly changed and challenged to change. (1997: 3-24)

Perhaps the Rainbow Covenant contracted in Assissi in 1986 is an example of how the shift can be made from creation mystique to ortho-praxis based on reciprocity. It was achieved through rituals of confession, repentance, covenant renewal and conscientization. Media facilities were employed to educate and inject a new idea into the postmodern worldview, highlighting a long history of eco- concerns in the world. An ecumenical mobilization of religious leaders, scientists and decision-makers ensured that the message entered into the inner core of global culture.

A similar model can be documented for Africa by following the career of Inus Daneel of Zimbabwe. This part of the reflection depends much on his work. Faced with harsh environmental degradation that threatened the ability of the nation to recover from the ravages of the liberation war, Daneel bemoaned the lack of adequate Christian theology to address an urgent and life-threatening issue. Yet his deep knowledge of Shona religion and culture assured him that African traditional religion is a "force with very specific implications for the development of a theology of the environment" (Daneel, 1991).He set out do three things: (a) probe the wisdom of Africa to seek the intuition that has lain at the roots of earth-keeping in African traditional religion and philosophy all along; (b) rebuild an African indig-enous theology which would be appropriate, realistic and praxis-oriented and (c) create a radical transformation of attitude, a ministry to nature. He chose a vigorous program of reforestation and eco-care of rivers as targets. He realized that during the war of liberation, traditional medicine men and apostles of African Independent Churches were very crucial in provid-ing empowerment for survival in the harsh terrains. He sought to tap their resources for a new war of liberation from denuded environment. Firstly, he mobilized the AICs into a co-operative called, *Fambidzano(co-operative of black churches)* in 1972. In 1988, he formed *Zimbabwe Institute of Reli-gious Research and Ecological Conservation (ZIRRCON)*. He mobilized an army of village chiefs, headmen, spirit mediums and guerrilla fighters who had utilized the wisdom of the fathers and the guardian ancestral spirits for mystical support in fighting and surviving the war. As the Christians felt uncomfortable to unite forces with the shamans, he formed a distinct *Association of Zimbabwe Traditional Ecologists (AZTREC)* for the shamans and *Association of African Earth-Keeping Churches (AAEC)* for the Christians. Using Zirrcon as the controlling unit and fund-raiser, he started an ecumenical venture in afforestation, wildlife conservation and protection of water resources. He has at various times recounted an intriguing tale of a wonderful adventure. (Daneel, 1989, 1991a: 2-26; 1991b: 129-142; 1991c: 225-246; 1991d: 99-1332332; see, Kritzinger, 1992: 99-115)

One dimension to Daneel's problems was that coming from a Reformed tradition, he sought a theology that will bestride primal religion, African Independency and Protestantism. He has met with robust and undeserved rebuke for his daring. The focus here will suffice with the tapping of the resources in primal worldview to inject an ideology of eco-care. The tree-planting component has been the most successful of the enterprise and will be our focus. The backdrop is a stricken land. He lifted the emphasis on the sacramental and ritual character of African primal worldview. He asked the mediums for their diagnosis. They averred that the spirits of the land have been neglected, sacred groves allowed to deteriorate and murder committed and hidden in the land. When skulls were dug out during a dam construction in 1992 (and in the middle of an awful drought) their ominous diagnosis assumed a political crisis. The next flag point was to incorporate ancestral rituals because these were most prevalent in that culture theater. He, then, invited the AICs who normally celebrate the *Ungano Yembeu, the seed conference,* at the October Paschal (called, *Paseka)* at the beginning of the rainy and planting season. The liturgy brought all the elements together in a manner as to transform the worldview towards a pro-active fight against eco-denudation through ritual of regeneration. The first part consisted of dancing around the heap of seedlings that are to be planted. This was designed to invoke *Mwari*, God, as the Lord of all creation. Instead of a remote God, He was immanent and fully present. Then, the liturgy tapped the ritual of baptism in a stream used to emphasize conversion, repentance and washing away of sins. Sins were related to the operation of forces that bedeviled social harmony and well-being. Such forces are attributed to the operation of witches (*varoyi).* At the tree-planting eucharist, there was an insistence on public confession for ecological sin imaged as witchcraft (ecological varoyi).Ecological degradation was attributed to breakdown of moral order which, in turn, spiraled into the breakdown of the economy. Those who chop down trees without replanting them were as witches; so were those who ploughed on the banks of rivers causing the rivers to silt. In some cases, night vigils of confession were adopted. For African Indigenous Churches (AICs) who regard "crossing river Jordan" in baptism as crucial, the eucharistic re-enactment required a commitment to help restore creation as a part of God's plan- as a sign of genuine conversion and repentance in recognition of the gifts of God's grace. Finally, at the gate- test, the unrepentant ecological *varoyi* will be cast out by the Spirit-filled prophets just as the mediums used to detect wizard-traitors at secret *pungwe* meetings during the war of liberation. (Daneel, 1991c: 228; 1993: 322) From a different set of symbolism, the chopped trees were imaged as the dead who were murdered and whose ghosts, *ngozi*, were crying for appeasement. When the vengeful spirit possesses anyone, the person would become an agent in doing terrible things. So insensitive eco-ethics could be a form of *ngozi* possession. The eucharistic confession and sacrifices begged the spirit to go away and have rest. After deliverance and cleansing, the Holy Spirit as the life-giver, fountain of life and healer was invoked to renew the community and bless the trees. The sacrality of the land and the ancestor- guardians were confirmed by sprinkling of holy water. Hundreds of thousands would troop out to plant trees all over the communities. And the voice of the officiating priest could still be heard saying, *Mwari saw the devastation of the land. So he called his envoys to shoulder the task of deliverance. Come ye messengers of Mwari, come...We are now the deliverers of the stricken land"* (cit, Daneel, 1993: 318) This is a significant shift from the attitude of fatalism found in peasant societies which watch helplessly as the biodiversity disappear. The AICs have developed Tree Hospitals, large tracts of nurseries, in the new vision of Earth Healing Ministries. The Headquarter of a church is often renamed as Zion City of Trees showing that the notion of sacred shrines or holy groves has been transferred from primal world-view. *Paskel,* the eco-liturgical innovation points to the ways in which a worldview can be transformed from the inside for eco-care. Walpole (1991: 128-133) describes a similar liturgy in the Phillipines which engages in "fasting for our forests." Cultural engineering will follow apace with the proliferation of the new eco- spirituality in Africa. As the people confess at the tree-planting eucharist in Zimbabwe:

> Look at the stagnant water
> where all the trees were felled
> Without trees the water-holes mourn
> without trees the gullies form
> For, the tree-roots to hold the soil are gone!
>
> I, the human being
> your closest friend
> have committed a serious offence
> as ngozi, the vengeful spirit
> I destroyed you, our friends.
> So, the seedlings brought here today

are the "bodies" mutumbu of restoration
a sacrifice to appease
the vengeful spirit
We plant these seedlings today
as admission of guilt
laying the ngozi to rest
Strengthening our bonds with you
our tree friends of the heart.

Indeed, there were forests
abundance of rain
But in our ignorance and greed
we left the land naked
Like a person in shame
our country is shy
in its nakedness. (cit. Daneel, 1993: 326)

This prayer and ritual have transformed the African's relationship with nature to a more organic form. Perhaps this was there but muted. It now provides the exit to a dilemma. The worldview of those who planted the iron crosses around the erosion gullies, needs inner transformation to confess their responsibility and harness their religious perception of the problem for a more pro-active eco-care. The gods are not to blame.

Bibliography

ABIMBOLA, W.(1994), "Ifa: A West African Cosmological System" In Blakeley, van Beek and Thomson, (eds.), *Religion in Africa: Experience and Expression* (London: James Currey): 101-116.

AMADIUME, Iffi, (1988), *Female Husbands Male Daughters* (London: Zed Press).

ASANTE, E. (1985), "Ecology: untapped resource of pan-vitalism in Africa", *AFER*, 27, 5.

BERGER, P.L. (1967), *Sacred Canopy* (New York: Doubleday).

BIDNEY, D. (1968), "Cultural Relativism" In *International Encyclopedia of the Social Sciences* ed. D.L. Sills (New York: Macmillan).

CHOMSKY, N. (1968), *Language and Mind* (New York: Harcourt, Brace and World).

CHRISTENSEN, T.G. (1990), *An African Tree of Life* (Maryknoll, Orbis).

DANEEL, I. M.(1993) "African Independent Churches Face Challenge of Environmental Ethics", *Missionalia*, 21, 3: 311-332.

DANEEL, I. M., (1989) *Fambidzano-ecumenical movement of Zimbabwean Independent Churches* (Gweru, Mambo Press).

_____ (1991a) "Towards a sacramental theology of the environment in African Independent Churches", *Theologia Evangelica*, 24, 1: 2-26.

_____ (1991b) "African Theology and the challenge of earth-keeping", Pt1, *Neue Zeitschrift fur Missionwissenschaft*, 47, 2: 129-142; PT2, 47, 3: 225-46.

_____ (1991c) "The liberation of creation: African Traditional Religion and Independent Church Perspective", *Missionalia*, 19, 2: 99-121.

ELIADE, M. (1959), *The Sacred and the Profane: the nature of religion* (New York: Harcourt, Brace and Jovanovich).

ESCOBAR, A.(1991), "Anthropology and the Development Encounter", *American Ethnologist*, 18, 4: 658-682.

FORTES, M (1949), *The web of kinship among the Tallensi* (London).

_____ (1959), *Oedipus and Job in West African Religion*(Cambridge).

GABA, C. (1974), *The Scriptures of an African People: Ritual Utterances of the* Anlo (New York: Nok Publishers).

Van GEEST (1997), "Development and other religious activities", *Together: A Journal of the World Vision Partnership*, 55(July-Sept.): 1-8.

GRIAULE, M. (1975) *Ogotemmeli* (New York, Oxford University Press).

HIEBERT, P.G.(1985) *Anthropological Insights for* Missionaries (Grand Rapids: Baker Books).

HORTON, R (1962), "The Kalabari Worldview: an outline and interpretation"*Africa*, 32, 3: 197-220.

_____ (1993), *The Patterns of thought in Africa and the West* (Cambridge University Press).

IYAM, D. U., (1995), *The Broken Hoe: Cultural Reconfiguration in Biase, Southern Nigeria* (University of Chicago Press).

JACKSON, M.(1986), *Barawa and the ways birds fly in the sky* (Washington: Smithsonian Institute Press).

KALU, O. U. (1978a), "Precarious Vision: The African Perception of His World" In O.U. Kalu, ed. *Readings in African Humanities: African Cultural Development* (Enugu: Fourth Dimension Publishers)..

_____ (1978b) "Nsibidi: Pictographic Communication in Pre-Colonial Cross River Basin Societies", *Cahiers d'Etudes des Religions Africaines*, 12, 23/24: 97-116.

_____ (1991a) "Gods of our fathers: a taxonomy of Igbo deities", Paper presented at the Seminar on Igbo Worldview, Institute of African Studies, University of Nigeria, Nsukka, October 10.

_____ (1991B), "Gender Ideology in Igbo Religion", *Africa*, 46, 2: 184-202.

_____ (1993) *Gods* as Policemen: Religion and Social Control in Igboland" In J. K. Olupona and S. Nyang eds. R*eligious Pluralism in Africa* (Berlin: Mouton de Gruyter): 109-131.

_____ (1996) *The Embattled Gods: Christianization of Igboland, 1841-1991* (Lagos/London: Minaj Publishers), chapt. 2.

KINSLEY, D.(1995), *Ecology and Religion: Ecological Spirituality in Cross-cultural Perspective* (New York, Prentice Hall).

KRAFT, C. H. (1989), *Christianity With Power: Your Worldview and Your Experience of the Supernatural* (Ann Arbor, Mich.: Vine Press).

KRAFT, M.G. (1995), *Worldview and the communication of the gospel* (Pasadena: William Carey).

KRITZINGER, J. J. (1992), "Mission and the Liberation of the Creation: A Critical Dialogue With M.L. Daneel", *Missionalia*, 20, 2: 99-115.

MANDELBAUM, D.G. ed., (1958) *Selected Writings of Edward Sapir in Language, Culture and Philosophy* (Berkeley: University of California Press).

MBITI, J. (1969), *African Religion and Philosophy* (London: Heinemann).

MACGREGOR, J. (1989), "The Paradox of wildlife conservation in Africa", *African Insight*, 19, 4: 201-212.

OJO, G. J. A. (1966), *Yoruba Culture: A Geographical Analysis* (London: University of London Press).

OLUPONA. J. K. (1991), *Kingship, Religion and Rituals in a Nigerian Community* (Stockholm: Almqvist and Wilksell Intl.).

_____ (1996) Platvoet, Cox and J. K. Olupona, eds., *The Study of Religions in Africa* (Cambridge: Roots and Branches).

OTTENBERG, S. (1971), *Leadership and Authority in an African Society* (University of Washington Press).

PLATVOET, Jan (1996), "Religions of Africa in their historical order" In *The Study of Religions in Africa:* 46-102.

RAE, ELEANOR (1994), *Women, the Earth, the Divine* (Maryknoll, NY: Orbis Books).

RAMIREZ-FARIA, C. (1991), *The Origins of Economic Inequality Between Nations* (Cambridge, MA.: Unwin-Hyaman).

RUETHER, R R (1996) *Women Healing Earth: Third World Women on the Ecology, Feminism and Religion* (Maryknoll, NY, Orbis).

D. Ackerman and T. Joyner, "Earth-Healing in South Africa": 121-34.

S.C. Mvududu, "Revisiting Traditional Management of Indigenous Woodlands": 143-160. Phiri, I. A.. "The Chisumphi Cult: The Role of Women in Preserving the Environment", : 161-170 Hinga, T., "The Gikuyu Theology of Land and Environmental Justice": 172-84.

SHIAWOYA, E.L.(1986), "Small-scale Farmers, Local Governments and Traditional Rulers in Agricultural Production" In A. Akinbode et als *The Role of Traditional Rulers and Local Governments in Nigerian Agriculture* (Ilorin, ARMTI).

STONE, G.D., (1996), *Settlement and Ecology* (Tucson: Arizona State University Press).

TUCKER.M. E. and GRIM, J. A., eds.. (1993), *Worldviews and Ecology* (Lewis-burgh: Bucknell University).

TUCKER, M.E. (1997) "The Emerging Alliance of Religion and Ecology", *Worldviews*, 1, 1: 3-24.

TIMBERLAKE, L. (1985), *Africa in crisis-the causes, the cures of environmental bankruptcy.* (London, Russell Press).

WALPOLE, P.W. (1991) "Fasting for our Forests," *Euntes Digest*, 24, 2: 128-133.

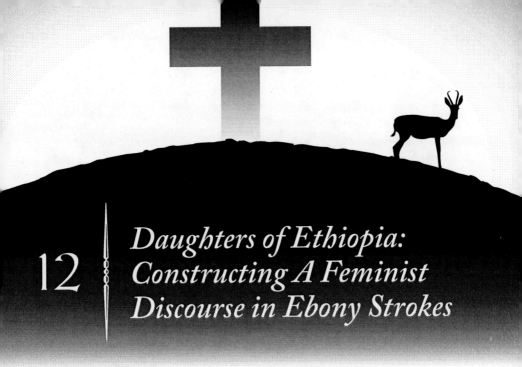

12 | Daughters of Ethiopia: Constructing A Feminist Discourse in Ebony Strokes

Naming the Theme and its Boundaries

The Circle for African Women theologians (hereafter the Circle)" that Mercy Amba Oduyoye pioneered has changed feminist discourse in African Christianity. It has achieved its first goal which is to conduct research, write and publish from African women's perspective. This reflection explores how the Circle could benefit from conversation between African and African American women theologians. It provides a male outsider perspective. One recalls the enormous impact of a robust conversation with African Americans in Accra in 1977.[1] It changed African theology.

Women constitute a core aspect of explosion of Christianity in contemporary Africa. However, the story of black women reflects the impact of dispersion into the New World that created new challenges in new environments and in the ancient homeland. The reflection urges that black women should intentionally develop creative and sustained linkages as they reflect about God's relationship with women confronted by challenges in varied ecosystems. It is argued that these black women come from the same stock, are perceived same by non-black peoples, share the same intrinsic values and spirituality, and should bond together for survival. There is need for a long conversation. They bring different gifts to the table because there are differences that emanate from different life experiences engendered by years of living in different cultures. Both affirm that their experiences set them apart from white women and their feminist causes. For some, this is because white women are oppressors. For others, the concerns are that white women presume that their condition is the norm; they paint negative images of the African woman as if they were mules, and presume that African women need to be liberated from their hostile environment so as to be like white women. There is resentment about the patronizing, biased, exotic, and essentializing profiles of the condition of the African women. [2]

At the core, black women complain that cultural norms are deployed to construct and silence women. This has two implications: there is no universal women's experience. The conversation must be attentive to systemic and cultural differences. Contextual theology must be built on adequate cultural mapping. The African social condition is very different from the North American. Homer Ashby has illustrated this with the example of marriage.[3] Moreover, African and African American women share the same frustration that emergent theologies ignored female input. Sheron Patterson's *New Faith* puts it sarcastically:

> Imagine this: A question is presented to you, but before you can answer it, an Anglo woman or man or an African American man speaks on your behalf. Your opinions are not heard and do not matter.[4]

The conversation may expose differences. For instance, some African women complain that cultural assimilation in a white world may have informed how some of the African American women have internalized white images and attitudes towards Africa. This explains the critical tone, frustration, and a sense of betrayal in the crusade mounted by Walker against circumcision that is portrayed as "genital mutilation" in her work (part fiction, part factual), *Possessing the Secret of Joy* (1992) and her film documentary, *Warrior Mask: Female Genital Mutilation and Sexual Blinding of Women (1993)*.[5]

It is alleged that she generalized about Africa as if the practice existed all over the continent; that some of her data are inaccurate and borrowed from French anthropological images; that she characterized the procedure as a male, patriarchal activity when it is in fact carried out by women; and claims that mutilation was the source of enslavement as many women ran away into slavery to avoid mutilation! The venom is rather disturbing. But it raises many other issues: should African American writing on Africa be allowed the space to be critical or should it romanticize "mother Africa"? Besides, the profile of women in indigenous communities carved by African women authors gyrates between the autonomous woman achiever and the woman in veil, invisible, and exploited by patriarchy.

A conversation would afford Alice Walker the opportunity to respond for several reasons: first, she has the right to be critical. Second, African women differ in their images of womanhood: some emphasize invisibility, others the autonomous achiever. For the latter, the indices are goddess worship, matrilineal inheritance structures, dual sex system, gender flexibility in social roles, gender bending that confers considerable authority on women, and neuter linguistic elements in references to sexes.[6] A number of cultural practices are deployed to validate the assertion, such as title-taking among women, woman-to-woman marriages/female husbands, the status and role of daughters of the family, female inheritance of their fathers' houses, replacement of sons with daughters or making sons of daughters, the privileging of age rather than sex as the determinant in social deference; gender freeness within the divine sphere as some gods are male in some communities and female in others, open priesthood, and the fact that women do not take their husbands' names. Third, the celebration of the ebony kinship between African Americans and Africans has been informed by the nature of "discerning black identity." The battle between black nationalists and integrationists has been long –drawn with no clear victor. W.E.B. DuBois elucidated it as the two souls of black folks-the Negro and the American- and the need to benefit from the dual cultural heritage. It is important for this conversation to understand the lay of the land on either shore of the great lake.

Fourth, rapid social and cultural changes continuously reshape feminist discourse, and therefore, doing feminist theology requires a cultural map or in-depth anthropological data. African feminist literature images a strong force of externality in gender construction by arguing that colonialism and Christianity reshaped the gender ideologies in contemporary African societies and churches by reinforcing the contested elements of patriarchy in the indigenous cultures, turning them into enduring structures that enervate other moderating influences. Put in another way, modernizing cultural forces destroyed the salient values of indigenous communities without replacing them with adequate alternatives.

Plurality of voices

A key aspect of the background to the conversation is that the women theologians do not come to the table with consensus. In fact, there are internal debates among African women theologians and among African American female scholars about the goals of the feminist struggle and even the terminology: is it for the consolidation of elite women in powerful positions (that may be dubbed as femocracy)? Or, are all sectors of womenfolk served? Should feminism privilege academic rigor or social engagement? There is no consensus about the diagnosis of the female predicament or the prescriptions for an exit, or the attitude to the past. Some urge a creative resort to the past for inspiration from "our mothers' gardens"; others urge a radical discontinuity because of alleged exploitation of women by patriarchal ancestors and the traditions that they bequeathed. Amba Oduyoye describes this as

> women standing up, abandoning the crouched positions from which their life-breath stimulated the wood fires that burned under the earthenware pots of vegetables they had grown and harvested."[7]

In *Beads and Strands* she urges a " departure from inflexibly ascribed positions whose hierarchical ordering was accepted as natural and permanent."[8] Oduyoye's position is perhaps more subtle than the bald statements. She uses the *art of remembrance* to do theology from the interior of African religious worldview. The quest for salvation must be rooted in the indigenous language, cultural practices, and religious idiom of the people. For African Americans, the attitude to the slavery era is quite crucial. As Linda Thomas puts it,

> the tasks of womanist theology are to claim history, to declare authority for ourselves, our men, our children, to learn from the experience of our forebears, to admit shortcomings and errors, and to improve our quality of life. [9]

It requires excavating the life stories of women including the "empowering dimensions of conjuring and syncretistic black religiosity" and "doing roots". Cultural excavation can become empowering in the struggles of the present, or in the task of regaining a sense of balance amidst the rapid changes of our times. The Jim Crow period is like the colonial moment in African story.

On naming the movement, some African American women would rather abandon the term, *feminism* to white women, and articulate their peculiar experiences as *womanist*, a powerful word that emerges from the interior of black culture and colorful imagery. To say that a girl is *acting womanish* is to affirm that the person is beginning to exercise agency, act as a grown up, and show creative, adult sense of initiative. Mitchem has, therefore, examined the signal texts, the class and communal dimensions to the construction, and the pastoral and theological implications. Others demur for fear of abandoning the feminist turf to white women and thereby installing boundaries that enclose the black cause in conceptual ghettoes where people rummage through colored pain. Behind this debate are class factor, academic orientations, life experiences, the allure of separate development, and the challenge of fighting and winning from the inside of the dominant culture. For Africans, argues Oyewumi, *sister* is a more powerful metaphor because it means the knitting of a sustaining network that is non-kin based, akin to such relationships as *ore* among the Yoruba, or the *chienjira* among the women of the southern Malawi. It enjoys confidence, intimacy and reliability.

On the task of the bonded sisters, the Circle started with public enlightenment activities through female cultural production, especially literary publications. Members have published almost two dozen books in the last decade, focusing on social problems such as poverty, family, violence and health issues as these affect women. Literary production by African American women has intensified. But many perceive agency as an effective mobilization of women through projects that raise consciousness, demonstrate woman capability, and nurture a sense of worth. It is argued that when sisters share their experiences in environments of trust, they become empowered to reverse their vulnerable conditions. [10]

The content of womanist theology is same as for any other forms of black pastoral theology. Homer Ashby has enumerated the indicators of the decline in African American participation in a white-dominated society.[11]

He examined issues about health, politics and economics. He dealt with the construction of black identity, connecting a disconnected people, and building hope for the future as the people try to find their way home. The list would resonate with African conditions characterized by declining economies, brutal civil wars, failed development, and the scourge of HIV/AIDS. African image in the Western new media has sunk to a new low. The argument by the Circle scholars is that women bear the brunt of the violent social environment and ravaging poverty. The level of violence committed by men complicates health issues for women.[12] Rapes committed by various marauding armies in Uganda created a large corps of children affected by HIV/AIDS, either as carriers or as orphans. This is the problem and content of any God-talk. Any viable methodology should be one that enables a black woman to contribute to the quest for strategies that create wholesome life in the midst of the darkness at noontide. Women must conscientize others to break the silence that perpetuates violence.[13]

Methodology is the essence of all theologies. The questions asked, and how they are answered, determine the message and its impact. Both African and African American women theologians privilege *experience* as the framework for doing feminist theology. This harks back to the debates about contextualization and inculturation in doing post-colonial theology. It is attentive to the pilgrim and indigenous principles in the gospel's encounter with different cultures and communities, or how local identities contest global processes. It touches the heart of theology as human reflection on God's relationship to human beings and the world of nature. For Delores Williams in her *Sisters in the Wilderness* there is need to see, affirm and connect between the academic reflections and community and the experiences of ordinary black women.[14] Therefore, where one stands, what one is experiencing becomes the starting point in doing theology. But it perhaps underlies the fragmentation at the backdrop to the conversation. Individual experiences of the social and religious cultures vary; so do their quests for cultural fulfillment. So, some women choose to be *reconstructive* by rejecting the Bible as the canon; others, are *radical reformers* who mine the radical elements within the gospel for empowerment; and still others have deployed Biblicism as the mooring for *loyalist* postures. It should be added that the loyalist posture may be found prominently among Roman Catholics as well as among charismatic evangelical women. However, it is not a supine, submissive posture but one that insists that men should obey Pauline demands on them to nurture, feed, enfold, protect and love their spouses. This may, in fact, be an argument for 'mutual submission'. In spite of differences within each camp and among the camps, the protagonists urge intense dialogue as a method of doing feminist theology.[15]

The ties that bind

This is because various strands of feminism share much in common: academically, feminist discourses have benefited from the same intellectual tradition, especially deconstructive, postmodernist discourse. Patriarchy, *the government of the fathers*, is color -blind and has operated effectively in different social, political and economic organizations through centuries and cultures. It may have been stronger in pre-industrial and agricultural societies but is still effective underneath the modern lifestyles and family structures. One of the Greek derivatives from the word, patriarchy, yielded the term *macho* to the English vocabulary and conveys the image of violence, struggle, force and may explain its cultural register that includes violence against women and psychological pressures on children by fathers. Anti-patriarchy is a key plank in the feminist enterprises. It is beyond the protest against capitalism because underneath the broad oppression against those who do not control the means of production is a specific oppression of the womenfolk. The register of feminist discourses, therefore, includes rebuilding the brokenness of women's psyche and self image, regaining safe environments, removing the veil of invisibility, enhancing participation in politics and decision-making in the public spaces, recovering agency in making decisions about one's health, marital status, sexual orientation, job satisfaction, remuneration, and the organization of social structures that matter.

African and African women, across the big lake, have certain identical attitudes towards men: they want to build sustainable homes (in spite of the high level of unmarried adults in the African American black population), encourage the survival of the folk (ranging from the extended family to the community), partner with the men and succor them in responding to external forces that emasculate the men-folk, and be respected. It is common knowledge that women bear the brunt of the humiliation of their sons and husbands. This is often captured by the tendency to "stand by my man." This could be quite risky but sustained with the memory of strong mothers, their gardens, nurturing practices, pains, wise words, ritual practices, incantations, and prayers. Indeed, attention should be paid to the fact that African and African women theologies have borrowed inspiration and discourses from broad international feminists groups. For instance, in spite of the quest for identity by African feminist theology, it has gained inspiration from the interventions of United Nation programs, new theological orientation of the World Council of Churches, and the development of Third World and Black theologies. This does not deny the impact of specific experiences in each ecosystem.

However, feminist theologies have shifted emphases through time, and the causes and methods have benefited from broader social trends and multi-disciplinary resources. A distinction must be made between secular feminist scholarship and Christian feminist theology because they have different goals, assumptions and methods. For instance, the negritude discourse has shaped African secular feminism including a nuanced response to Diop's contention that originally African societies were matrilineal. [16] The secular feminist enterprise has paid attention to matters of theory and yielded immense data on women in African indigenous communities and.

In contrast, the Circle represents the mobilization of Christian women who are "calling the church to account". Mercy Oduyoye declares that she is writing as a Christian woman. Hers is a genre of Christian social ethics in which the Bible is very central. For her, the exodus event is a basic paradigm for reflecting on women and patriarchy. She shares the passion with Linda Thomas because "the exodus story is a hermeneutical device used to draw a parallel between the oppressed Israelites and the oppressed African American community."[17] Delores Williams concurs but is intrigued with the story of Haggai in the wilderness. Others choose the ambiguous image of Esther. Itumeng Mosala cautions about the implications of the text of Esther because Queen Vashti appears like the heroine of female assertion and agency.[18] The women are aware of their demographic importance. *If it were not for the women*, perhaps churches will be empty. The numerical strength of women (which Linda Thomas estimates to be two-thirds) has an inverse ratio to their power in decision- making processes and exercise of ritual authority. The rationalization of the anomaly is made more intriguing by grounding gender ideology in certain exegesis of the canon while, at the same time, sourcing the ethics in the ecclesia from the wider society. This is the argument in the three cycles of Oduyoye's *Daughters of Anowa (1995)*. She explores how gender ideology in the language and proverbs, cultural and socio-political practices of the Akan of Ghana and Yoruba of Nigeria inform the gender practices in the churches. Ironically, when liberal values spur a paradigm shift in the society, the ecclesia would deploy the canon to insulate a conservative ethic that benefits the males.

This tendency has determined the trend in feminist discourse. The first goal is to return to the canon, and (since the Greek for *canon* means boundary), dissolve its enfolding boundaries by attacking its source: who wrote these scripts and with whose regnant bias? Admittedly, some move from here to reconstruct the image and roles of women to show that these were broader than acknowledged. Others would rather discard the entire canon as irredeemable. Elizabeth Schussler-Fiorenza is the high priestess of the reconstructive genre, as best illustrated in her *Bread Not Stone*. [19] The social sciences provide many tools for merging the erstwhile canon into new social realities and analysis and thereby opening ecclesial boundaries to legitimize contemporary social values that seemingly affirm life. It is a long road and numerous wayfarers stop at many watering grounds along the route. As R.B. Hays argues in *Moral Vision of the New Testament* when one dissolves the canon, the conversation stops.[20] Sometimes, distinctions are made about the mode of reading the Bible, whether from hermeneutics of *trust* or hermeneutics of *suspicion*. The core issue is the option: either to work from the inside, as the radical reformists do, or attack the canon from the outside. Either option requires an elaborate engagement with biblical theology.

Two interesting aspects of African and African American women theologies are, first, the lack of adequate number of women theologians trained in the Biblical field. The situation is worse for Africans. African Biblical scholarship has been generally weak. Knut Holter has demonstrated this with the study of African doctoral dissertations in the Old Testament:[21]

Decadenal Analysis of Number of
African Old Testament Doctoral Dissertations

Decade	All Africa	Nigeria	Dem. Republic of Congo
1960	3	1	-
1970	13	8	1
1980	28	10	2
1990	43	15	5
TOTALS	87	34	8

Two countries provided a half of the total for the continent. The statistics do not indicate the number written by women.

Second is that most of the black female authors still believe in the church; they are mostly inside-combatants who prefer to use the short dagger; neither do they to create the 'women's church' that reads only the Woman's Bible. Some attack its patriarchal ideology by urging women ordination. They file into seminaries in large numbers, change denominational affiliations to those places that ordain women, and seek larger roles and stronger voices in ecclesial structures of power. There are more black women in seminaries in the United States than men and this is going to be significant for the future. In 2004, sixty percent of the student admission into McCormick Theological Seminary, Chicago, was female- a trend that characterized the last seven years of the second millennium. The situation in Africa is somewhat different: the percentage of female enrollment in Nigerian universities rose significantly in the period between 1980-1990, from 6000 to 27, 000. This trend reflects the high drop-out rate of males in secondary schools. Departments of Religion/Religious Studies may enjoy high female enrollment figures especially for the Diploma courses. But female enrollment in postgraduate schools, seminaries and Bible Colleges are lower than would be the case in universities. Most of the university female graduates in Religious Studies become teachers and social welfare workers, few seek vocation in the churches. However, the high visibility of women in Western theological education, with the attendant implications for the future of the ministry could prove useful in doing theology. [22]

One index in reading a womanist is to watch where the author stands on womanist relationship to men in the church. Some are so keen on designing an exclusive, identifiable theology that they become suspicious of men. Many, however, opt for partnership with men rather than engage in the demonization of men. They reject the oppositional theology that pits the males against the females, and would subtly argue that patriarchy hurts all because it fails to mobilize all available resources for the building up of the whole. African women are wary about gender constructs that profile communities as if they were perpetually engaged in gender wars.[23] From this perspective, attention should be paid to plurality of voices or the differences in the goals of the feminist struggles, their methods, nuances, strategies, and prescriptions. Changes in culture wars in America, the rise in women education, and the growth of feminist/womanist literature have changed the trend in theological discourse. These changes have a great impact on the rate and direction of change in gender status within African American churches. Recently, many American black churches have ordained women bishops. In Africa, many denominations ordain women but conservatism is still rife. Can the changes among African American churches catalyze change in the African continent? Linkages are important.

Charismatism and gendered space

In contemporary religious landscapes, charismatic influences predominate. But black religiosity everywhere has always been charismatic because of an indigenous charismatic worldview and religious practices. Those in the diaspora have retained a large dosage of this. Therefore, attention should be paid to the impact of charismatism in feminist theology for at least seven reasons. First, there is much interest in religion and human sexuality; thus, it could be useful to examine the sexuality agenda of different types of religious forms. The relationship between doctrinal affirmations, ecclesial heritage, and gender ideologies among churches is of great interest precisely because doctrines and ecclesial heritage legitimize polity and are expressed in liturgy and ethics. Second is charismatism and religious space. Some have argued that the charismatic experience dissolves boundaries, creates freedom, and enlarges the space for women. Among many benefits, the criterion for accessing authority is less on biological sex and more on possessing and exercising spiritual gifts or *charismata*. Thus, a woman who prophesies and performs miracles wins acceptance in spite of her biological sex. This is what happened to the Corinthian women. But they frightened the men, too.

Studies of early holiness movement and Pentecostalism show that women played large roles till the turn of the 20th century. Wesley licensed women lay preachers as an "extraordinary calling". Many holiness groups ordained women or permitted their ministries. Some women were widely acclaimed evangelists, missionaries, founding mothers of monasteries, prayer houses and denominations. They asserted what Susie Stanley called, *holy boldness*, and Evelyn Higgibotham, *righteous indignation.* As Elizabeth Agumba's poem put it: " nobody can send me out of the church/for I have a message for the disciples of Christ."[24] The women insisted that they had a calling, a mandate to preach, a control over their voices, and that Christ died for the whole people of God and not for a half. They published autobiographies and books. But, as fundamentalists attacked the trend, the leash was shortened. Only the Salvation Army survived the onslaught. Autobiographies and biographies are rich sources for doing feminist theology. Quite intriguing in the enterprise is to distinguish between white and black women precisely because the double jeopardy of race determined their varied experiences in the ministry. One must not miss the irony in the story of the 'washer woman evangelist', Amanda Smith (d.1915) whose riveting autobiography, written in 1893, recounts how she was rejected by her black church and patronized by white churches! [25]

Third, there is a basketful of ironies: evangelical and charismatic spirituality fed on the freedom in Christ but bred conservative ethics, biblicism and the canonization of select Pauline 'verses of terror', family values, and submission of women. Even the Promise Keepers of our times are alleged to have become a bastion of male chauvinist effort to restore non-liberal values about the status of women. The jury is still out on this assertion because some scholars are worried about the anti male diatribe in feminist discourse that misses nuances as in the activities of the Promise Keepers. In Africa, sociologists have argued that Pentecostal environment is safe and protective of women. This explains female ardor.

Fourth, in Africa, the African Indigenous Churches were hailed as creative expressions of African religious genius at the interface of Christianity and culture. But a close look at their gender ideologies does not show that the status of women may have benefited from either the indigenous gender ideology or from the liberating aspects of pneumatic theology. In Nigeria, only one group ordains women. Menstrual taboos and other hurdles are placed at the doors of these churches against women.

Fifth is a resurgence of women spirituality. This has arisen from contradictory sources such as the emphasis on the earth mother and goddesses in nature or ecological awareness, as well as from the intensification of Marian devotion. There has been a proliferation of apparitions. The upsurge of interest in spirituality has been signaled by the growth of retreat centers and large roles for women. In Protestant circles, the growth of sodalities such as Women's Aglow and many others encourage the mobilization and empowerment of women through prayer, pilgrimages, and devotional activities.[26] This trend explains the numerical strength of women support for charismatic organizations. It is related to a sixth factor, namely, a theological trend that could be dubbed as the renaissance of Christology in feminist theology. Women find Jesus to be more friendly than the traditions of churches, and since the Holy Spirit glorifies Jesus, women have been at the forefront of the charismatisation of mainline churches in the southern hemisphere. The trend is perceptible in Hisako Kinukawa's *Women and Jesus in Mark.* [27] In Africa, Christology is important in theology for a number of reasons: Jesus is a figure that needs to be inculturated into a worldview that is more theistic and charismatic. Theologians have debated through failed images whether he is an ancestor, guest, chief or king. His maleness has been a contentious point in white feminism. This triggered the insistence on inclusive language; but this has no relevance in the African language structure. Liberation movements find Jesus as a champion of antistructure, a revolutionary, and a model in the struggles for social justice. Quite typical is Steve Biko's enthusiasm with the sacking of money- changers from the temple. The real robbers were not the hungry, petty pick -pockets in the streets but were the merchants and bankers who operated even in the temple! For Oduyoye, the salvation achieved by Jesus could be imaged from various stances in traditional Akan society: from a certain perspective, he is the *Osagyefo*, the liberator; a great friend and guarantor, *Adamfo Adu;* and he is the *Ponfo Kese* the one who pays the debt to redeem someone who may have been pawned into slavery.[28]

Seventh, many have pointed to the *laicization* of churches that reshapes power and authority at the infra political zone. One dimension is that rapid growth has weakened the capacity of old institutions to control devotees as effectively; liturgical experimentations proliferate, and the power of women groups such as Mothers' Union, Women's Guild and other sororities within the churches may have become stronger. Their financial capacity has increased the power of local congregations and competed against centralized church institutions. Among Protestants, the level of giving may have gone up but congregations prefer to spend their money. There has been a definite power shift rooted in changing spirituality. Finally, womanist theology has emphasized the power of women in shifting attention from individual salvation to confrontation with structures of injustice, a practice of theology of engagement. Black feminist theologies of various hues remember the contributions of women in the struggle for racial justice; they strive to be praxis-driven, proactive efforts that confront structures that dehumanize women. Knowledge must be commitment.

Conclusions

In conclusion, there are a number of reasons for stimulating a long conversation between African and African women theologians. The first is ideological: a survey of the literature shows that most collections of essays that engage Third World women have been organized by white women. Some of these encourage them to produce data on the earth goddess, marine spirits and other fertility goddesses in the effort to construct feminist spirituality. Rosemary Ruether could rightly point out that while black women are castigating white feminists, some white women are the ones connecting into the wider transcontinental scene, and mobilizing Third World women to do theology from pluralistic contexts. The second is academic: the emerging theologies need stronger and broader interpretative bases. Those who have done fieldwork in the African context have garnered data that enriched their understanding of religion and especially Christianity. Moreover, each theology benefits from a plurality of voices when experiences are re-read from broader templates. Third is the need to engage global cultural and economic forces as they impact a variety of contexts. These forces create the contexts, challenges, and content of theology for the 21st century. Fourth, Christian women must engage Muslim women because many women live and breath in religious pluralistic contexts. A dialogical theological method becomes imperative. Novels and activities of Non-Governmental Organizations have produced enormous data on women under Moslem regimen, especially under the *sharia* laws. Most of contemporary Africa is Moslem and the growth of the Nation of Islam in the United States compels attention from scholars.

Fifth, African American women have paid more attention to charismatic religiosity than the African women. Amba Oduyoye who has provided solid leadership and fondly acknowledged as "the grandma of African Women Theologians" perhaps set the example. She was one of the founders of the charismatic Christian Union (CU) during her undergraduate days at the University of Ghana, Legon. Many of the leaders of contemporary Pentecostal movements in West Africa drank from the CU cistern. But she soon tired of it and preferred her Methodist roots. She has consistently avoided engaging the explosion of Pentecostal spirituality with the seriousness it deserves. Off-the-cuff comments about their iconoclastic cultural ethics are followed with diatribes about prosperity preaching. Meanwhile, white sociologists have spawned theories about the salient impacts of charismatism on women. As the theologian, Cherly Bridges Johns argues, if women's advocacy taps into the pneumatic resources in the Scriptures, they will discover that the "Pentecost story contains the

263

story of the conscientization of women"; that the mission of the Pentecost involves both men and women as co-laborers and joint heirs as members of God's new *ekklesia*. The Holy Spirit empowered many spirit-filled women to perform priestly, charismatic roles, obey the call to move into mission fields without male or institutional support, and in revolutionary manner posture themselves in the line of God's eschatological design. [29] Much more attention to this facet is required because this force is reshaping the religious landscape. There has been a stunted tradition of researching only about African Independent Churches. As observed earlier, charismatic spirituality may be offering more space for women. This opens a vast research potential. Finally, African American womanists would enrich their theology through the recovery of African roots. This requires that they establish valid linkages and networks that obviate safari scholarship. It may require a conscious ideology of using the resources in their environment to build lasting bridges with fellow women theologians in Africa. Scholars may borrow a leaf from some black churches that have excavated history and found that there was a period when African Americans pioneered the evangelization of Africa.

Notes

1. Kofi Appiah-Kubi and Sergio Torres eds. *African Theology Enroute* (Maryknoll: Orbis, 1978).

2. M.O. Okume, " What Women, Whose Development: A critical analysis on reformist evangelism on African women" In Oyeronke Oyewumi ed. *African Women And Feminism: Reflecting on the Politics of Sisterhood* (Trenton, NJ: Africa World Press, 2003): 67.

3. Homer U. Ashby Jr., *Our Home Is Over Jordan: A Black Pastoral Theology* (St Louis, Mo: Chalice Press, 2003):107.

4. Sheron C. Patterson, *New Faith: A Black Christian Woman's Guide to Reformation, Recreation, Rediscovery, Renaissance, Resurrection, and Revival* (Minneapolis: Fortress Press, 2000):27, 28. See Musimbi Kanyoro's speech in Oduyoye, *Transforming Power* (Accra: Sam-Woode Ltd, 1997):chapter 2.

5. Oyewumi, *African Women and Feminism:*160;Alice Walker, *Possessing the Secret of Joy* (New York: Pocket Books, 1992); *Warrior Masks* (San Diego: Harcourt Brace, 1993).

6. Ifi Amadiume, *Male Daughters, Female Husbands: Gender and Sex in an African Society* (London: Zed Press, 1987); Oyeronke Oyewumi, *The Invention of Women: Making an African Sense of Western Gender Discourses.* (Minneapolis: University of Minnesota Press, 1997); D.U. Iyam, *Broken Hoe* (Chicago: University of Chicago Press, 1995).

7. Amba Mercy Oduyoye, *Daughters of Anowa: African women and Patriarchy* (Maryknoll: Orbis, 1995): 2.

8. Amba Mercy Oduyoye, *Beads and Strands: Reflections of an African woman on Christianity in Africa* (Maryknoll: Orbis, 2004):4.

9. Linda E. Thomas, ed. *Living Stones in the Household of God: the Legacy and Future of Black Theology* (Minneapolis Fortress Press, 2004):38.

10. cit. Stephanie Y. Mitchem, *Introducing Womanist Theology* (Maryknoll: Orbis, 2002): 85; see, my review of Mitchem's book in *Mission Studies: Journal of IAMS*, 20, (2003):188-189.

11. Ashby, *Our Home Is Over Jordan:* 9.

12. See chapter by Isabel Phiri on the trauma experienced by women under the apartheid in South Africa. Mary Getui and M.M. Theuri, eds. *Quest for Abundant Life in Africa* (Nairobi: Acton Publishers, 2002).

13. See, O.U Kalu, "Silent Victims: Violence Against Women in Nigerian Tertiary Institutions, " UNIFEM-UNDP Research, Lagos, 1996; Expanded in O.U Kalu, *The Scourge of the Vandals: The Nature and Control of Cults in Nigerian Universities* (Enugu: University of Nigerian Press, 2001):115-135. It included a study of women-on-women violence.

14. Delores S. Williams, *Sisters In The Wilderness: The Challenge of Womanist God-talk* ((Maryknoll, Orbis, 1993).

15. For fuller analysis see, O.U Kalu, *Power, Poverty and Prayer: the challenges of poverty and pluralism in African Christianity, 1960-1996* (Frankfurt: Peter Lang, 2000):161-193.

16. Ifi Amadiume, *Reinventing Africa: Matriarchy, Religion and Culture* (London: Zed Books, 1997):176.

17. Thomas, *Living Stones:* 41.

18. In R.S Sugirtharajah, ed. *Voices from the Margin* (Orbis, 1995):168-178.

19. E. Schussler-Fiorenza, *Bread Not Stone* (Boston: Beacon Press, 1984).

20 R.B. Hays, *The Moral Vision of the New Testament* (Harper San Francisco, 1996).

21. Knut Holter, *Old Testament Research for Africa: Critical Analysis and Annotated Bibliography of African Old Testament Dissertations, 1967-2000* (New York: Peter Lang, 2002).

22. Jeremiah A. Wright Jr., " Doing Black Theology in the Black Church" In Thomas, *Living Stones:*22.

23. See, N.J. Njoronge, "Resurrection People: Break the chains of injustice" *Reformed World,* 47, 1 (March, 1997):2-13.

24. "The search for my place in society" In Oduyoye ed., *Transforming Power,* 153-154.

25. See, Susie Cunningham Stanley, *Feminist Pillar of Fire: the life of Alma White* (Cleveland: Pilgrim Press, 1993); *Holy Boldness: Women Preachers' Autobiographies and the Sanctified Self* (Knoxville: University of Tennese Press, 2002).

26. Marie Griffiths, *God's Daughters: Evangelical Women and the Power of Submission* (Berkeley: University of California Press, 1997).

27. Hisako Kinukawa, *Women and Jesus in Mark* (Maryknoll:Orbis, 1994).

28. See, chapter Three: Jesus Saves in Oduyoye, *Beads and Strands.*

29. Cheryl Bridges Johns, "Pentecostal Spirituality and Conscientization of Women" In H.D. Hunter and P, D. Hocker, eds. *All Together in One Place* (Sheffield: Academic Press, 1993):161-165. See, also, Kalu, *Power, Poverty and Prayer,* (2000): chapter 7.

Part III

RELIGION AND VIOLENCE

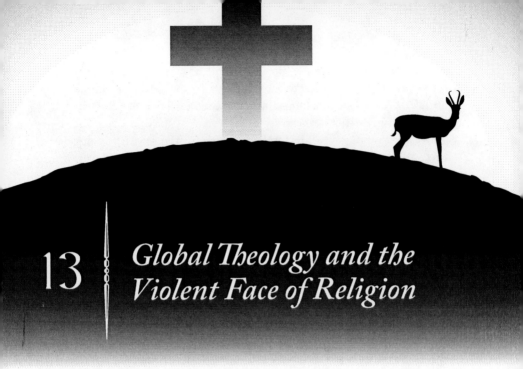

13 | *Global Theology and the Violent Face of Religion*

Introduction

In the 1970s when Professor Imasoghie[1] returned to Nigeria and joined the academy, his first impact was on deep reflections that sought to link theological discourse and theological education in West Africa to the conversations in the American academy. He was really engaged in doing global theology except that the globalization discourse had not gained currency. Recently a dictionary of global theology emerged reminding one of how the academic enterprise runs in cycles honing old issues in new ways. The first matter is about the meaning of global in global theology: whether it refers to a shared theology and certain accepted methods and conclusions for Christians all over the world. This is like the notion of universality as the Western world defined the methods of systematic theology, deployed enlightenment epistemology, and arrived at exportable conclusions inscribed in textbooks that should be accepted by the non-Western world.

Times have changed and theories of knowledge and theories of culture contact have equally changed-not just because of the shift of the center of gravity of Christianity to the global south—but because postmodernism in the West has recovered the power of *mythos* sufficiently to challenge the certitudes and pretensions of the enlightenment worldview. New ways of responding to narrative texts have opened new interpretations and exegeses. Indeed, the breakdown in the religious landscape of the West has opened new ways of reading the Bible and new ways of doing theology. More important, new themes have emerged as scholars pay attention to cultural shifts, social problems and the grains of living as Christians in a postmodern age. This is theology of life, the capacity to bring theological tools to grapple with life threatening issues, the search for alternative structures, building beloved communities and interventions that save the church from becoming irrelevant. Theology becomes a tool for the church's engagement with society or for linking faith to justice; or, as Bryant Myers put it, a theological enterprise that asks provoking questions that will enable churches to unite Christian witness and transformational development.[2] This perspective enables theology to be contextual by paying attention to local realities and the living problems of living churches, grappling with the difficulties generated by local terrains. The original question of theology re-emerges with urgency: where is God in this or that situation? How do we hear Him in His worlds and in His words? How does theology serve as a handmaid of theological education?

This understanding of global theology is crucial for Africa because it used to be said that Asian theology concentrates on religious pluralism and interfaith matters; Latin Americans on liberation theme tending towards Marxist analysis; and Africans on cultural theology-forever quarreling about what dead Europeans said about African indigenous cultures. This chapter argues that the future for African theology will be dominated by a new social awareness that involves past and emergent cultures as well as the realities in the political economy. This reflection will be less prescriptive and more illustrative by pointing to a theme that will be inescapable for African theology in the future, namely the increasingly ugly and violent face of religion in contemporary Africa.

Violence as the Emergent Theological Theme

The Roman Catholic Church in Africa is preparing for the Second African Synod as a follow-up to the first held in 1994 and celebrated in the Pope John Paul II's *Ecclesia in Africa*. (1995)The *lineamenta* urge that the focus will be on Reconciliation, Justice and Peace.[3] Some will protest that the theme should start with justice, move to peace, before reconciliation. At the WCC General Assembly in Vancouver in 1983, Allan Boesak intoned that there could be no peace without justice! To the writers of the *Kairos Document*, reconciliation was a dirty word precisely if someone's boot pressed another person's head firmly on the tarmac, it might be difficult for the broken jaws and distorted mouth to pronounce the word "reconciliation" properly. A conversation partner in the preparation urged that the Synod should reflect theologically and practically on the matter of violence; that the Synod in 1994 appears to have ignored the din and horrors of Rwanda at the background and in which the Roman Catholic Church was heavily implicated.[4] This foregrounds my perspective on the future of global theology. Congo, Rwanda and Burundi have not recovered fully from the past atrocities. The rest of Africa has been traumatized by waves of violence, a costly plague that has distorted the developmental path of the continent. Coups, counter coups, civil wars, mineral wars, political riots, religious violence have decimated the states in Africa. Some are no longer soft states but have become phantom states known by unrecognizable multicolored flags. No serious reflection on God's relationship to the people and the world of nature in Africa can be done without theologizing on violence and the churches' role in securing justice and peace that could lead to reconciliation and celebration of God's shalom. The cocktail of God, distress and growth of Christianity makes violence the hub of theological and pastoral projects, especially as the Second African Synod promises to examine the political, pastoral and pious dimensions to the church's presence in Africa.

The global dimension is that pundits claim that the 20th century was notably a violent epoch in human history but that most of the violent events were connected with competing ideologies. When Francis Fukuyama declared the end of history because of the fall of Communist Russia, he actually surmised the end of virulent ideological contests, the victory of capitalism and liberal democracy. He intoned that big business will pacify the clash of cultures; that the world will move together as it builds the bodies through which we can trust each other more; that trust will emanate from shared cultural values and shared interests precisely because self-interest is the basis of modern economic interdependence. He perhaps forgot the hypnotic drums of nationalism that summoned nations to ideological violence.

Indeed, the surprising dimension of our contemporary period is the heightened level of violence that is rooted in religion, indicating that the future will be dominated by religious violence in spite of the unabated forces of secularism, scientific development, consumerism and the pursuit of the good life. These forces require a certain urbane environment. Stock markets are very fragile and vulnerable to violent winds and the masks of modernity are sewed from the fabric of enlightened reasonableness. Violence is an emergent theme for global theology of the future: the resilience of religion in the public space; the rising crescendo of religious violence in the midst of modernity and globalization. Does the complexity of modern culture compel people to hold to some moorings from a religious past?

Violence brewed in one region of the world will affect many distant shores because of the dark sides of globalization as local identities reassert against global processes. Yet there will be differences in the nature, regional shapes, and patterns of religious violence in the global north and south because of different styles of appropriating the canons of world religions and because of the different ways in which indigenous worldviews gestate the resources of externality. The differences are fraught with immense political consequences. Philip Jenkins avers that Christians in the global south read, appropriate and believe the bible differently.[5] He could have added that that all canons are increasingly read from glistening holy eyes and that popular religion trumps the hermeneutics of suspicion whether among Muslims, Buddhist, Hindus or Christians. The radicalization of religion and the regional dimension are accompanied by the scourge of poverty in these religiously violent lands of the global south. Paul Collier, a specialist in African economics, has recently tried to connect poverty to violence by suggesting that new attention must be given to the "bottom billion," that is the billion people in the world in some fifty-eight countries (most of which are in Africa and Central Asia) who are not benefiting in any way from globalization, and are caught in a series of traps. He argues that five –sixth of global violent contentions occur in one-sixth of the world. This minority suffers from protracted warfare, dependency on one crop or one natural resource, landlocked with bad neighbors, and corrupt government that keep them on the bottom. The looming food crisis reported by UNESCO on April 15th of 2008 and the statistics on protracted warfare (80% of the poorest 20 countries have had war in the last years) prompts a special attention to the most disadvantaged and the negative effects of globalization that manufactures the tinder box for violence. Charismatic religious passion, often labeled as fundamentalist, is imploding in the global south just at the time when religion is declining in the global north. But the connectedness of the world means that no region is safe.

In the northern globe, religion has survived as a dimension of cultural heritage that is vicariously cultivated. By vicarious, says Gracie Davis, "I mean the notion of religion performed by an active minority but on behalf of a much larger number, (who implicitly at least) not only understand, but, quite clearly, approve of what the minority is doing."[6] She argues that there are effectively two religious economies in Europe: an incipient market in which voluntary membership is the norm. It is a minority's market. The second is governed by the idea of religion as a public utility in which membership remains ascribed rather than chosen. The tendency is to opt out. The turn from obligation to consumption dovetails with liberal ideology to promote experimentations with forms of spirituality beyond formal boundaries. Quite often, civil religious forms are invented to sustain fading and contested myths. In Eastern Europe, societies that are in transition suffer the same pangs of violence in the trauma of adjustment.

A key area missed by Davis is the phenomenon of apocalyptic and counter-cultural religious groups in the north who are studied under the rubric of new religious movements because the word *cult* is now taboo. Some are fragile groups – cultural opponents who are forced to violence because of internal weakness or the opposition of the society; others are assaulted by government law and order instruments and resort to self defense; still others are revolutionary utopian groups who initiate violence to overthrow legitimate government. There are secular apocalyptic groups (environmentalists and feminists, for instance) and religious apocalyptic movements, some harboring catastrophic or pessimistic views of human beings and society while others are more progressive in linking human endeavors to the future of the world. All share a cosmic perception in their engagement of society or use of violence. They perceive themselves as engaged in a human drama that is larger than life and connected to the inner core of reality. The whole of humanity has been drawn into the vortex of violence; even the rich regions of the world are witnessing an escalating violent conflict between sect and its detractors.[7]

The churches in the global south must reflect on the character of violence that has decimated the resources, manpower and ecosystems of communities. Millions are displaced and have become migrants, victims of violence even as they flee from ancestral homelands. In the Lingala, migrants term the adventure as "eating the crocodile" because many are eaten by crocodiles as they attempt to cross the seas. A global theology for the future must interpret the canon from the contextual realities where one can no longer saunter freely in African cities for fear of being mugged.

This paper explores the power of the emergent religious forms in generating loyalty and deep passions. Votaries abandon the gods of their fathers for the emergent forms and sacrifice sacred lives in defense, protection and promotion of the new religions that are invented as markers of cultural identity and the definition of the future of life. The concept of fundamentalism as a label for the new passionate religions may no longer suffice because the manifestations in the political, economic and theological realms yield contradictory conclusions. One irreducible dimension is the increased use of violence in religious matters and the spilling of such violence into political, social and economic realms. Secularism has failed to turn the public space into a neutral arena. The irony is that the religions preach peace, love and the supremacy of a supernatural ruler who dwells in a balmy realm. Yet we are confronted with the presumption of human beings essaying to protect the supernatural being with violence.

Discourses on Religious Violence

The intention here is to engage the theoretical discourses through a case study of the literature on religion and violence from Africa and specifically Nigeria where the Muslim north and "Christian" south are numerically balanced and where religious conflict acquired a violent face from the 1980s. For instance, when someone published a cartoon of the prophet Mohammed in Europe, some Nigerians in the northwestern corner, Maiduguri, attacked a Roman Catholic priest, killed him, and burnt many churches in a religious fury. Neither the victims nor the assailants had seen the cartoon and every indication is that the cartoonist is not a Christian. Later, another perplexing incident occurred in a secondary school in Bornu, northern Nigeria. A young, female Christian teacher was invigilating an examination and came upon a male pupil who was reading his Koran instead of writing the examination. She seized the material from him. He stalked out in fury, mobilized a group of Muslim students against the young woman for desecrating the holy book. They killed her, leaving a young daughter and a youthful husband. Since the 1980s, the spate of religious violence has increased and grown more brazen and bizarre. Scholars have canvassed a number of explanations that could serve as points for conversation and comparative analysis. Here, we are not dealing with the apocalyptic new religious movements but focus on a conflict within two of the ancient Abrahamic religions. There are five dominant discourses in the literature: the *conflict, instrumentalist, rainbow, competing fundamentalisms* and *state* models. Each has subsidiary dimensions and these are not necessarily discreet models.

The Conflict Discourse

The *conflict* discourse explains the linkage between religion and violence by arguing that religion has been a dysfunctional force in world politics and is the cause of the spate of instability. On the global scale, religious-related violence is a hallmark of the new millennium. The model locates the source of the dysfunctional role of religion in *the nature of religion* defined as the concern and quest for the ultimate, the source of the highest values in human experience. It canvasses seven dimensions: the recognition of the ironic fact that instead of wilting under the rays of science and technology, religion has been resilient in the modern public space and the level of religious has escalated in the midst of modernity. Depth psychological analysis avers that religious ardor/passion runs at deep levels of the human being and breeds loyalty; the depth of loyalty installs boundaries to exclude

274

others who do not participate or share the same religion; that religious prescription conjures certainty and assured reward. It is one source for nurturing difference and identification of the 'other'.

Some scholars aver that canons and theological interpretations harbor violence; that doctrinal and theological interpretations sustain non-salutary ethical practices. For instance, some canons offer rewards for using force to sustain religion while others instill the demand to do so. Some scholars emphasize the psycho-social analysis: that individuals engaged in religious violence perceive themselves as engaged in a cosmic battle larger than the individual; an antidote to perceived marginality and humiliation; an attempt to establish equality with rivals, opponents and oppressors; sacralizing violence as triumph over the force of Satan by saints and martyrs; with sanctions and links to ancient religious traditions; a postmodernist rebellion against modernity and secularism and Enlightenment; and a disregard for conventional mores. The sense of mission removes the sense of horrific acts such as murder, group suicide, terrorism and dissemination of hateful literature.[8]This explains the language of purity, ritual, sacrifice, restoration and scapegoating. Some scholars emphasize that the histories of various world religions are replete with horrific advocacy and use of violence because of intrinsic ethics of violence in boundary maintenance within religions. They draw attention to the history of violence and conflict in Muslim-Christian relationship throughout history.

Thus, Toyin Falola studied the history of violence in Nigeria and subtly raised the question whether religion innately contains a prescription for violence.[9] Does the binary worldview that divides the faithful from those proscribed to the sword instigate the use of violence for the preservation of orthodoxy? On the one hand, it argues that adhoc responses to cases of violence ignore the consistent history of violence in religious matters. On the other hand, it distinguishes between the academic and popular understanding of jihad. Interpretations of the word jihad indicate that it does not always invoke war but refers to thinking and self-reflection. It resembles the Greek word, dialogos. This academic exercise does not impress the ordinary person on a violent street. Popular belief and practice tend to privilege the declaration of jihad as self-assertion and restoration of orthodoxy that employs violence in defense of true worship. Jihad has always been an instrument for a revolutionary change; revolutionary change must perforce involve the use of violence.

Theories on the connection of violence and religion point to the fact that the twentieth century has been distinguished by "categorical violence"- a violence directed against people on the basis of their belonging to a certain religious group. Categorical violence has three distinctive features: excessiveness, the discourse on purification, and a ritual element. This recognizes the fact that non-religious ideologies could also produce violence. Categorical violence has been powered by a metaphysical meaning that is embodied in the notion of the good and true. Destruction is thought as divine and restorative. Thus, the restoration of orthodoxy in the face of alleged corruption or desecration of the pure could be achieved through divine destruction.[10] Close to this is scapegoating, the impetus to identify a contrast group onto which we can project, and which provides an explanation of the root problem. Scapegoating is like the ritualization of violence. Thus, if America attacks Iraq, a Muslim in northern Nigeria could attack a southern Christian as an escapegoat to be sacrificed in restoration of purity and in revenge for the Muslim blood shed in Iraq.

Scholars have borrowed from epidemologists the virus theory that says that violence spreads like virus as some infect others creating an infected environment in which the use of violence is an accepted option. Young people growing up in such an environment regard it as an acceptable response. A combination of these factors engenders the wider politics of difference and compels devotees to do difference in avoidable ways.

Since Africa is said to be suffering from the plague of "tribes and tongues," analysis pays attention to heritagist and historical factors that underlie ethnicity. The historical factors including territorial divide and ethnicity. The appeal to a prideful heritage and history of a particular religious tradition could be used as an arsenal in the competition in the modern political space. But it hides *fear* and insecurity as modernity challenges the roots of such heritage, and it could become a burden that constrains in the search of creative possibilities. Some communities have lost their indigenous traditions and use one or the other of the world religions as a marker of identity (either group or ethnic). David Laitin argues that while the Yoruba of south-western Nigeria use land as a cultural signifier, the Hausa/Fulani use religion and specifically Islamic religion as a marker and group identification especially when dealing with the outsider.[11] The mixture of religion and ethnicity complicates the quest for transformation.

However, the easy resort to violence in the post-1980 period and the excessiveness in religious violence in Nigeria may reflect the intricate weaving of religion into three other fabrics: a culture of violence in the society that reflected the militarization of society caused by years of military rule. Hassan Kukah argues that military rule denies access to other channels of organized opposition and imposes limitations on their ability to negotiate with the state; social dissenters find that violence is the only means of attracting the attention of military regimes that had little patience for discussion. Worse, during the long periods of military rule, there were neither parliamentary nor other viable institutional mediators between the people and the government.[12] The decimation of civil society muffled critical voices, and created the monologic state.

Another strand of this discourse argues that this period was characterized by social breakdown or social suffering that increased the level of social violence. Oil boom was gradually giving way to oil doom. For instance, it has been shown that armed robbery and the resort to secret societies increased when the World Bank installed the structural adjustment programs as a consequence of economic failure and insisted that people should 'tighten their belts' on their lean waists. In Nigerian Universities, forty-one secret societies emerged in the decade 1980-1995. Unlike fraternities in American universities, these secret societies became deadly and vitiated the academic culture.[13] Violent groups in universities are funded by politicians and many are directly linked to traditional religious shrines. This fact should stimulate researches into the resilience of indigenous religion in the modern public space especially during social stress. Secret societies resort to indigenous cultus, "medicine" and amulets in religious conflicts. The line between reverence for and the magical perception of the canon became blurred among the less educated or in popular religion. Such "medicines" arouse devotees to engage in violent acts. [14]

Finally, conflict theories adduce that there are three levels: the manifest, the underlying cause, and the ideological core in each conflict situation. Many argue that in spite of political and ethnic dimensions in religious violence, the specifically religious dimension should not be ignored precisely because religion looms large as the ideological core, buried deep in the human psyche.

The Instrumentalist/Manipulation Discourse

The social sciences tend to privilege the functionalist dimension in the explanation of religious violence. The *instrumentalist* model blames *class* as the underlying catalyst of conflict; that competition, struggle and corruption among the elite compel the *manipulation of religion*. Thus, many of the conflicts are not related to religion specifically but the elite pose as devotees and defenders of Christianity or Islam. They are not what they pretend to be but are engaged in *elite violence* perpetrated against the people and driven by more mundane interests such as the acquisition of political power embedded in the power arrangements. They are haunted by the strains in operating a federal structure and the sharing of resources in a constitutional arrangement that allocates much power to the center. Meanwhile, the collapse of economies, the long period of military rule (that vitiated the federal structure by imposing the military unitary command), legitimacy crises and the scourge of poverty increase the level of competition in the public space.

For instance, the Human Rights Watch calculated that in Nigeria, 481 large-scale incidents of political violence claimed over 15, 000 lives and destroyed properties within years, 1999-2006. Meanwhile, small-scale incidents became regular features of the political landscape. [15] In 2008, the fear of violence threatened the run-off presidential election in Zimbabwe. All over Africa, ostensibly elected leaders obtained their positions by demonstrating an ability to use corruption and political violence to prevail in sham elections. In violent and brazenly rigged polls, government officials have denied millions of citizens any real voice in selecting their political leaders. In place of democratic competition, struggles for political office have often been waged violently in the streets by gangs of thugs recruited by politicians to help them seize control of power. In recent years, thousands have lost their lives in the crossfire or as paid proxy fighters for the political leaders. At the same time, corruption and mismanagement have led to the waste of revenues from mineral resources that could have been expended to tackle poverty and improve access to basic health and education services. The experience of Nigeria has been repeated in the Democratic Republic of Congo, Kenya, Liberia, Sierra Leone, Ivory Coast, Uganda, Somalia, Sudan, Zimbabwe and many others. From the Horn of Africa to the Atlantic and Indian Oceans, political violence has proved the single most important blockage to the socio-economic transformation of communities. Elite aggression is a complex social and agnostic behavior to acquire power resources. It could be satisfying, self-rewarding, perceived as necessary for maintaining status and for ensuring control of the public space. This reflection argues that both elite and collective violence, as aspects of political violence, often mask religious forces; that religion is manipulated by political actors.

It also argues that conflict has been engendered by the response of Muslim elites to the power located at the center of the federal structure. There are two subtle dimensions to this discourse: the first is the Islamic conception of power versus the practice in the modern African states; the second is about Muslim response to modernity and its structures and ethics. According to Lamin Sanneh, Islamic conception of power asserts that the state's power should be used to serve and preserve religion. It denies the separation of powers and the ambiguous doctrine of two swords/two kingdoms entertained by Christians. Religion suffuses the whole of reality. The flip side, of course, is the danger that the state could co-opt religion for legitimation. Ancient Muslim sages cautioned about this and adopted a middle axiom that distanced the *seriki* or turban from the crown.[16] Many observers agree with Bala Usman who alleges that the religious leaders have already fallen into the embrace of the elite, that Muslim elite manipulate the religious leaders who mobilize the masses to serve the ulterior interest of the elite; they spin political and social facts as devices to alert the masses about their presumed marginalization by infidels-a vindication for jihad and violent response.[17] As an aside, people have always wondered why violent activities follow the Friday *jumat* prayers.

From here, the model argues that if only there were adequate economic resources, good governance, and just distribution of wealth, everyone would live happily together. The Mervyn Hiskett model focused on the *almajiri* as examples to argue that the unemployed youth provide the fodder for religious violence.[18] This is used to explain the incredibly violent Maitatsine riots that rocked Kano and other northern communities during the half decade 1980-1985. The *Yantsine* represents a populist genre of Islam that attacked both Muslim elites as well as Christian southerners in Kano, Maiduguri, Kaduna, Yola and Gombe. The argument follows that social order could be secured by ensuring that these youths, attached to Muslim teachers or *mallams,* are given employment and saved from the indignities of religious- sanctioned begging. Some Muslim governors have recognized the force of this argument and installed programs to alleviate the fate of the *almajiri*. But some scholars would demur against the demonization of the *almajiri*.

Moreover, the model fails to explain the anti-Christian riots in Kaduna and Zaria nurtured by university students who dreaded the possibility of a southern President of the Students' Union in 1987. The Muslim Students' Society was formed in that University in 1977 and sought to turn the University into a Muslim community. The Hiskett model does not explain the fact that the combination of ethnicity and religion caused over ten ethno-religious conflicts in Northern Nigeria between 1980 and 1992.The un-Islamised communities upon whom the northern elite imposed Muslim rulers, took the occasion to rid themselves of such leaders. This explains what happened at Zango-Kataf. Arguably, a sustainable environment may ease tension but the socio-economic argument does not adequately recognize the power of religion in fostering bigotry, superiority complex, and conflict; or how the reverence for the Koran that spurs devotees to become protectors against desecration. Above all, it does not explain why poverty and unemployment do not elicit anti-Islamic violence in the southern region of the country.

Three groups of scholars urge the instrumentalist model: first is the socialist-oriented scholarship that has privileged this model because they cast religion to the periphery in social analysis, and caricature it as false consciousness or humbug. It was prominent in the conclusions of a committee empanelled by government who produced *The Report of the Political Bureau: Federal Government of Nigeria, March, 1997*. This group will prefer a public space free of religious language and interests. The second strand consists of internal critics within Islam - those educated Muslim youth who feel that the elite have neither been faithful to the doctrines of the religion or helpful to the masses. Prominent among this group is Sanusi Lamido Sanusi a scion of the ruling family in Kano. He trained in the West as a banker but is also a recognized *mallam*. His trenchant critic of the Muslim elite has poignancy because of his class. [19]Writing in the northern-based newspaper, *Weekly Trust* (June 22-28, 2001), Lamido observed that "whether it is in the name of religion, region or ethnicity, the Nigerian elite everywhere strives to keep people in perpetual ignorance of their real enemies." Underneath Lamido's position are: first, a theological root that argues that Islam is about delivering justice and not a tool of simplistic politics of identity, and definitely not a tool for self-seeking. A second dimension is his concern about internal disunity among Muslims because the *izalatu*, Wahhabbist fundamentalists are violently opposed to the *tariqas or sufi orders* whom they accuse of engaging in doctrinal abuses. Acting as youthful advocates for purity, they decry the compromises among the elite who no longer obey the *ribah* laws, care for the poor, or encourage learning among the *umma*. Their goal of the *izalatu* is to restore the pristine traditions of Islam. The protagonists in the *sharia* controversy tend to employ Wahhabist rhetoric. According to Lamido, neither the appropriation of religion as the referent for political identity by the northern Muslim elite nor the violence of the extremists augurs well for the genuine Muslim interest. A third strand consists of secularist commentators who appeal to modernity discourse and borrow from enlightenment worldview.

The Rainbow Discourse

The *rainbow* model contains at the least four sub-sets that urge inherent doctrinal resonance between world religions, the primacy of pluralism, the need for religious toleration, the nationalist goal for indigenizing the world religions, and even the acceptance of secularity as creating a free public space for the practice of religions without the trammels of state restrictions. The first position argues that each religious tradition has in -built models in their doctrines for peaceful co-existence; that they preach peace, love, the sanctity of human life and other salient ethics; that scholars should mine the interiors of the faith traditions, identify and promote religious transformations through these pathways. The richness and diversity of the religious traditions could be compared to the colors of the rainbow that combine to enhance the cultural life of the nation. It appeals to the shared origins and ethical resonance among the *Abrahamic religions* and the prominence of Abraham, Moses, the patriarchs and Jesus in the Koran and shared cultural ingredients, feasts and fasting periods. From here, it argues that respect for human dignity should build a bridge for co-existence. Precedents could be found in the Neoplatonic mysticism of Nicholas of Cusa, who pioneered ecumenism and sought to understand God and all reality in some inclusive harmony and interdependence of all parts of nature. Some point to the promising Christian/Buddhist conversations between Karl Rahner and Masao Abe.

The rainbow discourse was the staple in conferences of the Nigerian Association for the Study of Religion through two decades, from the mid 1970s to early 1990s. The Abiola Foundation funded the Association when the leadership was located in the University of Ilorin to research in this area in the 1980s. Perhaps Abiola typifies the irony in this posture. To garner the Muslim support for his political ambition, he built mosques and Muslim schools; to build a broader political base, he gave money for research on peaceful-co-existence; and yet he mediated the implosion of international Islamic influence in the country; and still yet he did not enjoy the full confidence of the northern Muslims because he had no Arabic pedigree.

But a shade of this model propagated by secular-oriented/reformist Muslims subtly harps on *indigenization of religion*. It argues that both Islam and Christianity came into the nation at certain points in time and bear the traditions and cultures of the religious messengers; that the Arabs were just as hegemonic and racist as the Western change agents; that these religions need to be inculturated and translated to answer the needs of specific African peoples and environments. Some argue that the Muslim laws emerged in ancient Arabic contexts that jar prominently with the needs of contemporary Nigeria. Indeed, just as Wahhabism was rejected in Saudi Arabia at the early period, so have many Muslims continued to reject it. This response delayed the introduction of the *sharia* in northern Nigeria. However, the Saudi rulers later found its conservative cultural practices to be useful for their own political goal; they adopted the ideology, and have propagated it as if it was the core of Muslim orthodoxy. The Wahhabis represent an extreme minority sect among the *sunni* Muslims. The nationalist perspective points to the external factor in the escalating religious conflict and urges that a proper historical understanding of Islam might create a wholesome social space.

The argument is that if left alone, Nigerians could solve their religious problems; that external enemies of the nation have funded religious conflict in Nigeria; that these forces essay to destroy the national unity by recruiting indigenous Nigerian agents who serve as conduits for foreign Muslim countries that have increased their investments in Nigeria. This discourse points to the fact that from mid-1980s, Arab countries have intensified the funding of mosques and Islamic education, and charitable infrastructure in Nigeria. In 2004, the Nigerian government accused some Arab embassies for using their mosques to mobilize dissidence. The government alleged that some affiliates of the al Qaeda movement started operations in northern Nigeria in 2001 as charitable non-profit organizations.

Without resort to statistics, it is arguable that Islam has grown rapidly in Nigeria. An aside is the debate that surfaced in the 19th century: whether Islam is more suitable for Africans than Christianity. Anti-colonialists had instigated the debate to annoy the missionaries and play on their fear of Islamic expansion that could swallow up Christianity. The protagonists pointed to the adaptability of Islam to local cultures; its capacity to tolerate popular practices that arise out of ignorance of the religion. The absorption of Ifa divination into Muslim divinatory process is a good example. Attention has been drawn to the impact of the untranslatability of Islam. The insistence on the use of Arabic language explains the varieties of Islamic practices among many communities. Vernacularization deepens the people's understanding of a religion.

However, an apologetic discourse deploys the moral high ground to argue that Islamic ethics against drinking alcohol produced better, disciplined communities. It was not only that Christians permitted the consumption of alcohol but that "Christian" European traders promoted the gin trade, and coastal African communities became vulnerable to moral instability. The sharia is buttressed on its capacity to promote a higher level of individual and communal morality and physical security.

From here, the model has progressed in different directions: some deploy the concept of *religious pluralism*, as does Simeon Ilesanmi.[20] The weakness of the discourse on pluralism is the scant attention paid to three dimensions of religious pluralism:

- In some contexts, there are possibilities for cooperation in public life, constructive encounters and open witness. All stakeholders must endeavor to maintain the peaceful environment.
- In others contexts, there are tensions growing where there used to be harmony. People respond to this deterioration in diverse ways, some by determining to build bridges, while others are confirmed in prejudices and negative perceptions.
- In some contexts the relationships between people of different faiths are openly hostile.

Two comments: first, the practice of religious pluralism requires a clear identification of the context because each context requires a different strategy and response. The second is that the northern Nigerian context has become extremely hostile for Christian witness. Others argue that increased religious conflict indicates that modernity has witnessed the illogical reality of the growth rather than death of religion. All religions are growing and the salience of religion in the political space of the Third World has become quite alarming, according to Jeff Haynes.[21] Therefore, conflict arises from the competition by a multiplicity of religions each clothed with its invented history and unique claims. The older ones seek to establish a dominance that is stoutly resisted by new religious movements. Market and rational choice theories tango here. Pluralism is portrayed as the enlargement of sacred space that increases the level of competition. Pluralism in the African context is somewhat different from the Western experience. Thus, Ruth Marshall-Fratani points to the peculiarity of pluralism in Nigeria which means

> a plurality of citizenship, each with its own moral vision, invented history, symbolic forms, models of power and authority, and institutional expressions, all interacting in the context of an authoritarian power whose control over public goods and accumulation is constantly under the pressure of their claims, and whose legitimacy is challenged by their alternate vision.[22]

Faced with the dilemma of pluralism, political scientists such as Jibrin Ibrahim argue in favor of *secularity* of the state ideology.[23] Often, the secularist argument is blurred by the plea for *toleration* but it harks to the old argument that only the separation of state and religion will protect minority religious groups.

The Competing Fundamentalisms Discourse

This model argues that the increasing conflict may be a result of "competing fundamentalisms". Paul Gifford in his *The New Crusaders* (1991) images both Pentecostalism and radical Islamic groups in Africa as fundamentalists.[24] Commentators connect the violent response of incensed Muslims in the last two decades with the implosion of Pentecostal-charismatic spirituality. From the mid 1970s, charismatic evangelical activities intensified in the northern regions that had been the preserved Muslim enclaves. A good example is the crusade by the German-born, Reinhard Bonnke in the ancient city of Kano in 1990. For one week, over a million people gathered every night in the Stadium. He sent vans through the city to bring the blind, deaf and street beggars. It is claimed that he healed many. When he planned to return two years later, a riot broke out to signal Muslim resistance. Muslim youths have at the same time come under the ideological and resource influences of international Muslim radicalism. Nigeria as an oil-producing country remained central to Muslim interest and the politics of the OPEC. The conjuncture of the two trends (the rise of youthful Islamic radicalism and youth charismatic/ Pentecostalism) may have intensified the violent atmosphere. It should be emphasized that the demonization of Islam in Nigerian Pentecostal rhetoric and the lack of a dialogical theology and praxis among this rapidly growing form of Christianity may have caused much harm and hindered conflict transformation.[25]

The *d'awaah* and the *great commission* are like hypnotic drums to a modern form of the crusade. The demarcation of Nigeria into sharia and non-sharia states is an intentional territorialization of Islam, veritable attempt to demarcate sacralized spaces and boundaries against infidels. But charismatic spirituality rejected the compromises of the old mission-founded churches, and demonized "the religion of the bond woman". Southerners have turned the strangers' quarters, *sabon gari,* in Muslim North into Zion cities bustling with economic and charismatic Christian activities. They organize evangelistic tours to heal and convert Muslims. They see no reason why Muslims could operate freely in the south while Christians are restricted to operate in the north. Some Muslims detect a disgusting whiff of Zionism in their doctrine. The Christian Association of Nigeria that Enwerem discusses in his *Dangerous Awakening* counters the leadership of the *Jam'atu Nasril Islam* (Victory for Islam) and the Nigerian Supreme Council for Islamic Affairs led by the revered Sultan of Sokoto (heir of the Sokoto Caliphate). [26]The new Christian daring elicits violent responses. The environment is made volatile and the problem becomes increasing intractable to all theories of conflict transformation. Countering the verses in the Qur'an that respects the total freedom of human beings to practice religion without compulsion are many that urge the duty of a Muslim to establish the religion on earth, including by violent means. Some scholars explain that the advocates of violence use an exegesis that gives universal import to Qur'anic verses revealed within and in relation to specific historical contexts.

The World Bank estimated that sub-Sahara Africa, with more than fifty states has a Muslim population of over 250 million or a fifth of the world's Muslims. The region also has the world's largest proportion of people living on less than one dollar a day. Traditionally home to the moderate and more tolerant Islamic *sufi* sect, the region is suddenly grappling with large pockets of radical Islamists seeking to establish strict Islamic law among some of the region's more disenfranchised communities. The report connects the economic environment to radicalism. Differentiating between revivalist and radical Islamism, it argued that the revivalists trend is not necessarily as politically explosive as the radical trend whose anti-structure and use of violence has recently become explosive and ominous as exemplified by Somalia, Eritrea, and Kenya. Historically, radical elements have not ruled in any of these states and therefore provide a critical voice that attracts the marginalized sectors of the population disillusioned by poverty, corruption and political alienation. The marginalized contribute to the spread of radicalism. The larger conclusion is that contemporary extremists do not necessarily draw inspiration from the intellectual legacies of Islam but from their historical circumstances, selecting aspects of that heritage to serve their political ideology.

The State and Transformation Discourse

The argument goes full circle: there are three dimensions of conflict intervention: prevention, resolution and healing. It is argued that the state has the responsibility to prevent and resolve conflicts even when ill-equipped to heal. The state should prevent conflict by creating an enabling environment, alleviate poverty, create an economic environment that provides employment, and ensure good governance by promoting a federal character in the allocation of infrastructure and resources. The enforcement agencies should anticipate the breakdown of order and respond to open conflict situations. Beyond security, the ethics of governance is essential because corruption deprives the state of moral capacity.

In practice, however, the security forces are often compromised partisan agents. In one case, investigators found that the governor of the state had been alerted about an incident but failed to take adequate preventive measures. Often, the Intelligence and Security services failed.

A second line of reasoning is that the demand for government patronage and the call on the secular government to referee religious activities cause much confusion. The political culture created the unconscionable situation when a Muslim-led government was urged by Muslim leaders and buckled under their pressure to register Nigeria as the 46th member of the Organization of Islamic Countries without the approval of the Executive Council of the State. It caused a massive political crisis.[27] A partisan government compromises its capacity to enlighten the public or create a dialogical environment that would encourage people to be rooted in their religions and open to others. It is admitted that the provisions in the various canons that enhance peaceful co-existence are ignored in the heat of the virulent rivalry.

Conflict transformation compels the recognition of the new reality or character of the public space, followed with deliberate policies that permit religious tolerance and religious freedom. Participation in the global community of nations, the demands of new market forces, and the reputation of the nation demand a different way of doing difference. However, it is realized that separation of religion and state as practiced in America may not be suitable for many African communities because the ethnic components operate from worldviews that do not demarcate the profane from the sacred. Therefore, policy should serve to articulate the moderating role of the state in such a manner as to leave the public space free. The problem for religious leaders is how to create and maintain distance from government. But this is not possible when every religious group tends to seek land, money, the patronage of pilgrimages, and a variety of government support. Besides, in Nigerian political culture, government officials are encouraged to use their positions in aid of their faith traditions. Faith plays an enormous role in political campaigns. Furthermore, the dividends of democratic structures include the enlargement of the number of actors and vested interests in the public space.

Some, therefore, urge that the ethics for peace should be deliberately engineered into the public space by either mining the indigenous religious traditions or by adopting a moderated secularist ideology. The reason is simple: the Nigerian Constitution declares that the nation is a secular state. This concept was derived from the West but jars prominently against the grain of indigenous political thought, and was stoutly rejected by both Muslims and Christians. However, the Christians appeared ready to accept secularity as a compromise for peace, if the state served as a referee. They rejected the stark form of secularity proposed by social science scholars in Nigerian universities. It is interesting to observe how a Muslim military ruler "settled" or neutralized the socialist voices through a policy of recruitment. General Ibrahim Babaginda's regime installed many of the scholars in newly created research centers such as the Center for Democratic Studies and Center for Inter-Governmental Relations, Abuja. The government also ensured that constitutional conferences do not discuss the religious question.

This constitutional anomaly of the religious questions hung like an albatross and became obvious during the federal government's intervention in the sharia controversy in the years, 1999-2002. Its ability to intervene was hedged by the provisions in the Constitution of 1996 which a dictatorial military regime led by a Muslim ruler had surreptitiously foisted upon the nation. This constitution permits the states of the federation to institute such religious provisions as the sharia by two-thirds majority vote in the state house of assembly. Beyond the constitutional dimension are such realities of the political culture as: the unregulated religious space, increased intervention of media in fostering competition and accent on otherness, nurturing of micropolitics based on religion, and the effects of an enlarged political space as a result of democratic process: increase in the number of participants, vested interests, discordant voices, and the promotion of culture of violence.

Thus, the federal government must perforce midwife religious politics because it has no legal force to do otherwise. The federal government has, therefore, intervened through policy such as the creation of an advisory body, the Supreme Council for Religious Affairs to culture peaceful co-operation among religious leaders. It has also tried to provide for the two religions in an even-handed manner. For instance, it created a Pilgrims Board that supervises pilgrimage to Mecca and Jerusalem; it donated to chapels and mosques in the Abuja and Lagos; and above all, it empanelled the Oputa Judiciary Panel to receive complaints of abuse by former military regimes and compensate those who lost property during religious riots. This attempt to bring religious values into governance borrowed a leaf from South Africa but has failed to accomplish much. For instance, the recommendations of the Oputa panel never saw the rays of light. As an aside, the healing effort in Rwanda, Somalia and Eritrea came from grassroots communities that used indigenous methods of conflict resolution. This method worked prominently in Zango-Kataf when the leaders of the warring ethnic groups exchanged their garments and swords in the market place. The federal government designed a number of affirmative action policies around allocation of resources, administrative posts, admission into federally-owned institutions, and employment in establishments. Meritocracy was jettisoned in favor of ethnic and religious criteria. These policies ensured that the state's role in religious politics remained prominent.

Conclusion: Dialogue and Accountability as Antidotes

The effort here has been to provide the church in Africa with an analytical resource for doing a theology of life. From a larger perspective the reflection argues that globally, the transformation of religious conflict would rest on a tripod:

i.   re-imagining the public space (socio-economic transformation and good governance);

ii. healing the public space through projects such as truth commission and re-negotiating social contract through national conference;

iii. centering the religious space by promoting a culture of interfaith religious education through (a) creating dialogue contexts that mine the interior theological bases of various faith traditions, and (b) deliberately engineering salient ethics for peaceful existence in the entire continent.

These prescriptions could be the bases of theological reflections by exploring the politics of Jesus as well as the models of conflict transformation in indigenous knowledge. Religious conflict transformation cannot be imposed from top-downwards; it can hardly be imposed by a constitution, or by the associations formed by the competing parties, or by the federal government. It will emerge from the quality of relationship generated by the common people and by paradigms of evangelization that enables the church to offer the water of life instead of being a river between communities. This may require new models of priestly/ministerial formation and the deliberate cultivation of a dialogical Christian presence. [28] Dialogue means living together, arguing or debating, reflecting and sharing. It is risky but it is practiced daily in the market places, schools, offices, and within political and social groups. When people interact, stereotypes dissolve. Stories abound that in the midst of religious violence, Muslim neighbors risked their lives to save southerners. Only the people could transform conflict in spite of the manipulations of the elite who control the media as instruments of fostering religious divides. Dialogue can be an antidote to religious conflicts when the government focuses on the elimination of violence as an acceptable mode of inter-religious response (just as health officials focus on the elimination of a specific form of virus infection). Some commentators have suggested the use of education to sensitize the citizens about the various religious traditions, especially practical education that brings people from various faiths together. This is crucial because it is built on fostering healthy relationships and enhancing knowledge. It can be concluded that violence, stereotyping and scapegoating in communities are often bred by ignorance, physical and mental isolation. The church must re-appropriate its missional vocation and should perceive theology both as a reflection and as engagement. This is how theological education can become a new dimension of doing theology by engaging the public space in a mode of "in actione contemplativus"- a spirituality that worships Christ and celebrates His reign by fully engaging the forces that dehumanize and incite violence.

Notes

1. This essay was written as a chapter in a festschrift honoring Professor Imasoghie's contribution to African theology and theological education.

2. Joe Holland and Peter Henriot, eds., *Social Analysis: Linking Faith to Justice* (Maryknoll, NJ: Orbis, 1980); Bryant L. Myers, *Provoking Questions: Uniting Christian Witness and Transformational Development* (Monrovia, CA: World Vision, 2006).

3. Synod of Bishops, II Special Assembly for Africa-*The Church in Africa in Service to Reconciliation, Justice and Peace: Lineamenta* (Vatican City, 2006).

4. Jay J. Carney, "Waters of Baptism, Blood of Tribalism, " *Africa Ecclesial Review,* 50, 1/2 (March-June, 2008): 9-31; C. Ritter, J. K. Roth, W. Whitworth, eds *Genocide in Rwanda: Complicity of the Churches?* (St Paul, MN: Paragon Press, 2004).

5. Philip Jenkins, *The New Faces of Christianity: Believing the Bible in the Global South* (New York: Oxford University Press, 2006).

6. This is best explained by Gracie Davis, *Religion in Modern Europe: A Memory Mutates*(Oxford: Oxford University Press, 2000). Quotation is from "Is Europe an Exceptional Case?" *International Review of Missions* , 95, nos. 378/379 (July/October, 2006): 247-258. see page 248; Andrew M. Greeley, *Religion in Europe at the End of the Second Millennium: A Sociological Profile* (London: Transaction, 2003).

7. Mark Leach, Mitchell Berman, Lea Eubanks, "Religious Activities, Religious Orientation and Aggressive Behavior", *Journal of the Scientific Study of Religion*, 42, 2 (June 2008): 311-319; Sarah M. Pike, *New Age and NeoPagan Religions in America* (New York: Columbia University Press, 2004); Helen A Berger, ed., *Witchcraft and Magic: Contemporary North America* (Philadelphia, PA: University of Pennsylvania Press, 2005); Gary Jensen, *The Path of the Devil: Early Modern Witch Hunts.*(Lanham, MD: Rowman & Littlefield Publishers, 2006).

8. Mark Juergensmeyer, *Terror in the Mind of God: The Global Rise of Religious Violence* (Berkeley: University of California Press, 2000); Catherine Wessinger, *How The Millennium Comes Violently: From Jonestown to Heaven's Gate*(New York: Seven Bridges Press, 2000); Marc H. Ellis, *Unholy Alliance: Religion and Atrocity in Our Time* (Minneapolis: Fortress Press, 1997); Leo D. Lefebure, *Revelation, The Religions and Violence* (Maryknoll, NY: Orbis Books, 2000).

9. Toyin Falola, *Violence in Nigeria: The Crisis of Religious Politics and Secular Ideologies* (Rochester: Rochester University Press, 1998).

10. Charles Taylor, "On Religion and Violence", *The Arts and Science Review* (University of Toronto), 2, 1(Spring 2005): 31-35.

11. David Laitin, *Hegemony and Culture* (Chicago: University of Chicago Press, 1986).

12. Matthew Hassan Kukah, *Religion, Politics and Power in Northern Nigeria* (Ibadan, Nigeria: Spectrum Press, 1994).

13. Ogbu U. Kalu, *The Scourge of the Vandals: The Nature and Control of Cults in Nigerian Universities* (Nsukka: University of Nigeria Press, 2001).

14. see, Stephen Ellis and G. ter Haar, *Worlds of Power: Religious Thought and Practice in Africa* (New York: Oxford University Press, 2004).

15. See, Human Rights Watch, Nigeria, *Revenge in the Name of Religion: The Cycle of Violence*.vol.17, no.8(A), May 2005.

16. Lamin Sanneh, *Piety and Power: Muslims and Christians in West Africa* (Maryknoll, NY: Orbis, 1996): ibid., *The Turban and the Crown: Muslims and West African Pluralism* (Boulder, CO: Westview Press, 1997).

17. Bala Usman, *Manipulation of Religion in Nigeria* (Kaduna, Nigeria: Vanguard Press, 1987).

18. Mervyn Hiskett, "The Maitatsine Riots, Kano, 1980: An Assessment", *Journal of Religion In Africa*, 17, 3 (1987): 209-223; Elizabeth Isichei, "The Maitatsine Rising in Nigeria, 1980-1985: A Revolt of The Disinhertited" ibid., : 194-208.

19. See, www.gamji.com for his articles.

20. Simeon Ilesanmi, *Religious Pluralism and the Nigerian State* (Athens: Ohio University, 1997).

21. Jeff Haynes, *Religion and Politics in Africa* (London: Zed Press, 1996).

22. Ruth Marshall-Fratani, "Mediating the Global and the Local in Nigerian Pentecostalism" *Journal of Religion in Africa*, 28, 3 (1998)278-315.see, p. 301.

23. Jibrin Ibrahim, "Religion and Political Turbulence in Nigeria", *Journal of African Studies*, 29 (1991): 116-136

24. Paul Gifford, *The New Crusaders* (London: Pluto Press, 1991).

25. Ogbu U. Kalu, "Sharia and Islam in Nigerian Pentecostal Rhetoric, 1970-2003", *Pneuma*, 26, 2 (2004): 242-261; Ogbu U Kalu, "Saffiyya and Adamah: Punishing Adultery with Sharia Stones in Twenty-First -Century Nigeria", *African Affairs* (London) 102 (June 2003): 389-408.

26. I.M. Enwerem, *A Dangerous Awakening: Politicization of Religion in Nigeria* (Ibadan, Nigeria: IFRA, 1995); Afe Adogame, "Politicization of Religion and the Religionization of Politics in Nigeria" In *Religion, History, and Politics in Nigeria: Essays in Honor of Ogbu U. Kalu* eds., Chima Korieh and Ugo Nwokeji (Lanham: University Press of America, 2005): 128-139.

27. H.A. Adigwe, *OIC: The Implications for Nigeria* (Onitsha, Nigeria: Catholic Archdiocese Publications, 1986).

28. Iheanyi Enwerem, "Political Activism and Priestly Formation", *African Ecclesial Review*, 50, 1/2 (2008): 31-57; Cyril Orji, "Incarnation, Self Transcendence and the Challenge of Inter-religious Dialogue", *AFER*, 50, 1/2(2008): 95-114; E. Katongole, "Violence and Social Imagination: Re-thinking Theology and Politics in Africa", *Religion and Theology*, 12, 2 (2005).

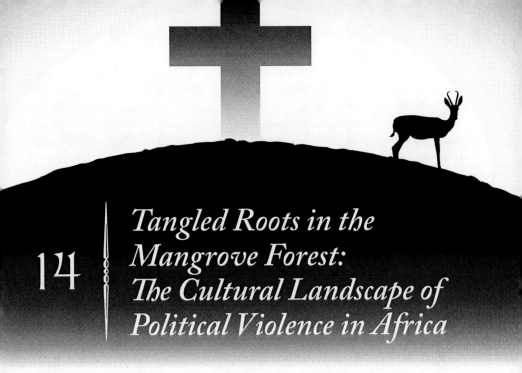

14 | Tangled Roots in the Mangrove Forest: The Cultural Landscape of Political Violence in Africa

Introduction: The Ethnography of Political Violence

I grew up in Calabar, a town that nestles on the banks of the Cross River in southeastern Nigeria, situated about eighteen nautical miles from the Atlantic Ocean. The Cross River builds up from numerous creeks bounded by a marshy terrain and the mangrove forest sporting gigantic outcrops of tangled roots. I was always amazed how these tangled roots supported and nurtured such huge trees and luscious green forests. Recently, I began to see a comparison between the cultural roots of violence in Africa with the imagery of tangled roots in the mangrove forests of the Cross River. As the tangled roots are nourished by the nutrients in the marshy waters, so are the complex forms of violence in the political culture nurtured by the nutrients of the religious cults. I became keenly aware that the study of religion and violence could become so heuristic that it might miss the crucial function of turning knowledge into commitment unless it uses a specific context or benefits from an ethnography that explores how religious and cultural roots inform and nurture the phenomenon of violence in the African public spaces, and how this model of exploration of the substratum of the political landscape could serve in policy making and social transformation of violent contexts. This method asserts that the African context is different from the cultural terrain in the northern globe and offers new theoretical possibilities as we reflect on the relationship between knowledge, power and culture. At the theoretical level, we are dealing with cultural framing as a means of engaging the dynamics of contention or violence. Cultural framing leads to emphasis on relational processes, acknowledges the importance of environmental and cognitive mechanisms, but urges that in Africa, the most sustainable mobilization of interest groups and identities are often forged through cults.[1]

The political field constitutes the best mirror precisely because it provides a composite site where the various forces in social structures and institutions intersect. The political field encapsulates the core dynamics in their relationship. To use Foucault's concept of power as consisting of forces that exist in various fields, all the forces (economic, social, cultural, ethnic, gender and class) surge together into the political space. Since power is not always repressive, Foucault recaptured the capacity of power to be productive and to serve the public good. [2] Political violence becomes an attempt to grab, control, and redirect the dynamics of the forces along vested interests. The interests may be advocacy for certain ideals, agitation based on ethnic or atavistic allegiances, attempts to seize and determine the outcome of electoral process, monopolize the governance of the *polis*, or to achieve the sectarian ascendancy of a particular religious passion and belief system.

Political violence in Eastern Europe and the Middle East could provide examples of the interlocking relationship between religion and political violence. This reflection will use the less familiar African case study. The backdrop consists of two dimensions: first the high incidence of political violence in Africa in the post-1989 period; and second, the tendency to root political violence in rituals of indigenous religion. This period is important because it has been dubbed as the *second liberation of Africa* and analyzed with the "new realism" discourse. It was surmised that after the collapse of Communist Soviet regime and the victory of capitalism, a new democratization process will be deployed to rid Africa of local dictators and install a neoliberal, democratic political economy. In some quarters, optimists raised the hope of an African Renaissance. A new realism greeted the failed dream and wallowed in the pessimism that African pathology was incurable. The argument here is that the cocktail of religion and political violence intoxicated the new political players and blocked the realization of the hopes of a second liberation. The elitist politics engendered by neo-liberal ideology excluded, dis-empowered and disenfranchised the masses. Thus, a chemical analysis of the cocktail has immense value for the wellbeing of communities in Africa. Some questions will guide: what are the characteristics of political violence? What are the causes? How is political violence connected to religion especially in the African context? The conclusion is to argue that theories of religious violence based on Western epistemology and enlightenment worldview may be unhelpful for many regions of the global south where religious violence is endemic.

The African case study should begin with certain theoretical musings. We observe two levels of political violence or intra-state conflict: elitist violence as the ruling elite predate on the ruled, and collective violence when the ruled use violence to express frustration and aggressive instincts. Such instincts may arise from failed expectations, unearned entitlements, relative deprivation and poor resource distribution. Elite predation is expressed at various levels of the dynamics of politics-electoral processes and habits of governance. The quality of politics is clarified in patterns of state presence, pursuit of legitimacy and the space allocated to the civil society. This space could be restricted by the reality or absence of social contract and responsibility of power (ordinarily called culture of accountability). Political actors weave the political culture with ideologies of leadership ethics, use of media and exploiting identity markers such as ethnicity, religion and class. These, in turn, may be affected by historical facts such as the colonial experiences, level of past conflicts and level of military interventions and militarization of the society. This political represents internal forces that aid analysis of elite predation. External geopolitics factors are equally important especially under the globalization canopy. We should, therefore, paint a brief canvass of both the globalization and democratization processes and how these forces underscored the environment that breeds political violence. While globalization may be a cultural free, it has enormous economic consequences. Collective violence is greatly a response of economic forces-production, population pressure, resource mobilization, distribution of wealth and the impact of international economic order or supra state shifts in perceived entitlement. Admittedly, it is argued that aggression and frustration may not lead to collective violence. The people devise subterfuges to mask their pains with jokes about leaders and policies. Others exit the scene of disasters. People emigrate denuding the inhospitable state of productive human resources, or at least seemingly so. It is now argued that emigrants are like exiles who mourn the loss of home and dislocation and re-engage through financial remittances. But we cannot avoid the connection between poverty and collective violence as could be illustrated with food riots of the mid-2008 and xenophobic assault on immigrants in South Africa and Kenya.

Electoral Process, Governance and Elite Violence

Political violence has become the most visible aspect of political competition across the continent. Many elections have been marred by political violence that takes many forms-from assassinations to armed clashes between gangs employed by rival politicians. Politicians recruit, pay and arm the gangs to intimidate opponents, the public and disrupt elections. Such gangs attack polling booths, carry away the ballot boxes and stuff them with the fake ballots of the patrons. The goals are to spread fear, ensure that supporters of political opponents are denied access to exercise their rights. Gangs control the public space by sending the wrong people into powerful political positions. When immoral people control the governance of nations, the opportunities for healthy development are lost. Worse, the gangs may grow stronger than those who hired them and could scuttle the prospects of consolidation after the elections. For instance, the Human Rights Watch calculated that in Nigeria, 481 large-scale incidents of political violence claimed over 15, 000 lives and destroyed properties within years, 1999-2006. Meanwhile, small-scale incidents became regular features of the political landscape.[3] In 2008, the fear of violence threatened the run-off presidential election in Zimbabwe.

All over Africa, ostensibly elected leaders obtained their positions by demonstrating an ability to use corruption and political violence to prevail in sham elections. In violent and brazenly rigged polls, government officials have denied millions of citizens any real voice in selecting their political leaders. In place of democratic competition, struggles for political office have often been waged violently in the streets by gangs of thugs recruited by politicians to help them seize control of power. In recent years, thousands have lost their lives in the crossfire or as paid proxy fighters for the political leaders. At the same time, corruption and mismanagement have led to the waste of revenues from mineral resources that could have been expended to tackle poverty and improve access to basic health and education services. The experience of Nigeria has been repeated in the Democratic Republic of Congo, Kenya, Liberia, Sierra Leone, Ivory Coast, Uganda, Somalia, Sudan, Zimbabwe and many others. From the Horn of Africa to the Atlantic and Indian Oceans, political violence has proved the single most important blockage to the socio-economic transformation of communities.

Elite aggression is a complex social and agnostic behavior to acquire power resources. It could be satisfying, self-rewarding, perceived as necessary for maintaining status and for ensuring control of the public space. This reflection argues that both elite and collective violence in Africa are expressed in a peculiar manner: In Africa, political violence often masks religious forces. Some may argue that religion is manipulated by political actors. But this begs the question as to why religion should energize the ethnic, class, and gender fault-lines. Why do people avoid ideas, public debates and media advocacy and agitation as in the global north? A cultural discourse or ethnography of violence points to the importance of worldview and resilience of primal values in the modern public space. In Africa, political violence, like the tangled roots of the mangrove forests, succor failed states, collapsed economies and scorched political terrains. This is because political violence masks a religious substratum. Resilient indigenous religions and cults still dominate the political cultures in the modern public spaces and inspire the roles of godfathers and gangs in politics. These tap into the violent dimensions of religion when religion is used as an instrument to instill fear and achieve one's goal by force in a competitive, pluralistic public space. This is an aspect of *counterfeit modernity*. The direct connection between cults and violence is that religious cults confer the illusion of invincibility, protection and numinous power to control others and destroy opponents. It empowers (or beguiles?) dictators, corrupt politicians and gangs.[4]

Political violence in the contemporary Africa is also an aspect of the negative side effect of democratization project or the dark face of the globalization process. First, the asymmetrical power relationship in the globalization process exacts a price. Second, as the globalization process confronts various forms of assertive local identities, violence ensues. As the African versions of carpet baggers, certain individuals pose as political godfathers by seizing, mobilizing, controlling and funding the apparatus of negative politics. Political godfathers often expose the deep connections between money, corruption and cultism. They do not just build political machines but weld them with oaths and covenants made with rituals in shrines.

Africans inflict political violence on themselves, and are also victims of political violence from the West. On one front, most wars in Africa are mineral resource wars in which Westerners arm Africans and mercenaries to perpetrate mayhem. On a second front, there is need for an adequate analysis of the relationship between the renaissance of neo-paganism (often referred to as churchless religion)[5] and political violence in the global north. Sarah Pike and others point to the commodification of witchcraft through films, television, music and art or the profitability of ritual seasons such as Halloween in the market place. Less attention has been paid to the ritual significance of political violence against other religions and against immigrants in the global north. Gary Jensen' theory in the *Path of the Devil* may be used to see right-wing extremists' violence in three interlocking dimensions: in terms of a sacrificial ceremony in which through organized ritual someone is put forth to pay for the veritable sins of the disordered world; in terms of a strategic persecution in which a group is persecuted in order for dominant or status quo interests to be maintained; and in terms of scape-goating in which anxiety over social crises is displaced onto a particular religion or people.

The concept of "social suffering" has also been used to make the connection between religion and politics in Africa because severe stress in the political economy compels people to turn to the things that mattered and sustained order in the past. Ancient religious traditions that had suffered from lack of patronage during the heydays of modernity are easily revamped. Thus, in universities, instead of fraternities, students form violent cults rooted in indigenous religion. Politicians hire them to terrorize the public.[6] Competitors in the modern public space feel compelled to "fortify" themselves with cultic power from indigenous sources and ancient pasts.

The harvest of military coups in Africa between the years 1960-1990 yielded a rich tradition of corruption and militarization of the society. The ethical register of the military consisted of easy dispensation with the rule of law, personality cult, graft and nepotism, a culture of impunity, abuse of human rights, language of force, availability of weapons of destruction and sexual immorality. Democratization project could not exorcize this violent spirit because of mimicry as the general society imitated the military overlords. Meanwhile, many military officers are still engaged in formal politics, hold political positions, and call the political tune from behind the curtains precisely because they amassed enormous wealth and could control many hungry politicians.

Violence is intricately woven to poverty. Democracy cannot function on empty stomachs. Poverty could be noted in its many forms: spiritual, material, capacity to attack the theology of life and as a deficit in contemporary world civilization. Once in a while, the poor go on a killing rampage bowdlerizing the veneer of civilization.

The Religious Substratum of African Political Culture

I have argued elsewhere and Stephen Ellis and Gerrie ter Haar have elaborated in their book, *The Worlds of Power* that in Africa, there is a substratum of religious cult beneath the contemporary political structures. Religion provides the dynamo, the engine that moves and shapes the modern political culture through the force of cultural "villigization" of the modern public space. Most of the inhabitants of the towns carry medicine made in the villages to empower their successful foraying in the towns. As Ellis and ter Haar observed, many Africans today who continue to hold beliefs derived from the traditional cosmologies apply these to everyday life even when they live in cities and work in the civil service or business sector. Religious worldviews do not necessarily diminish with formal education. [7]

Among Muslims, mallams and seriki provide such services for a fee. The syncretism in their rituals has been noted. The sacralization of political order and ethics in primal society informs the political culture in the modern public space. The political elite tap the resources of primal religion in their competitions in the modern space. Legitimacy crises intensify the process and provide enormous opportunities for primal religiosity to influence the dynamics of modern politics. Thus, the political space is literally bedeviled with an occult explosion. For instance, a close look at militant groups will show that every militant group in Africa uses indigenous cultic rituals to bond, motivate and keep members from desertion: the *Lord's Army* among the Acoli of northern Uganda, the *Kalare* among the Gombe of central Nigeria, the *Egbesu* among the Niger Delta communities who are allegedly fighting against oil companies for a viable environmental ethics, the *Munguki* (Kikuyu) of Kenya and the *al-Shabab* ("The Youth") that serves as the militant wing of the Union of Islamic Courts in Sudan.

Rosalind Hackett adds another dimension by showing how new spiritual science movements from the global north have invaded Africa-the Freemasons, Rosicrucians and others have immense political significance. They are forms of cultural invention, some deriving and all "consonant with the world-affirming and pragmatic orientation of traditional religious beliefs and practices."[8] They weld the elite in the monopoly of political power. Abner Cohen and Paul Gifford have demonstrated that the American Liberians consolidated over a century's monopoly of power by resting the political structure of Liberia on a tripod of Freemasonry, Church and Party.[9] The point, however, is that primal cults have been resilient in the modern public space. It was not only President Kamuzi Banda of Malawi, an elder of the Presbyterian Church, who danced with secret cults in the national stadium, President Jerry Rawlings of Ghana proactively resurrected indigenous cults in an attempt to use cultural renaissance as a tool for refurbishing legitimacy. Meanwhile, President Nicophore Soglo of the Republic of Benin declared *vodoo* as the national religion as an election campaign gimmick. He still lost.[10] Many African leaders espouse Christianity in the open but dance with secret societies behind the scene and commit ritual murders in the secret. Kenneth Kaunda of Zambia patronized a shrine, *The David Universal Temple* operated by an Indian guru, M.A. Ranganathan, President Bongo of Gabon belonged to the *Bwiti* and

Ndjobi secret societies and William Tolbert of Liberia served as the president of World Baptist Alliance and the Supreme *Zo* of the *Poro* society. A host of others including Houphet Boigny, Idi Amin, Sanni Abacha used secret rituals to maintain themselves in power.[11] Traditional religion ranked high as the dominant religion in eight West African nations. This is the ethnographical backdrop for understanding contemporary political culture and politics of violence. Leaders perpetrate violence and protect themselves from violence with traditional cults.

This factor can be explained from the persistence of the indigenous worldviews. In Africa, the sacralization of the cosmos legitimates the political space and dynamics of the political culture. The rulers and the ruled often act from a sense of the presence and ultimacy of the spiritual forces. This fact is seen in the four models of social control: the socialization process inculcates the acceptable norms of the community. Covenanting rituals, with what Victor Turner calls "forest of symbols" bond the new born child with the spirits at the gates of the community. Van Gennep has examined the physical, psychological, and sociological dimensions of socialization. Shorter adds that the process continues into adulthood, imparting the wisdom of the ancestors, religious rituals, and wisdom for living well and fully for one's sake and for the sake of the community. The proverbs, riddles, songs, and dances exude with moral guidance. [12] The tensile strength of the covenanting ritual is demonstrated by the fact that it may involve withdrawal from the community and periods of exclusion and communion with the spirits of the land.

The community restricts people from flouting the salient values with prohibitions, gossip, joking relationship, satire and cultic action. Punishment crashes on the heads of the obstinate; the offended deities are then appeased with sacrifice and rites of purification. Those who uphold salient values are rewarded with honor, a chieftaincy title, praise names and an eagle's feather to the accompaniment of the flute and big drum. Political values in a traditional society were rooted in the social control models. The foundation is morally sanctioned by the gods for the well-being of all. Truthfulness, decency, moderation, and wisdom are acceptable leadership values. There was no secular theory of obligation. To accede to authority and leadership roles, the individual must be "animated", imbued with a close relationship to the gods of the community. As a chief, the animation rites imbue the ruler with the "tongue of the tiger," sharp and capable of judging rightly without favor or swerved by patronage of the rich. Many studies have used the ritual of enthronement of rulers to buttress the religious roots of legitimacy in primal society. [13]

Our interest is not to mine the political structure of African cultures but to emphasize a certain ambience, namely, that the modern political culture has sought to corrode primal ethics and yet the spiritual dynamics of the primal order has invaded the modern political space. Put the irony in another way, contemporary African rulers turn to traditional cults for legitimacy but use the resources without due moderation and boundaries because they perceive the modern public space with amoral lenses.

The political elite source legitimacy from the primal space yet they fail to absorb the salient values. For instance, before the rise of the emergent urban space, a leader in a traditional community served as a ritual agent even in the situations where there are priestly guardians of communal shrines. Priestly functions were invested in the paterfamilias, first sons, kinship heads, village, clan leaders, and female priestesses. The community respected the elders as guardians of the moral code. Gerontocracy, the rule of elders, predominated because elders and ancestors were perceived as being in close proximity. In any community, the ritual power nodes were the diviner, seer, the herbalist/ healer, and witchcraft expert who provide protective enhancement and destructive medicine, charms, and amulets. General practitioners may combine some of these roles! An elastic structure enables the recruitment of spiritual forces from foreign communities for witchcraft detection and protective and achievement-enhancing medicine. Guilds and secret societies also co-existed sharing wisdom, craft, cult, and medicine. They mobilized around certain interests; for instance, healing, wealth, influence, esoteric knowledge, mutual aid, and entertainment. In some communities, leaders can only emerge from among the members of the secret societies. The argument is that political violence has escalated because the ancient political values have been eroded by modernity and yet modernity has not routed the religious pillars of the indigenous world.

The key theoretical frame here is the concept of *three publics*-the interlocking village, western and emergent urban publics, each purveying contesting values. The cultural flows and dynamics among the three publics inform the political culture. The urban culture is neither western nor indigenous. Its power is illustrated by the expectation of villagers that their kith and kin should go to the emergent public and bring their own share of the "national cake" by hook and preferably by crook. If a fraudulent public official were prosecuted, his village elders would go on a delegation to protest. Dishonest individuals can now take chieftaincy titles without fulfilling the moral prerequisites. The immoral ethics of the emergent public have debauched the salient values of the primal culture and provided the fodder for power adventurers and predatory military rulers. The flow of urban values into the village ensures the collapse of the religious and moral force that propped up the village society.

Yet a closer look betrays the ironic "villagization" of the modern political space. Political actors pose as warriors from their villages to compete for national resources on behalf of their communities. They, therefore, seek legitimization in the primal society. They undergo rituals of empowerment by taking chieftaincy titles and becoming membership in cults and secret societies. They patronize indigenous and Islamic ritual agents who provide protective charms and amulets. Thus "fortified," they are able to detect poison, ward off witchcraft spells, and operate with immense vital force. The emergent public is imaged as a precarious context in which success can be achieved only with magico-religious power derived from any efficacious sources. The preparation for the foray into the emergent zone starts from the village. This has the benefit of building a grassroots support by showing the villagers that their political representative is one of them and shares the village's value system and cults. One can appear as a champion of African culture, dance with the masquerade, and pose as a nationalist of no mean order!

In a context in which economic power is derived from political power, the elite utilize primal cult and spiritual force in self-aggrandizement. They assume titles which position them as the "*the leopard which guards the village, the voice of the people, the light, the sun, the moon, the lightning that shows the way, the war leader*" of the people. There is a teasing cluster of imageries around money, power and light on the darkened path of communities. Armed with village legitimacy, they offer themselves as a good investment for the godfather. This was important in consolidating the powers of military rulers and dictators who were always in the market for clientele and ready to pay cash for some form of legitimacy. An intimacy of power can be easily crafted. The parasitic relationship vitiates traditional institutions, robbing them of their salient values and disabling the rural masses of the will to protest. It fosters impunity and enculturates the culture of violence. The inability of the political elite to withstand the dictator (military or civilian) or to protect the masses from the humiliations of poverty can be explained by the dynamics between the primal and emergent publics. The political elite meander between both and thereby vitiate the power of civil society. Thus, the greedy political elite, the dictator and the godfather deploy the religious institutions and values of indigenous world to foster violence and keep the states in perpetual chaos and legitimacy crises. The ritual substratum of African political culture explains the impunity of the predatory elite.

Ethnographic data from some ethnic groups in Nigeria illustrate how the elite manipulated the power of indigenous cults as political tools. There are certain powerful cults which have emerged from the primal religious domain to dominate the modern political space. The *Ogboni* from Yorubaland and the *Nyamkpe* from the Cross River basin in south-eastern Nigeria are two glaring examples. Both are powerful secret societies whose votaries developed through rungs or degrees of initiation. The *Ogboni* cult controlled Yoruba society and could discipline a king. It became dominant because Nigerian contact with whites, traders, commissars, or missionaries first took place in the Yoruba environment. The indigenous people used their secret society as a means of mobilizing adequate responses to the new dispensations. Gradually, other Nigerians sojourning in Lagos found that the society conferred protection, access to wealth, power, and upward mobility in professions and politics. It became a trans-ethnic religious force dominating modern sectors such as business, professions and politics. The judiciary, civil service, military, government, and even top ecclesiastical posts were lorded over by *Ogboni* members. In 1914, an Anglican archdeacon, Venerable T.A .J. Ogunbiyi, founded the Reformed Ogboni Fraternity in an attempt to remove the "pagan" rituals and enable Christians to participate without qualms. He emphasized the benefits of the bonding in the brotherhood. Each initiate swears to be "in duty bound to help one another in distress, to succor, in adversity to warn against danger and be charitable under all circumstances". Thus, two *Ogboni* cults co-exist as a powerful secret society from the primal religion and serve as a power node in modern political space. The secrecy, class, wealth, and bonding enable them to wield enormous influence. The *Nyamkpe* played a similar role by webbing a host of communities around the Cross River basin and expanded into the vast territories of the Igbo of southeastern Nigeria.

Globalization, Democratization, Militarization and Collective Violence

From a different perspective, political violence has been fuelled by the negative side-effects of the *democratization* project. First, this terminology is applied only to the southern globe; it is an external impetus, a "political conditionality" demanded by the Bretton Woods organizations as a strand of the Structural Adjustment Program that every southern nation must accept and implement so as to adjust their macro-economic structures along neo-liberal economic lines. This enables the easy collection of spurious debts. It seeks to introduce market economy and democracy. Among its deficits, democratization disempowers the ordinary people functioning in the micro-economic and infra-political zones. Second, democratization is linked intimately to the globalization process which has deepened the poverty level of Africa.

Suffice it to summarise that globalization is a relational concept that explains how technological, economic and cultural forces have fostered culture contacts which have reduced vast distances in space and time and brought civilizations and communities into closer degrees of interaction. Everybody may not be amused but find the process ineluctably absorbing. In the 1960s when Marshall McLuhan talked about the "global village," he pointed to the impact of communication and technology on cultures; how, from Gutenberg's invention of the printing press, massive communication technology gradually turned the world into multi-sites webbed together by electronic languages and symbols in such a manner that whatever happens in one part of the globe is immediately known in another part.[14] Thomas L. Friedman put it more graphically in his book, *The World Is Flat: A Brief History of the Twenty-first Century.*[15] Friedman's list of "flattening influences" includes such milestones as the advent of the Netscape web browser, work-flow software, outsourcing, offshoring, and supply-chaining. He demonstrates that technology has become even more complex since McLuhan's ring tone, "the media is the message," enthused the public! The electronic media have knotted many cultures, societies and civilizations together into unavoidable contact, depriving them of their isolation and threatening their particularity. All are caught in the complex embrace and the delicate balance between particularity which could lead to isolation and universality which could lead to homogenization.

Technology has reshaped human economies, cultures and lifestyles. Friedman uses China to illustrate the benevolent face of the process, showing how isolated societies and economies have grown through the power of globalization. When Marco Polo visited China in the 13th century, he found a rich land known for its invention of paper, printing, gunpowder, and the compass. China's per capita income exceeded that of European nations. Its ships dominated the Indian Ocean right up to the shores of East Africa. In the 15th century, however, China retreated into a splendid isolation, its inventive spirit faded, and by the 19th century it lagged behind Europe and was forced to accept a humiliating colonial domination. Internal turmoil followed. China changed course under Deng Xiaoping's leadership in the late 1970s and fueled by a commitment to education, technological innovation, and global commerce, it regained its positions as a world economic superpower. Lurking underneath the success story are the ethical dimensions: the inequalities in wealth distribution, the divinity of the market, a certain spirit that commodifies human relationship, breeds inordinate consumption habits and pollutes the environment- a fate that China has been forced to confront as a prize for hosting the World Olympic Games.

The galloping process of globalization not only affected the theory of knowledge but had two other results. Beyond the fact that it has created a new landscape and human challenges for production, dissemination and utilization of knowledge, it has generated a new "global culture" and the intensification of cultural and value clashes. As cultures are pressed together, the problem of identity looms large. The discomfort of enforced intimacy could be illustrated with fact that globalization has been used to explain the phenomenon of intensified religious violence in the 21st century. Religion is manipulated as a marker of identity and ultimacy, invested with the symbol of a prideful heritage, deployed as a tool for boundary maintenance and propped as the mooring for scape-goating the "other." A combination of these factors engenders the wider politics of difference and compels devotees to do difference in avoidable ways.[16] Some scholars emphasize the psycho-social analysis of religious violence: individuals who engage in religious violence perceive themselves as engaged in a cosmic battle larger than the individual; an antidote to perceived marginality and humiliation; an attempt to establish equality with rivals, opponents and oppressors in the new global space that threatens everyone with a homogenized culture. Theories on the connection of violence and religion point to the fact that the twenty-first century has been distinguished by "categorical violence"- a violence directed against people on the basis of their belonging to a certain religious group.

Categorical violence has three distinctive features: excessiveness, the discourse on purification, and a ritual element. We recognize the fact that non-religious ideologies could also produce violence. Categorical violence has been powered by a metaphysical meaning that is embodied in the notion of preserving the good and true against relativizing global forces. Destruction is thought as divine and restorative. Thus, the restoration of orthodoxy in the face of alleged corruption or desecration of the pure could be achieved through divine destruction.[17] Sacrifice is an essential ingredient of scapegoating, the impetus to identify a contrast group onto which we can project, and which provides an explanation of the root problem.

The concept of fundamentalism as a label for the new passionate religions may no longer suffice because the manifestations in the political, economic and theological realms yield contradictory conclusions. Two irreducible dimensions are the increased use of violence in religious matters and the spilling of such violence into political, social and economic realms. Secularism-another icon of globalization process- has failed to turn the public space into a neutral arena. Thus, the concept of globalization may harbor internal contradictions: at once multi-directional, complex and inherently paradoxical; incorporating movement, flows, counter-movements and blockages.

Some, therefore, argue that the new global culture is not from any particular region; others believe that it is a product of and an internal requirement of capitalism; that much of the global violence is connected to the competition for resources, a drama heightened by the character of new economic order and aroused appetites. The allure to and capacity for consumption capacity explain why many fear American domination dubbed as "McDonaldization," propped by a political and economic ideologies-liberal democracy and market economy. [18]When Francis Fukuyama declared "the end of history" in 1989 because of the fall of Communist Russia, he actually surmised the end of virulent ideological contests and the victory of capitalism and liberal democracy. He intoned that the impact of 1989 was not just political but unleashed cultural, technological and economic forces that reshaped the globe; that big business will pacify the clash of cultures; that the world will move together as it builds the bodies through which we can trust each other more; that trust will emanate from shared cultural values and shared interests. He further argued that beyond theories, basic self-interest is the basis of modern economic interdependence; that in a market-dominated world, the primary human interaction is competition, not support and solidarity. He virtually prophesied that the new world order and its asymmetrical power relations will intensify the scourge of poverty among the weaker communities such as Africa. Stronger economies will create an osmotic pull engendering massive emigration or brain drain.

Some may demur alleging an incomplete social analysis. Indeed, Friedman's earlier book, *The Lexus and Olive Tree: Understanding Globalization* explored the tension between globalization on the one side, and culture, geography, tradition, and community on the other. He noted both the benefits and problems of globalization and explored the problems of glocalization, arguing that certain forms of glocalization could be self-defeating. What is certain is that globalization has acquired many characteristics based on the lenses used to interpret how certain cultural forces and values (economic, cultural, social and political) have woven the *oikoumene* into a certain order sharing identical values and bound by economic, cultural, religious forces which are so strong that some inherited values must be surrendered and development trajectories modified or abandoned. This is an emergent "global culture" utilizing technology, commerce and monetary power to weld disparate peoples and cultures. Sometimes the cord is so strong that a sneeze at one end causes flu at the other end. Sometimes the bind is so ineluctable that even losers cannot extricate themselves.

The caveat is that matters have shifted from the global village concept to a rather bewildering disintegration and flux. First, questions arise about the pace and direction of change. Global cultural flow is not unidirectional. Pietra Rivoli, *The Travels of a T-Shirt in the Global Economy* illustrates this with the fact that textile factories were once in England, then New England, then the southeastern United States, then Japan, then Hong Kong. [19] Now subsidized cotton grown in Texas is sent to China to be made into T-shirts and then shipped back to the United States. Second, at the core, globalization is a power concept bearing the seeds of asymmetrical power relations. There is no guarantee of equality or benefit for all. Third, globalization could be perceived as a liberal ideology, with a mind of its own, imbued with post modernity, dislocations and hybridity. It is akin to the New Testament concept of *kosmos, the world order*, controlled by an inexplicable, compulsive power, dazzling with allurements or *kosmetikos*. Some wonder whether friendship with it is not enmity with God's design because it breeds poverty at the periphery.

From these perspectives, its pursuit of democratic order is designed to create friendly political and socio-economic environment for consumer market economy. But the down side of democratization process in the Third World countries includes the liberalization of the media space, the increase in the number of discordant voices in the public space, increase in violence especially ethnic, religious and political violence and a chaotic political culture that disables the consolidation that should follow the post electoral process. On the positive side, globalization of domestic politics has made it possible for intervention into local issues by the transnational advocacy groups or the disaporic communities. For instance, the whole world participated with detailed information in the debates and negotiations around the recent political violence in Kenya in early 2008. Similarly, some laud the embedded concepts of economic interdependence and mutual interest without attention to the vulnerability of the Third World countries. The region is the Cinderella in this global dance and dreads the possibilities of homogenization, Americanization, propagated by the ubiquitous multinational companies that serve as the vanguards of the new global order penetrating into nooks and corners of the globe.

Globalization has exacerbated the center-periphery concept in international relations. Livelihood studies theorize the new social and gender identities that transformed families, the decomposition of households and the increased diversification and increased multi-locality of livelihoods under globalization. On the whole, globalization discourse has taken three routes through the cultural, economic to the socio-political and geopolitical concerns. Attention has been paid to the cultural and geopolitical dimensions. But for Africa, the most important aspect of the globalization process is the economic import. Just as the industrial revolution in 19th century England had negative side-effects and bred enormous social problems that Charles Dickens chronicled in his novels *Oliver Twist, Bleak House* and *David Copperfield,* and whose victims were etched in Hogarth's paintings, so have the socio-economic impacts of globalization become a disaster for the marginalized and created poverty, health problems and other unsavory consequences. The increased level of political violence is a function of the pressure of survival and pangs of adjustment in the nego-tiation between globalization processes and local economies. The failure of poverty alleviation programs and rhetoric has ensured that poverty could fuel political violence because socio-economic distress yields the gangs that are recruited as fodders by politicians, godfathers and dictators. The spate of military coups that followed the bugles of independence militarized the societies and the new urban gangs merely imitate the soldiers.

The Dreadful Cocktail: Poverty and Collective Violence

Paul Collier, a specialist in African economics, has recently tried to connect poverty to violence by suggesting that new attention must be given to the "bottom billion," that is the billion people in the world in some fifty-eight countries (most of which are in Africa and Central Asia) who are not benefiting in any way from globalization, and are caught in a series of traps. He argues that five –sixth of global violent contentions occur in one-sixth of the world. This minority suffers from protracted warfare, dependency on one crop or one natural resource, landlocked with bad neighbors, and corrupt government that keep them on the bottom. The looming food crisis reported by UNESCO on April 15th of 2008 and the statistics on pro-tracted warfare (80% of the poorest 20 countries have had war in the last years) prompts a special attention to the most disadvantaged and the nega-tive effects of globalization that manufactures the tinder box for violence.

Recently, South Africa demonstrated the connection when xeno-phobic riots broke out against immigrants from other African countries. Violence against immigrants, like some windswept fire, spread across one neighborhood after another in one of South Africa's main cities, and the police said the mayhem left many people dead -- beaten by mobs, shot, stabbed or burned alive. Thousands of panicked foreigners - many of them Zimbabweans who have fled their own country's economic collapse –and Mozambicans deserted their ramshackle dwellings and tin-walled squatter hovels to take refuge in churches and police stations. The outbreak of xeno-phobia began in May 2008 in the historic township of Alexandra and soon spread to other areas in and around Johannesburg, including Cleveland, Diepsloot, Hilbrow, Tembisa, Primrose, Ivory Park and Thokoza. At the root is poverty because the new elite have become more rapacious than the old, and strangely, the poor take it out on themselves rather than fighting the rich. Beneath is the old fact that the level of witchcraft accusation rises as a function of social stress, social suffering and a disordered cosmos. The witchcraft spirit is used to explain the diminishing vitality of life by pointing to the strange "other" as the cause. Eradication measures are taken to eliminate the cause. In the rainbow nation, witchcraft eradication of the public square took the form of killing immigrants and looting their business premises while the unprepared government was entrapped by neo-liberal capitalist policies that failed. The state reeled with unbecoming caparisons and ineffective responses, ordering a royal commission to inquire into the causes of the barbaric acts in a land once ruled by Nelson Mandela. The real cause is poverty!

Collective violence is often expressed with cultural idiom. Neil Whitehead urges that we should examine how cultural conceptions of violence are used discursively to map and amplify the cultural force of violent acts, or how those acts can produce a shared idiom for violent death. [20] Collective violence borrows and re-enacts the symbolic, ritual and performative qualities of witchcraft eradication as rioters act in the belief that the destruction of the bodies of the condemned was integral to the reproduction of society-paradoxically achieving the healing of the society through the exclusion and destruction of the victims. Thus, the Mungiki sect in Kenya like the Talibans and the Egbesu in the Niger Delta of Nigeria deploy religious rituals to express political protest and ethnic identities. The same could be said for the Al-Shabab (the youth) fighters in Somalia who serves as the military wing of the effort to establish a Sharia-dominated Islamic state.

This raises the question about the psychology of religious violence where the rioters attempt to establish social and economic equality as an antidote to perceived marginality and humiliation or sacralizes violence as a triumph over forces of evil, a posture that numbs the conscience against horrific acts. Sometimes a dose of apocalyptism (whether secular or religious) is added to the brew as the rioters perceive themselves as engaged in a cosmic battle which is larger than the individual. The religious substratum of the cultural landscape in Africa has in many ways fuelled the rising intensity of religious violence in the continent. The cost of violence may negatively impact the development of a continent that is already embattled.

Notes

1. This reflection utilizes but modifies the contentions in Doug McAdam, Sidney Tarrow and Charles Tilly, *Dynamics of Contention* (New York: Cambridge University Press, 2001).

2. Michel Foucault, *The Archeology of Knowledge* Trans A.M Sheridan Smith (New York: Pantheon Books, 1972); Colin Gordon, ed., *Power/Knowledge: Selected Interviews and Other Writings, 1972-1977*(New York: Pantheon Books, 1980):109-133.

3. See, Human Rights Watch, Nigeria, *Revenge in the Name of Religion: The Cycle of Violence.*vol.17, no.8(A), May 2005.

4. Mark Leach, Mitchell Berman, Lea Eubanks, "Religious Activities, Religious Orientation and Aggressive Behavior", *Journal of the Scientific Study of Religion*, 42, 2 (June 2008):311-319.

5. Sarah M. Pike, *New Age and NeoPagan Religions in America* (New York: Columbia University Press, 2004); Helen A Berger, ed., *Witchcraft and Magic: Contemporary North America* (Philadelphia, PA: University of Pennsylvania Press, 2005).

6. Gary Jensen, *The Path of the Devil: Early Modern Witch Hunts* (Lanham, MD: Rowman & Littlefield Publishers, 2006); Ogbu U Kalu, *The Scourge of the Vandals: The Nature and Control of Cults in the Nigerian University System* (Enugu: University of Nigeria Press, 2001).

7 Stephen Ellis and Gerrie ter Haar, *Worlds of Power: Religious Thought and Political Practice in Africa* (New York: Oxford University Press, 2004), 51.

8. R.I.J. Hackett, *Religion In Calabar: The Religious Life and History of an Nigerian Town* (New York: Mouton de Gruyter, 1989), 164.

9. Paul Gifford, *Christianity in Doe's Liberia* (Cambridge: Cambridge University Press, 1993); Abner Cohen, *The Power Culture of the Elite* (Berkeley: University of California Press, 1981).

10. See Ogbu U Kalu, *Power, Poverty and Prayer* (Frankfurt: Peter Lang, 2000).

11. Ellis and Haar, *Worlds of Power* (2004), chapter 4.

12. A.van Gennep, *The Rites of Passage* (Chicago: University of Chicago Press, 1960), 165ff; Aylward Shorter, *Songs and Symbols of Initiation* (Nairobi: Catholic Higher Institute of East Africa, 1987); Victor Turner, *The Forest of Symbol* (Cornell University Press, 1967),

13. J. K. Olupona, "Religious Pluralism and Civil Religion in Africa, " *Dialogue and Alliance*, 2, 4 (1989):41-48; idem., *Kingship, Religion and Rituals in a Nigerian Community* (Stockholm: Almquist and Wiksell International, 1991).

14. Marshall McLuhan and B. Powers, *The Global Village: Transformation in World, Life and Media in the 21st Century.*(Oxford, Oxford University Press, 1967).

15. Thomas L. Friedman, *The World Is Flat: A Brief History of the Twenty-first Century* (New York: Picador, 2007: first published in 2005); *The Lexus and the Olive* (New York: Random House, 1999).

16. Fukuyama, *Foreign Affairs*<http://foreignaffairs.org/19951101fabook46664/benjamin-r-barber/jihad-vs-mcworld-how-the-planet-is-both-falling-apart-and-coming-together-and-what-this-means-for -democracy.html>

17. Charles Taylor, "On Religion and Violence," *The Arts and Science Review* (University of Toronto), 2, 1(Spring 2005):31-35.

18. Rebecca T. Peters, *In Search of the Good Life: The Ethics of Globalization* (New York: Continuum, 2004).

19. Pietra Rivoli, *The Travels of a T-Shirt in the Global Economy* (London: Wiley, 2006).

20. Neil L. Whitehead, "Violence and the Cultural Order", *Daedalus* (Winter, 2007):40-50; idem *Dark Shamans*(Santa Fe: School of American Research Press, 2004).

Part IV

THEOLOGICAL EDUCATION

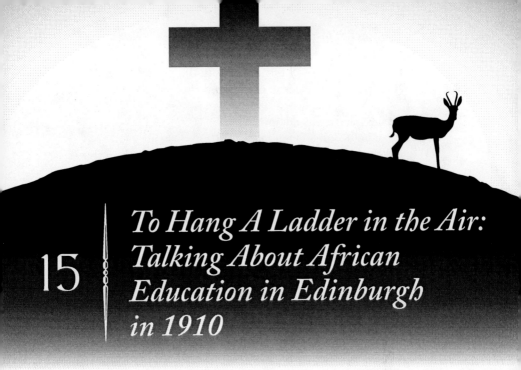

15 | To Hang A Ladder in the Air: Talking About African Education in Edinburgh in 1910

The African Road to Edinburgh: Introduction

The conference in Edinburgh in 1910 was the most important European gathering of missionaries in the 20th century. Among its significance is the birthing of the World Council of Churches; its impact on missionary thought remained strong in the future that appeared scorched by the violence of the First World War and its untoward aftermath. The text generated by its nine committees constitutes a significant perspective into the missionary's mind. The effort here is to read the report of Committee Three on education from the African's lens because education was the instrument for colonizing the Africans' mind. The text could best be read as an example of Africans' encounter with the rain of the gospel and how they responded by the end of the first millennium.

As there was no African present at the conference, white missionaries spoke for them. My people are very concerned about the prospects of a discussion where those concerned were absent or whose 'mouths' were literally not there. The verdict runs the risk of being so prejudicial that the conversation could be presumed to be a hostile gossip. Happily, the voices that spoke for Africa were so scattered by the ancestors, so discordant that the conferees soon realized the vastness of the neglected continent, how complex and incomprehensible the problems, and how challenging the context could be for the integrity and future of the missionary enterprise.

In spite of the high ideals about education, the Commissioners felt like people trying to hang a ladder in the air and concluded that,

> so varied are the conditions with which missionary workers are confronted in different parts of Africa that only a few conclusions apply to the whole region which is dealt with in this chapter. But these conclusions are concerned with matters of outstanding importance.[1]

The task assigned to Commission III at Edinburgh was global though limited to China, India, Japan and Africa. Latin America was imaged as a preserve of the Roman Catholics. Its focus was on education. The reflection here revisits the deliberations about Africa, the voiceless continent. It examines how the West talked about African education during the Edinburgh Conference of 1910. The reason is that the indigenous folks from the other nations participated. Some, like Reverend V.S Azariah from India, made stirring speeches. His plea for friendship that was more than condescending love struck at the heart of the racism, cultural hubris and disparity of wealth that distorted missionary relationship with host communities. Besides, much has been written about these places that constituted the focus of missionary enterprise. Europeans were intrigued by China, Japan and India. Indeed, the Commissioners observed that, "more than one of our correspondents in China emphasizes the marvelous power possessed by Chinese civilization of influencing those who came in contact with it." [2] They acknowledged the power of Confucian thought and the need to approach "the Chinese mind along the lines of deeply laid convictions of truth which we need not disturb otherwise than to set them in their places as related to the higher truths of Christianity."[3] As J.R. Mott confessed in *Decisive Hour of Mission*,

> The great and highly organized religions present a stronger resistance than the simpler nature-worship of barbarous tribes, and they would therefore require a larger and better-equipped staff of workers.[4]

Later, when the Continuing Committee, the International Missionary Council, could not meet in China, it met in India.

On Japan, the Commissioners acknowledged that their education system was advanced, the literacy level was high, and "the percentage of children without schooling is far less than in Great Britain;"[5] that many Japanese Christians are superior in culture, native ability and education to the missionaries. "Thirty years ago, the missionary was first, today he is influential only when he is ready to co-operate with the Japanese and to give them initiative."[6] It would, therefore, require missionaries of the highest ability and training to function in such an environment.

The Indian context should have resembled the African in its complexity and in the depth of loathing that the conquering British had for the indigenous religions. But the Commissioners pointed to the allure of India beyond the opportunity for manifesting the arrogance of power as depicted in E.M. Forster's *A Passage to India*. Two dimensions mattered: first was

> the deep and subtle powers of the Indian mind bent continuously towards the fundamental problems of religion, the unequalled capacity of the Indians for meditation and inwardness, their wonderful devotion to the ascetic discipline-the qualities which have made men call the Indian thinkers 'God-intoxicated'.[7]

The second was ironically the success of "Christian colleges (that) have in a wonderful way been assimilated by the people themselves and become in a sense indigenous."[8] The Asian countries possessed enough to invite attention and dialogue.

Africa was truly at the periphery and its conditions conjured an image that was exotic, at the lowest rung of the evolutionary process of both religion and civilization, and as if from the penumbra of the missionary zone. After listening to twenty-eight correspondents that included some prestigious veteran missionaries, the Commissioners were dumbfounded and concluded that it appeared that the core elements of a meaningful education did not exist, especially in the development of industrial skills, training of girls, higher education and evangelization of the culture (or national life).

It should, therefore, be germane to reconstruct the profile of African Christianity through the 19th century to the end of the first millennium in 1900. This may aid our understanding and re-evaluation of what they were talking about in Edinburgh in 1910. Second, a short comment on the significance of the conference in missionary discourse provides another introductory background. Here, we are confronted with the problem of images and lenses. The image of African education could be explained by the lens through which the conferees *read* the African cultural landscape, the responses to the presence of the gospel and their needs. There is little doubt that the core of the conference was the problem of *legibility*, the way people read other people. As the Commissioners observed,

> it is only of recent years that we have been learning to look with sympathy on forms of religion which are strange to us. We are an insular race.[9]

Quite important in this regard is Mott's account of the conference in 1912 based on the documents generated by the conference. He reviewed the profiles of the mission fields, articulated the strategies, and recommended the directions for the future in bold terms. Reading non-Western contexts with Western lenses has remained an enduring aspect of the ecumenical relationship with non-Western world and a source of the ambiguity, paradoxes and complexities in their relationship especially as the center of gravity of Christianity has shifted to the southern hemisphere.

Third, on the specific matter of education, three dimensions would be privileged: the ideology- broad aims and specific goals -of missionary education; the interior of the educational process and its enemies; and ecumenism as an antidote. Since some of these are complex, they may not receive the adequate treatment that they deserve.

Christianity in Africa in 1900

Perhaps to understand the import of the neglect of Africans at the conference, we could analyze the shape of Christianity in Africa at the turn of that century. The story of Christianity in Africa took a specific, enduring turn in the 1880's as a reflection of currents in European geopolitics. After the British trade fair in the 1850's that exhibited the inventions and glory of industrialization; after the German invasion of France in the 1870's and the Paris commune that fought it to a standstill, competing nationalism consumed Europe and this was played out in the acquisition of colonies. Arguments abound whether colonies were acquired in a fit of absent-mindedness; whims and caprices of officials in the Colonial Office; spurred by men-on –the field; the urging of missionaries; an effort to protect the natives or paltry returns in commerce. The literature has attempted to debunk the economic arguments for colonization. But all agree that the Berlin conferences of 1884/5 to partition Africa among competing nations dramatically changed the geopolitical terrain and the relationship between Europeans and the rest of the world.

The effects were in the mindset and attitudes; at once hegemonic, filled with hubris and salted with a conquering spirit. Jingoism filled the air to drown the protests of the enemies to the imperial idea. It also had much to do with space, expansionism and enlargement of European space and migration to non-Western world. Without this, one may not appreciate either the popularity of Rudyard Kipling or the children stories of G.A. Henty and the attraction of Romantic poets as Coleridge. Armchair theorists such as Frazier wove the myth of *The Golden Bough*. One of the provisions of the Berlin treaty included the need to demonstrate actual presence instead of mere claims of areas of influence. European interest in Africa and the non-Western world increased and its presence opened the innards of communities to foreign gaze. Chiefs were now treated in a cavalier, imperial manner; middlemen were brushed aside; maxim guns became important in the pacification projects. Even the romantic notion of savages turned into pejorative insistence of African lack of capacity and the need to control and tutor the half-man, half child. Trusteeship replaced the vision of using indigenous agents to evangelize. There was an enlargement of scale in missions: number of missionaries, number of participating nations; areas evangelized; level of participation by females and amount of funds raised for the enterprise.

Competing interests bred virulent rivalry that spurred the pace, direction, strategies and. Right up to Edinburgh Conference in 1910, the European missiologists remained hostile to the new spirit in the 19th Century missionary enterprise. Race and control dominated missionary encounter in Africa resonating from the mood in the secular imperial age. Often ignored is the African story in the encounter.

Missionary message, presence and attitudes determined some aspects of the patterns of African responses. The power of the Word and the translation into indigenous languages determined the charismatic elements. Some scholars have emphasized control and hegemony in the relationship; that racism generated counter racism; European nationalism bred imitation. Others have argued that in culture contact, all parties are agents who give, take, negotiate and appropriate according to basic needs; that even when the playing ground appears unequal, translation goes on; the vulnerable party always has command of the infra-political zone to articulate feelings and that Africans were not passive proselytes; indigenous religions remained resilient, birthing the new. In spite of the control system that essayed to make the victims legible, Africans wrote their own hidden scripts. Still others argue that it was a contest between rival narratives; each party engaged in universe maintenance. In the moral economy designed by the intimate enemies (missionaries and colonial order), Africans responded variously by loyalty/collaboration, voice and exit.

Yet the story of missionary enterprise is characterized by its varieties and fluidity; and missionary presence was always vulnerable though the control system bred dependency and disunity in many communities. Yet the exigencies of the mission field continuously compelled modifications of missionary hardware. Therefore, its story is a fragmentary one precisely because the size of the continent, number of players and vested interests proved so daunting that they took opposing positions on socio-economic, political and cultural themes. Some have argued that the contributions in education, medicine and translation of the Bible into indigenous languages catalyzed the changes in African Christianity. The point has often been made that when people read the word in their languages, the power catalyzed tremendous changes. Each regional context presented its own challenges as culture became the contested ground. The argument here is that both education and the effects of translation became more apparent after the First World War when the character and provenance of education changed, and when the flares of revivalism grew more intense. In 1900, the Commissioners would have been confronted with a rudimentary education system that was operated haphazardly.

Periodization is important in the reconstruction of Christian presence in Africa. The missionary enterprise was unsuccessful in many parts of Africa till the second half of the century. This may explain why African Christianity was not central in missionary discourse when they met in the Edinburgh Conference of 1910. J.R.Mott enthused about changes in education and socio-economic development in the continent that he described as "the most plastic part of the world."[10] But in 1900, African Christianity was like the tender offshoot of an emergent non-Western plant. The maturity and galloping changes would occur later in the 20th Century. The argument here is that those changes benefited from these forces of regeneration that started during the 19th century. In the Horn of Africa, indigenous agency struggled to maintain the independence and orthodoxy in Ethiopia, confronted by Jewish, Protestant and Catholic efforts to "clean" up Ethiopian Christianity. The return of court Christianity by 1856 and the victory at Adwa in 1896 sealed the nationalist rebuttal. In southern and Central Africa, missionary villages as enclaves served as the means of evangelization and encrusted a certain ideology of education that concentrated on primary level education. Its ideological contradictions became apparent with the years. Venn's indigenous ideal in West Africa, that produced the novelty of Adjai Crowther's bishopric in 1864, collapsed by 1891 betraying the rising tide of "scientific" racism that thwarted the evangelical spirituality of yesteryears. White settler Christianity dominated in Eastern Africa, escalating a diatribe against indigenous culture to a breaking point. Metropolitan Christianity in Belgian Congo rivaled Portuguese underdevelopment of Angola and Mozambique through religious instruments. French secularism and British protection of Islamic emirates would arouse missionary outcry.

The Africans responded to missionary structures through *loyalty* and collaboration in certain places, serving as native agents. Critical *voices* were heard in other places while some would *exit* either out of cultural nationalism or through charismatic and prophetic initiatives that appropriated the pneumatic elements of the gospel. Sometimes, these manifested in curious ways as Nxele and Ntsikana did among the Xhosa; or when Shembe saw transforming visions in 'Boss' Conrad's barn. Others joined the early Pentecostal movements that came from the West, especially between 1906-1910. When racism snuffed off the Spirit, the Africans built their own 'Zions' on the smoky ashes. At other times, anti-structural rebuttal appeared in cultural, religious and political protests and even exit as in the foundation of "African Churches" that seceded from mainline churches from the 1880's. In all cases, the forces that catalyzed the first phase of growth of Christianity in the period, 1914-45, had appeared in nascent forms by 1900. Unfortunately, their salience was unrecognized when whites talked about Africans in Edinburgh in 1910.

Wade Harris typifies the African Road to Edinburgh. In the year that whites met to talk about Africa, a bearded man, decked in a long white *soutan*, walked from his native Grebo Island across Liberian coast, through Ivory Coast to the Gold Coast. He carried a long staff, a Bible and a bowl of holy water. He preached; he created choruses and taught these to large crowds. He baptized, healed and performed other miracles. He was very ecumenical; he founded no churches but convinced many to burn their idols and go to the nearest churches. The Methodist Church in the Gold Coast exploded numerically because they took the old man seriously. The Roman Catholics in Francophone colonies also benefited. Others engineered problems for him using the colonial governments. On his return through Ivory Coast, he found that shipmasters had not stopped the practice of using Kru men to offload their ships on Sundays. He had warned them; and now, decided to punish their recalcitrance. He threw his holy water at some ships and these caught fire. The French authorities put him under house arrest. Undoubtedly, his missionary journey achieved more within months than the labors of many expatriate missionaries through many years.[11]

Images and Lenses: The Significance and Structure of Edinburgh Conference, 1910

Edinburgh Conference in 1910 has become the referent point in missionary discourse because of a variety of reasons. It was not the first attempt by those engaged in the massive missionary resurgence of the period to meet and compare notes. The conference in New York in 1900 touched on a number of similar issues. It was simply the largest and best organized of such conferences. Twelve hundred delegates from over one hundred and fifty missionary organizations participated. The combined genius of two people whose personalities complemented each other produced an efficient administrative structure: John Mott enjoyed the glare while J.H. Oldham, who had some hearing difficulty, preferred to stay in the background. In constituting the eight commissions, they deployed people from academia, church leadership, administrators of missionary organizations and people with missionary experience. They paid attention to geographical and denominational spread, gender and participation by indigenous people from the key areas of the mission field.

For instance, on Commission III on Education in Relation to the Christianisation of National Life, the Right Rev Dr C. Gore, the Bishop of Birmingham, a High Church Anglican, chaired while Rev Professor Edward Caldwell Moore of Harvard University served as his Vice-Chairman. Out of twenty members in the Commission, twelve came from Britain, six from the United States, one from Canada, Professor R.A. Falconer, President of the University of Toronto, and one from India, a Scot, Rev Dr John Morrison who was formerly the Principal of the Church of Scotland College, Calcutta. In fact, twelve of them were leaders of Western academic institutions including Universities of Oxford, London, Manchester, Harvard, Chicago, Columbia, Toronto and Rutgers, and four others were connected with colleges. Two were Administrative Secretaries of key missionary societies. The membership deliberately excluded missionaries.

The strategy for gathering data privileged active participants in the mission field. They sent out questionnaires to about 223 correspondents whose names were submitted by missionary societies from Europe and North America: 69 in China, 62 in India and Ceylon, 33 in Japan and Korea, 28 in Africa, 14 in Mohammedan lands in the Near East, and 17 special interest groups that included 8 from Dutch East Indies, Sumatra and Java. This last category included Dr T.J. Jones of Hampton Institute, Virginia, who was an expert in Industrial Training, and would later become very important in designing the plan for African education in the mid 1920's. The size and distribution of correspondents may indicate the priority and perception of the size of the mission field. However, in China, the correspondents included only one indigenous person, Cheung wan Man, a medical doctor with the Southern Baptist Convention at Shiuhing. India had five, Japan and Korea, five and Africa, none.

In Africa, the regional distribution of correspondents created a lens that could distort the image: twelve came from South Africa, seven from Nyasaland, five from the whole of West Africa, two from East Africa and one each from Madagscar and Mozambique. Within West Africa, three came from Nigeria and one each from Sierra Leone and Liberia. Within Nigeria, one came from the northern region, the intrepid medical doctor, Dr Miller, who confronted the exclusion of missionaries from the Moslem emirates, and two came from Calabar: one Presbyterian and one Primitive Methodist, ignoring the vast south-western region where the educated, religious nationalists were very strong.[12] From hindsight, the strategy of using participant observers served better than arm- chair theorists but the distribution flawed the results. It is argued that the distortion in sampling factored the distortion of the image of Africa and African Christianity in the conference.

The Commission received replies from over 200 and distributed these by regions to separate sub-committees. "The English members of the Commission met in London for a week (November 1-6, 1909), discussed these reports, and determined the lines to be taken by the report as a whole."[13] They submitted their work for the input from the American members, who suggested changes. At a meeting between the British members and a representative of the American members in London on April 22nd, 1910, the report, conclusions and recommendations were harmonized to be presented with the assent of the entire commission. One approach to the document is to examine the roles of individuals behind the scene and trace how disagreements were ironed out. Another approach, as adopted here, analyzes the document in the spirit and words of the protagonists, that "the conclusions or recommendations represent the deliberate opinion of the whole Commission." There is every indication of a high level of responsibility, attention to the data and a certain level of frankness in dealing with the role of education in the missionary enterprise. It was the lens that distorted the image!

The fourteen questions administered were exhaustive and shall be considered along with other aspects of the interior of missionary education. Suffice it to say that the Commission was sensitive to the pioneering hardship of missionary work, and endeavored to balance the achievements with new theories of education. As the Report put it,

> It has seemed to us that we should probably best assist those who are actually engaged in the educational work of missions by formulating such a series of conclusions or recommendations... not to make final pronouncements or to arrogate authority to ourselves in any sense, but rather to stimulate thought and to provide a basis for discussion.[14]

The significance of Edinburgh 1910 in missionary discourse is the astonishing level of self-criticism that made the movement resilient. The Conference espoused high ideals. Having acknowledged the achievements by missionaries, it moved quickly to observe that education, as pursued under missionary auspices, has exhibited certain *weaknesses in its methods,* and is exposed to certain *perils,* which make it necessary to review its *principles and its processes.*[15]

This startling acknowledgment opens up the discussion on the gap between the ideal that the Commission perceived and the practice that the missionaries pursued. The very title of the Unit was theologically loaded as it proposed to examine how education could be used as an instrument to engage in mission to culture, baptizing the nations or Christianizing the national life. In re-imagining the conference, it is argued that the Commissioners started a conversation on African education that combined with geopolitical realities to nudge missionary practices in new directions.

The Ideology of Education in Edinburgh 1910

The Commission espoused an ideal of education that resonated with Roman Catholic ideals and practices. In spite of the collapse of their early mission to China, their indigenising principles remained classic. In many parts of Africa, Roman Catholic education enterprise outpaced the Protestant. In southern Nigeria, Bishop Shanahan boasted that if he captured the hearts of the children, the heart of the country would be safe in Roman Catholic hands. He prosecuted the education apostolate with such vigor that inspectors from Lyon in 1929 wondered whether the Holy Ghost Fathers had not deserted evangelism. The absence of their input in the conversation in Edinburgh was regretted. But apparently, Protestants at Edinburgh arrived at the same conclusions. As Mott put it, a German proverb says that, "What you would put into the life of a nation, put into its schools."[16] Education was the instrument that mediated the missionary message.

Imagining the educational process

First, the Commission delineated the contexts or types of education that are required: primary, higher education, teacher training, ministerial formation, industrial, education of girls, and education for Muslim evangelism because Islam is reaching out and Christians must penetrate its hearts. Second, it derived the rationale for missionary education by exploring the lessons from the early church. The early church recognized the *pilgrim/universal* and *indigenous/local* principles in Christianity. It sought to be universal and catholic without becoming exotic or foreign. In the early church,

Christianity became indigenous in each race and place from the first, because it was entrusted to native teachers and rulers almost at once. There was somewhat later accommodation to such national religious customs as were thought to admit of a Christian interpretation and use. The result was the diffusion of a Catholic religion exhibiting local variations of customs and presentation.[17]

Education was crucial to Christianity for several reasons: a commonly shared elementary education saved the catholicity of the Christianity from becoming exotic or representing a foreign influence. Christianity was a religion of ideas and institutions that could only be maintained through teaching. It inherited from Judaism a profound respect for teachers and special instructions in catechism that were designed as a process of training and initiation into the religion. When the center of gravity shifted from Palestinian roots into the Graeco-Roman world, it came into an empire well furnished with schools that it utilized. People were versed in both secular and Christian literature. Some leaders were wary about the idolatrous dimensions to secular education but recognized the utility for Christian evangelism. Those who engaged in "spoiling the Egyptians" in their apologetics, demonstrated the usefulness of secular education. The implication is that the goal of education is evangelization and the method or process utilized cultural pathways.

The Commission recognized the changed environment. In some places, there is no commonly shared public education that could serve as a framework; so, each mission designs its process. The Commissioners may have been blind to indigenous models of education and socialization that could serve as inculturating pathways; they ignored the voices of educated Africans crying for indigenisation of the gospel; but conceded that the ideal method of propagating Christianity in the contemporary period is that,

> the Gospel should be received by each race through the ministry of evangelists from nations already Christian but that the church should pass as rapidly as possible under the control of native pastors and teachers, so that while all churches hold the same faith, use the same Scriptures, celebrate the same sacraments, and inhere in the same universal religion, each local church should from the first have the opportunity of developing a local character and colour.[18]

Converts, they argued should, with their children, continue to share the education and social life of their own races and nations; and bring the distinctive genius and its products within the circle of the Holy Spirit, to the glory and honor of all nations. They not only promoted the Venn policy shared with Rufus Anderson but moved towards a compromise with the German *volkskirche* principle that Gustav Warneck and other German missiologists urged. It was an espousal of a brand of ecumenism in which all nations and cultures stood equidistant to the kingdom of God. But one suspects that they proffered this idea for Japan and China and hardly for Africa.

The ecology of learning

Third, they explored the counteracting forces in the ecology of learning, for instance, the tendency of Western people to reproduce "strongly defined and intensely western forms of Christianity." This creates a gulf between the mental equipment of missionaries and that of the indigenous people. Missionaries pay little attention to presenting the gospel in the form best suited to the context and spirit of the people. This tendency to plant "the religion of conquerors or foreign devils and unwelcome intruders" betrays a lack of the wisdom of the apostles, especially when conquest, perception of the other, insularity, lack of sympathy for and study of other religions may have caused alienation.[19] This has created the peril that the replacement of the indigenous vernacular and culture may create an exotic religion and promote false ethics that replace communal ethics with western individualism.

They pointed to the teaching-learning environment that privileges imparting ideas and exercising the memory and intelligence of the student. The Commissioners observed that the missionaries

> did not estimate how little the imparting of information, with the appeal to only the too facile memory to receive and repeat it, would really do in the way of reforming the fundamental habits of thought or instinct in their pupils.[20]

It is exciting to find that the Commissioners said in 1910 what made Paulo Freire famous in 1970. Here is the banking model described by Paulo Freire. The banking model is built on a jaundiced image of the host community, perceiving it as a "pathology of the healthy society" represented by the home of the missionary. The teacher "mythicizes" the indigenous social structure and creates a platform for causing division, manipulation, cultural invasion, alienation, conquest and all manners of induced actions. The teacher's high profile is that he knows all things, thinks, teaches, talks, disciplines, enforces, chooses the program, confuses authority of knowledge with professional authority and deposits knowledge that the students bank by memorizing mechanically. The teacher withdraws from the bank when he chooses. The teacher is the subject and the learners are mere objects. The goal of the teacher is to change the consciousness of the students to ensure that the students internalize the teacher and his world.[21] Using India as an example, the Commissioners argued that the product contents of missionary education are imitative, dependent, weak native Christianity, lacking initiative.[22] Paulo Freire dubs this model as "cultural invasion" in which

> the actors draw thematic content of their action from their own values and ideology; their starting point is their own world, from which they enter the world of those they invade.[23]

The opposite is "cultural synthesis" in which

> the actors who come from another world to the world of the people, do so not as invaders. They do not come to teach or to transmit or to give anything, but to learn, with the people, about the people's world.

The actors integrate with the people and become co-authors of the action that both perform upon the world. For him, this model of transformation, dialogue and liberation does not deny the encounter of two different worldviews, but argues that each can affirm the other in a process of "mutual humanization"; that knowledge of the indigenous culture frees it from alienation and enables it to be transformed in a creative manner.[24]

The Commissioners did not go this far but called for a reversal of the contemporary trend. Education should be a social process that trains students for social functions. It should train the whole being-body, soul and spirit- through music, poetry and dance. It should engage and develop the psychological roots of the child such as the instincts of one's nature or the subconscious nature. Education should train the individual into conscious and intelligent participation in the great social movements and challenges of one's environment. As the South African educationist, Bongani Mazibuko said, "It is stressing the affective and experiential, rather than the narrowing rational and academic, that students are affirmed and empowered."[25] As a practical measure, the Commission urged missions to train native Christian leaders as teachers and church officers as people who will bear the responsibility of building the church, produce the indigenous literature and use the vernacular in instruction in the elementary schools because " a man's mother tongue is that which reaches his heart, and always offers the best approach to the deepest subjects."[26] Simply put, foreign language makes Christianity a foreign production.

Fearing that the divisions and rivalry among western Christianities may confuse the non-western world, they suggested that the best approach is to teach the original and fundamental elements of Christianity, using the vernacular. The challenges in Japan brought this matter home because the Japanese feelings for the ancestors, patriotism and their assertion for leadership in the church not only compelled the need for highly educated missionaries but people who were open for dialogue in the vernacular. Even in India where the religious base was heavily pantheistic, there was still the possibility of a dialogue that sifts the best values such as the peaceful or passive ethics of the Hindu as a pathway to the character of Jesus, a critique of western aggressive culture and ethics and the representation of "a full-orbed type of Christian life, embracing the eastern and western emphases."[27]

The undergirding ideology of education was based on the reading of the peoples, the times and conditions in the various mission fields. The geopolitical environment was suffused with intense nationalism all over Asia: Japan emerged as a major power player in 1905; China showed an astonishing awakening of national consciousness, enormous changes in the social infrastructure, and rapid proliferation of education; Indian Christians brought the political nationalism into the church. R. Suntharalingham has traced the politics of national awakening in South India in the prelude to the conference.[28] For instance, in 1888 the Madras Native Christian Association was founded and two years later, their newspaper, *Christian Patriot* appeared. Edwin James Palmer, the Bishop of Bombay, confirmed in 1909, a report that

> the modern young man wants a national church, first and foremost, to attain independence from all foreign sway and its concomitants…There is a sort of idea floating around that India could start with a clean state and evolve something wholly new and Indian, based as some of its advocates openly say, on the 'religious treasure' of non-Christian India.[29]

The Christians were pressurized by the temper of Hindu nationalism that stereotyped Christians as unpatriotic, denationalized people who pandered to foreign churches that bore such names as the *Church of England* or *Lutheran Church*. In Africa, Ethiopianism continued to garner strength in western and southern Africa. In 1891, the firebrand, Wilmot Blyden, gave a lecture in Lagos entitled, *The Return of the Exiles* in which he intoned that "*Africans must evangelize Africa*" or, as Mojola Agbebi would say, the sphinx must solve its own riddle! The Niger Delta pastorate had split from the Church Missionary Society in that year. A young Ghanaian Methodist lawyer, J. Casely-Hayford wrote his play, *Ethiopia Unbound* in the year that white people met to talk about Africans in Edinburgh. There was ferment in the young mission fields but the din did not interrupt the discussions. [30]

As J.R Mott read the signs: beyond the strategic position of Japan, there was an openness to receive the gospel in Africa and a significant conversion rate occurred in Korea and Manchuria. China remained attractive to missionaries because of its population density. The challenge from Islam in both Moslem countries and Equatorial Africa contested the enterprise. Moreover, Christianity needed to deal with certain neglected regions as Sudan and the Pacific Islands, and buffer the marginalized caste groups in India.[31] In this task, education was a core instrument and the distribution of Christian literature was imperative. This included devotional materials, apologetics, literature for moral formation and general, scientific materials that would provide information and aid reading abilities.

But there appears to be three different perceptions of the goal of education among the conferees in Edinburgh 1910. The first was the *assimilationist* that argued that the African indigenous civilization was low; education could be deployed to uplift the culture to the European level. By the mid-1880's this benign view suffered a defeat. Mott may represent a second posture held by the *'cultural invaders'* when he enthused that,

> As already seen, the influence of western learning has been in the direction of undermining the faith of the student class in the non-Christian religions and of breaking up the social and ethical restraints of the old civilizations.[32]

As Jacob Ade Ajayi would argue in 1965, the goal of missionary education was "the making of an elite" class of detribalized, educated people who will interpret Christianity to their people. [33]The Commissioners may not have been averse to the civilizing project of the missionary enterprise but nuanced their *indigenizing* position differently. The task was to explore how to Christianize the national life through education or how to respond to the challenging social and economic structures that would determine the fate of Christianity. The handwriting on the wall was boldly nationalistic and suggested the need for a native agency trained to shoulder the burdens of self-governing, self-funding, self-propagating churches. Education should be

> an instrument for raising native Christian Churches, which shall be in the fullest sense national, and capable of a growing independence of foreign influence and support.[34]

To achieve this, they recommended changes in the content and method of education, with emphasis on agricultural and industrial training. This should culturally and economically equip people who will lead the churches and the nations, and respond to challenges of their ecosystems.

The problem of industrial education emanated from three sources: there was a concern about the effect of "book-learning" that did not enhance the full productive capacity of the person; the second was a racial commentary on the pretensions of educated Africans who served as clerks and imitated white people. The third was related to western enthusiasm with industrialized economy. In 1900, a conference in New York had insisted that the industrial spirit, when properly directed, would champion liberty, serve as handmaid of education, an auxiliary to the gospel and aid missions.[35] The problem was how to ensure that the indigenous people participated in its benefits and avoided its vicious effects. The Commissioners suggested a gender sensitive model of education to mobilize the women and girls. However, they merely envisaged "raising up a pure girlhood and womanhood such as is only possible in truly Christian home." This wove the traditional community's goals to new white needs for domestic servants, nurses and teachers. The curriculum consisted of domestic science, hygiene, cooking, laundry, sewing, cleaning, spinning, lace-making, basket weaving, dispensary assistance.[36] The only missing subject was hewing wood.

The education ideology in response to Islam was more creative than the confrontational habits of evangelical Sudan parties. They urged for special education facilities in Moslem countries manned by evangelists trained on how to witness without injury to the sensibilities of the Muslims. The strategy would privilege edification, leavening and living the faith without preaching it.[37] Behind the contrasting ideologies of the 'cultural invaders' and the 'indigenizers' was a certain reading of the contentious matters of race, indigenous cultures, mission and the future of Christianity. Racism so vitiated the force of the missionary enterprise that J.H. Oldham wrote a book, *Christianity and the Race Problem* in 1926 and many imaged him as a friend of Africa.[38]

The Commissioners, however, privileged a technical or professional view of education as an instrument and avoided the larger issues. In their view, contemporary missionary education suffered from a wrong method, wrong subject matter, wrong articulation of goals, and a challenging environment. That environment consisted of imploding materialism introduced from the West, destruction of old values that had not been adequately replaced by a new moral system; vagaries of official policies and practices, symbolized by Education Codes, that could harm education; insurgent nationalism; and inadequately trained teachers.

Returning to the old premise that teachers constituted the point men in the enterprise, they asserted that,

> Nowhere has experience more conclusively shown that the essential thing in education is the personality of the teacher. The clearness of his moral convictions, his unselfishness in the sphere of his duty, his personal example, are the character-forming influences which make education a living thing.[39]

They paid close attention to the training, requiring that it should become more professional than based on spiritual fitness. Thus, the training of the missionary became a major consideration in reforming and revitalizing missionary education. This broad ideology determined the contours of the questions sent to respondents in Africa.

The Interior of Missionary Education in Africa in 1910

The Questions of education

Using the social science model of the shape and flow of Christian education, the fourteen categories of questions could be schematized under four headings: the purpose (broad aims and specific goals) of education; the teaching-learning process focused on the facilitator/teacher, the learner/student, and the environment. On the teacher, they queried about the technical training and moral quality. On the learner, they identified the various contexts of education and rehearsed the same questions for various contexts of the process (elementary, higher, teacher training, education of girls, industrial and Muslim contexts of education). They sought to assess the product-content or result of the process: whether it had caused Christian conviction, permeated indigenous thought, feelings and outlook and whether it had percolated a certain influence directly, indirectly or by general diffusion on the learner's community; whether "the course of education is being gradually brought into more vital relation to the real needs of the different categories of native pupils"?[40] Specifically on the learner, the Commissioners wanted to know whether the process has catalyzed a higher ideal in life, equipped the learner for leadership roles and enhanced physical development. Most of the questions focused on the environment of learning: on curricula, especially use of indigenous and other Christian literature; on the mode of communication, either English or vernacular; and the social ecology of learning characterized by competing power nodes,

Government policies and actions, the white settler communities and their racism, indigenous nationalism, and dysfunctional missionary rivalry.

The Answers From the Fields

The discussion of the responses of protagonists in the mission fields, could start with J.R Mott's typical hyperbole that galled the Germans. He intoned that,

> it is not necessary to call attention to the economic, social and educational development of the natives races of South Africa, which development, along with the political evolution, has advanced steadily through the past two or three generations. Suffice it to say that in no period has the progress been more marked, judged by every test, than during the last two decades. This progress is observable in almost every part of what is known as the Sub-Continent, the parts of Africa lying south of the Zambesi.[41]

In reality, 1910 was a dark year for the black population of South Africa as the Afrikaans declared a political status that denied the indigenous people of their political and socio-economic status. They were compelled to appeal for Britain's intervention in 1912, the year that Mott's book came out. So, what was the advancement catalyzed by missionary education?

The correspondents showed that missionary education in 1910 was prominently at the elementary level, with little effort at the higher or secondary school level and a few Teachers' Colleges. Industrial education was either non-existent or rudimentary and girls' education remained at the lowest priority. The correspondents usually skipped the opportunity to dialogue on broad ideology of missionary education. They were more interested on the specific goals of education. These focused on enabling the pupils to read the Bible and devotional literature; moral re-orientation that would subvert the traditional worldview and culture, imaged as the bondage of superstition, and victory for the civilizing mission. This would, in turn, foster a closer dependency on the gospel bearers, broaden the vistas of Western civilization and produce interpreters or native agents and teachers. The intellectual and moral equipping of the native agents was the missionaries' contribution to the leadership of native churches. It was also hoped that technical education would attach a breed of intelligent natives to the periphery of the new capitalist society, engage them in "useful living" and improve their earning power. The brass ceiling of missionary education was moral formation, skill acquisition, and production of native teachers.

The reasons were not hard to find. As Rev D.D. Stormont, Principal of Blythswood Institution, Butterworth, insisted: education in the Cape Colony certainly has taught the people to improve their hygiene, physical surroundings, acquire higher ideals in life and capacity to dissent from tribal ties and family control. But the unintended consequence has intensified individualistic ethos, assertion of independence often amounting to license, and opposition to Europeans. Admittedly, this last fact is linked to wider socio-economic factors such as erosion of "tribal life" or social control system, effects of alienation of land, and urban morality. Stormont basically admitted that missionary education did not provide an adequate coping mechanism in the face of dire socio-economic changes in the lives of the indigenous people. The product-content left much to be desired because the key component in the teaching –learning process was faulty. The native teacher, he wrote, is unchastely, conceited, and lover of ease and money, unless he apprentices for a very long time under the European who could provide him with money and morals.[42] Stormont did not comment on the European teacher as the Commissioners would have liked; but he was impressed by the effect of missionary education that has liberated the impulse of individualism in the 'native' by crushing by tribal norms. There is little of industrial training in the Cape Colony but it must be seen in perspective. Industrial education is no prophylactic against moral weakness because those who show less capacity for academics turn to industrial education; these function as second rate people with lower moral quality of life.

Interestingly, the other leaders of institutions in the southern African region echoed Stormont. Henderson of Lovedale repeated the goals of moral regeneration and character formation, confessed the little engagement in higher education, unfocussed goal of generating Christian influence in the communities, and low priority of industrial education because the youth find it unattractive. Even less attention was paid to girls' education because they would rather stay at home. Blame polygamy, early marriage and love of ease.

Rev J. D. Taylor of Adams Mission Station, Natal, devoted immense effort in answering the questionnaire. He perceived the moral dimension of missionary education, the access to the Bible, arousal of interest in higher education, and spread of Christian influence. But he rated the enterprise as a failure because of poorly trained native teachers, who despoil primary schools and lack earnestness in giving religious education. Blames go to parents who use child labor and encourage indolence and absenteeism as well as the Government that under-funds education. He explained missionary reluctance to engage in higher education precisely because the products so far are

> leavening the native population with new ideas and ambitions-
> a process which is at the present stage unsatisfactory in many
> of its results, and is causing a ferment of half-comprehended
> ideas.[43]

The teaching-learning environment, observed Taylor, is vitiated by an over-emphasis on academics, undue attention to examination results by government inspectors, lack of textbooks suitable for local conditions, and multiplication of low quality schools by competing societies. Industrial education has low priority because the Government plays to the gallery of white labor organizations who resent the skill acquisition by blacks. The dark picture in South Africa is completed by Rev L. Fuller of Johannesburg who saw less of the academic emphasis and more of a religious emphasis in primary education, and would not encourage higher education for natives because it will afflict them "with a horror of hard work, either mental or physical", and make them "rather immoral and very far from religious." [44]

In Nyasaland, the chorus continued as if orchestrated or reflected the editorial agenda behind the records. Dr Robert Laws of Livingstonia appeared to be the most optimistic about missionary education that has widened the horizon of those who have learnt to read, enculturated higher ideals and standard of life, and created a fruitful evangelistic agency. Miss M.W. Bulley of the Universities Missions to Central Africa, Likoma, explained the catch phrase, 'higher ideals'. It means "bringing the natives in touch with European ideas", building a disciplined character and breaking ties with traditional norms. Or, as Dr Hetherwick of Blantyre Mission put it, "gradual purifying of the atmosphere of native thought and morality, and imparting a higher ideal of life to the native and his race." [45] All agreed that higher education was practically non-existent and industrial education was confined to producing artisans who work for the mission stations. According to Rev. H.H. Weatherhead of King's School, Buddu, Uganda, the training of indigenous teachers remains unorganized and on small scale because the salaries are low and young people would prefer other occupations. The Native Church apparently paid low wages to the clergy in Uganda as in the Sierra Leone. In 1950, the World Council of Christian Education, in New York, conducted a very elaborate global survey of the practice of Christian Education, and produced a source book for the convention in Toronto. Virtually all respondents linked evangelism to Christian education and stressed moral formation and destruction of indigenous religions as their aims.

Internal Diagnosis: Problems and Prospects

The missionaries pointed to some of the problems and possible solutions. On the social environment, they pointed to the political resurgence, Ethiopianism, that spread throughout the Zambesi, Cape Province, Natal and Nyasaland; the effect of increased demand for labor in the mines and its attendant moral consequences; growth of Islam; the spread of materialism and urbanization; and the competition by governments, some of whom were hostile as the French in Madagascar, or suspicious of missionaries as the Portuguese in Mozambique. Besides, Africa suffered from conflicting policies by the British, French, Portuguese and Belgians.

The missionaries did not always agree on how to improve the results of missionary education. J. K. McGregor, United Free Church, Calabar, blamed the lazy 'natives', their distaste for manual labor, and preference for high salaries as interpreters and civil servants. Others wanted a review of the teaching-learning environment. Dr. Weatherhead raised the question "whether (missionaries) may not have laid too much stress on Bible teaching in the past to the exclusion of the practical side of education." [46] Rev W.T.Balmer of the Wesleyan Methodist Missionary Society, Freetown, Sierra Leone concurred, adding that Sierra Leone was now educating the fourth generation of Africans; that the Native Pastorate handled much of the Christian work while missionaries served as supervisors. However,

> the weakness of the system of education which followed the British models too closely is now apparent...Education has been too much confined to instruction in the art of reading and writing, with the tacit assumption that manual labour is of less dignity and worth than the exercise of those accomplishment... Mere book knowledge is compatible with the retention of the corrupting notions of the natural world, and is even capable of aggravation of the corrupt ideas which prevail. Hence in the educational policy of Missionary Societies, emphasis should now be laid upon the giving of instruction in manual arts and upon the systematic study of nature.[47]

Beyond content, the use of vernacular as a means of instruction and the use of indigenous literature became contentious. The Commissioners had been scandalized by the fact that

> so little has as yet been done in this direction that there is not even a school history of South Africa dealing with the subject in any way suitable for natives or from the native point of view. The

333

musical gift of many of the African native tribes is remarkable. As at Hampton and Tuskegee in the United States, vocal music may be made a great factor in this connection. Much good is done by the introduction of hymns in the vernacular as an alternative to such of the native songs as are low and indecent.[48]

The debate on the use of English squared off Dr Stormont against M. Junod of Lourenco Marquez who had delivered a very thoughtful paper entitled, *Native education and native literature* at Bloemfontein Missionary Conference in 1909. Stormont had delivered his counter view on *Literature for native Christians* at a conference in Johannesburg in 1906. Three issues were raised: use of English as a branch of study; use of English as a means of instruction; and at what level of education. The protagonists said little about the translation of the Bible or catechisms into indigenous languages. Yet, this was the primary literature for learning to read; except in Francophone colonies where people were designated as illiterates if they could not read in French, and even if they could read in Bambara or any other indigenous language. The debate turned into the contest between a monocultural and a multicultural approach to education.

Arguing for the former, Stormont insisted on the use of English as a branch of study and means of instruction at all levels, because it will help the blacks in their relationship with whites; it is necessary for commerce and civilized life; good government and public morality; and it will be economical as students could acquire cheap literature from Europe. He represented those who fought against vernacularization because

> there is no native literature in Africa. Tradition is largely based on myths and vague ideas. Thus, there is practically no stock on which to graft Christian ideas.[49]

The Nigerian representatives disputed this because enormous translation work had been a part of the missionary task in West Africa. As W.H. Mobley has shown, the indigenous educated elite in the Gold Coast had graduated by 1900 from producing literature of tutelage to critical literature. P.E. H. Hair has studied the enormous translation work in West Africa and commended the high quality of the Efik Bible translated by the Presbyterians, thirty odd years before Edinburgh conference. Translation work was a priority for Adjai Crowther who co-operated with Schon to publish a number of such translations; he also encouraged missionaries on the Niger to do so. J.D.Y Peel has argued that the Yoruba Bible created the identity of the Yoruba. The ingenious capacity of T. J. Dennis who gathered a group of indigenes to produce the Ibo Bible (1907-1911) has been celebrated as the achievement of the Church Missionary Society in Nigeria. John S. Mbiti, therefore, explored the translations and impact of the Bible on Africa in 1987. Three years later, Lamin Sanneh reinterpreted the African church historiography on the touchstone of translation.[50] Educationists recognize that first grounding in the vernacular is essential for transmitting and preserving indigenous knowledge and for developing mental and communication skills. The irony was that many communities wanted to learn English. When the CMS insisted on using vernacular as a means of instruction, village chiefs chose to patronize the Roman Catholics who easily obliged to teach in English. Pundits wager that this fact explains the pre-eminence of the Roman Catholics in education and numbers of votaries in civil service and professions. But all these appear as historical hindsight.

Among the protagonists of this era, William Beck of the American Lutheran Church, Monrovia, Liberia, concurred with Stormont that he "finds native tongues barren of words to express Christian thought."[51] Dr Laws added his weighty voice to urge that the vernacular suffered from an imprecise interior and encouraged tribalism. Those who deploy the political theory of mobilization in nation building, always look for a *lingua franca* that would wipe away competing power nodes and the differences of "tribes and tongues." Missionary ideology in the settler communities was a mobilizing concept. Vernacularization was not one of its ideals. The total rejection of the resources of indigenous knowledge destroyed the potential of a liberating education.

H. A. Junod (Mission Romande, Switzerland/Rikatla, Mozambique) countered that the mother tongue must be retained because it is the medium of thought and emotion; for producing native teachers who will teach their compatriots because English is as foreign to them as Latin was to Europeans; their vernacular is composite and contains all that is necessary for communication. J.E. Hamshere (CMS, Freretown) opined that Swahili was sufficient for those in British East Africa. At this point, P.S. Kirkwood of Livingstonia beat his chest in guilt and picked up enough courage to disagree with the venerable Dr Laws:

> Let us remember how much our own national growth in Christianity was hastened by translation of the Scriptures into our mother tongue. We must get at the hearts as well as the heads of the natives. For that we need the vernacular... our students when they pass to the village schools as teachers are apt to attach an altogether exaggerated importance to English, both as a medium of instruction and as a branch of study.[52]

Vernacular, some argued, could be the needed antidote to the nagging problem of "narrow ignorance and overweening self-conceit" among educated Africans. Europeans found their insolence to be insufferable and caricatured them as "Black Englishmen." In Joyce Cary's novel, *Mister Johnson*, the Europeans deserted the African who dared to dress in white and inch his way into the charmed circle.

However, many missionaries conceded that translating the Bible into indigenous languages was one kettle of fish, using the vernacular as a medium of instruction was another. The myriads of languages and dialects may necessitate the use of English at the higher levels of education while vernacular could be used to teach at the lowest grades. Rev. W.T. Balmer of Sierra Leone had the brilliant idea that the best means of cleansing the impurities of the vernacular was "having it used properly and vigorously in schools and colleges, where its use can be brought under direct Christian oversight."[53] Few were prepared to engage in such sanitary work. Some looked into the seeds of time and predicted that the future belonged to western civilization; the blacks cannot do without European supervision; and the appropriate language of the future should be English. The debate among the correspondents said more about the minds of missionaries and the temper of the era than the subject matter.

Conclusion: Ecumenism as an Antidote

The Commissioners were overwhelmed by the discordant voices emanating from the mission fields, impressed by the breadth of the continent and complexities of its problems, and filled with "anxieties as to the present results of some of the educational work upon which men and women are unselfishly spending themselves in many regions of the African mission field."[54] Scholars, therefore, speak about African Christianities that grew out of these realities as well as the patterns of appropriation of the gospel from many cultural contexts. Edinburgh Conference proffered few solutions: it sought to bring modern educational theories into missionary practice. In considering the immense challenges, it suggested an ecumenical endeavor as antidote, urging missionaries to co-operate in building inspectorate divisions in the system, operating joint training of teachers so as to harmonize the instructional methods, intensifying the care of alumni, improving the education of the girl child, and especially emphasizing handwork, manual labor, sports, industrial skill acquisition and agricultural education. The North American ideals of Hampton and Tuskegee Institute would continue to beckon throughout the colonial period. But the Commissioners were aware of the need to review the education ideology at the home base of mission and the training of those who will go out as teachers. Many missionary societies did not differentiate between gospel bearers and teachers, or provided them with the requisite skills. A study of ministerial formation institutions that prepared missionaries in various parts of Europe and America will be quite instructive. Government inspectors complained about the rapid opening of schools in the heat of rivalry without adequately trained teachers. Missionary co-operation would, by delimiting areas of operation, diminish competition; by bonding save resources and avoid duplication; and by dialogue engage the colonial governments' policies, and harmonize cultural policy in response to the tensile strength of indigenous religions and cultures. Examples abound that from 1911, the conference inspired many co-operative efforts.[55]

But Christian missionary enterprise remained unsuccessful till after the First World War because its cultural hardware and dark image of the African hosts restrained its capacity to exploit the inculturating pathways. Ironically, education and translation would fuel both charismatic spirituality and nationalism and change the character of Christianity in the aftermath of the conference. The gospel would expand under the indigenous bearers just as it did in the early church. All these lay in the future. The challenge of re-imagining the Edinburgh Conference is to reconstruct it with a keen eye to context. It was 1910 and hindsight does no justice to the protagonists. Christianity had not encountered many African communities in the hinterland of the coastal regions. The European mind gloried in the Enlightenment worldview and Social Darwinism. The missionary was a child of his age and struggled to balance an evangelical spirituality with the racism of the age and the challenge of a civilizing mission. The exigencies of the mission field, the compelling desire to work with the colonial governments, and the resilience of indigenous structures complicated the scene. Indeed, some of their strategies were sourced from the model employed in dealing with delinquent children in 19th century Europe. A missionary would often adapt the familiar principles of education. William H. Taylor's study of the Scottish Presbyterian Mission to eastern Nigeria, argued that, "the first Calabar mission schools were to borrow many of their practices from the Ragged Schools that had been started in Edinburgh by philanthropist and theologian Thomas Guthrie and from the Scottish Sunday School movement."[56] Africans were read as "docile bodies", to borrow from Michel Foucault. A body is docile that may be subjected, used, transformed and improved; or plastic according to Mott. Chosen young, three factors, time, space and the constitution of a new individuality, contributed directly to the culmination of this African docile body.[57]

This makes the conference significant in revealing the strength of the missionary enterprise as its capacity for self-criticism. The Commissioners and the men-on –the –spot differed over the ideals, content and method of education. The Commissioners set out to revamp the entire educational apparatus of evangelism by indigenising it. That was a tall order. Yet on closer look, the Commissioners did not go far enough in distinguishing *training* from *education*. They diagnosed that the primary pedagogy for learning did little to impress upon the learner the importance of knowing self. It was directed more toward a formation that promotes social maintenance instead of promoting a liberating agenda that reveals the divinity of the human spirit. It fitted individuals into the colonial caste system maintained by the pedagogical approach termed as "action-reaction". Most often this is manifest in "presentation of information-information regurgitation" or banking model. It did not encourage reflection and analysis as much as it promoted singularity of thought, uniformity of ideas, and monolithic universality of response. It privileged training over against education. Training is skill based, whereas education is identity based. Training focuses on learning mechanics; education focuses on learning one's place in the world through an emphasis on one's history or high culture. Education nurtures the human being and expands the person's understanding of the self through the identification of a cultural-social location.

The historian must, however, put their ideals in the context of the period. What is the significance of reconstructing this era? The result provides an interesting cameo of an era, an insight into the adventurous western imagination at the turn of the century, and the backdrop to what happened later. Indeed, the revolution in education in the aftermath of the Conference becomes more significant. As education exploded, it became clear that it was the African who initiated the modern face of Christianity. Mary Slessor wrote soon after the Edinburgh Conference that the chiefs at Itu "want their boys educated and they want someone to guide them safely through the new world in which they are being enclosed by the white man of whom they know so little and whom they fear."[58]

This is more astonishing because Edinburgh Conference did not represent the actual face of Christianity in Africa because of the lenses used in reading the people and their responses to the presence of the kingdom of God in their midst. By focusing on the settler communities of southern and central Africa, it missed the ferment in the western theatre and the signals of transcendence all over the continent. It ignored the key players in the indigenising movement, misrepresented Ethiopianism and paid scant attention to the rising tide of charismatic revivals. Finally, education became the strongest weapon in western underdevelopment of Africa because of its power of eradication. It is intriguing to note how some of the missionary ideas of the early period survived till the decolonisation period and served as the backdrop of the hostility to missionary control of education. The study of the past always has meaning for the present and future. It is always useful to know where the rain met us.

This lecture is gratefully dedicated to Graeme Brown, my Latin teacher at the Hope Waddell Training Institution, Calabar.

Notes

1. *World Missionary Conference, 1910, Report of Commission III: Education in Relation To The Christianisation of National Life* (Edinburgh and London: Oliphant, Anderson and Ferrier, 1910): 213. Hereafter referred to by volume only.
2. III: 248.
3. ibid., 250.
4. John R. Mott, *The Decisive Hour of Christian Missions* (New York: Student Volunteer Movement For Foreign Missions, 1912): 120.
5. III: 254.
6. ibid., 253.
7. ibid., 259.
8. ibid.
9. ibid., 257.
10. Mott, *The Decisive Hour*, 25.
11. Gordon M. Haliburton, *The Prophet Harris* (London: Oxford University Press, 1973).
12. III: vii-xx.
13. ibid, . 3.
14. ibid., 4.
15. ibid., 6.
16. Mott, *The Decisive Hour*, 114.
17. III: 240.
18. ibid., 244.
19. ibid., 245, 257.
20. ibid.
21. Paulo Freire, *Pedagogy of the Oppressed* (New York: Continuum, 1970): 58-60.
22. III: 258.
23. Freire, *Pedagogy of the Oppressed*, 181.
24. ibid., 182-3.

25. III: 247; see, Roswith Gerloff ed., *Mission Is Crossing Frontiers: essays in honour of Bongani Mazibuko* (Pietermaritzburgh: Cluster Publications, 2003): 14.
26. ibid., 252.
27. ibid., 261.
28. R. Suntharalingam, *Politics and Nationalist Awakening in South India, 1852-1910* (Jaipur-New Delhi: 1990).
29. cit Klaus Korschorke, ed. *Transcontinental Links In the History of Non-Western Christianity* (Weisbaden: Harrasowitz Verlag, 2002): 205.
30. E.A Ayandele, *The Missionary Impact on Modern Nigeria, 1842-1914* (London: Longmans, 1966).
31. Mott, *The Decisive Hour*, 109-110.
32. ibid., 114.
33. J. Ade Ajayi, *Christian Missions in Nigeria; The Making of an Elite* (London: Longmans, 1965); see , John P. Ragsdale, *Protestant Mission Education in Zambia, 1880-1954* (Toronto: Associated University Press, 1986).
34. III: 8.
35. see a discussion in Efiong S. Utuk, *From New York to Ibadan: the impact of African Questions on the making of ecumenical mission mandates* (New York: Peter Lang, 1991).
36. III: 208-211.
37. ibid., 233ff.
38. See, Brian Stanley's article on "Church, State and Hierarchy of Civilization" and Andrew C. Ross, "Christian Missions and the Mid-Nineteenth Century Change in Attitude to Race" in Andrew Porter, ed., *The Imperial Horizons of British Protestant Missions, 1880-1914* (Grand Rapids: Eerdmans, 2003): 58-105.
39. ibid., 166.
40. ibid., 168.
41. Mott Decisive Hour, 22.
42. III: 175.
43. ibid., 180.
44. ibid., 183.
45. ibid., 187.
46. ibid., 197.
47. ibid., 197-198.
48. ibid., 203.
49. ibid.203; see, Stormont, 204.
50. W.H Mobley, *The Ghanaians' Image of the Missionary* (Leiden: EJ Brill, 1970); J. S. Mbiti, *Theology and Bible in Africa* (Nairobi: Oxford University press, 1987): Lamin Sanneh, *Translating the Message* (Maryknoll, NY: Orbis, 1989); John Peel, *Religious Encounter and the Making of the Yoruba* (Bloominghton, IN: Indiana University Press, 2002); P .E .H. Hair, *The Early Study*

of Nigerian Languages (Cambridge: Cambridge University Press, 1967). See the chapter on translation work in N. Omenka, *Schools as means of evangelization* (Leiden: E.J.Brill, 1991).

51. III: 207.

52. ibid., 206.

53. ibid., 207.

54. ibid., 166.

55. O. U. Kalu, *Divided People of God: Church Union Movement in Nigeria, 1875-1966* (New York: NOK Publishers, 1978). Deeply impressed by the Edinburgh Conference, Wilkie of the UFC initiated the regular meetings between the CMS, Qua Iboe Mission and the CSM in Eastern Nigeria from 1911. These inspired the church union movement.

56. William H. Taylor, *Mission to Educate* (Leiden: EJ Brill, 1996): 11.

57. M. Foucault, *Discipline and Punish* (Paris: Gallimand, 1979): 136; V. Y. Mudimbe, *Tales of Faith: Religion as Political performance in Central Africa*((London: The Athlone Press, 1997): 50-51.

58. *Record, 1911: 168* cit. ibid., : 125.

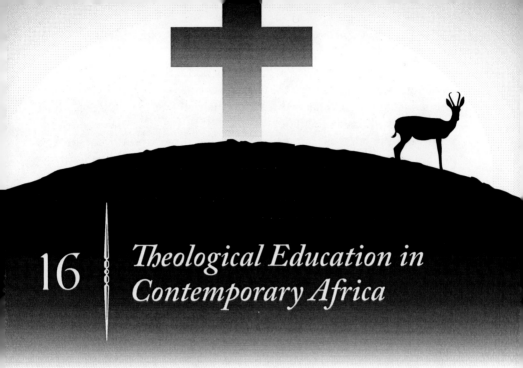

16 | *Theological Education in Contemporary Africa*

Introduction

L et me begin with a disconcerting story. I read about a new theological school in Lagos. The provost and founder obtained a diploma from a bible school run by a Pentecostal church named Christ Ambassadors, a bachelor and masters from a certain Shepherd University in Lagos, and a doctorate from another institution named International Pentecostal University in Lagos. It hit me that I had never heard about any of the institutions listed in the curriculum vitae of the eminent churchman and educationist. I started inconclusive inquiries precisely because none was approved and listed under the National Universities Commission. Other people in Nigeria have suffered from following big advertisements to nondescript facilities. There is a story that a Nigerian saw a glossy advertisement for a university and traced the address. In utter surprise, he inquired whether this address was the correct one for the advertised university. The receptionist roughly countered: "are you looking for a building or for a degree?"

The context is the explosion of Christianity in contemporary Africa. Statistics show that much of the growth in southern Christianity is occurring in Africa. But growth, like decline, could be a traumatic experience as the old structures are challenged and new theological ideas and practices contend with traditions in the religious landscape. A number of key indicators could be used to analyze the religious scene that some commentators have likened to the early Christian period; others have deployed the market model to characterize the new Christianity as a market place where competing agents package and redesign their religious products to attract consumers with increasingly refined palates. In the consumerist environment, some goods are packaged cheaply for those who do not wish to pay high costs. In Nigeria where over 400, 000 students annually sit the examination for entry into universities, about a third score very well, but the universities can only absorb about 3, 000 students, many patronize private unaccredited institutions.

Examined from a continental perspective, education attracts an enormous patronage in Africa. This chapter examines the impact on contemporary African Christianity. A key index is ministerial formation precisely because how Christian groups recruit, train, equip and morally "form" their leadership agents may determine the quality and faithfulness of Christianity in Africa and its missional vocation. The vocation is exhibited in the character of Christian being or presence in a community, concrete participation in the lives of the people, and a consistent sharing of the gospel message that heals, nurtures, and transforms the physical and spiritual lives of communities. Thus, the quality, curricula, facilities and the entire gamut of theological formation of the agents are, therefore, crucial. From a certain perspective, ministerial formation is a stage in the conversion process. The nature of conversion involves a process of learning the mission, vision and practices of a particular religious community so as to win others to its core affirmations and life style. The agent must be an adept. Within this perspective, theological education becomes an instrument of a broad-based formation that ensures that agents are properly 'formed' or converted so that they could serve as the representatives of the reign of God through the transmission of the gospel and a particular faith tradition. Some argue that there is sometimes a thin line between ministerial formation and indoctrination process however voluntary the individual's participation may be. In our contemporary period we re-conceptualize ministerial formation by insisting upon the capacity to acquire a good grasp of the canon, critical thinking, passion for evangelization, moral stability, sound ethical conscience and skills for engaging the public space and popular culture.

The effort here is to assess contemporary theological education in Africa from this perspective. But as a historian I cannot avoid starting with its roots in missionary practice precisely because African institutions are still struggling to transform inherited habits and structures. Churches in Africa inherited a certain model of ministerial formation based on a series of traditions, some from the early church and others from secular theories of education as Europe resolved its cultural wars. Christianity inherited education and ministerial formation from earlier traditions when priests were the purveyors of modernity in communities, the preservers of the oil of civilization and transmitters of high culture. Arguing that the early church had benefited from secular education, the resources of walled education became the key strategy of ministerial formation.

From the inception of the missionary enterprise, emphasis was put on theological education. Thus, the early uneducated missionaries who were dubbed as "Godly mechanics" of the nineteenth century were retrained as the numbers of graduate missionaries increased. In spite of the fact that "faith missions" opened the doors for many individuals to enter the missionary affray in the 19th century without the support and restrictions imposed by missionary bodies, enormous efforts were made to train missionary agents. The case for academic formation of ministers continued unabated as the missionary enterprise grew. For instance, as we have shown in an earlier chapter on Edinburgh Conference 1910, it was argued that the level of education in Japan was so high that the field required very highly trained missionary personnel. Similarly, China and India sported religions and cultures that demanded academic aptitude from the missionary agents.

Initially, it was presumed that animistic religions of the pagan regions such as Africa would be less demanding until the realization of the broad cultural challenges and character of the peoples forced a re-thinking. Missionary records are filled with lengthy discussions about training of both missionary personnel and indigenous agents because missionaries privileged the development of the life of the mind. Soon, education became the gateway of missionary success as exponential rates of growth demanded more personnel than the Europeans could muster.

From the colonial period to the 1970s, missionaries controlled the education systems of African countries to such an extent that the new African states became critical of the control and Euro-centric curricula of schools and dared to oust the missionaries in a rapid secularization process that followed the early independence period. From the 1980s, some of the African theological educators drew attention to the fact that walled education that privileged academic training may be too expensive for African churches to maintain if they should ever develop to be self-sustaining. Theological Education by Extension (TEE) was proffered as an alternative aspect of the indigenization project and the decolonization of African churches. It had its systemic challenges. But its failure to gain a strong acceptance was related to an image of inferiority. The cult of certificates among Africans and the insistence on reproducing an African Christian elite as the inheritors of the Western missionary enterprise, among whites, contested any alternative measures.

Then, an explosion started like a storm in the prairies, with uncontrollable gusts. Charismatic-Pentecostal spirituality exploded in the 1980s. Many young people, educated, professional men and women sought to wear the surplice. New ideas spawned around the five-fold ministry in Paul's letter to the Ephesians. Commentators contested the sufficing requirements for ordination by deploying curious forms of biblical exegesis. The main problem was that the numbers of new converts overawed the available manpower and infrastructure. Contests over doctrine, polity, liturgy and ethics yielded new visions and strategies for ministerial formation. *Elijah's mantle* became a dominant imagery for describing and legitimizing the formation of new Christian churches under the new leadership that had not tasted formal theological training.[1] The models of ministerial formation in Africa became scrambled: apprenticeship, unaccredited Bible schools, short-term crash courses offered by well-meaning global partners, awards of doctorates, outright sale of certificates by wolves in sheepfolds, and a host of other strategies emerged.

The changes in the patterns of theological education emerged from shifts in the perception of the church and its mission within Africa. For instance, when the character of African Christianity became more charismatic, its understanding of the meaning of the church and its missional vocation changed. The new forms tended to be pro-active, evangelistic, mission-oriented, and growth-driven. This temper created a leadership environment that indulged in biblicist rhetoric and leadership imagery that excavated the Hebrew bible for legitimization. For instance, a leader may image his ministry as engaged in promoting the "Abrahamic Covenant People", or the "Moses Servant Spirit", or leading the "Joshua Generation." The leader will pretend to be either Abraham or Moses or Joshua.

The emphasis on the leadership of the Holy Spirit creates conditions in which people could declare that the Spirit has called and given them visions. No one could query the authenticity. When people could be led by the Spirit to start new evangelistic ventures ("building new altars") without years of formation, the old system would be scrambled. The leader, as "the man of God", passes his anointing to his followers as Elijah passed his mantle to Elisha; except that the apprentice may not wait to see his master taken up into the sky. Yet, " the man of God" syndrome fits into the indigenous cultural tradition of power and authority; it resonates with the power of the white missionary over the "native" church. But it could create a very dictatorial and manipulative style of leadership under the guise that "God is not a democrat" and that frequent consultations with the eldership is a sure way to lose the vision that God gave to the leader. It could also breed half- baked leaders who may have not trained adequately for the mission.

Three developments have become important in recent times: first, new groups such as the African Theological Fellowship have organized to create sustainable, respectable models of postgraduate courses along the old Western academic models but with revised curricula that privilege doing theology in the vernacular. Second, the most intriguing dimension of the religious landscape is the emergence of Christian Universities. At one level, it is not a phenomenon common only to southern Christianity. Western Christians indulged in massive foundations of Christian institutions in the 19th century. The new dimension in Africa is that the churches that had been pushed away from their control of primary and secondary school education by new independent African states, rebounded by re-entering the affray at the cost -intensive level of tertiary education. In West Africa, there are about a dozen private universities in Ghana and over thirty in Nigeria. Most are Christian unlike Kenya where only about 45% are so, A new entrepreneurial concept of education has emerged and the competition in the religious market has escalated. Muslims also have founded universities, claiming that they brought the idea to Timbuktu in the golden yesteryears of African civilization. Third, a large group of unaccredited universities have sprouted, arguing that the state does not have any accrediting power over institutions that are purely religious. In Nigeria, they banded under the aegis of Association of Christian Theological Schools.

This study is a historical reconstruction of the trend of ministerial formation in contemporary Africa from around 1975 to the present. The new trends demonstrate how global flows and local processes combine to produce new cultural trends. Inheriting Elijah's mantle illustrates one of the traumas of explosive growth of Christianity in Africa.

TEE and Its Enemies: Ministerial Formation, 1975-1985

The problems of ministerial formation in Africa after 1975 are connected to the missionary structures that developed under the colonial canopy. There are two dimensions: the first is the training of missionary personnel; the second is the training of indigenous agents. The reflection here will concentrate on the latter. Missionary education was built on a number of pedestals all of which were based on the patterns of education in various European metropoles. They were primarily designed as a means of evangelization, to enable the new converts to access the Bible and other forms of Christian literature, and to nurture indigenous Christian leadership. The broad aim was to improve manners and contribute to the civilizing mission but the specific goal was to generate manpower for missionary institutions. Literacy was important for a literary religion. The Protestant insistence on access to the Bible merely doubled the need for educated converts. For the Roman Catholics, memorizing the catechism would suffice.

The question arose about the language of instruction. Some opted for the vernacular; others thought that the vernacular lacked the finesse, vocabulary, and the future as a viable mode of teaching-learning process. Access to the Bible in the vernacular however compelled the translation of the Bible into many indigenous dialects. A compromise was reached that instruction could use the vernacular at the lower levels of education, and the European language of the overlords would be employed in cleaning up the converts at the higher rungs of the educational ladder.

Vernacular translation served well when the missions followed the colonial expansion into the hinterlands creating the need to witness in the vernacular and to respond to the challenges created by enlargement of scale. This growth occurred just when geopolitical factors hindered European capacity to supply the required level of manpower, 1914-1945. In some places, the inhospitable climate exacerbated the problem. Mosquitoes intensified the mortality rate of missionary personnel before quinine was discovered as a prophylactic. The need for "native agents" turned attention to ministerial formation because teachers served as ministers; church and school operated as the same units. The dominant strategy was a combination of apprenticeship and walled education. People who served missionaries as cooks, stewards, interpreters, porters, houseboys and house girls could later become church servants, evangelists, deacons, and a few may climb to the noble heights as pastors. All missionary bodies were hesitant to ordain indigenous people as pastors. Some Protestant bodies did but many Roman Catholic Orders persevered in using foreign agency till the twilight of the colonial period. Racism was rife. The schools were, therefore, designed to train indigenous leaders as teachers of village schools and mission agents and pastors. The regimen and curricula ensured this limited range.

Education was not a consumer good but an investment good. Opinions varied: some wanted to replicate the training that they received at home and produce a native elite that would interpret Western values to their people. Others would leave the native agents as close to their natural habitat as possible and avoid too much literacy. Still others, as the French Holy Ghost Fathers, deployed the method used in juvenile delinquency homes in France, best described by Michel Foucault in *Discipline and Punish*. (1979) The goal was re-formation of personality and morals. He imaged the enterprise with an apt term, *docile bodies*. A body is docile that may be subjected, used, transformed and improved. Africans were perceived as plastic. Chosen young, the construction of a new individuality would be achieved by the allocation of space, use of time and other forms of regimens in enclosed school spaces or compounds.

Enclavement was a major form of missionary presence and strategy for ministerial formation. Educationists would later add the holistic concepts that ensured that physical and industrial education, hygiene, and the training of girls would become parts of the broad ideology. At all times, the strategy rejected "book learning" as the chief goal of ministerial formation, and provided an antidote to the racial concern for the pretensions of the educated Africans. It did more, as J.R. Mott and other cultural invaders enthused,

> the influence of Western learning has been in the direction of undermining the faith of the student class in the non-Christian religions and of breaking up the social and ethical restraints of the old civilizations.[2]

They reformatted both the person and the environment, and privileged training rather than education precisely because training tended to assist people learn skills for operating in a particular system. Education, on the other hand, impresses upon the learner the importance of knowing self. This could prove to be subversive and may query the curricula, the strategy and the arrangement of the learning –teaching environment. Conformity remained at the heart of missionary education until the 1940's when secular intervention differentiated between training of teachers, secondary and industrial education. Ironically, missionary critics insisted that the fauchet-sponge model of education in classroom-based academic environment encouraged head knowledge, stunted creativity and did little for moral development because many of the products remained lazy and immoral.

Among Protestants, there were no seminaries manqué until the early 1950s. In many places, the idea arose in response to the need to train deacons and rural evangelists as competing missionaries surged into the interior of communities. Roman Catholics decided earlier than this to counteract Government interference by designing seminaries that served as both grammar schools and priestly formation. A certain disillusionment about African capacity combined with European traditions to install a system that involved many years of orchestrated process of indoctrination to attain priestly initiation. By 1948, the colonial governments established universities that challenged missionary domination and responded to African demand for higher education.

In summary, missionary pattern of ministerial formation was propped on the general education system because of the close connection between church and school. Primary schools and Teachers' Colleges produced pastors. Roman Catholics combined priestly formation, novitiates and educational institutions. Recruitment into the ministry was from the ranks of house servants and school children. The goals were manpower development, inculcation of religious knowledge and Western civilization, and a deliberate moral reshaping of the neophytes with Victorian values. The curricula not only ignored the cultural environment but set out to undermine indigenous values and cultural traditions. It rejected the traditional power and authority structures and set out to create new leadership and ministerial systems along European models. The preference for residential or walled institutions had many advantages that enhanced control but removed the students from their world and its wealth of indigenous knowledge.

The first challenge to missionary education came from the inside. The first educated Africans objected to the cultural hubris of missionary leaders and dared to give voice to African discontent and to exit from missionary structures by founding their own educational institutions without foreign aid. They promoted indigenous cultures but failed to design an alternative indigenous strategy of education. A second challenge emerged much later when the proponents of theological education by extension sought to revise the missionary heritage by placing the students within their cultural settings so that the process of education may enhance coping abilities and the quality of witness. Walled education became increasingly expensive as the infrastructure had to be modernized. Funding of education has remained an enduring problem. Indeed, when Protestants founded seminaries, the tendency was to mobilize their resources and eschew denominational competition. Thus, Fort Hare in South Africa, Trinity College, Legon (Ghana), Trinity College, Umuahia (Nigeria), St Paul's Limuru (Kenya), Faculte de Theologie, Yaounde (Cameroon) were joint ecumenical ventures. The tensile strength of rivalry, however, ensured the emergence of purely denominational institutions. Bible Schools emerged among smaller denominations and institutions for formation of rural evangelists and deacons. Many of the Colleges/Seminaries only offered Diploma Certificates. Later, the Roman Catholics and some Evangelicals founded degree-awarding institutions affiliated to Western institutions such as Concordia University and Urbana University, Rome. Newly independent states would later attack the off-shore degrees and insist on affiliation to local universities by the early 1980s.

Indigenizing education involved paying attention to the environment of learning, attention to the cultural imperatives, designing a relevant curriculum, cutting costs, and reframing the goals of ministerial formation to integrate the academic, moral and leadership expectations. It was argued that people would learn more creatively by combining learning and working, or practicing the "praxis –reflection-praxis" model. This argument was best made for the African scene by Ross Kinsler who had imbibed much of the ideology of the education for liberation in Latin America. From the vantage point of Program for Theological Education Unit of WCC, he could survey Third World problems in ministerial formation and could see clearly the dangers of dependency. Dependency bred vulnerability and the Peter Pan syndrome that vitiated growth and selfhood. The piper would always call the tune, and wealth of indigenous resources and cultural knowledge would be ignored in educating those who will minister among their peoples. In the early 1980s the advocacy for TEE assumed an evangelical tone as a panacea for African ministerial formation. It sought to privilege human experience in the learning process, based on responses to environment and culture, to ensure self-development, liberation, creativity and spiritual growth. This was the solution for forming a viable leadership cadre. [3]

The problems for the alternative model, TEE, were that someone had to write the curricula, create access to the materials, and enable dialogue and communal reflection. Costs remained high and the curricula could not escape the clutches of Western orientation unless indigenous scholars wrote a new script. But a host of missionaries were deployed to work on TEE ministry and write the materials. Logistics based on the level of infrastructure vitiated the possibilities of distributing and retrieving instructional materials, and supervising the students. For instance, one vaunted ideal was to refurbish the Lutheran radio and taping stations in Nigeria as a base for contacting the students through audiotapes and radio. It failed because of lack of funding. In South Africa, the government later built a long distance educational University (UNISA), furnished with the adequate technology and manpower that could promote the ideals that TEE envisaged for ministerial formation. Moreover, a balanced education should enlarge the students' vision through diverse cultural resources and opportunities. Critics claimed that TEE tended to encourage closed, narrow boundaries. A participant would forever hover around the rural location of birth. With increasing urbanization and upward mobility tendency, few accepted the limited boundaries.

Meanwhile, the defenders of residential education insisted that it offered consistent supervision and accountability; allowed for a combination of academic studies, devotional life (personal and communal) and practical work to be carried out in a consistent, regular and in-depth manner; and facilitated progressive development and assessment of learning outcome. Residential institutions encouraged spiritual development-in-community (that is a vital component of congregational life) in an environment that nurtures fellowship between candidates for the ministry. Students practiced ministry in communities during the field work periods. [4]

But the death knell was sounded by traditionalism, the internalization of long years of missionary tradition. People adjudged TEE to be inferior, offering certificates that are not accredited by the state. The problem of accreditation in African ministerial formation has remained an enduring problem. Each nation state designs its own rules and it has been impossible to weave a transnational accreditation system. This was only one of the problems that faced an alternative ecumenical model that was experimented in the period, 1965-85.

In response to nationalism and the efforts to decolonize the African churches, an outbreak of ecumenism occurred in many African countries. It may have been a survival strategy or passive revolution. But by the early 1980's most of the talks about church unity sponsored by the WCC occurred in Africa. The Church of South India provided a model for Africa. Many failed by the end of that decade because of those non-theological factors that usually ruined ecumenical endeavors. Years of intense rivalry could not be wiped away by musing on how pleasant it could be for brethren to come together. Moreover, the motivation came externally as African theological institutions and Departments of Religion in African Universities were grouped into regional associations: Southern Africa, Eastern, Central, Western, Francophone. The goals were to engage African scholars in comparing notes across denominational lines about indigenous ministerial formation patterns in the entire continent. The focus included reviewing the curricula, manpower development, improving library facilities, acquisition of books published outside the regions, Bible translation and writing of Bible commentaries by Africans for African congregations, encouragement of scholarship and journal publications. Most crucial were the opportunities for scholars from different denominations, subcultures and disciplines to meet annually from the different countries in a region. Matters became even more intriguing when in 1980 the regions were organized around the Conference of African Theological Institutions. Membership was by regional institution so as to enable them address wider continental problems.

Critics pointed to the domination by academics and lack of contact with local congregations. This was misplaced criticism precisely because most of the teachers in the University Departments were ordained pastors and priests and provided leadership both in reflection and re-directing the churches towards the indigenous routes. Indeed, such organizations enabled Western bodies to link coherently with the continent. It neutralized the virulent aspects of denominationalism. The collapse of these agencies by the late 1980s was due primarily to leadership failure. Many individuals were pressed to serve many constituencies and failed to concentrate on this task. Moreover, by this period, as the union talks collapsed, Western bodies inaugurated revamped denominational identities. The Vatican, The Lutheran World Federation, the Anglican Communion led the hunt to disable ecumenical ministerial formation in Africa.

They intensified the training of their personnel in European countries. When African Bishops pointed to the disadvantages of such foreign training, the Propaganda Fidei experimented with Catholic Higher Institutes located in Port Harcourt, Nigeria for West Africa, Nairobi for Eastern Africa and Dakar for Francophone Africa. They initiated the *doctorat troisieme cycle* programs for Francophone Africans in Younde and Congo Kinshasha. These efforts indicate a clear awareness that 'mis-formation' was at the root of the failure of African Christian leadership and weakened the presence of the churches.

They realized that when Western institutions admit and fund Africans, the curricula are not designed to serve African needs. Diversity in racial population of Western seminaries does not imply diversity in perspectives. Many Africans have to suppress their thoughts and feelings so as to gain the certificate or 'golden fleece'. A certain patronage system allows foreign students to graduate with low performance on the understanding that they are going back to their homes. This is the background to two new developments, namely, the insurgence of new formation patterns by Evangelicals and Pentecostal/Charismatic groups. As mentioned earlier, the spiritual temper and polity of these groups compelled new expectations and strategies in ministerial formation. Second, as Cephas Omenyo entitled his study, there has been a massive operation of the *Pentecost Outside Pentecostalism*. He demonstrates the charismatisation of mainline churches in Ghana. This is true for many African countries with immense implications for ministerial formation.[5] Third, this trend has catalyzed enormous growth of Christianity in Africa and created the need for more pastors than could be produced by walled schools.

Scrambled Ministerial Formation and the Rise of Christian Universities

The complexity and trauma of growth are most perceptible in emergent forms of ministerial formation. The quality of Christianity in Africa would depend on how churches train their leadership. A report by the Presbyterian Church (USA) on the Presbyterian Church in Malawi in 2004 brings out this most clearly. It observed that

Malawi is largely rural. The majority of the people are subsistence farmers, very dependent on weather conditions. In the last several years the country has experienced serious food shortages, sometimes due to drought and sometimes due to torrential rains. Government has not always been quick and efficient in responding to crises, and famine has occurred in areas of the country. Despite the harshness of life in Malawi, rapid church growth has continued. In the CCAP there is a perpetual shortage of ministers and lay leaders. There is just one theological college for the church, Zomba Theological College. It is limited in the number of candidates it can take from each synod and so, from time to time the synods have instituted their own emergency training courses for ministerial candidates.

Massive and unstoppable church growth is yielding a large cache of candidates wanting to go into the ministry. But the churches are dealing with the bulging membership with a ministerial formation strategy based on inherited patterns, walled institutions. It used to take a careful selection of candidates for the ministry, followed with a number of years of training, to produce a minister. Now, the numbers of believers, Christian forms and groups have expanded at such an incredible rate and size that the greatest need is trained personnel. Competition, conflicting theologies, and jealousy for turf add to the problem. Many cannot wait for long years of training. Many churches have resorted to de-schooling in theological education. Confident of a spiritual experience and a divine call, many people start their own ministries without formal training. It is dubbed as setting up a new altar. Thus, large numbers of church leaders with good qualifications in professional areas as medicine, architecture, academics and finance, desert their professions for full-time ministry.

In this scrambled pattern of ministerial formation, many pastors train their own leaders. Apprenticeship is often imaged as gaining a mantle. Some form an in-house Bible College within their churches where the pastor teaches all subjects and there is no need for an outside accreditation. In American black churches, such people are called "ministers in training." Others build seminaries. But the quality could be so low that an informant told me that the operators of a Christ Apostolic Church seminary merely taught the students pulpit protocols and bell-ringing. There are many seminaries with reasonable infrastructure and staff. Few are accredited because there may be no accrediting body for non-degree programs. For degree programs, some state governments are serious in restraining the grant of degrees. Approved colleges must be affiliated to state –owned universities. Many church leaders obtain degrees by taking correspondence courses from American or South Asian institutions. Singapore is a popular spot. Others simply buy certificates from fake operators. There are groups of Americans who travel through the Third World granting degrees as a way of building a worldwide network. They are the same people who ordain bishops. In some of the bizarre cases, the operators would arrive in an African country, hire a hall in an academic institution, pay in foreign currency, and organize a graduation ceremony with gowns, mortarboards and pomp. Many African countries such as Nigeria prohibit the award of offshore degrees. In Nigeria, some seminaries endeavored to form an association, Nigerian Theological Education Council, that could serve as an accreditation body in 1999. It failed to gain state recognition. In eastern Africa, some seminaries operate under the Accrediting Council for Theological Education in Africa that is run by the Association of Evangelicals in Africa, with headquarters in Nairobi. They recognize the challenge of quality control in the seminary education.

A new phenomenon has emerged as the growth of private higher education in Africa has been spurred by the intervention of churches. Admittedly, some of the private universities are secular. As Bev Thavers says,

> In East Africa, evidence points to the emergence of secular-based private higher institutions with profit motive that are managed by a new group of 'education entrepreneurs' deploying market principles in education…The application of market ideology to higher education is related to a global ideology that defines education as a private good for economic growth.[6]

In many countries, a majority of the new universities belong to religious organizations. The reasons for the explosion are: first the retreat of soft states. The hubris of African states evaporated with the collapse of economies and population growth. For instance, with a population of over 130 million, Nigerian government can no longer afford the provision of adequate tertiary education. The states can no longer afford to monopolize the education sector. It would appear that the IMF and World Bank urged African governments to adopt an ideology of liberalization, privatization and commercialization in their broad economic policies and practices. This has affected education policies and funding very dramatically. Second, the ideology of education has shifted. Education must be perceived as an investment good; it should pay its way as any other enterprise; and be available for those who could pay.

Third, the collapse of morality in state institutions has coincided with the awakening of Christian responsibility to regain a voice in a fundamental area of national life. Fourth, population increase, modernity and globalization have combined to yield a large population demanding education. There is so much desire for education in Africa that the number of tertiary institutions cannot adequately meet the need. For instance, in 1999, Central University College started in Accra with an enrollment of 428 students, increased to 952 by 2000, and over 2000 in 2003/4 academic session and currently has a student population in excess of 4, 000. If the growth rate of Central University was alarming, Covenant University located at Ota, Ogun State of Nigeria, opened its doors in 2003 with 1, 360 students: 693 females and 667 males. Its numbers and facilities tripled thereafter. Regent University of Science and Technology, Accra, garnered a student population of over 1, 000 within the two years, 2005-2007. In all cases, the Bachelor degree in Business Administration that includes a computer training component proved to be the most attractive sector. Some perceive this demand for computer training as being driven by global market economy. These forces necessitated the privatization of education. Churches that had been pushed away from primary and secondary levels of education during the heydays of national independence have re-entered the education field to invest at the tertiary level.

New Christian Universities: Visions and Mission Statements

Beyond serving as a response to globalizing forces, the visions of the universities emerge from a Pentecostal theology that privilege practical Christianity. The core moral and theological values are independence, human dignity and excellence. People do not need to be poor because they are Christians but should develop all their God-given resources and should strive to succeed in life. A vital relationship with Christ must result in an abundant and improved quality of life. Regent University of Science and Technology says that it is

> dedicated to preparing purpose-driven human resources in science and technology application for holistic socio-economic development and spiritual renewal...providing well-rounded educational opportunities, ...recognizes higher education as a national asset, and is making every effort to work with industry, employers, government, research agencies, as well as other academic and professional institutions in Ghana and around the globe.[7]

The new Christian institutions avoid the temptation to articulate the goals of the institutions in a market entrepreneurial manner. They prefer a moralistic biblical tone more appropriate for seminaries. For instance, Bishop

David Oyedepo, describes the vision of Covenant University (Otta, Lagos Nigeria) with the concept of Total Man:

> This concept centers on developing the man who will develop his world. It is designed to produce students who are intelligently conscious of their environment and who know how to maximize their potentials in life. The programs of the University are first directed at the person before addressing his profession.[8]

He insists that the curricula would ensure

> sound cultural and moral ethic, managerial and sensitive skills and self-development training designed to achieve integrated, holistic life-centered perspective.

He describes the task as the *Nehemiah Complex*, rebuilding the ethos of education in the nation that has collapsed. Thus, the context of contemporary Christian education is characterized by both an expanding demand for education, dwindling government resources, moral discourse and market orientation. Christian intervention has a theological underpinning.

For manpower development in the churches, many of the new universities image themselves to be responding to the challenges of an increased demand for an educated leadership who are locally trained and contextualized at a cheaper cost. Many church leaders do not have formal theological education and are hungry. For instance, a Master degree program designed for ecclesiastical leaders at the West African Theological Seminary, Lagos, was over subscribed by bishops from Nigeria, Liberia, Sierra Leone and Kenya. Daystar University's mission statement therefore states that:

> At Daystar, five African students can be educated for the cost of sending one student overseas. By educating committed leaders in an African context to address the needs and issues of the continent, Daystar is an important solution to Africa's 'brain drain', reversing the loss of its talented young people. Daystar University provides some of the finest Christian education available in East Africa so its graduates are prepared to boldly lead communities, businesses and churches well into the 21st century.[9]

It brags that many of the alumni are serving the nation in parliament and education sector, relief agencies and the entire society "with leadership rooted in Christian values." This harps on a typical theme that the problem of the continent is lack of a leadership with a strong ethical orientation.

It is, therefore, critical for these institutions to distinguish between entrepreneurial goals and Christian goals especially because higher institutions are cost intensive, and to respond to the challenges of funding, faculty development, adequate infrastructure and quality control. Many have embarked on unapproved postgraduate courses. As they grow, many of the mission statements posted on the websites may be challenged. For instance, Benson Idahosa University, Benin, has a vision to "raise an army of professionals and academics who would go in Christ's name to the ends of the world with the fire of the Holy Ghost to impart truth by precept and example." This leaves the impression that the institution will be engaged in training pastors. But recently, it decided to branch out into Law, Medicine, Applied Science and Management Science. The concern is that many Christian institutions find it difficult to maintain the Christian commitments when they turn into universities.[10]

Two dimensions of the phenomenon included the resilience of the culture of paper qualification and the number of churches involved. For many pastors a doctorate degree becomes a signifier or sign of the quality of a particular church. In Nigeria, the National University Commission has approved over thirty church-related universities and many secular and Muslim ones in the last decade. Among the Christian universities, some are Roman Catholic, Anglican, Christ Apostolic, Methodist, Baptist, Seventh Day Adventist, Evangelical Church of West Africa and many are owned by Pentecostal groups. The trend can be documented for the entire continent. It is still spreading because many churches revamp old Teachers' Colleges and Bible Colleges.

Values as An Acrostic for Evaluating Theological Education

The pattern of ministerial formation has been scrambled, creating a trauma for African Christianity. Who could control all these institutions and ensure an accredited performance, a liberating curriculum, and manpower development for the churches? In 2000, the Vice Chancellors of five private universities met in Dar es Salaam to establish the Tanzania Association of Private Universities to bring some order into the new system. Competition is rife among the churches and hinders useful co-operation because to found a higher institution has become the mark of a successful church in the African environment. We must, therefore, conclude by raising the question whether the new Christian universities will serve the cause of theological education in Africa in the 21st century.

The first concern is that the new universities are not seminaries or even divinity schools devoted to studying comparative religions. But they have religious roots, and sports departments devoted to continuing what the old bible schools did. This explains the tendency by the national accrediting boards to approve the theological components of Christian universities while suspicious about their other intentions. The *visions* must be stated in two ways to show both broad aims and specific goals. Beyond the hortatory statements, the numerical growth in a bulging market hide the deep problems of organizing universities along Christian principles or replicating what missionaries achieved by using educational institutions for ministerial formation. This would require a disciplined regimen that may be unsustainable in the emergent cultures of African societies. Examples abound in South Korea and in the northern globe of such experiments. It is not clear that there is sensitivity to the pluralistic shape of the religious landscape. Every department needs to state its own vision in measurable ways.

This leads to the second problem of *academics and accreditation*: recruitment and development of faculty, staff and students, salaries, infrastructure and location, funding, curriculum, accreditation and learning outcome assessment. Many institutions find it difficult to recruit adequate faculty because the state universities garner the best; the level of emigration of African academics; the remuneration and employment packages. Adjunct faculty alleviate the situation but accreditation panels reject this option. In a broad university structure, the religious department may not have sufficient numbers to pay for adequate number of faculty. Recruitment of students in non-denominational universities is tricky and may depend on the capacity to offer scholarships. New universities require roots in congregations, alumni bodies and creative advertisement before they could compete. Infrastructure is essential because location in urban areas may enable a higher recruitment and enable the institution to deploy resources in academic infrastructure. Debate rages about urban/ suburban location and single/multi-campus options. Covenant, Daystar, International Central and Idahosa's universities are moving towards single, large campus options in semi-urban locations. Implications include deploying resources from purely academic recurrent expenditure to housing of faculty, staff and students. It may affect the possibility of utilizing adjunct faculty from other institutions and the corporate world. Libraries and laboratories constitute the most urgent need for all institutions to ensure the quality of teaching, research, the combination of theory and practice and reputation.

Our people say that money provides good meals. Funding in the universities come from seven possible sources: denominations, bank loans, fees, external sources, endowments/philanthropy, research/consultancy and alumni. My guess is that the last three play little role. None has launched a professional fund-raising campaign. Fees rank highest especially for professional courses. Generally, fees are higher in private universities than in state-owned universities. Some, like the Church of the Pentecost in Ghana, raise special funds for its university from congregations located at home and abroad.

An area that needs discussion is contextualized curriculum. The theology departments must design a different type of curricula that privilege the African worldview and cultures. Here the concept of Africentricity must be fully discussed and deployed because it addresses the problem of identity and education. An educational model that is not rooted in the African world and spirituality perpetuates colonial mentality and dependency on the resources of externality. African institutions must rear people who critically engage both indigenous and contemporary realities, who read fellow Africans and turn knowledge into commitment. For those entering the ministry, schools must use field placement to connect students to congregations from the third year in a four-year program or second of a three-year program. Faculty must dialogue about new methods of pedagogy and include more visual aids, information technology, dialogue and non-magisterial approaches. The universities must emphasize the practical curricula adumbrated in their mission statements. They should mobilize the alumni through associations, regular mailing of newsletter, and continuing education events. Accreditation is shaping as the bane for the many of the private universities. This problem differs from country to country. In Ghana and Kenya, no one would dare start an institution that is not approved by state agencies. The dilemma in Nigeria is that after rejecting state control, the Christian institutions cannot accept the governance of any external agency. The poorly-equipped institutions band together to check-mate any form of accountability and quality control.

Leadership is an essential value—honest, creative administrative leadership is crucial. The product—content depends on the ethos of the institution. Every effort should be made to inculcate salient Christian values that include healthy gender relationship, courtesy, and sensitive non-exploitative ethics. Schools should reward creativity and active leadership traits. We must continuously ask ourselves: What measures are used to maintain cleanliness, accountability and hard work? How does an institution instill Christian values in students engaged in technical studies? In Yonsei Universities, attendance at chapel is compulsory. When Covenant University imposed a pregnancy and HIV/AIDS test for its graduating students in 2007, the National University Commission intervened to declare the moral control as an abuse of human rights of the students.

Unity and avoidance of duplication is the bane of the religious landscape in Africa. Rivalry, struggle for turf in a competitive religious market place, and personality cult have vitiated the capacity for sharing of resources. There are no cross-registration of courses among institutions located in the same city! The scandal of disunity and the death of ecumenism in African religious landscape are signified by the competing universities.

Ethical dimension of education appears in every mission statement. Yet the advisory system is not properly developed to ensure mentoring. Enormous responsibilities are placed on the students to be accountable and disciplined. For instance, matriculants at Regent University sign a matriculation oath pledging a "wholehearted commitment to Regent vision" because the institution has been "established on the authority of God's word." In Ghana, the national accreditation board specified certain peer assessment measures. Regent University interpreted these heavily by insisting that "all lecturers will have to sign an attendance register in the office of their respective heads of department. They are also required to keep a journal/log book in which they will record, inter alia, time spent" on various functions including teaching, tutorial, mentoring/counseling, lecture preparation, research, project supervision and many others that draw attention to the *social commitment* of the institution.[11] Discipline will be essential for the survival of the new universities. They will need to engage the public space as a means of gaining credibility and visibility in an intensely competitive market. In conclusion, neither the church officers that are spearheading the investment in Christian universities nor the congregations are certain that the universities are the primary training grounds for equipping the manpower for the churches. But they have the potential for intervention in postgraduate training and for re-moralizing the education systems of African nations.

The First Regent Divinity Lecture, Regent University of Science and Technology, Accra, Friday, June 5th, 2007

Notes

1. Ogbu U Kalu, "Elijah's Mantle: Ministerial Formation in Contemporary African Christianity", *International Review of Mission*, 94, no.373(April, 2005):263-277.

2. John R. Mott, *The Decisive Hour of Christian Missions* (New York, NY: Student Volunteer Movement for Foreign Missions, 1912), 114.

3. Ross Kinsler, *The Extension Movement in Theological Education: A Call to the Renewal of the Ministry* (Pasadena, CA: William Carey Library, 1978); Gert

J. Steyn, "The Future of Theological Education by Extension in Africa," *Missionalia* 32, no. 1 (2004).

4. Graham A. Duncan, "Theological Education: Mission Birth-African Renaissance," *Missionalia* 28, no. 1 (2000), 35.

5. Cephas Omenyo, *Pentecost Outside Pentecostalism* (Zoetmeer:Boekecentrum, 2002).

6. Jeffrey S. Hittenberger, "Globalization, Marketization, and the Mission of Pentecostal Higher Education in Africa, " *Pneuma* 26, no. 2 (2004); Beth Tavers, "Private Higher Education in Africa: Six Country Case Studies, " in *African Higher Education: An International Reference Handbook*, ed. Damtev Teferra and Philip G. Altbach (Bloomington, IN: Indiana University Press, 2003), 53-60. My field work was conducted in the summer of 2005 and 2007.

7. Message from the President, Brochure, 2nd Matriculation Ceremony, February 27th, 2007, p. 7.

8. www.covenantuniversity.com/aboutmain.htm; David Oyedepo. "Influencing the External Environment" (paper presented at Meeting the Challenges of Higher Education in Africa: The Role of Private Universities, Nairobi, Kenya, 2003).

9. www.daystarus.org.

10. www.idahosauniversity.com.

11. Regent University of Science and Technology, Accra, *The Voice of Regent*, May 2007, 18.

Ogbu Kalu:
Curriculum Vitae

OGBU UKE KALU
Henry Winters Luce Professor of World Christianity and Mission
McCormick Theological Seminary, Chicago

Awards, Honors, Fellowships, and Membership (Abridged)

Honors and Awards
- D.D., Presbyterian College, McGill University
- Vice-Chancellor's Research Leadership Prize, University of Nigeria
- Mwalimu (Professor) Toyin Falola Award for *African Pentecostalism: An Introduction* (Oxford University Press, 2008)
- *Festschrift*: Chima J. Korieh and G. Ugo Nwokeji (eds.) *Religion, History and Politics in Nigeria: Essays in Honor of Ogbu U. Kalu* (Lanham: University Press of America, Inc., 2005)

University of Nigeria, Nsukka: Positions and Membership of Boards and Committees

- Member, the Senate of the University of Nigeria, Nsukka (UNN), 1976-2001

- Coordinator, Humanities Section, Division of General Studies, UNN, 1976-1978
- Director, Division of General Studies, UNN, 1978-1980
- Dean, Faculty of the Social Sciences, UNN, 1980-1982
- Member, Governing Council of the University, UNN, 1980-1984
- Head, Department of Religion, UNN, 1984-1986
- Director, Institute of African Studies, UNN, 1983, 1995/6
- Chairman, Management Information Service Unit, UNN, 1994-1998

McCormick Theological Seminary: Membership of Boards and Committees

- Board of Trustees, McCormick Theological Seminary
- Director, Chicago Center for Global Ministries
- Associate Dean, D.Min. Program
- Member, Admission Committee
- Member, Search Committee
- Professorial Review Committee

Membership of Academic/Professional Associations:

- Vice President, *Association of Midwest Professors of Mission*
- Member, *American Society for Church History*
- Member, *Society for Pentecostal Studies*
- Member, *History of the World Christian Movement Project* (Pew Trust funded)-
- Executive Member, *Currents in World Christianity* (Cambridge University)
- Chair, Executive Board, Section on Evangelicalism and Globalism, 1998
- Member, Mid-West Association of Professors of Mission
- Member, American Missiological Society
- Member, Igbo Studies Association
- Member, International Association for Mission Studies

Editorial Board Membership

- *African Theological Journal* (Tanzania)
- *Journal of Religion in Africa* (Leeds)
- *Bulletin de Theologie Africaine* (Zaire)
- *Kabiara* (University of Port-Harcourt)
- *Ikenga* (University of Nigeria)
- *Journal of Religion and Theology* (Anglican Communion, Nigeria)
- *Studia Historiae Ecclesiaticae* (Church History Society of Southern Africa)
- *Bulletin for Contextual Theology* (University of Natal, Pietermariztburg, South Africa)
- *Nigerian Journal of the Social Sciences* (University of Nigeria) (Editorial Consultant), 2002

Editorship

- *West African Religions*
- *Nigerian Journal of Social Studies*

External Examiner and Faculty Assessor in African Institutions

- Nigeria: University of Jos, Ife, Ibadan, Ilorin, Port-Harcourt, Calabar, Bendel State
- Other African Countries: University of Ghana, Legon, Cape Coast, Cape Town
- Chief Examiner, West African Examinations Council (1978-1983)

Offices in Ecumenical Organizations

- Secretary General, West African Association of Theological Institutions
- Member, Board of Management, Institute of Church and Society, Ibadan
- Chairman, Conference of African Theological Institutions, (Nairobi, Kenya), 1980-1984
- Present Coordinator, Church History Projects for WAATI and CATI, 1980 - present

- Coordinator, History of the Church in Africa, a multivolume series sponsored by the Ecumenical Association of Third World Theologians and Roman Catholic Mission, (Aachen, West Germany), 1986- present
- Secretary and Coordinator, Association of African Church Historians, 1986-Present
- One of three Executive Directors, Working Commission on the History of the Church in the Third World, London, 1989-present
- Member, Governing Council, Spiritan School of Theology, Enugu (Holy Ghost Fathers, Roman Catholic Church), 1996-present
- Co-Director, International Project on Evangelicalism and Globalism, 1997-present
- Member, Executive Board, Currents in World Christianity, University of Cambridge; Chair, Executive Board, Section on Evangelicalism and Globalism, 1998
- Life Member, Gideon International Bible Society (The Gideons International in Nigeria)
- Zonal Patron (East), Scripture Union, Nigeria.

Church Leadership and Activities

- Elder, Presbyterian Church of Nigeria (PCN), 1976-Present
- Secretary, Board of Faith and Order, PCN, 1980-1986
- Member, Administrative Council, PCN, 1980-1986
- Member, Board of Christian Education, PCN, 1986-1990
- Member, General Assembly Board of Faith and Order, 1991-Present
- Chairman, Book Project, 150th Anniversary of the PCN, 1993/95
- Member, Intercessors for Africa Prayer Project, Nigeria, 2002

Theological Education & Congregation Life in Chicago

- Dean of Studies, Progressive Bible Institute, Progressive Community Church, Bronzeville, Chicago
- Member, Steering Committee, Center for African-American Theological Studies, Chicago
- Member, Prayer for City of Chicago Project

I. Name: KALU, OGBU UKE

Institution: McCormick Theological Seminary, Chicago
5460 South University Avenue,
Chicago, IL.60615, USA
Tel.773-947-6354 <okalu@mccormick.edu>

II. Present position

(i)   Henry Winters Luce Professor of World Christianity and Mission, 2001-present;
(ii) Associate Director, Chicago Center for Global Ministries, June 2002-2005;
(iii) Director, CCGM, June 2005-2009.
(iv) Member, Board of Trustees, McCormick Theological Seminary, 2006-2008

III. University Education

- 1963/64-1966/67   University of Toronto, Canada
- 1967/68   McMaster University, Canada
- 1968/69-1969/70   University of Toronto, Canada
- 1970/72   Institute of Historical Research, University of London
- 1972-1974   Princeton Theological Seminary, USA

IV. Academic Qualification

- 1967   B.A. Hons, History, University of Toronto, Ontario, Canada
- 1968   M.A. Summa cum laude, History, McMaster University, Ontario, Canada
- 1972   Ph.D., History, University of Toronto
- 1974   M.Div., Princeton Theological Seminary
- 1997   D.D., Presbyterian College, Montreal, Que. Canada

V. Scholarships and Prizes

Secondary School: Owuwa Anyanwu Native Authority Scholarship

1963-1967	University of Toronto: Presbyterian Church of Canada Scholarship
1967-1968	University Teaching Fellowship, McMaster University
	• University Scholarship (Faculty of Arts, 1967),
	• Nominated for Woodrow Wilson National Fellowship
1968-1969	The Waring Fellowship, University of Toronto
1968-1969	University of Toronto Open Fellowship
1968/69-1969/70	Province of Ontario Graduate Award
1970-1972	Canada Council for the Arts Fellowship: University of London, UK
1972-1974	Princeton Theological Seminary Fellowship
1973	Ecumenical Commission Research Grant
1974	Grier-Davies Award, Princeton
1986	Vice-Chancellor's Research Leadership Prize, University of Nigeria
1995	UNIFEM/UNDP Grant on "Silent Victims: Violence Against Women in Nigerian Universities." Social Science Council of Nigeria Research Grant
1999	Pew Trust Research Enablement Grant
2000	Ford International Scholar Award

VI. Teaching Career

1974-1976	Lecturer Grade 1
1976-1978	Senior Lecturer
1978-2001	Professor of Church History, University of Nigeria, Nsukka
1987	Visiting Lilly Professor, Christian Theological Seminary, Indianapolis, Indiana, USA

1988	Visiting Professor for World Missions, Presbyterian Theological Seminary, Seoul, South Korea.
1992/93	Senior Research Fellow, Center of the Study of Christianity in the Non-Western World, and Visiting Professor, New College, University of Edinburgh, Edinburgh
1995	Visiting Professor, University of Pretoria, South Africa
1996	Charles Johnson Scholar, and Visiting Professor Knox College, University of Toronto and Presbyterian College, McGill University, Montreal, Canada.
1997	Visiting Professor, Faculty of Religious Studies, McGill University.
1998	Visiting Professor, Emmanuel College, University of Toronto
1999	Visiting Professor, Harvard Divinity School and Senior Research Fellow, Center for the Study of World Religions, Harvard University
2000	Visiting Professor, *Ls Religionwissenchaft*, University of Bayreuth, Germany

VII. Honours and Distinctions

- Fellow of the Historical Society of Nigeria (FHSN)
- Men of Achievement (Cambridge) Vol. VII
- Who's Who in America: Contemporary Authors, Vol. 93- 96
- The International Author's and Writer's Who's Who, Vol. IX
- A **Festschrift** in my honor: *Religion, History and Politics in Nigeria Essays in Honor of Ogbu U. Kalu* ed. Chima J.Korieh and G. Ugo Nwokeji (Lanham: University Press of America Inc., 2005)

Distinguished Lectureships

- Paul B Henry Lecture, Calvin College, 2003.
- Burgess Lecture, 2003, Luther Seminary, 2003.
- Towards Edinburgh 2010 Lectures, New College, University of Edinburgh and Glasgow, 2004

- African Studies Lectures, Harvard University, 2004, 2005, 2006, 2007
- African History Lectures, Trinity International University, 2004
- World Christianity Lectures, Westmont College, Santa Barbara, CA, 2005
- Convocation Lecture, Lutheran Theological Seminary at Philadelphia, 2006
- Regent Divinity Lecture, 2007 (5th June, 2007), Regent University of Science and Technology, Accra, Ghana
- ERANOS TAGUNG and Lecture, Ascona, Switzerland, August 10th, 2007
- ERANOS TAGUNG and Lecture, Ascona, Switzerland, June 10th, 2008

VIII. Membership of Boards of Academic Journals

(I) Member, Editorial Board of:

- *African Theological Journal (Tanzania)*
- *Journal of Religion in Africa* (Leeds)
- *Bulletin de Theologie Africaine* (Zaire)
- *Kabiara* (University of Port-Harcourt)
- *Ikenga* (University of Nigeria)
- *Journal of Religion and Theology* (Anglican Communion, Nigeria)
- *Studia Historiae Ecclesiasticae* (Church History Society of Southern Africa)
- *Bulletin for Contextual Theology* (University of Natal, Pietermariztburg, South Africa)
- *Kosimme: Journal of Arts and Religion*, Alvan Ikoku College of Education, Owerri, Nigeria
- *Journal of World Christianity* (Harvard)

(ii) Editor:

(a) 1975-1987   *West African Religion*
(b) 1977-1980   *Religions*
(c) 1979-1982   *Nigerian Journal of Social Studies*

IX. Membership of Professional Bodies

- American Society for Church History
- Society for Pentecostal Studies
- President, Mid-West Association of Professors of Mission
- International Association for Mission Studies
- American Society of Missiology
- Igbo Studies Association
- 1978-1983 **Chief Examiner**, West African Examinations Council

X. Offices In Ecumenical Organisations

1970-1981	Secretary General, West African Association of Theological Institutions
1977-1988	Board of Management, Institute of Church and Society, Ibadan
1980-1984	Chairman, Conference of African Theological Institutions, (Nairobi, Kenya)
1980-1996	Coordinator, Church History Projects for WAATI and CATI
1986-Present	Coordinator, History of the Church in Africa, a multi-volume series sponsored by the Ecumenical Association of Third World Theologians and Roman Catholic Mission
1986-1996	Secretary and Coordinator, Association of African Church Historians
1989-Present	One of three Executive Directors, Working Commission on the History of the Church in the Third World, London
1996-2001	Member Governing Council, Spiritan School of Theology, Enugu (Holy Ghost Fathers, Roman Catholic Church)
1997-Present	Co-Director, International Project on Evangelicalism and Globalism.
1998-2001	Member, Executive Board, Currents in World Christianity, University of Cambridge;

	Chair, Executive Board, Section of CWC on Evangelicalism and Globalism.
1998-Present	Member: History of World Christian Movement Project (Pittsburgh Theological Seminary) Funded by Luce Foundation.
2002-05	Associate Director, Chicago Center for Global Ministries (CCGM)
2005-2009	Director, CCGM
2002-2003	Vice President, Midwest Association of Professors of Mission
2003-2004	President, Midwest Association of Professors of Mission

XI. Offices in University of Nigeria, 1974-2001

1976-2001	Member, the Senate of the University
1976-1978	Coordinator, Humanities Section, Division of General Studies
1978-1980	Director, Division of General Studies
1980-1982	Dean, Faculty of the Social Sciences
1980-1984	Member, Governing Council of the University
1984-1986	Head, Department of Religion
1983, 1995/6	Director, Institute of African Studies
1994-1998; 2000-2001	Chairman, Management Information Service Unit

XII. Offices in the Presbyterian Church in Nigeria (PCN)

1976-Present	Elder, Presbyterian Church of Nigeria
1980-1986	Secretary, Board of Faith and Order, PCN
1980-1986	Member, Administrative Council, PCN
1986-1990	Member, Board of Christian Education, PCN
1991-Present	Member, General Assembly Board of Faith and Order
1993/95	Chairman, Book Project, 150th Anniversary of the PCN

IX. Publications

Published books

1. Editor, *Christianity in West Africa: The Nigerian Story*. (Ibadan: Daystar Press, 1978), 348 pp.

2. *Divided People of God: Church Union Movement in Nigeria, 1875-1966*. (New York: NOK Publishers Ltd/Doubleday, 1978).

3. Editor, *Readings in African Humanities: African Cultural Development*. (Enugu: Fourth Dimension Publishers, 1978).

4. Editor, *The History of Christianity in West Africa*. (London: Longman, 1980), 378 pp.

5. Editor, *African Church Historiography: An Ecumenical Perspective*. (Editor), (Bern, Switzerland: Evangelische Arbeitsstelle Oekumene Schweiz, 1988).

6. *Surviving in the Wilderness: Cameos of a Groping Faith*. (Enugu: Gospel Communications Inc., 1992).

7. *The Embattled Gods: Christianization of Igboland, 1841-1991* (London & Lagos, Minaj Publishers, 1996), 358 pp. *Republished* by Africa World Press, Trenton, NJ, 2003

8. Editor, *One Hundred and Fifty Years of Presbyterian Witness in Nigeria, 1846-1996*. (Enugu: Presbyterian Church in Nigeria, 1996).

9. M. Hutchinson and O.U.Kalu eds., *Global Faith: Essays on Evangelicalism and Globalism*. (Sydney: Center for the Study of Australian Christianity, 1998).

10. With O.N. Njoku and C.N. Ubah (Co-editors), *A Tapestry of the African Past*. Woven in Honor of A. E. Afigbo (Lagos: Vista Books, 1996)

11. *Power, Poverty and Prayer: The Challenges of Poverty and Pluralism in African Christianity, 1960-1996.*(Frankfurt am Main: Peter Lang, 2000). Republished by Africa World Press, Trenton NJ, 2005

12. *Scourge of the Vandals: The Nature and Control of Cults in the Nigerian University System* (Enugu: University of Nigeria Press, 2001)

13. Editor, *African Christianity: An African Story* (Pretoria: University of Pretoria, Perspectives Series, 2005. Republished: Africa World Press, Trenton, 2007). Declared as one of the Fifteen Outstanding Books of 2005 for Mission Studies. International Bull of Mission Research, 30, 1(Jan 2006), 43.

14. David Esterline and Ogbu U. Kalu, *eds. Shaping Beloved Community: Multicultural Theological Education* (Louisville: Westminster John Knox Publishers, 2006)

15. Editor, *Interpreting Contemporary Christianity: Global Processes and Local Identities* (Grand Rapids: Eerdmans, 2008).

16. *Clio In a Sacred Garb: Essays on Christian Presence and African Responses, 1900-2000* Published under the *African Christian Initiatives Series,* edited by Professors Inus Daneel and Dana Robert (Trenton, NJ: Africa World Press, 2008). 346pp

17. *African Pentecostalism: An Introduction.* (New York: Oxford University Press, New York, 2008). 357pp. Won the Africa Book Award, Association of Third World Scholars, 2008.

18. Editor, *After the Christendom: Emergent Themes in Contemporary Mission* (Louisville, KY: Westminster John Knox Press) forthcoming

Completed Manuscript

19. *Religious Policy and Practice in Jacobean England, 1604-1634.* 224pp.

Articles, 1975-1994

I. African Traditional Religion

1. "Precarious Vision: The African's Perception of His World: in *Readings in African Humanities,* Chapter 3. Also in E. M. Uka (Editor*), Readings in African Traditional Religion.* (Bern: Peter Lang, 1991): 11-18.

2. with Humphrey N.Nwosu "The Study of African Culture," *Readings in African Humanities,* Chapter 1.

3. "Nsibidi: Pictographic Communication in Pre-Colonial Cross-River Basin Societies", *Cahiers d'Etudes des Religions Africaines,* XII, 23/4 (Jan- Juliet, 1978): 97-116.

4. "Gods in Retreat: Models of Religious Change in Africa", *Nigerian Journal of the Humanities.* (University of Benin), 1, (Sept. 1977): 42-53

5. "The Traditional Religious Structures of Igboland: in G. E. K. Ofomata (Editor), *A Survey of Igboland.* (Onitsha: Africana-FEP Publishers, 1987): 476-507.

6. "Religion and Political Values in Nigeria: A Pluralistic Perspective: in *Religious Pluralism in Africa.* (New York: Pergamon, 1985).

7. "African Traditional Religion in Western Scholarship; in E. M. Uka (Editor), *Readings in African Traditional Religion: Structure, Meaning, Relevance, and Future.* (New York: Peter Lang, 1991): 91-108.

8. "The Study of Traditional Medicine, Healing and Religion" Keynote Address, Conference on Traditional Medicine, Healing and Religion. The Nigerian Association for the Study of Religion, Obafemi Awolowo University, Ile-Ife, Nigeria. (1986).

9. "Gods as Policemen: Religion and Social Control in Igboland", in J. K. Olupona (Editor), *Religious Plurality in Africa, Festschrift to Prof. J. S. Mbiti* (Leiden: Mouton de Gruyter, 1993): 109-131.

10. "Religion and Social Control in Cross-River Igboland", *Nigerian Journal* of *Theology,* 2, 1, (1988): 1-18.

11. "Under the Eyes of the Gods: Sacralization and Control of Social Order in Igboland", *Ahiajoku Colloquium,* (Owerri: Ministry of Information and Culture, 1988): 35-58.

12. "Ritual and Efficacy in Traditional African Medicine", 2nd Traditional Medicine Fair, National Arts Theatre, Lagos, 9-10th April, (1989). Organisers: Professors Sofowora and Wande Abimbola.

13. "Gender Ideology in Igbo Religion: The Changing Religious Role of Igbo Women", in A. E. Afigbo, *Igbo Women in Socio-Economic Change.* (Lagos: Vista Books, 1992). Also in *Africa,* 46, 2 (Guigno, 1991): 184- 202.

14. With U. Onuwa and E. Inyama, "Gods of Our Fathers: A Taxonomy of Igbo Deities", Seminar on Igbo World View, Institute of African Studies, University of Nigeria, Nsukka, Nigeria.1989.

15. "Responsibility of Power: Ethical Values and the Igbo Tradition of Politics", in U.D. Anyanwu & J.C. Aguwa (Editors), *The Igbo and the Tradition of Politics.* (Enugu: Fourth Dimension Publishers, 1993): 9-20

16. With W.J. Kalu, "Gender Roles Among the Igbo of South-Eastern Nigeria", *International Handbook of Gender Roles,* ed Leonore Loeb Adler (Wesport: Greenwood Press, 1993): 228-243.

17. "The Study of African Traditional Religion: A Select Bibliography till 1990", in E.M. Uka (Editor), *Readings in African Traditional Religion*, (New York: Peter Lang, 1991): 355-381.

18. "The Cross, the Crescent and the Serpent: Historical Strands of Religious Interaction in Nigeria", in R.D. Abubakre et als eds. *Studies in Religious Understanding in Nigeria* (Lagos: The Nigerian Association for the Study of Religions, 1993): 129-154.

II. English History

19. Ph.D. Dissertation. "The Jacobean Church and Essex Puritans, 1604-1628" (Department of History, University of Toronto, 1972).

20. "When the Bishop Came to Essex in 1605: Analysis of Bishop Vaughan's Episcopal Visitation", *Transactions of Essex Archaeological Society*. (Chelmsford, Essex, Spring, 1973).

21. "Puritans and Bishops in Jacobean England: A Methodological Perspective", *Church History*, University of Chicago, 45, 4, (Dec. 1976): 469-489.

22. "Continuity in Change: Bishops of London and Religious Dissent in Early Stuart England", *Journal of British Studies*, 18, 1, (Fall 1978): 28-45.

III. Historiography

23. "Kirchengeschicte in Afrika Heute", *Theologische Zeitschrift*, (University Basel), Jahr. 38 heft, 5, (Sept-Okt. 1982): 433-454.

24. "Over a Century of Christian Presence in Africa: A Historical Analysis", in Appiah-Kubi and Torres (Editors), *African Theology En Route*. (New York: Orbis Books, 1979): 13-22. A longer version in *Bulletin de Theologie Africaine*, 1, 2 (Jan. 1979): 113-126.

25. "Moral Judgment in History", *Nsukka Journal of Humanities*, 2, (Dec. 1987): 21-38.

26. "African Church Historiography: An Ecumenical Perspective", *Encounter*, 50, 1, (Winter 1989): 69-79; A longer version in *African Church Historiography*. (Bern, 1988): chapter 1.

27. "Color and Conversion: The White Factor in Christianization of Igboland, 1857-1970", *Missiology*, 18, 1, (Jan. 1990): 61-74.

28. "The Irony of Colonialism: Formulation of Cultural Policy in Colonial Nigeria", *Tradition and Modern Culture*. ed. Edith Ihek-weazu (Fourth Dimension Publications, 1985): 125-138.
29. "Odd Couples?: The Study of Christianity as an Academic Discipline", *Religions*, 1, 1, (Dec. 1976): 51-57.
30. "Afrika-Mission in der Koloiazeit/De Berliner Kongokonferenze von 1884/5 und die Entwick lun des Christentums in Westafrika", *Evangelische Mission Jahrubuch*, (Hamburg, 1985): 94-106.
31. "The Berlin-West Africa Conference and the Development of Christianity in West Africa", *Ikenga: Journal of the Institute of African Studies*, 61/2 (1984): 58-66.
32. "Broken Covenants: Religious Change in Igbo Historiography", *Neue Zeitschrift fur Missionwissenschaft*, 46, 4, (1990): 298-311.
33. "Writing the History of the Church in The Third World: The African Agenda", Africa's Position Paper, Workshop on the History of the Church in the Third World, London, July 1989.
34. "Images and Lenses: The Igbo in Early Missionary Records 1841-1945", in A. E. Afigbo (ed.) *The Image of the Igbo* (Lagos: Vista Books, 1992): 120-140.
35. "African Church Historiography", *African Historiography: Essays in Honor of J. F. Ade Ajayi*. ed Toyin Falola (London: Longman, 1991): 171-184.
36. "Decolonizing Church Historiography: The African Experience, 1986- 1996", Keynote Address, Workshop on African Church History, Harare, August 1992.
37. "Beyond Nationalist Historiography: White Indigenizers of the Igbo Church, 1876-1892", in *A Tapestry of the African Past Woven in Honor of Adiele Afigbo* (Lagos: Vista Books, 1993).

IV. African Church History

38. "Church Unity and Religious Change in Africa", in R Gray, et als. *Christianity in Independent Africa*. (London: Rex Collings, 1978): 164- 178.
39. "Protestant Christianity in Igboland, in *History of Christianity in West Africa, The Nigerian Story*: chapter 10.
40. "Church, Mission, and Moratorium", *The History of Christianity in West Africa* (London, Longmans, 1980): 365-374.
41. "The Shattered Cross: The Church Union Movement in Nigeria, 1905- 1966", ibid., : 340-363.

42. "Church Administration in Nigeria", *Problems In Administration In Nigeria*. Ed H.N. Nwosu (Fourth Dimension Publishers, 1985): 222-248.

43. "Moratorium and All That", in *The Future of the Historical Missionary Enterprise*. (New York: IDOC Publications, 1974): volume 9, 52-8.

44. "Peter Pan Syndrome: Church Aid and Selfhood in Africa", *Missiology*, (Continuing Practical Anthropology), 3, 1, (January, 1975): 15-29.

45. "Not Just New Relationships but a Renewed Body", *International Review of Missions*. (Geneva), 64, 254, (April, 1975): 143-147.

46. "The Politics of Religious Sectarianism in Africa", *West African Religion*, 16, 1, (January, 1975): 16-25.

47. "Traditionalization and Modern Evangelical Strategy in Nigeria", *West African Religion*, 16, 2, (1975): 22-31.

48. "Tradition in Revolutionary Change", *Ikenga*: Journal of The Institute of African Studies, 3, 1/2, (January-July, 1975): 53-58.

49. "Waves From the Rivers: The Spread of Garrick Braide Movement in Igboland, 1914-1934", *Journal of the Historical Society of Nigeria*, 8, 4, (June, 1977): 95-110.

50. "Missionaries, Colonial Government and Secret Societies in South Eastern Igboland", *Journal of the Historical Society of Nigeria*, 9, 1, (December, 1977): 75-90.

51. "Battle of the Gods: Christianization of Cross-River Igboland, 1903- 1950", *Journal of the Historical Society of Nigeria*, 10, 1, (1979): 1-18.

52. "Children in the Missionary Enterprise of the 19th Century", *Calabar Historical Journal* (University of Calabar), 2, 1, (1978).

53. "Requiem to a Lost Register", *Journal of Niger Delta Studies*, 1, 4, (1979).

54. "The Rhythm of Religious Dissent: An African Perception of the Survival of Puritanism in 17th Century England"" *African Theological Journal*, 8, 1, (1979): 34-49.

55. "Early Primitive Methodists on the Railroad Junctions of Igboland, 1910- 1931", *Journal of Religion in Africa*, 16, 1, (Leiden, EJBrill, 1986): 44-66.

56. "The Religious Factor in Nigerian History", *Teaching History in Nigerian Schools*. ed. J.A Atanda (Historical Society of Nigeria Special Publication, 1986).

57. "Religion in Nigeria: An Overview", *History of Nigeria Since Independence: The First 25 Years.* (Presidential Committee on the History of Nigeria: ed J. A. Atanda, et als.(Ibadan: Heinemann Educational Books Ltd., 1989), Vol. Ix: 11-24.

58. "Christianization of Igboland, 1857-1967", *Groundwork of Igbo History*, ed. A.E Afigbo (Lagos: Vista Books Ltd., 1992): 487-521.

59. "Education and Change in Igboland, 1857-1967", *Ibid.:* 522-541.

60. "Ebony Kinship: Black Americans in the Evangelization of Africa, 1820- 1920", *Leadership Development in the Black Church*, ed. in Rufus Burrow (Indianapolis, 1988).

61. "Christian Witness in the Third World of the 1980s", *Occasional Publications of the Center for the Study of World Missions*, Presbyterian Theological Seminary, Seoul, South Korea, 1988.

62. Reviews in Church History:

   (1) I. R. A. Ozigbo, *Igbo Catholicism* In *Nsukka Journal of History*, 1, 1, (December 1989): 172-177.

   (2) F. K Ekechi, *Tradition and Transformation in Eastern Nigeria* In *Journal of Religion in Africa*, 20, 3, (October 1990): 312-313.

   (3) I. Okpewho, *Myth in Africa*, In *JRA*, 19, 1, (1989): 86-88.

   (4) R. Gray, *Black Christians and White Missionaries* In *JRA*, 22, 2 (May 1992): 186-187.

63. "Evangelizing Africa in the Year 2000 AD: The Ecumenical Dimension", in J. S. Ukpong (Editor), *The Church in Africa and the Special Africa Synod*, (Port Hacourt: Catholic Institute for West Africa, Publications, 1993): 30-50.

64. "Wind of God: Evangelical Pentecostalism in Igboland, 1970-1990", The Pew Charitable Trusts Seminar. Center for the Study of Christianity inn Non-Western World. New College, University of Edinburgh, December, 1992.

65. "The Balm of Gilead: Christianity and Inner Healing of War Wounds in Igboland, 1966-1986", *Healing the Social Wounds of War* ed. Murray Last (Edinburgh: University of Edinburgh Press, 1993): chapter 14.

66. "Testing the Spirits: A Typology of Christianity in Igboland Revisited, 1890-1990", The Pew Charitable Trusts Seminar, Center for the Study of Christianity in Non-Western World, New College, University of Edinburgh, January, 1993.

67. "Church-State Relations in Nigeria, 1900-1990", Special Edition, *Horizon: Journal of Theology*, 1992.

68. "The Dilemma of Grassroot Inculturation of the Gospel: A Case Study of a Modern Controversy in Igboland, 1983-1989", *Journal of Religion in Africa*, 25, 1, (Feb. 1995): 48-72.

V. Theology

69. "Conscientization and Religious Education: Pauolo Freire Revisited", *Religious Periscope: A Journal of Religious Studies*, 1, 1, (September, 1988): 40-51.

70. "J. M. Lee and Social Sciences Approach to Religious Education", *West African Journal of Education*, 21, 1, (1980): 123-138.

71. "Theology of Power in Contemporary Nigeria", *Ikenga; Journal of Institute of African Studies*, 7, 1/2, (1985): 1-10.

72. "Religion as a Factor in National Development", *Readings in Social Sciences: Issues in National Development*.ed. E.C.Amucheazi (Enugu: Fourth Dimension Publishers, 1980): 307-319.

73. "Theological Ethics and Development in an African Context", *Missiology* (California), 4, 4, (October, 1976): 455-464.

74. "Theology of Unity in the Letters of Ignatius of Antioch", *ORITA: Ibadan Journal of Religious Studies*, 11, 1, (June, 1977): 15-27.

75. "The Living God and the New Humanity: An African Response", *The Augsburg Confession in Asia Today*.ed. Y.Tokuzen (Geneva: LWF Publication, 1983): 69-92.

76. "Some Aspects of the Theology and Strategy of Mission in the Africa of the 1980's in *Christian Theology and Strategy for Mission*. (Geneva: LWF Publication, 1980).

77. "Religion and Youthful Intellectuals", *Nigerian Magazine*, Literary Section, (Lagos: Federal Ministry of Culture, 1985).

78 "Luke and the Gentile Mission: A Study of Acts 15", *Nigerian Journal of Biblical Studies*, 1, 1, (April, 1986): 59-73.

79. "Political Theology for Christian Young Men", Pilgrim, (1976): 11-18.

80. "Ecumenism in Nigeria Today: Its Goals and Aims" Lecture: Annual Synod, Anglican Diocese on the Niger, Onitsha, 1986.

81. "Princeton and the Overseas Student: Comments on Selfhood and Aid", *Princeton Alumni Bulletin*, 16 (1973): 4-11.

82. "Dialogue as an Antidote", S Abogurin (Editor), *Under the Shelter of Olodumare: Essays in Honor of E. B. Idowu* (Ibadan University Press, 1989).

83. Liberty to the Captives: Cameos of Liberation Theology", Occasional Publications of the Center for the Study of World Missions, Presbyterian Theological Seminary, Seoul, South Korea, 1988; ALSO IN *The Journal of Interdenominational Theological Center* (Atlanta), XVI, 1/2 (Fall 1988/Spring 1989): 192-205.

84. "Dialogue of the Deaf, Dumb and Jelly Fish: Reflections on Religion and National Stability", Public Lecture: Federal Government Polytechnic, Oko, 1988.

85. "The Flow of the Spirit: Reflection Luke 1: 46-55", WCC Commission: *Come Holy Spirit, Renew the Whole Creation* (Geneva, 1989).

86. Assembly of the First-born: Ecumenism in Africa in the Year 2000", Commissioned by a WCC Agency for a book on Ecumenism in the Year 2000 (1989).

87 "The Protestants' Protest for Human Rights: A survey of New Trends, 1960-1990", *Bulletin of Ecumenical Theology*, 4, 1-2, (1991), 70-88.

88. "Unconquered Spiritual Gates: Inculturation Theology in Africa Revisited", *Journal of Inculturation Theology*, 1, 1, (1994): 25-37.

VI. Minor Publications: Poems

(a) "Swallow", *Victoriana Acta*, Toronto, 90 (1966), 9.

(b) "A Night Scene", *Victoriana Acta*, Toronto, 91 (1967), 17.

(c) "The Biting Point", *Omabe*, (Nsukka), 26 (1978), 27.

(d) "The Kenyan Stork", *Omabe*, (Nsukka), 28 (1979), 38

VII. Lexikon and Dictionary

90. (a) "Afrika" In *Neue Kirchengeschichte in Lexikon fur Theologie und Kirche* ed Johannes Weitzel (Freiburg: Verlag Herder, 1992).

(b) G.H.Anderson (ed) *Biographical Dictionary of Christian Missions.*(Grand Rapids, Eerdmans, 1998) (i) J. C. Taylor, 1871- 1880: p.685 (ii) Joseph Shanahan, 1871-1943: p.614 (iii) T. J. Dennis, 1869-1917: p.176 (iv) E. M. Lijadu, 1862-1926: p.402.

91. *Die Religion in Geschicte und Gegenwart*, J. C. B. Mohr, Paul Siebeck, Tubingen (i) Brotherhood of the Cross and Star (ii) Mojola Agbebi.

VIII. Field Work Reports in Rural Socio-Economic Studies

92. (i) Federal Ministry of Water Resources (FMWR): Pre-feasibility Study of Anambra River Basin (With Nippon Koei, Japan) (1977). (ii) Anambra-Imo River Basin Development Authority (AIRBDA): Feasibility Study of Niger Flood Plain North (with motor Columbus Inc., Switzerland), 1978. (iii) Anyangba-Otuocha Feasibility Project, 1978. (iv) Amadim-Olo Project, 1979. (v) Agba Umana Project, 1979. (vi) Niger Flood Plain South Project, 1982. (vii) Federal Ministry of Industries; survey of small-scale industries, zone Middle Belt Nigeria (with Industrial Consultancy Bureau, Studies 1 & 2), 1982. (viii) Federal Ministry of Water Resources with Government of Japan: Water Resources Inventory, Phase I, 1992. (ix) FMWR, NALDA MODULE Project Isu-Arochukwu Feasibility Study, (University of Nigeria Consultancy, Abia State Project), 1992. (x) Anambra State Ministry of Agriculture: State-wide Irrigation Project, Phase I, (Prime Services Engineering, Enugu), 1994. (xi) ASMA: ut supra, Phase II, 1995. (xii) Social Science Research Council of Nigeria, Ford Foundation Project on University Governance, Phase II, 1995-1997. *"Scourge of the Vandals: A Social Control Model Approach to Secret Cults in Nigerian Universities, 1970-1997". This is a- 212 pages study.* (xiii) UNDP/UNIFEM: *Silent Victims: Violence Against Women in Nigerian Tertiary Educational Institutions*, 1996.

Articles, 1995-2004

93. "Christianity as a missionary faith in Africa, from beginnings to the Second World War", Presented at Seminar on *Searching for God in Europe and Africa*, Faculty of Divinity, Cambridge University, 1995.

94. "The Golden Age of Christianity in Africa? Early Christianity in North Africa Revisited" *Nsukka Journal of Religious Studies*(Continuing West African Religion), 1, 1, (1996): 34-49.

95. "The Vine and Brambles: Christianity, State and Development in Nigeria, 1900-1995", *Studia Historiae Ecclesiasticae*, 22, 2, (Dec. 1996): 88-113.

96. "Federalism, State and Religion: The Nigerian Experience, 1960-1995", in R. A. Akindele (ed.) *The Foundation of Nigerian Federalism*, vol. III (National Center for Inter-Governmental Relations, Abuja, 1995).

97. "After the Former Rains: Paradigm Shifts in the Study of Christianity and Culture in Nigeria", In *1948 Plus 50: Theology, Apartheid and Church* ed. J. W. Hofmeyr, C.J.S. Lombard, P.J.Maritz, (Pretoria: University of Pretoria, 2000): 168-182.

98. "The Cry At Midnight: Inculturating the Parable of the Ten Maidens, Matthew 25: 1-13" *Biblical Principles and Moral Foundations for Nigerian Society* (Nigerian Association for Biblical Studies, 1997): Chapt. 8.

99. The Economic Development of Ohafia (a Cross River Community) In Time Perspective" In *Ikoro* A Special Publication, Ohafia Udumeze Lecture Series, Lagos), 1, 1, (November, 1996): 19-30.

100. "The River Highway: Christianizing the Cross River Igbo" in O. U. Kalu, ed., *A Century and Half of Presbyterian Witness in Nigeria, 1846-1996.* (Enugu: Presbyterian Church of Nigeria, 1996): 50-95.

101. "The Game of Numbers: Vertical Growth of Presbyterianism in Post- Civil War Nigeria, 1970-1996". (as in 100 item): 120-137.

102. "Power, Poverty and Prayer: The Church in the African State at the edge of the 21st Century", *Toronto Journal of Theology* (University of Toronto), 15, 1 (1999): 69-87.

103. "Who is Afraid of the Holy Spirit? The Pentecostal/Charismatic Debate in the Presbyterian Church of Nigeria", Commencement Lecture, Presbyterian College, McGill University, May, 8th, 1997.

104. "Tools of Hope: Stagnation and Political Theology in Africa, 1960- 1996"in M. Hutchinson & O. U. Kalu (eds.) *A Global Faith: Essays in Evangelicalism and Globalism.* (Sydney, 1998): 181-213.

105. "The Third Response: Pentecostalism and the Reconstruction of Christian Experience in Africa, 1970-1995", First presented at the Yale- Edinburgh Seminar, Yale Divinity School, New Haven, June, 1997. Published in *Journal of African Christian Thought*, 1, 2 (Dec., 1998), 1-21 ; and *Studia Historiae Ecclesiasiticae*, 24, 2(Dec, 1998): 1-34.

106. "Gathering Figs from Thistles? Slavery and the Christianization of Igboland, 1900-1950", *Nigerian Heritage: Journal of the National Commission for Museums and Monuments*, 8 (1999): 11-27

107. "Why Pilgrims Travel in A Convoy: Godly Globalism" Commencement Address. Presbyterian College, McGill University, May, 8th 1997.

108. "The Sacred Egg: Worldview, Ecology and Development in West Africa", in JAGrim(ed) *Indigenous Traditions and Ecology: The Interbeing of Cosmology and Community* (Cambridge, MA: Center for the Study of World Religions and Harvard University Press, 2001): 225-245.

109. **Book Reviews: 1997-2004**

   i.   Adrian Hastings, *The Church in Africa, 1450-1950*.In *Cristianesimo nella storia*, Bologna, vol 18, (1997): 724-726.

   ii. Lamin Sanneh, *Piety and Power: Muslims and Christians in West Africa* In *International Bulletin for Missionary Research*, 22, 1, (1998): 34-35.

   iii. Mark Shaw, *The Kingdom of God in Africa: A Short History of Christianity in Africa*.In *International Bulletin of Missionary Research*, 1997).

   iv. Julian Kunnie, *Models of Black Theology*. *Toronto Journal of Theology*, 1997).

   v.   Joseph C. McKenna, *Finding a Social Voice: The Church and Marxism in Africa* In *Church History*, Duke Divinity School, 1998.

   vi. Paul Gifford, *African Christianity: Its Public Role* In *International Bulletin of Missionary Research* 24, 1 (Jan. 2000): 36.

   vii. T.Falola, *Violence in Nigeria: The crisis of religious politics and secular ideologies*, In *Journal of Religion in Africa*, 31, 1, (2001): 242-243.

   vii. J.D.Y. Peel, *Religious Encounter and the Making of the Yoruba*, In *JRA*, 34, 1-2,, (2004): 201-204.

   viii. Carl Sundberg, Conversion and Contextual Concepts of Christ, In *Mission Studies*, 21, 1, (2004): 150-152.

   ix. C.A. and F. Quinn, *Pride, Faith and Faith: Islam in Sub-Saharan Africa* In *International Bulletin for Missionary Research*, 28, 2, (2004): 84.

   x.   Roswith Gerloff, *Mission is Crossing Frontiers*, IBMR, 28, 4, (2004).

xi. Cephas Omenyo, *Pentecost Outside Pentecostalism*, *Pneuma*, 26, 2, (Fall, 2004): 376-379.

xii. Stephanie Y. Mitchem, *Introducing Womanist Theology*, *Mission Studies*, 20, 2 (2003): 188-189.

110. "Gospel, Culture and Mission: Revisiting an Enduring Problem" *Skrief En Kerk*, Jaargang 19, 2, (1998): 283-300.

111. "Preserving a Worldview: Pentecostalism in the African Maps of the Universe", *Pneuma, Jnl of Society for Pentecostal Studies*, 24, 2, (Fall, 2002): 110-137.

112. "The Practice of the Victorious Life: Pentecostal Political Theology and Practice in Nigeria, 1970-1996", *Mission: Journal of Mission Studies*, 5, 2 (1998): 229-255.

113. "The Estranged Bedfellows?: The Demonization of the Aladura in African Pentecostal Rhetoric". *Missionalia*, 28, 2/3 (Aug/Nov.2000): 121-142.

114. "The Gods are to blame: Religion, Worldview and Light Ecological Footprints in Africa". 6th International Congress of Ethnobiology, Whakatane, Aotearora, New Zealand, Nov., 1998. Published in *Africana Marburgensia*, 32, 1/2 (1999): 3-26.

115. "Harsh Flutes: The Religious Dimension of the Legitimacy Crisis in Nigeria, 1993-1998" In Toyin Falola ed. *Nigeria in the Twentieth Century* (Durham, NC: Carolina Academic Press, 2002): 667-685.

116. "Doing Mission Through the Post Office: The Naked Faith People of Igboland, 1920-1960". *Neue Zeitschrift fur Missionwissenchaft*, Luzern, Switzerland, 56, 4(2000): 263-280 117. "Daughters of Ethiopia: Gender, Power and Poverty in African Christianity, 1980-1996". *Currents in World Christianity Papers, University of Cambridge*, Position Paper no.100. Presented at NAMP Seminar, Princeton Theological Seminary, November, 1998.

118. "Passive Revolution and Its Saboteurs: African Christian Initiative in the Era of Decolonization, 1955-75".In Brian Stanley (ed)*Missions, Nationalism and the End of Empire* (Grand Rapids, Eerdmans, 2003): 250-277. Originally in: *Currents in World Christianity Papers, Cambridge University*, Position Paper no.114, 2000.

119. "Decolonization of African Churches: the Nigerian Experience, 1955-1975". First presented at the XIXTH International Congress of Historical Sciences, University of Oslo, Norway. Published in *Nigerian Heritage*, 10 (2001): 35-59.

120. "Religion and Globecalisation: The Pentecostal Model in Africa". First presented at SSR Annual Conference, Houston, October, 2000. Published In James L.Cox and Gerrie ter Haar (eds) *Uniquely African? African Christian Identity from Cultural and Historical Perspectives.*(Lawrenceville, NJ: Africa World Press, 2003): 215-240 Also In *Studia Historiae Ecclesiasticae, 28, 2 (Dec.2002):* 46-74.

121. "Charismastichen Bewegung und die Wiederentdeckung des traditionellen Afrikanischen Weltbildes In *Neue Christliche Spiritualitat in Ghana"* (Evangelisches Missionwerk in Sudwestdeutschland: informations-brief, 4, 2000): 9-15.

122. "African Christian Art (Kunst Christliche)" in *Das Afrika: Ein Kontinent in 1000 Stichworten,* ed. by Jacob E. Mabe (Stuttgart: J.B.Metzler, 2001): 31-33.

123. "Ancestral Spirituality and Society in Africa" in J.K. Olupona(ed.) *African Spirituality: Forms, Meanings and Expressions* (New York: Herder and Herder Books, 2000): 54-84.

124. "Religion, Ethnicity and Development in Africa" *Reforming the Reformed Tradition: African Presbyterianism in the 21st Century* ed.N.Onwu (Enugu: Presbyterian Church, 2001): 19-40.

125. "Jesus Christ, Where are You?: Themes in West African Church Historiography at the Edge of the 21st Century". *Missionalia, 30,* 2(August, 2002): 235-264.

126. The Stigma of War: Reconciliation and Healing in the Nigerian-Biafran War" Lecture: *Ethnic Nationalism and Democratic Consolidation* (University of Nigeria, 2001).

127. "Clio in a Sacred Garb: telling the story of people-gospel encounters in our time". Inaugural Lecture: Henry Winters Luce Chair, McCormick Theological Seminary, Chicago, May 22nd, 2000. Published in *Fides et Historia, 35,* 1(Winter/Spring, 2003): 27-39.

128. "Shape, Flow and Identity in Contemporary African Historiography". *Trinity Journal of Church and Society,* 12, 1/2 (July/ Dec.2002): 1-21.

129. "Experiencing Evangelical Christianity in Africa, 1770-2000: An Africanist Perspective", *Ghana in Africa and the World* ed.Toyin Falola (Lawrenceville: Africa World Press, 2003): 335-379.

130. Review Essay: Allan Anderson and J.W. Hollenweger eds. *Pentecostalism After A Century: Global Perspectives on a Movement in Transition.*(Sheffield, Sheffield Academic Press, 1999) In *Mission Studies,* 19, 1, 37 (2002): 187-189.

131. "Poverty and Its Alleviation in Colonial Nigeria". In A. O. Oyebade, ed., *Studies in Colonial Nigeria* (Trenton: Africa World Press, 2003): 423-445.

132. "Poverty, Religion and Social Engagement" First presented in the *African and African Diaspora Lectures,* Western Illinois University, Macomb, Nov 17, 2004. Published in www.wiu.edu/iaddp2004.

133. "Safiyya and Adamah: Punishing Adultery With Sharia Stones in 21st Century Nigeria". *African Affairs, Journal of the Royal Africa Society,* London, 102(June, 2003): 389-408.

134. "Pentecostal-Charismatic Reshaping of African Religious Landscape, 1970-2000". *Mission Studies: Journal of International Association of Mission Studies,* 20-1, 39, (2003): 84-111.

135. "Black Missionaries and White Abolitionists: Joseph and Mary Gomer in the Good Hope Mission, Sierra-Leone, 1871-1894" *Neue Zeitschrift fur Missionwissenchaft* 59, 3(Summer 2003): 161-174.

136. "World Christianity and Mission: the Voice of Africa", *Trumpet* Chicago, 3, 4 (Nov.2002): 16ff.

137. "Faith and Politics in Africa: Emergent Political Theology of Engagement in Nigeria, 1970-2002". Paul B. Henry Lecture, 2003, Paul B. Henry Institute for Christianity and Politics, Calvin College, Grand Rapids, Michigan.Winter, 2003.

138. "Sharia and Islam in Nigerian Pentecostal Rhetoric, 1970-2003". *Pneuma, Journal of the Society for Pentecostal Studies,* 26, 2 (Fall 2004): 242-261.

139. "The Trauma of Growth: Reflections on African Christianity in the 21st century". Presented in International Christian College, Glasgow, Scotland, May 2nd, 2004.

140. "Ethiopianism in African Christianity" in Toyin Falola, ed. *Dark Webs: Perspectives on Colonialism in Africa* (Durham NC: Carolina Academic Press, 2005): 137-160.

141. "The Prophet, The Watchman and the Madman: Confession in Barmen Declaration and Kairos Document", Presented at the MTS Continuing Education Seminar on 20th Century Confessions, March, 10, 2003.

142. "Underdog Consciousness in Doing Church History: Collaborative Church Historiography in the Third World, 1970-1992". Presented at the American Society for Church History. Annual Conference, January, 3rd, 2003.

143. "Remembering South Africa: Kairos Document, Religious Commitment and National Identity". Presented at World Mission Institute, Chicago, April 22-24, 2003.

144. "Presbyterians and Early Pentecostalism in Nigeria, 1966-1975 Revisited." In Afe Adogame ed. *Pentecostalism and Globalisation* (University of Bayreuth, Germany/Trenton NJ: Africa World Press) Forthcoming.

145. "*To hang a ladder in the air*: talking about African education in Edinburgh in 1910" Presented as Edinburgh, 1910 Lectures, New College, University of Edinburgh, May, 1st, 2004. see, Towards 2010 http: //66.70.177.170/downloads/kaluedinburgh_1910. pdf.156; Published In *Mission, States, and European Expansion in Africa* ed Chima Korieh (New York: Routledge, 2007): 101-126.

146. "*Nthowa Yifupi?* Edinburgh 1910 and Ethiopianism in African Christianity" Presented at CSCNW, New College, University of Edinburgh, Scotland, May, 3rd 2004.

147. "*Bakufuzu*: Revival Movements in African Christianity" in *Clio in a Sacred Garb: Essays in Christian Presence and African Responses* University of South Africa Press. Forthcoming.

Articles, 2005-2008

148. "Poverty in Pre-colonial and Colonial West Africa: Perception, Causes, and Alleviation" In Emmanuel Akyeampong ed. *Themes in West Africa's History* (Oxford: James Currey, 2006): 163-185.

149. "Ethiopianism and the Roots of Modern African Christianity" In *World Christianities c1800-c.1914* Brian Stanley and Sheridan Gilley eds. *The Cambridge History of Christianity*, vol viii (Cambridge: Cambridge University Press, 2005): 576-592.

150. "African Christianity: From the World Wars to Decolonisation". In D.H. McLeod, ed. *World Christianities c.1914-c.2000.The Cambridge History of Christianity*, vol.ix (Cambridge: Cambridge University Press, 2005): 197-218.

151. "Elijah's Mantle: Ministerial formation in Contemporary African Christianity" in *International Review of Missions*, Geneva, 94, no.373 (April, 2005): 263-277.

152. "A Trail of Ferment: in African Christianity: Ethiopianism, Prophetism and Pentecostalism" in Klaus Koschorke, ed, *African Identities and World Christianity in the 20th Century* (Wiesbaden: Harrassowitz Verlag, Germany, 2006): 19-47.

153. "Constructing Feminist Discourse in Ebony Strokes" *African Women, Religion, and Health: Essays In Honor of Mercy Amba Ewudziwa Oduyoye*. eds. Isabel Phiri and Sarojini Nadar(Maryknoll: Orbis, 2006): 261-278.

154. *"Ndi Afe Ocha*: The Early Aladura of Igboland, 1925-1975"In Toyin Falola ed *Christianity and Social Change in Africa: Essays in Honor of J.D.Y. Peel*(Durham, NC: Carolina Academic Press, 2005): 335-360.

155. "Poverty, Pluralism and Christian Social Engagement: Patterns In Contemporary African Christianity." In A.R.N'Allah ed., *Globalization, African Culture and the Academy: Indigenous African and Diaspora Discourses.*2006. Forthcoming.

156. "The Andrew Syndrome: Models for Understanding Nigerian Diaspora" *African Immigrant Religions in America* eds. J.K. Olupona and Regina Gemignani (New York: New York University Press, 2007): 61-85.

157. "Baptism and New Life." In *Amazing Gift of Your Baptism: A Resource Book*. Evangelical Lutheran Church in America 2005, no 7.

158. "Yabbing Pentecostals: Paul Gifford's Image of Ghana's New Christianity." *Trinity Journal of Church and Theology*, (Legon, Ghana), 15, 1 (January, 2005): 3-16.

159. "The Legacy of James Cone in Africa: Confessions as Political Praxis In The Kairos Document." Presented at the Samuel De Witt Proctor Conference, Atlanta, Feb.15, 2005. Published: *Verbum et Ecclesia*, 27, 2 (2006): 576-595.

160. Multicultural Theological Education on a non-Western Context." In D.Esterline +O.U. Kalu eds *Shaping Beloved Community: Multicultural Theological Education* (Louisville: Westminster John Knox, 2006): 225-242.

161. Lecture: Westmont College, Santa Barbara, CA, Feb 25th, 2005 (a)Power Encounters in Sacred Spaces: African Responses to Christianity, 1900-1960; (b) Faith in Doing Church History (Faculty Seminar, Westmont College).

162 "Worship-full Hearts: an interpretation of women's spirituality in the gospels." In Charles Farhadian ed *Christian Worship Worldwide: Expanding Horizons, Deepening Practices* (Grand Rapids: Eerdmans, 2007): 197-204.

163. "The Other 55th in Chicago: Reflections on Is.55" *Crystal Sermons* ed Awa K Ume (Lagos, 2006), vol 1: 77-83.

164. "Constructing A Global Pentecostal Discourse: An African Example." In *Into All The World: Black Pentecostalism in Global Contexts* Harvard Divinity School, April 18th, 2005.

165. Encyclopedia articles: submitted in 2004/5

Cambridge Dictionary of Christianity ed M Patte: Charismatic Movements (2000 words); History of Christianity in Africa (2400 words); Protestantism in Western Africa (300 words).

Dictionary of Mission Theology ed John Corrie (Nottingham, UK: InterVarsity Press, 2006): New Religious Movements (2700words), pp42-46; Charismatic Movements (1200 words), pp. 29-31.

Encyclopedia of Western Colonialism since 1450 ed Thomas Benjamin 3vols (Detroit: McMillan Reference USA, 2006): Christian Missionaries in Africa (3000 words); Indigenous Religion and Western Presence in Africa (1000);Sierra Leone (1000 words); Islam, Colonial rule in Subsahara Africa (2000 words).

International Encyclopedia of Religious Biography ed J.Gordon Melton. Consultant.

Lion History of World Christianity ed: J.S.Mbiti (1000 words).

166. "African Christianity" In John Bowden ed *Christianity: The Complete Guide* (London: Continuum, 2005): 2-12.

167. Religion and Conflict Transformation: Discourses on Muslim-Christian Conflicts in Nigeria." *Violence and Islam,* University of Bayreuth, Germany, June, 2006.

168. Book Reviews:

Paul Gifford, *Ghana's New Christianity: Pentecostalism in a Globalising Economy.* In *Pneuma,* 27, 1 Spring 2005: 189-191.

M.A Oduyoye, *Beads and Strands;* Ka Mana, *Christian Churches of Africa,* Kwame Bediako, *Jesus and the Gospel in Africa* In *International Bulletin of Missionary Research,* 29, 1 Jan 2005: 48-49.

Frieder Ludwig+Afe Adogame, eds. *European Traditions In The Study of Religion in Africa* (Wiesbaden: Harrassowitz Verlag, 2004) *Journal of African History,* 46, 3(November, 2005): 511-513.

Richard Hall, *On Afric's Shore: A History of Maryland in Liberia, 1834-1857*(Baltimore: Maryland Historical Society, 2003, 644pp) *IBMR, 31, 3, 2007: 158-159.*

Luke Ndubuisi, *Paul's Concept of Charisma in 1Corinthians 12*(Frankfurt: Peter Lang, 2003) *Pneuma*, 28, 2, 2006: 358-361.

David Maxwell,*African Gifts of the Spirit: Pentecostalism and the Rise of a Zimbabwean Transnational Religious Movement*(Oxford: James Currey, 2006) *H-NET University of Michigan, 2007 (5*, 800 words).

Matthew Ojo, *The End_Time Army: Charismatic Movements in Modern Nigeria*(Trenton, NJ: Africa World Press, 2006) *Africa Studies Review,* 2007.

Tabona Shoko, *Karanga Indigenous Religions in Zimbabwe: Health and Well-being.(*Aldershot, UK: Ashgate, 2007) *Pneuma: Jnl of Society for Pentecostal Studies.*2007.

Keith Augustus Burton, *The Bible and African Christianity: The Blessing of Africa* (Downers Grove. IL: Inter Varsity Press, 2007).*Religious Studies Review(A Publication of the Council of Societies for the Study of Religion)* 2007.

Barbara M Cooper, *Evangelicals in the Sahel* (Bloomington: Indiana University Press, 2006) *Journal of Modern African Studies,* 47, 2 (2009).

Robert Mbe Akoko,*Ask and You Shall be Given: Pentecostalism and the Economic Crisis in Cameroon* (Leiden: African Studies Centre, University of Leiden, 2006) *Pneuma.*

168. "The Changing Faces of Evangelicalism in Africa: A Response to George M. Marsden." Consultation on *The Changing Face of American Evangelicalism* Institute for the Study of American Evangelicalism, Wheaton College, October 13th, 2005 In press, edited by Edith L. Blumhofer.

169. "Modeling the Genealogy and Character of Global Pentecostalism: An African Perspective." Society for Pentecostal Studies, Pasadena, March, 2006. Published: *Nerd Geref Teol Tydskrif,* 47, 3(2006): 506-533.

170. Encyclopedia, 2006-2009

Encylopaedia of Missions and Missionaries ed Jonathan Bonk (New York: Berkshire Publishing/Routledge, 2007): "Political Economy"1250 words (pp. 345-347) *Global Dictionary of Theology* eds William A Dyrness and Matti-Velli Karkkainen (Downers Grove: InterVarsity Press, 2008): "African Theology"2500 words.

The Atlas of Global Christianity ed Kenneth Ross and Todd Johnson Edinburgh University Press, 2007: "Modern West African Christianity (3,600 words).

"Christianity in West Africa" *Introducing World Christianity* ed Charles Fardian. Blackwell Press, 2007 (7,000 words).

"Christianity in Sub Saharan Africa from 1800 to the Present" In Lamin Sanneh ed. *Blackwell Companion to World Christianity* (Oxford, UK: Basil Blackwell, 2009) 5500 words.

171. "The Rain and The Sojourner: Igbo Scholarship and The Challenge of Contemporary Experience." Keynote Address, 4th International Conference of Igbo Studies Association, Howard University, Washington, DC, March 31st, 2006. Published In *Mbari: The International Journal of Igbo Studies*, 1, 1(January 2008): 1-24.

172. "Babel, Multiculturalism and Theological Education: Models in Contemporary Africa," Convocation Lecture, Lutheran Theological Seminary at Philadelphia, April 4th, 2006.

173. "Pentecostalism and Mission in Africa, 1970-2000", *Mission Studies, Journal of International Association of Mission Studies*, 24, 1 (2007): 9-45.

174. "The Big Man of A Big God: Pentecostalism, Media and Popular Culture in Africa" *New Theology Review (American Catholic Journal for Ministry)*, 20, 2 May, 2007: 15-26.

174. "Pentecostalism, Media and Cultural Discourse in Africa" *Media Development, Jnl of World Association of Christian Communication*, 14, 1 (2007): 41-45.

175. "*Sankofa*: Pentecostalism and African Cultural Heritage" *The Spirit in the World: Emerging Pentecostal Theologies in Global Contexts* ed. Veli-Matti Karkkainen (Templeton Foundation- sponsored project, 2007.Grand Rapids: Eerdmans): chapter 8. In Press.

176. "African Traditional Religion and Its Modern Fate" *World Religions: Continuities and Transformations* eds. Peter Berger and P.B.Clarke (London: Routledge, 2007): word count: 7,500.

177. "Holy Praiseco: Negotiating Sacred and Popular Music and Dance in African Pentecostalism" Lecture: African Studies Program, Harvard University, March, 20, 2007. To be published in *Pneuma*.

178. "Anatomy of Reverse Flow in African Christianity: Pentecostalism and Immigrant African Christianity" *African Christianity and Neo-Diaspora* ed. Frieder Ludwig (Trenton, NJ: Africa World Press, 2007).

179. "From the End of History to the Beginning of Poverty: Poverty and Social Engagement in Contemporary African Christianity" in *African Identities and World Christianity in the Twentieth Century* ed.Klaus Koschorke (Wiesbaden: Harrassowitz Verlag, 2008).

180. "Hinterland Slave Trade and the Christianization of Igboland, 1900-1950"In Chima Korieh, ed, *The Igbo and Igbo Diaspora in the Atlantic World: History, Culture and Identity*(Trenton, NJ: Africa World Press, 2007), chapter 4.

181. "The Challenges in Contemporary Theological Education in Africa" *Regent Divinity Lecture, 2007.*Regent University of Science and Technology, Accra, Ghana, 5th June, 2007.

182. "Black Joseph: Early African American Charismatic and Pentecostal Linkages and their Impact on Africa." *Black Tongues of Fire: The Changing Discourses of Afropentecostalism* ed Amos Yong and Estrelleda Alexander (New York: New York University Press). *African American Pentecostal and Charismatic Movements in USA* Colloquium. Regent University School of Divinity, October 13th 2007.

183. "Osondu: The Igbo Quest for Jesus power: in Toyin Falola and Matt Childs eds *Igbos in the Atlantic World.*

184. "A Drum for A Warrior Hunter: Osofo J.Wright and the Re-engagement of Africa" Plenary Lecture, March 1st 2008.Published in US/African Dialogue website.

185. "Emerging Images of Humanity: Religion and Violence in the 21st Century" *Eranos Tagung,* Ascona Switzerland, 2007.

186. "The Entangled Roots of the Mangrove Forest: The Cultural Landscape of Political Violence in Africa" *Eranos Tagung,* Ascona, Switzerland, 2008.

187. "Children's Bread: Contested Healing–Coping Strategies in African Pentecostalism" Society for Pentecostal Studies, Duke University, Durham, March 13, 2008. To be published in a festschrift for Professor Tite Tienou.

188. Globalization and Mission in the 21st Century in Kalu, ed. *After the Christendom: Emergent Themes in Contemporary Mission* (Louisville, KY: Westminster John Knox Press, 2009).

189. Discursive Interpretations of African Pentecostalism *Fides et Historia,* 2009.

Index